Begums, Thugs and White Mughals

BEGUMS, THUGS AND WHITE MUGHALS

FANNY PARKES

ELAND
London

First published by Pelham Richardson, London
in 1850 as *Wanderings of a Pilgrim in Search of
the Picturesque, during four-and-twenty years
in the East; with Revelations of Life in the Zenāna*

This edition published by Eland Publishing Limited
61 Exmouth Market, London EC1R 4QL in 2005

ISBN 978 0 907871 88 0

Cover image shows *Colonel Mordant's Cock Match*
by Johann Zoffany © Tate, London 2005

Text set in Great Britain by Antony Gray
Printed by GraphyCems, Navarra, Spain

Introduction

'WE ARE RATHER OPPRESSED just now by a lady, Mrs Parkes, who insists on belonging to our camp,' wrote Fanny Eden in January 1838. 'She has a husband who always goes mad in the cold season, so she says it is her duty to herself to leave him and travel about. She has been a beauty and has remains of it, and is abundantly fat and lively. At Benares, where we fell in with her she informed us she was an Independent Woman.'

Fanny Eden was the sister of the Governor General, Lord Auckland, and the First Lady of British India. Fanny Parkes was the wife of a mentally unstable junior official in charge of ice making in Allahabad. The different status of the two women made friendship between them impossible, and posterity has been far kinder to the Eden sisters than to Fanny: Emily Eden's *Up the Country* has long been regarded as one of the great classics of British Imperial literature and has rarely been out of print since it was first published in 1866; the critic Lord David Cecil went as far as placing the author 'in the first flight of English women letter writers'. Fanny Eden's *Journals* (recently republished as *Tigers, Durbars and Kings: Fanny Eden's Indian Journals, 1837–1838*) are also much read and much reprinted, though they have never had the celebrity of her sister's work. In comparison Fanny Parkes' *Wanderings of a Pilgrim in Search of the Picturesque* had no second edition, and has only recently re-emerged into print. In contrast to the fame of Emily and Fanny Eden, few have ever heard of Fanny Parkes. Fewer still have read her.

Yet anyone who today reads the work of these three women together can hardly fail but to prefer Parkes' writing to that of her two more famous contemporaries and rivals. While the Edens are witty and intelligent but waspish, haughty and conceited, Parkes is an enthusiast and an eccentric with a burning love of India that imprints itself on almost every page of her book. From her first arrival in Calcutta, she writes how 'I was charmed with the climate; the weather was delicious; and . . . I thought India a most delightful country, and could I have gathered around me the dear ones I had left in England, my happiness would have been complete.' The initial intuition was only reinforced the longer she stayed in South Asia. In the twenty four years she lived in India, the country never ceased to surprise, intrigue and delight her, and she was never happier than when off on another journey under canvas exploring new parts of the country: 'Oh! the pleasure,' she writes, 'of vagabondizing over India!'

Partly it was the sheer beauty of the country that hypnotised her. Indian men she found 'remarkably handsome', while her response to Indian nature was no less admiring: 'The evenings are cool and refreshing . . . the foliage of the trees, so luxuriously beautiful and so novel, is to me a source of constant admiration.' But it was not just the way the place looked. The longer she stayed in India, the more Fanny grew to be fascinated by the culture, history, flowers, trees, religions, languages and peoples of the country, the more she felt possessed by an overpowering urge just to pack her bags and set off and explore: 'With the Neapolitan saying, "*Vedi Napoli, e poi mori,*" I beg to differ entirely,' she wrote, 'and would rather offer *this* advice – "See the Taj Mahal, and then – see the Ruins of Delhi." How much there is to delight the eye in this bright, this beautiful world! Roaming about with a good tent and a good Arab [horse], one might be happy for ever in India.'

It is this sheer joy, excitement and even liberation in travel that Fanny Parkes manages so well to communicate. In the same way, it is her wild, devil-may-care enthusiasm, insatiable curiosity and love of the country that immediately engages the reader and carries him or her with Fanny as she bumbles her way across India on her own, wilfully dismissive of the dangers of dacoits or thugs or tigers, learning the sitar, enquiring about the intricacies of Hindu mythology, trying opium, taking down recipes for scented tobacco, talking her way into harems, befriending Maratha princesses and collecting Hindu statuary, fossils, butterflies, zoological specimens preserved in spirits, Indian aphorisms and Persian proverbs – all with an unstoppable, gleeful excitement. Even when she dislikes a particular Indian custom, she often finds herself engaged intellectually. Watching the Churuk Puja, or 'hook swinging', when pious Hindus attached hooks into the flesh of their backs and were swung about on ropes hanging from great cranes for the amusement of the crowds below, 'some in penance for their own sins, some for those of others, richer men, who reward their deputies and thus do penance by proxy', Fanny wrote that: 'I was much disgusted, but greatly interested.'

No wonder the Eden sisters turned their noses up at Fanny Parkes, complaining that she clung onto their party, taking advantage of their protection while touring the lawless roads of Northern India and taking the liberty of pitching her tent next to theirs: she was a free spirit and an independent mind in an age of imperial conformity. Behind the jibes of the Eden sisters ('There is something very horrid and unearthly in all this,' wrote Fanny Eden on

March 17th, 'nobody ever had a fat attendant spirit before . . . ') lies a clear
uneasiness that 'Bibi Parkes' (as they call her) is a woman whom they would
like instinctively to look down upon, but who is clearly having more fun –
and getting to know India much better – than they are.

The mental gap between the world of the Eden sisters and that of Fanny
Parkes widened as time went on. The longer she stayed in India, the more
Fanny Parkes became slowly Indianised. At one point in December 1837, after
visiting an Indian Rani where Parkes acts as interpreter for the Eden sisters,
Parkes urges 'with considerable vehemence' that the Eden sisters should con-
form to Indian custom and accept the symbolic gifts offered to them as they
leave, thus pleasing the Rani and avoiding giving offence. The Eden sisters
worry that this might be seen as corruption and want to follow Company
regulations and refuse the presents. There is a standoff, and eventually the
Edens do turn down the gifts so giving huge offence to their host. Already
Fanny Parkes is instinctively embracing Indian custom and trying to adapt
herself to the Indian scene, trying to avoid rudeness and unpleasantness. The
Eden sisters are more worried about what others will think: instinctively they
want to play by the imperial rules, to keep within the accepted boundaries.

Parkes' slow 'chutnification' (to use Salman Rushdie's excellent term)
continued long after Parkes left the Eden's camp. Over the following years,
Parkes – the professional memsāhib, herself the daughter of a colonial official
(Captain William Archer), who came to India to watch over her colonial
administrator husband – was gradually transformed into a fluent Urdu
speaker, and spent less and less of her time at her husband's *mofussil* posting,
and more and more of her time travelling around to visit her Indian friends
and assimilating herself to the world she discovered. Aesthetically, for example,
she grew slowly to prefer Indian dress to that of the English. At one point
watching Id celebrations at the Tāj she notes how 'crowds of gaily-dressed and
most picturesque natives were seen in all directions passing through the
avenue of fine trees and by the side of the fountains to the tomb: they added
great beauty to the scene, whilst the eye of taste turned away pained and
annoyed by the vile round hats and stiff attire of the European gentlemen, and
the equally ugly bonnets and stiff and graceless dresses of the English ladies'.

Later, visiting the women in Colonel Gardner's Khasgunge *zenāna*, she
again raises Indian ways over those of Europe:

[Mulka Begum] walks very gracefully and is as straight as an arrow. In
Europe how rarely – how very rarely does a woman walk gracefully! Bound
up in stays, the body is as stiff as a lobster in its shell; that snake-like

undulating movement – the poetry of motion – is lost, destroyed by the stiffness of the waist and hip, which impedes the free movement of the limbs. A lady in European attire gives me the idea of a German manikin; an Asiatic, in her flowing drapery, recalls the statues of antiquity.

She becomes increasingly unorthodox in her views and can barely believe the philistinism of the Government in Calcutta and recoils in horror when she sees what the English have done to the beautifully inlaid Mughal *zenāna* apartments in the Agra Fort: 'Some wretches of European officers – to their disgrace be it said – made this beautiful room a cook-room! and the ceiling, the fine marbles and the inlaid work, are all one mass of blackness and defilement! Perhaps they cooked the *sū'ar*, the hog, the unclean beast, within the sleeping apartments of Noorahān – the proud, the beautiful Sultana!'

She is even more angry when she hears that the Turkish 'baths in the apartments below the palace, which most probably belonged to the *zenāna*, were broken up by the Marquis of Hastings: he committed this sacrilege of the past . . . [Then] having destroyed the beauty of the baths of the palace, the remaining marble was afterwards sold on account of the Government; most happily the auction brought so small a sum, it put a stop to further depredations'.

Gradually, over the twenty-four years she lived in India, and as her *Wanderings* took shape, Fanny's view begin to change. Having assumed at first that good taste was the defining characteristic of European civilisation and especially that of her own people, she finds her assumptions being challenged by what she comes to regard as the rampant philistinism of the English in India, and by the beauty of so much of Indian life, not least its architecture. (In this, incidentally, she would have agreed with Robert Byron who was equally horrified by what the English had done to India a hundred years later: 'In a country full of good example,' he wrote, 'the English have left the mark of the beast.' He also wrote with horror about 'how the whole of [British] India is a gigantic conspiracy to make one imagine one is in Balham or Eastbourne . . . [as for Darjeeling] imagine Bognor or Southend roofed in corrugated iron and reassembled in the form of an Italian hill town . . . ')

Every bit as bad, in Fanny's eyes, was the attitude of the British who employed a band at the Tāj so that visiting Company officials could have the opportunity to dance a jig in the marble platform in front of the tomb: 'Can you imagine anything so detestable?' she wrote. 'European ladies and gentlemen dance quadrilles in front of the tomb! I cannot enter the Tāj without feelings of deep devotion: the sacredness of the place, the remembrance of the fallen grandeur of the family of the Emperor, the solemn echoes, the dim light, the beautiful architecture, the exquisite finish and delicacy of the whole… all produce deep and sacred feelings; and I could no more jest or indulge in levity beneath the dome of the Tāj, than I could in my prayers.' On leaving the enclosure, she writes, movingly: 'And now adieu! Beautiful Tāj – adieu! In the far, far West I shall rejoice that I have gazed upon your beauty; nor will the memory depart until the lowly tomb of an English gentlewoman closes on my remains.'

Over time, these emotional and aesthetic responses to India slowly con- solidated themselves into something more structured, and in due course they profoundly altered Fanny's political outlook. By the late 1830s she came to be increasingly critical of the East India Company her husband served. In her published work that criticism was by necessity muted, but her allegiances are clear. At a time when many of her contemporaries were calling for the British to annex the 'degenerate' Kingdom of Oude (or Avadh as it is more usually spelled today) Fanny was quite clear that, 'the subjects of his Majesty of Oude are by no means desirous of participating in the blessings of British rule. They are a richer, sleeker, and merrier race than the natives in the territories of the Company.' She rails against the authorities for failing to reward her friend William Gardner for his gallantry (largely, though she does not say this, because of the degree to which Gardner was believed to have 'gone native'.) She points out how many have died painful, unnecessary deaths from small- pox as 'Lord William Bentinck did away with the vaccine department, to save a few rupees; from which economy many have lost their lives.'

At the end of her travels, when Fanny finally looks forward to seeing her family in England again, she turns to a Persian aphorism to express the intensity her feelings: 'The desire of the garden never leaves the heart of the nightingale.' Yet when she finally sets foot on English soil again, her return is not a moment for rejoicing but for depression and disappointment: 'We arrived at six o'clock. May-flowers and sunshine were in my thoughts. [But instead . . .] it was bitterly cold walking up from the boat – rain, wind and sleet, mingled together, beat on my face. Everything on landing looked so wretchedly mean, especially the houses, which are built of slate stone, and also slated down the side; it was cold and gloomy . . . I felt a little disgusted.'

When she arrived home, her mother barely recognised her. It was as if the current of colonisation had somehow been reversed: the coloniser had been colonised. India had changed and transformed Fanny Parkes. She could never be the same again.

*   *   *

In 1822 when Fanny Parkes arrived in India, British attitudes to the country were undergoing a major transformation.

In the late eighteenth century, the more intelligent of the British in India tended to respond to their adopted country with amazement and fascination. Under the influence of Sir William Jones, the Chief Justice of the new Supreme Court at Calcutta, there was a sudden explosion of interest of what Jones called 'this wonderful country'. In 1784, Jones had founded an Asiatick Society 'for inquiring into the History, Civil and Natural, the Antiquities, Arts, Sciences and Literature of Asia'. Its patron was the most enlightened of all the British Governor Generals, Warren Hastings, who shared the new enthusiasm for Hinduism and who declared 'in truth I love India a little more than my own country'. Under Jones and Hastings, the Asiatick Society became the catalyst for a sudden explosion of interest in Hinduism, as it formed enduring relations with the local Bengali intelligentsia and led the way to uncovering the deepest roots of Indian history and civilisation. In India, Jones wrote that he had discovered Arcadia. Valmiki was the new Homer, the Ramayana the new Odyssey. The possibilities seemed endless.

Yet in the early years of the nineteenth century, this optimism and excitement began to wane, and senior figures in the Company became openly disdainful of all things Indian. Partly the reasons for this were political. In the eighteenth century the Company was a small, vulnerable coastal power that depended on the goodwill of Indian rulers. Many Indian armies were better equipped and better trained than those of the Company: the armies of Tipu Sultan for example had rifles and canon which were based on the latest French designs, and their artillery had a heavier bore and longer range than anything possessed by the Company's armies. But by the 1830s the British had become the paramount power in India. For the first time there was a feeling that technologically, economically and politically, the British had nothing to learn from India and much to teach. As with the contemporary US since the fall of the Soviet Union, it did not take long for imperial arrogance to set in.

Religion played a major role too. Perhaps the most powerful of the new breed of hard-line critics of Indian culture was one the Company's directors, Charles Grant. Grant was among the first of the new Evangelical Christians, and he brought his fundamentalist religious opinions directly to the East India Company Boardroom. Writing that 'it is hardly possible to conceive any people more completely enchained than they [the Hindus] are by their superstitions,' he proposed to launch missions to convert a people whom he characterised 'universally and wholly corrupt . . . depraved as they are blind, and wretched as they are depraved.' Within a few years, the missionaries –

initially based at the Dutch settlement of Serampore – were beginning to fundamentally change British perceptions of the Hindus. No longer were they inheritors of a body of sublime and ancient wisdom as Jones and Hastings believed, but instead merely 'poor benighted heathen', or even 'licentious pagans', some of whom, it was hoped, were eagerly awaiting conversion, and with it the path to Civilisation.

It was at this period too that the first development of ideas of racial purity, of colour and ethnic hierarchy, and the beginnings of straightforward racialism emerged: ideas which would of course reach there most horrifying denouement in the middle years of the twentieth century, but whose roots can be traced to developments in European thought a century earlier, and at least partly to developments in British India.

These new racial attitudes affected all aspects of relations between the British and Indians. The eighteenth and early nineteenth century had produced many 'White Mughals' – characters like the British Resident at the Mughal court, Sir David Ochterlony. When in the Indian capital, Ochterlony liked to be addressed by his full Mughal title, Nasir-ud-Daula (Defender of the State) and to live the life of a Mughal gentleman: every evening all thirteen of Ochterlony's consorts used to process around Delhi behind their husband, each on the back of her own elephant. With his fondness for *hookahs* and nautch girls and Indian costumes, Ochterlony amazed Bishop Reginald Heber, the Anglican Primate of Calcutta, by receiving him sitting on a divan wearing a '*choga* and *pagri*' while being fanned by servants holding peacock-feather *punkhas.*

Such people were few and far between by the 1830s, and their way of life was beginning to die out. The Bengal Wills show that it was at this time that the number of Indian wives or *bibis* being mentioned in wills and inventories begins to decline: from turning up in one in three wills in the 1780–85, the practice went into steep decline. Between 1805–10, *bibis* appear in only one in every four wills; by 1830 it is one in six; by the middle of the century they have all but disappeared.

Englishmen who had taken on Indian customs began to be objects of surprise even, on occasions, of derision in Calcutta. In the early years of the nineteenth century there was growing 'ridicule' of men 'who allow whiskers to grow and who wear turbans &c in imitation of the Musulmans'. Curries were no longer acceptable dishes for parties, and pyjamas – common dress in eighteenth-century Calcutta and Madras – for the first time became something that an Englishman slept in rather than something he wore during the day. By 1813, Thomas Williamson was writing in *The European in India* how 'The hookah, or pipe . . . was very nearly universally retained among Europeans.

Time, however, has retrenched this luxury so much, that not one in three now smokes.' Soon the hookah was to go the way of the *bibi*: into extinction.

Fanny stood in the middle of this process of change – this slow alienation of the British from the India they ruled – and was one of the last of the generation who was able to express unequivocal admiration for India. Even so her attitudes were subject to criticism from her peers. On her travels, she found that extreme Victorian religiosity was already beginning to make itself felt, and that attitudes were changing: 'Methodism is gaining ground very fast in Cawnpore,' she records. 'Young ladies sometimes profess to believe it is highly incorrect to go to balls, plays, races, or to any party where it is possible there may be a quadrille. A number of the officers also profess these opinions, and set themselves up as new lights.' In Calcutta she finds many of her contemporaries were 'determined to be critical' of anything Indian. When she visits an old Princess who was a cousin of the Gardners in the *zenāna* of the Red Fort in Delhi, British opposition to Fanny's sympathies comes out into the open. She lets slip that she is clearly regarded as suspect by the British in Delhi for mixing with (or even taking an interest in) the sad, impoverished descendants of the Great Mughals, and fires back at the criticism, both of her and her Mughal hosts:

'I heard that I was much blamed for visiting the princess . . . Look at the poverty, the wretched poverty of these descendants of the emperors! In former times strings of pearls and valuable jewels were placed on the necks of departing visitors. When the Princess Hyāt-ool-Nissa Begum in her fallen fortunes put the necklace of freshly-gathered white jasmine flowers over my head, I bowed with as much respect as if she had been the queen of the universe. Others may look upon these people with contempt, I cannot; look at what they are, what they have been!

'One day a gentleman, speaking to me of the *extravagance* of one of the young princes, mentioned that he was always in debt, he could never live upon his allowance. The allowance of the prince was Rs 12 a month! – not more than the wages of a head servant.

'With respect to my visit, I felt it hard to be judged by people who were ignorant of my being the friend of the relatives of those whom I visited in the *zenāna*. People who themselves had, perhaps, no curiosity respecting native life and manners, and who, even if they had the curiosity, might have been utterly unable to gratify it unless by an introduction which they were probably unable to obtain.'

With such criticism buzzing around her, it is hardly surprising that Fanny took refuge and found friendship among an older generation of Indianised

Europeans, men who had to some extent crossed cultures in exactly the way that she was now beginning to do.

In Calcutta, she immediately fell for the dashing French General Allard, a Sergeant Major of Joseph Bonaparte's bodyguard, who left St Tropez and ended up commanding two Regiments of dragoons and lancers for the Sikh leader Ranjit Singh in the Punjab, marrying a beautiful Kashmiri girl and more or less becoming a Sikh himself. 'He is the most picturesque person imaginable,' wrote Fanny after meeting him. 'His long forked beard, divided in the centre, hangs down on either side his face; at dinner time he passes one end of his beard over one ear, and the other end over the other ear. I was much delighted with the General: he asked me to visit him in Lahore, an invitation I told him I would accept with great pleasure, should I ever visit the hills, and he told me he would send an escort for me.'

Fanny forged a deeper relationship still with William Linnaeus Gardner, perhaps the single most intriguing character in Fanny's entire book. Gardner was born into a prominent American loyalist family on the banks of the Hudson. He had fled America after the Patriot victory in the War of Independence, and finished his education in France and Holland, before sailing to India to make his fortune. There he inherited his father's peerage, married a beautiful Mughal Princess of Cambay and, having fought for many years as a mercenary under a variety of Indian rulers, he eventually resumed his allegiance to the British Crown and formed his own irregular regiment, Gardner's Horse.

Gardner was very much a family man, and in his private correspondence, now in the India Office Library, he talks proudly of his multi-racial family: 'Man must have a companion,' he wrote to his cousin, 'and the older I get the more I am confirmed in this. An old age without something to love, and nourish and nurse you, must be cold and uncomfortable. The Begum and I, from twenty-two years constant contact, have smoothed off each other's asperities and roll on peaceably and contentedly. Now I hope both my boys will get me lots of grandchildren, for I find the grandpapa is the greatest favourite they have. The shouts of joy when I return after an absence of any time can be heard for a mile. My house is filled with Brats, and the very thinking of them, from blue eyes and fair hair to ebony and wool makes me quite anxious to get back again ... There's no accounting for taste but I have more relish in playing with the little brats than for the First Society in the World ... New books, a garden, a spade, nobody to obey, pyjamas, grand-children, tranquillity: this is the summit of happiness, not only in the East but the West too.'

Gardner's son James continued the family tradition by marrying Mulka

Begum, who was the niece of the Mughal Emperor Akbar Shāh as well as being the sister-in-law of the Nawāb of Avadh, and together they fathered an Anglo-Mughal dynasty, half of whose members were Muslim and half Christian; indeed some of them, such as James Jehangir Shikoh Gardner, seem to have been both at the same time. Even those Gardners who were straightforwardly Christian had alternative Muslim names: thus the Revd Bartholomew Gardner could also be addressed as Sabr, under which name he was a notable Urdu and Persian poet, shedding his clerical dress in favour of Avadhi pyjamas to declaim his achingly beautiful love poems at Lucknavi *mushairas*.

Fanny's description of her visit to Gardner's *jagir*, his estate, at Khāsganj, her detailed exposition of how an English nobleman lived in a culturally hybrid house with a Mughal zenāna, Mughal customs and mixed European and Mughal cuisine, and her account of Gardner's strange Anglo-Mughal wedding celebrations, is the most fascinating section of her travel book, a unique record of an attractively multicultural world that was soon to vanish. Indeed Fanny was clearly a little in love with the dashing Colonel: 'He must have been, and is, very handsome; such a high caste man! How he came to marry his Begum I know not. What a romance his love must have been! I wish I had his portrait, just as he now appears, so dignified and interesting. His partiality flatters me greatly!'

Even at this stage Gardner, though clearly a survivor – even a museum piece from a previous age – was nevertheless not alone in his tastes and sympathies. At the wedding of the Colonel's granddaughter, Fanny describes how the European guests, like their host, were all in Mughal dress. Later, 'two English gentlemen, who were fond of native life, and fascinated with Khāsganj, requested me to mention to Colonel Gardner their wish to become of his family; I did so.' It was the last gasp maybe, but the old inter-cultural hybridity was not yet completely finished.

William Gardner died on his Khāsganj estate on the 29th July 1835, at the age of sixty-five. His Begum, whose dark eyes he had first glimpsed through the chinks of a curtain in Surat thirty-eight years earlier, could not live without him. According to Fanny's account:

'My beloved friend Colonel Gardner . . . was buried, according to his desire, near the [domed Mughal] tomb of his son Allan. From the time of his death the poor Begum pined and sank daily; just as he said she complained not, but she took his death to heart; she died one month and two days after his decease. Native ladies have a number of titles; her death, names and titles were thus announced in the papers: "On the 31st August, at her Residence at Khāsganj. Her Highness Furzund Azeza Azubdeh-tool Arrakeen Umdehtool Assateen Nawāb Mah Munzil ool Nissa Begum Dehlmi, relict of the late Colonel

William Linnaeus Gardner. The sound of *Nakaras* and *Dumanas* [kettle drums and trumpets] have ceased." '

The following year Fanny returned, broken-hearted, and paid her respects at the grave of her beloved friend: 'I knelt at the grave of my kind, kind friend and wept and prayed in deep affliction.'

The family never recovered the position they held under William. Despite possessing a pukka peerage, the Barony of Uttoxeter, over time they squandered their wealth, became poorer and poorer and more and more provincial Indian, gradually losing touch with their aristocratic English relations. The penultimate Vicereine, Lady Halifax, had Gardner blood and records in her memoirs that she was a little surprised when alighting from the Viceregal train on her way up to Simla, to see the station master of Kalka break through the ceremonial guard and fight his way up to the red carpet. Shouldering his way through the ranks of aides and the viceregal retinue, he addressed Her Excellency the Vicereine:

'Your Excellency,' he said, 'my name is Gardner.'

'Of course,' replied Lady Halifax, somewhat to the astonishment of the viceregal entourage. 'We are therefore cousins.'

The Gardner dynasty, incidentally, still survives near Lucknow, today one of the most violent and backward parts of India. The present Lord Gardner, who has never been to England and speaks only faltering English, contents himself with farming his Indian acres and enjoying the prestige of being the village wrestling champion. Until he recently missed his chance, he threatened every so often to return 'home' and take up his seat in the House of Lords.

* * *

Fanny enjoyed travel books, and mentions those of several of her male contemporaries in her text. She was well aware that her sex made her vulnerable and so deprived her of opportunities open to them; but she also knew that she had one distinct advantage where she could trump her male rivals: her access to Indian zenānas. No Englishman could go into the quarters of Indian women, and Fanny was determined to make the most of the opportunity and to report from beyond a frontier that her rivals could not cross.

In Calcutta, in Lucknow, at Khāsganj and in Delhi, Fanny repeatedly visits the women of different harems and reports about the life, the pleasures and the sorrows of the women she encounters there. One women in particular she befriends, Bāiza Bāī, the dowager Maratha queen of Gwalior who had been deposed by her son and sent into exile at Fatehgar in British territory not far from Cawnpore.

Fanny found a common love of riding with the Queen, and describes learning to ride Maratha style, while trying to teach Bāzai Bāi's women how to ride side-saddle. Always impatient with Western notions of feminine decorum, Fanny records how 'I thought of Queen Elizabeth, and her stupidity in changing the style of riding for women'.

Far from fantasising the sensual pleasures to be had in the Eastern harem, as was the wont of many of the male painters and writers of her time, Fanny reports on her perceptions of the reality of the lives of Indian women, and especially the restrictions which she felt women in both East and West suffered in common: 'We spoke of the severity of the laws of England with respect to married women, how completely by law they are the slaves of their husbands, and how little hope there is of redress.' It is at such points that Fanny's *Wanderings* becomes an explicitly feminist text. In fact it is one of the great pleasures of the book that the more Fanny wanders, free of her husband, the more outspoken, sympathetic and independent she becomes.

If Fanny was able to break some contemporary stereotypes about the life led by the inhabitants of Indian zenānas, she was less perceptive with her passages on Thuggee: the strangling and robbery of travellers by what the British came to believe was an Indian-wide brotherhood of Kali worshippers. Fanny devotes a great deal of space to the sensational reports then being circulated in the British press about the prevalence of thugs who were said to take the lives of literally tens of thousands of travellers every year. Today few would dispute that merchants and pilgrim bands were indeed very vulnerable to attack and robbery during this period; but most modern historians now believe that the British officials put in charge of the 'Suppression of Thuggee' hugely exaggerated the scale of the problem and created a mythical All-India Thug Conspiracy where in reality there were only scattered groups of robbers and impoverished highwaymen. Some historians also allege that the British used the suppression of Thuggee as an excuse and a justification for widening their area of rule: it was no coincidence that James Sleeman, the man who led the British campaign against the Thugs, was also the man who wrote most insistently for the annexation of the Kingdom of Avadh.

Yet even here, while clearly fascinated by the threat and spectacle of thuggee, and excited by the idea of a conspiracy of sacred stranglers, Fanny sounds a note of caution, remarking on hearing about the mass execution of a group of twenty-five thugs that, 'it cannot but be lamented that the course of justice is so slow; as these men, who were this day executed, have been in prison more than eight years for want of sufficient evidence'. So saying, she leaves a question hanging in the air. If the thugs were so guilty, how come there was so little evidence? It was certainly an apposite query. In normal circumstances, courts in India did not accept the statements of informers who turned 'King's Evidence' on their fellow captives; but in the case of thugs, the colonial laws were altered to allow the conviction of thugs on evidence which would in other circumstances be regarded as wholly suspect and inadequate. The result was that accused thugs hoping for a pardon would produce lengthy and dramatic testimonials, giving evidence against scores of men they alleged to be former colleagues. The parallels with the Salem witch trial are obvious – and alarming.

The same Evangelical Victorian colonial attitudes that wished to sell the Tāj Mahal for marble, and demolish the monuments of Agra, was also the world that dreamed up India-wide conspiracies involving vicious blood-thirsty thugs. It was not a world where Indian and English could cohabit on any terms of equality, and Fanny Parkes was one of the last English writers to believe – or even to want to believe – that mutually respectful relationships were possible and even desirable. The inevitable clash came in the Indian Mutiny of 1857, when the East India Company's own troops finally rose in rebellion, joined in much of North India by great swathes of the civilian population. Nowhere was this more the case than in the supposedly 'degenerate' and 'effeminate' towns of Mughal Delhi and Lucknow, where the British only defeated the rebels with the very greatest difficulty and with unimaginable casualties on both sides.

The world beloved of William Gardner and General Allard, and indeed of Fanny herself, was swept away by the Mutiny. During the fighting, Gardner's Anglo-Indian descendants, like those of all the other White Mughals, were forced to make a final choice between one or other of the two sides – though for many the choice was made for them. After an attack on their property, the Gardners were forced to take refuge first in Aligarh then in the Fort of Agra, and so also ended up on the side of the British – though given a free hand they might just as easily have lined up behind their Mughal cousins in Delhi and Lucknow.

Afterwards, nothing could ever be as it was. With the British victory, and the genocidal spate of hangings and executions that followed, the entire top rank of the Mughal aristocracy was swept away and British culture was unapologetically imposed on India; at the same time the wholesale arrival of the memsāhibs ended all open sexual contact between the two nations. White Mughals like Ochterlony and Gardner died out, and their very existence was later delicately erased from embarrassed Victorian history books. Only now is their existence beginning to be unearthed. Moreover, at a time when respectable journalists and academics are again talking of the Clash of Civilisations, and when East and West, Islam and Christianity are again engaged in a major confrontation, Fanny's record of this fragile hybrid world has never been more important.

*   *   *

At the time of her travels, Fanny Parkes was criticised by her contemporaries for 'going native', for her over-developed sympathies for the cultures, religions and peoples of North India. Today she is under assault from the opposite direction.

Following the success of Edward Said's groundbreaking work *Orientalism*, a school of criticism has attempted to apply Said's ideas to the whole range of colonial writings and art. Some of these applications have proved more suitable than others, and there sometimes seems to be an assumption at work in academia – especially in the US – that all writings of the colonial period exhibit the same sets of prejudices: a monolithic, modern, academic Occidentalism which seems to match uncannily the monolithic stereotypes perceived in the original *Orientalism*.

Fanny has not escaped this academic pigeon-holing, and has recently been the subject of two academic articles which would have her implicated in the project of gathering 'Colonial knowledge' and 'imbricated with the project of Orientalism' – in other words an unwitting outrider of colonialism, attempting to 'appropriate' Indian learning and demonstrate the superiority of Western ways by 'imagining' India as decayed and degenerate, fit only to be colonised and 'civilised'. Anyone who reads Fanny's writing with an open mind cannot but see this as a wilful misreading of the whole thrust of her text, an attempt to fit her book into a mould which it simply does not fit. There are many writers of the period to which such strictures could be applied, but it seems misguided in the extreme to see Parkes as any sort of gung-ho colonialist. Fanny was a passionate lover of India and, though a woman of her time, in her writing and her travels did her best to understand and build bridges across the colonial divide.

As Colin Thubron has pointed out, 'To define the genre [of travel writing] as an act of domination – rather than of understanding, respect or even catharsis – is simplistic. If even the attempt to understand is seen as aggression or appropriation, then all human contact declines into paranoia.' The point is well made, and the attacks made on Fanny highlight the problem with so much that has been written about eighteenth- and early nineteenth-century India: the temptation felt by so many critics to project back onto it the stereotypes of Victorian and Edwardian behaviour and attitudes with which we are so familiar.

Yet these attitudes were clearly at odds with the actual fears and hopes, anxieties and aspirations of many of the eighteenth- and early nineteenth-century Company officials and their Indian wives. Their writings can be read with the greatest of ease in books such as Fanny Parkes', and in the fifty miles of

East India Company documents and letters stored in the India Office Library in London. It is as if Victorians succeeded in colonising not just India but also, more permanently, our imaginations, to the exclusion of all other images of the Indo-British encounter.

The travel book, by its very nature, records the transitory moment: as Thubron puts it, a good travel book 'catches the moment on the wing, and stops it in Time'. Fanny Parkes' wonderful book is an important historical text for its record of the last moments of this very attractive (and largely forgotten) moment of cultural and sexual interaction, of crossover 'chutnification'. The world described by Fanny – especially the syncretic culture of Lucknow and Delhi, and its satellite at Khāsganj – was far more hybrid, and had far less clearly defined ethnic, national and religious borders, than we have been conditioned to expect, either by the conventional Imperial history books written in Britain before 1947, or by the nationalist historiography of post-Independence India. It was a world where British mercenaries married Mughal princesses and where Anglo-Indian women entered the harems of Nawabi Avadh, where Muslims attended Hindu ceremonies and vice versa.

This edition of Fanny Parkes' writing represents my own personal selection of her work, but I hope it conveys the flavour of her writing and the largely forgotten world she so loved and enjoyed.

WILLIAM DALRYMPLE
Pages Yard, 17th September 2002

PUBLISHER'S NOTE

To make the book more manageable, we have made a number of changes to the text. The original edition, published in 1850 as *Wanderings of a Pilgrim in Search of the Picturesque*, ran to over eight hundred pages. Several passages have been omitted, and are marked by ellipses within square brackets – [. . .] The original edition was also riddled with inconsistent spellings, both of place names and Indian words. These have been standardized so that they correspond with the newly-created glossary and map.

To give meaning to the prices mentioned, 1 rupee in Fanny's day would have been worth roughly £6 today.

Contents

ILLUSTRATIONS

Glossary

ābdār water-cooler

amari seat with canopy for riding on elephant

ānā copper coin

angiya native bodice

angriah pirates, robbers

arak alcoholic drink

atr perfume

ayah lady's maid

baboo Hindu gentleman, Calcutta merchant

bahangi a stick with ropes, carried on the shoulder, used for carrying baggage

banglā a thatched house

baniyā a shop-keeper

barkandāz a policeman

batta extra pay

bibi a European woman, or the Indian wife of a European man

begum a lady

bihishti a water-carrier

brahman a member of the priestly caste

burj tower

chaprāsi messenger

chārpāi four-legged bed

chaunri fly-whisk

chītā hunting cheetah

churi bracelet

dāk mail coach, post service and bungalow

dāndi a boatman

darbār audience hall

darwān porter

darzee a tailor

dastūri payment over and above wages

dhobee a washerman

fakir a religious beggar

gūnth Himalayan pony

hackery a bullock cart

hakim a learned man, physician

harkāra running footman

hinnā henna, a dye

huqqa hookah, a water-pipe

howdah a seat on an elephant with no canopy

hākāk stone-cutter

hammām Turkish bath

jagir hereditary income from land

jamadār native officer, head of the running footmen

khānsāmān head table-servant

khas-khas root of a grass

khidmatgār table-servant

khraunchi a native carriage

kimkhwab silk brocade worked in gold and silver

lota a drinking vessel

lugoe to moor, attach

mahout elephant keeper, driver

Mahratta a famous Hindu warrior race

maidān   a plain or square
mānjhī   master of a boat
mashāl   a torch
mashālchi   a torch-bearer
mashk   a water bag
masjid   a mosque
masnad   a throne, large cushion
mate   assistant servant
mofussil   countryside
mohur   a gold coin
moonshee   an educated Indian
mug   people from Chittagong
   renowned for their cooking skills
mushāira   evening of poetry and
   music
musulmān   a Muslim
nāch   a traditional Indian dance
nālā   a small river, watercourse
nawāb   a Nabob, a Muslim title of
   rank
nilgāi   an antelope
omrāh   grandees of a Muslim court
pālkee   a palanquin
pān   leaves of the betel pepper
pankhā   a fan
pattū   a kind of woollen cloth
pindāri   a member of a band of
   plunderers

pitārā   a basket
pukka   substantial, permanent
pashmina   fine wool shawl
pūtli   a small puppet
roomal   a handkerchief
sā'is   a groom
sāleb misree   a medicine made from
   orchid root
sarāy   a native inn
sawāri   retinue of horsemen
shastra   Hindu scripture
sholā   a plant – *aeschynomene
   paludosa*
sipahi   an Indian soldier
sircār   a superintendent
surma   eye make-up, kohl
sati   a woman who burns herself on
   her husband's funeral, or the act
   thereof
tamāshā   fun, sport, spectacle
tanjan   a chair carried by natives
tatti   a screen or shutter
tattoo   pony
tufān   a hurricane
zenāna   female apartments

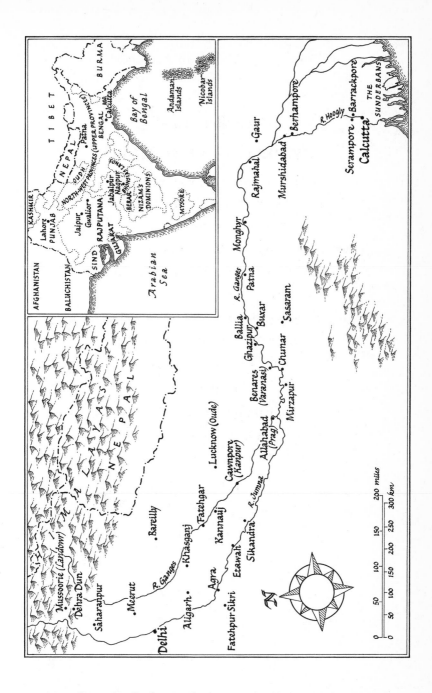

Map of central India showing the region covered by Fanny Parkes' travels

𝔗𝔬 𝔱𝔥𝔢 𝔐𝔢𝔪𝔬𝔯𝔶 𝔬𝔣

MY BELOVED MOTHER

AT WHOSE REQUEST IT WAS WRITTEN,

THIS NARRATIVE IS DEDICATED:

AND IF ANY OF THE FRIENDS,

WHOSE KIND PARTIALITY HAS INDUCED THEM TO

URGE ITS PUBLICATION, SHOULD THINK I HAVE

DWELT TOO MUCH ON MYSELF, ON MY OWN

THOUGHTS, FEELINGS AND ADVENTURES,

LET THEM REMEMBER THAT THIS JOURNAL

WAS WRITTEN FOR THE AFFECTIONATE EYE

𝔬𝔣 𝔥𝔢𝔯

TO WHOM NOTHING COULD BE SO GRATIFYING

AS THE SLIGHTEST INCIDENT CONNECTED

WITH HER BELOVED AND ABSENT CHILD,

فاني پاركس

[FANNY PARKES]

INVOCATION

Work-perfecting Ganésha! Salāmat.
Ganésh! – Ganésh!
Two-mothered! One-toothed!
Portly-paunched! Elephant-faced Ganésha!
Salām! !
Moon-crowned! Triple-eyed !
Thou who in all affairs claimest precedence in adoration!
Calamity averting Ganésh
Salām! !
Thou who art invoked on the commencement of a journey,
the writing of a book,
Salām! !
Oh ! Ganésh, 'put not thine ears to sleep!
Encourage me, and then behold my bravery;
Call me your own fox, then will you see me perform
the exploits of a lion!'
'What fear need he have of the waves of the sea,
who has Noah for a pilot?'
First born of Mahādēo and Parvatī!
God of Prudence and Policy!
Patron of Literature!
Salām! !
May it be said,
'Ah ! she writes like Ganésh!'

CHAPTER I

Departure from England

I N APRIL, 1822, *Monsieur mon mari* took me to Switzerland. For the first time, I quitted England. How beautiful was the Valley of Chamonix! How delightful our expedition on the La Flegère! The guides pronounced it too early in the year to attempt the ascent of Mont Blanc. We quitted the valley with regret, and returned to Geneva: but our plans were frustrated, and our hopes disappointed; for, on reaching the hotel, we found a letter requiring our instant return to England. The *Marchioness of Ely*, in which we had taken our passage to Bengal, was reported to be ready to sail in a few days: no time was to be lost; we started immediately, travelled night and day incessantly, and arrived, greatly harassed, in town. The illness brought on by the over-fatigue of that journey never quitted me for years. The vessel, however, was merely preparing for her departure, and did not sail until long after.

Happily the pain of separation from the beloved home of my childhood was broken by the necessity of exertion in preparation for the voyage.

June 13th – We went to Gravesend, to see the ship: it was scarcely possible to enter our destined abode, the port stern cabin; so full was it to overflowing – boxes of clothes, hampers of soda water, crates of china and glass – a marvellous confusion! After a time the hampers and boxes were carried below, the furniture cleated and lashed, and some sort of order was established.

We had carefully selected a ship that was not to carry troops: we now found the *Ely* had been taken up to convey four troops of H. M. 16th Lancers; the remainder of the regiment was to sail in the *General Hewitt*. Some of our fellow-passengers were on board on the same errand as ourselves.

June 18th – We had lingered with our friends, and had deferred the sad farewell until the last moment: half uncertain if we should be in time to catch the ship in the Downs, we posted to Deal, took refuge at the *Three Kings*, and had the satisfaction of watching the *Marchioness of Ely*, and the *Winchelsea* her companion, as they bore down. At eleven o'clock we went on board, and sailed the next day. There was such a glorious confusion on deck, that those who were novices in military and naval affairs might deem, as they gazed around, it could never subside into anything approaching order. Everyone, however, was saying it would be very different when the ship was at sea; of which, indeed, there was little doubt, for to go on as we were would have been impossible. Off the Isle of Wight the pilot left us to our captain's guidance; the breeze was favourable; we were sailing so smoothly, there was scarcely any motion. The last farewell tears dropped as I passed the Needles and the coast of Hampshire, whilst memory recalled the happy days I had spent there, and in the Forest, the beautiful Forest!

Such thoughts and feelings it was necessary to throw aside. I joined the party in the cuddy, scrutinised the strange faces, and retired to my cabin, with as solitary a feeling as if my husband and I had been exiles for ever.

The voyage began prosperously; I was satisfied with the captain, with my cabin, with my servant, and happy with my lord and master.

We regretted we had taken our passage in a ship full of troops, and anticipated we should be debarred taking exercise on the quarterdeck, and enjoying ourselves with walk and talk during the fine moonlight nights. In the *Ely* it appeared as if it would be impossible; were you to attempt it, you would be sure to blunder over some sleeping Lancer. However, the band was on board – some small consolation; and as the society was large, there was more chance of entertainment.

July 1st – Porto Santo looked beautiful, its head enveloped in clouds. The rocky island rises boldly out of the sea; its mountains are very picturesque. The sight of land and white châteaux was quite charming.

I now began to recover from the *maladie de mer*, and to regain my usual good spirits. Creatures of habit, we soon grew accustomed to the small space. The stern cabin, twelve feet by ten, at first sight appeared most extremely inconvenient; but now it seemed to have enlarged itself, and we were more comfortable. Still sleep would scarcely visit me, until a swinging cot was pro-cured. From that time I slept calmly and quietly, whatever pranks the old *Ely* might choose to play.

The comfort or discomfort of a voyage greatly depends upon your fellow-passengers. In this respect we were most fortunate; one-half the officers of the 16th Lancers were in the *Ely*. The old 16th to me were friends; my father, who had been many years in the regiment, was forced to quit it, in consequence of a severe wound he received in action in the Pays Bas, under the command of the Duke of York. My uncle had commanded the gallant regiment in Spain, and other relatives had also been many years with the regiment. Chance had thrown us amongst friends.

Perhaps no friendships are stronger than those formed on board ship, where the tempers and dispositions are so much set forth in their true colours.

[. . .]

July 22nd – What a strange, bustling life! This is baggage day; all the trunks are on deck – such a confusion! I am suffering from *maladie de mer*; the wind is contrary; we tack and veer most tiresomely; the ship pitches; we cling about like cats, and are at our wits' end, striving to endure our miseries with patience

The Bristol water is invaluable, the ship water very black, and it smells vilely. I knew not before the value of good water; and, were it not for the shower bath, should be apt to wish myself where Truth is – at the bottom of a well.

Yesterday such a noise arose on deck, it brought me to the scene of action in a minute: 'Come here! Come here! Look! Look! There they go, like a pack of hounds in full cry!' I did come, and I did look; and there were some hundred of skipjacks leaping out of the water, and following each other with great rapidity across the head of the ship. When many fish leaped up together, there was such laughing, shouting, pointing, and gazing, from four hundred full-grown people, it was absurd to see how much amusement the poor fish occasioned. I looked alternately at the fish and the people, and laughed at both.

A kind of rash teases me; in these latitudes they call it prickly heat, vow you cannot be healthy without it, and affirm that everyone ought to be glad to have it. So am not I.

Having beaten about the line for a fortnight, with a contrary wind, at length we entertained hopes of crossing it, and letters were received on board from Neptune and Amphitrite, requesting to be supplied with clothes, having lost their own in a gale of wind.

July 30th – Neptune and his lady came on board to acquaint the captain they would visit him in form the next day. The captain wished the god good-night, when instantly the deck was deluged with showers of water from the main-top, while a flaming tar-barrel was thrown overboard, in which Neptune was supposed to have vanished in flame and water.

July 31st – At nine o'clock the private soldiers who were not to be shaved were stationed on the poop with their wives; on the quarterdeck the officers and ladies awaited the arrival of the ocean-god. First in procession marched the band, playing 'God save the King'; several grotesque figures followed; then came the car of Neptune – a gun-carriage – with such a creature for a coachman! The carriage was drawn by six half-naked seamen, painted to represent tritons, who were chained to the vehicle. We beheld the monarch and his bride, seated in the car, with a lovely girl, whom he called his tender offspring. These ladies were represented by the most brawny, muscular, ugly and powerful fellows in the ship; the letters requesting female attire having procured an abundance of finery. The boatswain's mate, a powerful man, naked to the waist, with a pasteboard crown upon his head and his speaking-trumpet in his hand, who represented Neptune, descended from his car, and offered the captain two fowls as tropical birds, and a salted fish on the end of a trident, lamenting that the late boisterous weather had prevented his bringing any fresh. A doctor, a barber with a notched razor, a sea-bear and its keeper, closed the procession.

Re-ascending the car, they took their station in front of the poop, and a rope was drawn across the deck to represent the line. Neptune then summoned the colonel-commandant of the Lancers to his presence, who informed him he had before entered his dominions. The major was then conducted, by a fellow calling himself a constable, to the foot of the car: he went up, expecting to be shaved, but the sea god desired him to present his wife to Amphitrite. After the introduction they were both dismissed.

My husband and myself were then summoned: he pleaded having crossed the line before. Neptune said that would not avail, as his lady had entered the small latitudes for the first time. After a laughable discussion, of to be shaved or not to be shaved, we were allowed to retire. The remainder of the passengers were summoned in turn. The sentence of shaving was passed upon all who had not crossed the line, but not carried into execution on the officers of the ship. The crew were shaved and ducked in form, and in all good humour. In the meantime the fire-engine drenched every body on deck, and the officers and passengers amused themselves for hours throwing water over each other from buckets. Imagine four hundred people ducking one another, and you may have some idea of the frolic. In the evening the sailors danced, sang, recited verses, and spliced the main brace (drank grog), until very late and the day ended as jovially as it began. Several times they charmed us with an appropriate song, roared at the utmost pitch of their stentorian lungs, to the tune of 'There's na luck about the house'.

> We'll lather away, and shave away,
> And lather away so fine,
> We always have a shaving day
> Whenever we cross the line.

With sorrow I confess to having forgotten the remainder of the ditty, which ended –

> There's nothing half so sweet in life
> As crossing of the line.

'Rule Britannia' with a subscription for the ruler of the seas, was the finale, leaving everyone perfectly satisfied with his portion of salt water. It was agreed the rites and ceremonies had never been better performed or with greater good humour.

[...]

Neptune was accompanied on board by a flying-fish that came in at one of the ports, perhaps to escape from an albicore: a lucky omen. The gentlemen amuse themselves with firing at the albatross, as they fly round and round the vessel; as yet, no damage has been done – the great birds shake their thick plumage, and laugh at the shot.

The favourite game is pitch-and-toss for dollars. Boxing is another method of spending time. Chess and backgammon boards are in high request; when the evenings are not calm enough for a quadrille or a waltz on deck, the passengers retire to the cuddy, to whist or blind hookey, and dollars are brought to table in cases that formerly contained Gamble's most excellent portable soup! On the very general introduction of *caoutchouc* into every department of the arts and sciences, some of the principal shipbuilders proposed to form the keels of their vessels of indian-rubber, but abandoned the project apprehending the *entire effacement of the equinoctial line.*

August 1st – Caught a bonito and a sea-scorpion; the latter was of a beautiful purple colour, the under part white: also a nautilus and a blue shark; in the latter were four-and-twenty young ones. The shark measured seven feet; its young from twelve to fourteen inches. The colour of the back was blue, of the belly white; several sucking-fish were upon the monster, of which some were lost in hauling him on board: one of those caught measured nine inches and a half; it stuck firmly to my hand in an instant.

Our amusements concluded with viewing an eclipse of the moon.

A stiff gale split the mainsail and blew the foretop and mizentop sails to pieces: no further damage was sustained. I enjoyed the sight of the fine waves that tossed the vessel as if she were a cockleshell.

We caught two Cape pigeons, very beautiful birds; the moment they were brought on deck they suffered extremely from *maladie de mer!*

[...]

August 23rd – There is a ship alongside! A ship bound for England! It speaks of home and the beloved ones, and although I am as happy as possible, my heart still turns to those who have heretofore been all and everything to me, with a warmth of affection at once delightful and very painful.

August 27th – Lat. 32° 9' S., long. 4° 25' E. – A dead calm! Give me any day a storm and a half in preference! It was so miserable – a long heavy swell, without a ripple on the waves the ship rolled from side to side without advancing one inch; she groaned in all her timbers: the old *Marchioness* appeared to suffer and be as miserable as myself. The calm continued the next day, and the rolling also; the captain kindly allowed the jolly-boat to be lowered, in which some of the lancers and my husband went out shooting.

This day, the 28th of August, was the commencement of the shooting season: game was in abundance, and they sought it over the long heavy swell of the glasslike and unrippled sea. The sportsmen returned with forty head of game: in this number was an albatross, measuring nine feet from the tip of one wing to that of the other; a Cape hen, a sea-swallow, with several pintado and other birds.

When the boat returned, it brought good fortune; the wind instantly sprang up, and we went on our way rejoicing. This day a whale was seen at a distance; if it had approached the vessel, a captain of the Lancers had prepared a Congreve rocket for its acceptance.

September 1st – We spoke a Dutchman off the Cape, looking in a very pitiable condition: the same gale which had damaged her overtook us, and blew heavily and disagreeably for three days. The weather was very cold and wet, and we felt disappointed at not touching at the Cape.

September 10th – Lat. 36° 43' S., long. 45° 30' W., ther. 64° – Another calm, and another *battue*: the gentlemen returned from the watery plain with great *éclat*, bringing seven albatross, thirty pintados, a Cape hen, and two garnets. One of the albatross, which was stuffed for me, measured fifty-three inches from head to tail, and nine feet ten inches across the wings.

[…]

September 23 – A *school* of twenty or thirty whales passed near the ship; it was almost a calm; they were constantly on the surface, frolicking and spouting away. They were, the sailors said, of the spermaceti order, which are smaller in size, and do not spout so high as the larger race. I was disappointed. Two of the officers of the Lancers rowed within ten yards of a large whale, and fired a Congreve rocket into its body; the whale gave a spring and dived instantly. The rocket would explode in a few seconds and kill him: a good prize for the first ship that falls in with the floating carcase. They fired at another, but the rocket exploded under water and came up smoking to the surface. The boat returned safely to the ship, but it was rather a nervous affair.

September 25th – Another calm allowed of more shooting, and great was the slaughter of sea game. I must make an extract from Colonel Luard's work, speaking of a battle that took place on the 10th: 'The Cape hen was a large fierce black bird, and only having its wing broken, tried to bite every person's legs in the boat. When she was placed on the ship's quarterdeck, a small terrier belonging to one of the officers attacked her, and they fought for some time with uncertain advantage; the bloody streams from the dog proving the severity of the bird's bite: at last the terrier seized his adversary by the throat, when the battle and the bird's life ended together. In lat. 4° 13' S., long. 93° 11' E., the thermometer in the sun standing at 130°, and in the shade 97°, two small birds, in every respect resembling the English swallow, came about the ship. One of them was caught, and died; the other (probably in hopes of rejoining its companion) remained with the ship fourteen or fifteen days, frequently coming into the cabins and roosting there during the night. It was at last missing; and, not being an aquatic bird, perhaps met a watery death'.

During the time of the *battue* on the third day, three sharks were astern; we caught one that had a young one by her side. When opened on deck, a family of twenty-four were found, each about twelve or fourteen inches long; the mother measured seven feet. The shark is said to swallow its young when in peril, and to disgorge them when the danger has passed. The curious birds and fish we see relieve the tedium of the voyage.

We now looked impatiently for the end of our passage, and counted the days like schoolboys expecting their vacation. It was amusing to hear the various plans the different people on board intended to pursue on landing – all too English by far for the climate to which they were bound.

The birds were numerous south of the tropics; we saw few within them. The flying-fish are never found beyond the tropics.

October 11th – Lat. 4° 20' S., long. 93° 11' E. – The heat was very great; the vertical sun poured down its sickening rays, the thermometer in the shade of the coolest cabin 86°; not a breath of air; we felt severely the sudden change of temperature. The sails flapped against the mast, and we only made progress seventeen knots in the twenty-four hours! Thus passed eleven days – the shower bath kept us alive, and our health was better than when we quitted England. *Monsieur mon mari*, who was studying Persian, began to teach me Hindustani, which afforded me much pleasure.

In spite of the calm there was gaiety on board; the band played delightfully, our fellow-passengers were agreeable, and the calm evenings allowed of quadrilles and waltzing on the deck, which was lighted up with lanterns and decorated with flags.

We spoke to the *Winchelsea*, which had quitted the Downs seven days before us and experienced heavy weather off the Cape: it was some consolation to have been at sea a shorter time than our companion. But little sickness was on board; a young private of the Lancers fell overboard, it was supposed, during a squall, and was lost; he was not even missed until the next day: a sick Lancer died, and a little child also; they were buried at sea: the bill of health was uncommonly good. A burial at sea, when first witnessed, is very solemn and impressive.

We passed an English ship – the Lancer band played 'God save the King', the vessel answered with three cheers. It was painful to meet a homeward-bound ship; it reminded me of home, country, and, dearer still, of friends. The sailors have a superstition, that sharks always follow a ship when a corpse is on board: the night after the man fell overboard, the Lancer and the child died; the day they were buried three sharks were astern. I thought of the sailors' superstition; no sharks had been seen alongside for three weeks. The sunsets on and near the line are truly magnificent, nothing is more glorious – the nights are beautiful, no dew, no breeze, the stars shining as they do on a frosty night at home, and we are gasping for a breath of air! A sea-snake about a yard and a half long was caught – many turtle were seen, but they sank the moment the boat approached them. A subscription lottery was made; the person whose ticket bears the date of our arrival at Saugor will win the amount.

October 22nd – Becalmed for eighteen days! Not as when off the Cape; there it was cool, with a heavy swell, here there is no motion, the sun vertical, not a breath of air, the heat excessive. At length a breeze sprang up, and we began to move: one day during the calm we made seven knots in the twenty-four hours, and those all the wrong way!

> Day after day, day after day,
>   We stuck, nor breath nor motion;
> As idle as a painted ship
>   Upon a painted ocean.

Our voyage advanced very slowly, and the supply of fresh water becoming scanty, we were all put on short allowance; anything but agreeable under so hot a sun. Captain Kay determined to make the land, and water the ship, and made signals to our companion, the *Winchelsea*, to that effect.

October 30th – To our great delight we arrived at, and anchored off, Carnicobar, one of the Nicobar Islands, lat. 9° 10' N., long. 92° 56' E. Boats were immediately sent on shore to a small village, where the landing was good, and two springs of delicious water were found for the supply of the ship.

CHAPTER II

Carnicobar

HANDSOME SISTER, WITH A MAT FOR A PETTICOAT*

THE ISLAND where we landed was covered to the edge of the sand of the shore with beautiful trees; scarcely an uncovered or open spot was to be seen. Off the ship the village appeared to consist of six or eight enormous beehives, erected on poles and surrounded by high trees; among these, the coconut, to an English eye, was the most remarkable.

The ship was soon surrounded by canoes filled with natives; two came on board. The ladies hastened on deck, but quickly scudded away, not a little startled at beholding men like Adam when he tasted the forbidden fruit: they knew not they were naked, and they were not ashamed. I returned to my cabin. The stern of the vessel was soon encircled by canoes filled with limes, citrons, oranges, coconuts, plantains, yams, eggs, chickens, little pigs, and various kinds of fruit. The sight of these temptations soon overcame my horror at the want of drapery of the islanders, and I stood at the port bargaining for what I wished to obtain until the floor was covered. Our traffic was thus conducted – I held up an empty jam-pot, and received in return a basket full of citrons; for two empty phials, a couple of fowls; another couple of fowls were given in exchange for an empty tin case that held portable soup; the price of a little pig was sixpence, or an old razor: they were eager at first for knives, but very capricious in their bargains: the privates of the Lancers had glutted the market. On my holding up a clasp-knife, the savage shook his head. I cut off the brass rings from the window-curtains – great was the clamour and eagerness to possess them. On giving a handful to one of the men, he counted them carefully, and then fitted them on his fingers. The people selected those they approved, returned the remainder, and gave me fruit in profusion. Even curtain-rings soon lost their charm – my eye fell on a basket of shells, the owner refused by signs all my offers – he wanted some novelty: at length an irresistible temptation was found – an officer of the Lancers cut off three of the gay buttons from his jacket, and offered them to the savage, who handed up the shells.

* Fanny Parks starts many of her chapters with an Oriental Proverb – some more obtuse than others. She also drops them liberally into the text.

'*Figurez-vous*,' said the Lancer, 'the Carnicobarbarian love of that fellow, matted with straw and leaves from the waist to the knee, decked with three Lancer buttons suspended round her neck by a coconut fibre, and enraptured with the novelty and beauty of the tout ensemble!!'

The dress, or rather the undress of the men was very simple; a handkerchief tied round the waist and passed between the limbs so as to leave the end hanging like a tail: some wore a stripe of plantain-leaf bound fillet-like round their heads; the necks of the chiefs were encircled either with silver wire in many rings, or a necklace of cowries.

One of the canoes which came from a distant part of the island was the most beautiful and picturesque boat I ever saw; it contained twenty-one men, was paddled with amazing swiftness, and gaily decorated. Of the canoes, some were so narrow that they had bamboo outriggers to prevent their upsetting. The natives appeared an honest, inoffensive race, and were much pleased with the strangers. After dinner it was proposed to go on shore in the cool of the evening: the unmarried ladies remained on board. I could not resist a run on a savage island, and longed to see the women, and know how they were treated.

Really the dark colour of the people serves very well as dress, if you are not determined to be critical. On landing, I was surrounded by women chattering and staring; one pulled my bonnet, but above all things they were charmed with my black silk apron; they greatly admired, and took it in their hands. They spoke a few words of English, and shook hands with me, saying, 'How do? How do?' And when they wished to purchase my apron they seized it rather roughly, saying, 'You buy? You buy?' meaning, Will you sell it? They were kind after the mode Nicobar.

The natives are of low stature, their faces ugly, but good-humoured; they are beautifully formed, reminding one of ancient statues; their carriage is perfectly erect. A piece of cloth is tied round the waists of the women, which reaches to the knee. Some women were hideous: of one the head was entirely shaved, excepting where a black lock was left over either ear, of which the lobes were depressed, stretched out, and cut into long slips, so that they might be ornamented with bits of coloured wood that were inserted. She had elephantiasis, and her limbs were swollen to the size of her waist. They are very idle; in fact, there appears no necessity for exertion – fruits of all sorts grow wild, pigs are plentiful, and poultry abundant. Tobacco was much esteemed. Silver they prized very much, and called coin of all sorts and sizes dollars – a sixpence or a half-crown were dollars. The only apparent use they have for silver is to beat it out into thick wire, which they form into spiral rings by twisting it several times round the finger. Rings are worn on the first and also on the *middle* joint of *every* finger, and on the thumb also. Bracelets formed after the same fashion wind from the wrist halfway up the arms. Rings ornament all their toes, and they wear half-a-dozen anklets. The same silver wire adorns the necks of the more opulent of the men also. They are copper-coloured, with straight black hair; their bodies shine from being rubbed with coconut oil, which smells very disagreeably. Their huts are particularly well built. Fancy a great beehive beautifully and most carefully thatched, twelve feet in diameter, raised on poles about five feet from the ground; to the first storey you ascend by a removable ladder of bamboo; the floor is of bamboo, and springs under you in walking; the side opposite the entrance is smoked by a fire: a ladder leads to the attic, where another elastic floor completes the habitation. They sit or lie on the ground. Making baskets appears to be their only manufacture.

From constantly chewing the betel-nut, their teeth are stained black, with a red tinge, which has a hideous effect. I picked up some beautiful shells on the shore, and bartered with the women for their silver wire rings.

The colours of my shawl greatly enchanted Lancour, one of their chief men; he seized it rather roughly, and pushing three fowls, tied by the legs, into my face, said, 'I present, you present.'. As I refused to agree to the exchange, one of the officers interfered, and Lancour drew back his hand evidently disappointed.

The gentlemen went on shore armed in case of accidents; but the ship being in sight all was safe. I have since heard that two vessels, which were wrecked on the island some years afterwards, were plundered, and the crews murdered.

Many of the most beautiful small birds were shot by the officers. As for foliage, you can imagine nothing more luxuriant than the trees bending with fruits and flowers. No quadrupeds were to be seen but dogs and pigs; there are no wild beasts on the island. They say jackals, alligators, and crabs are numerous: the natives were anxious the sailors should return to the ship at night and as they remained late, the Nicobars came down armed with a sort of spear; they were cautious of the strangers, but showed no fear, and told the men to come again the next day. It must be dangerous for strangers to sleep on shore at night, on account of the dense fog, so productive of fever.

The scene was beautiful at sunset; the bright tints in the sky contrasted with the deep hue of the trees; the shore covered with men and boats; the beehive village, and the novelty of the whole. Many of the savages adorned with European jackets, were strutting about the vainest of the vain, charmed with their new clothing; Lancour was also adorned with a cocked-hat! The woman who appeared of the most consideration, perhaps the queen of the island, wore a red cap shaped like a sugar-loaf, a small square handkerchief tied over one shoulder, like a monkey mantle, and a piece of blue cloth round her hips; a necklace of silver wire, with bracelets, anklets, and rings on the fingers and toes without number. The pigs proved the most delicate food; they were very small, and fattened on coconuts: the poultry was excellent.

The natives make a liquor as intoxicating as gin from the coconut tree, by cutting a gash in the bark and collecting the juice in a coconut shell, which they suspend below the opening to receive it; it ferments and is very strong – the toddy or *taree* of India.

Little did I think it would ever have been my fate to visit such an uncivilised island, or to shake hands with such queer looking men; however, we agreed very well, and they were quite pleased to be noticed: one man, who made us understand he was called Lancour, sat down by my side, and smoked in my face by way of a compliment. They delight in tobacco, which they roll up in a leaf; and smoke in form of a cigar. I cannot refrain from writing about these people, being completely island struck.

It was of importance to the *Winchelsea*, in which there were a hundred and twenty on the sick list, to procure fruit and vegetables, as the scurvy had broken out amongst the crew.

We landed October 30th, and quitted the island November 2nd, with a fair wind: all the passengers on board were in good spirits, and the ship presented a perfect contrast to the time of the calm.

November 3rd – We passed the Andaman Islands, whose inhabitants are reported to have a fondness for strangers of a nature different to the Carnicobarbarians – they are Cannibals!

A steady, pleasant monsoon urged us bravely onwards: a passing squall caught us, which laid the vessel on her side, carried away the flying jib, and split the driver into shreds: the next moment it was quite calm.

November 7th – We fell in with the Pilot Schooner, off the Sand-heads the pilot came on board, bringing Indian newspapers and fresh news.

November 10th – We anchored at Ganga Sāgar. Here we bade adieu to our fellow-passengers, and the old *Marchioness of Ely*: perhaps a more agreeable voyage was never made, in spite of its duration, nearly five months.

Our neighbours in the stern cabin, very excellent people, and ourselves, no less worthy, hired a decked vessel and proceeded up the Hoogly; that night we anchored off Fulta, and enjoyed fine fresh new milk, etc.; the next tide took us to Bijbij by night, and the following morning we landed at Chāndpāl Ghāt, Calcutta.

The Hoogly is a fine river, but the banks are very low; the most beautiful part, Garden Reach, we passed during the night. The first sight of the native fishermen in their little dinghies is very remarkable. In the cold of the early morning, they wrap themselves up in folds of linen, and have the appearance of men risen from the dead. Many boats passed us which looked as if

> By skeleton forms the sails were furled,
> And the hand that steered was not of this world.

November 13th – In the course of a few hours after our arrival, a good house was taken for us, which being sufficiently large to accommodate our companions, we set up our standards together in Park Street, Chowringhee, and thus opened our Indian campaign.

CHAPTER III

LIFE IN INDIA

THE FOUR TROOPS of the 16th Lancers from the *Ely* disembarked, and encamped on the glacis of Fort William; the *General Hewitt*, with the remainder of the regiment, did not arrive until six weeks afterwards, having watered at the Cape.

Calcutta has been styled the City of Palaces, and it well deserves the name. The Government House stands on the Maidān, near the river; the city, and St Andrew's Church, lie behind it; to the left is that part called Chowringhee, filled with beautiful detached houses, surrounded by gardens; the verandahs, which generally rise from the basement to the highest story give, with their pillars, an air of lightness and beauty to the buildings, and protecting the dwellings from the sun, render them agreeable for exercise in the rainy season.

The houses are all stuccoed on the outside, and seem as if built of stone. The rent of unfurnished houses in Chowringhee is very high; we gave Rs 325 a month for ours, the larger ones are from Rs 400 to 500 per month.

The style of an Indian house differs altogether from that of one in England. The floors are entirely covered with Indian matting, than which nothing can be cooler or more agreeable. For a few weeks, in the cold season, fine Persian carpets, or carpets from Mirzapur are used. The windows and doors are many; the windows are to the ground, like the French; and, on the outside, they are also protected by Venetian windows of the same description. The rooms are large and lofty, and to every sleeping-apartment a bathing-room is attached. All the rooms open into one another, with folding-doors, and *pankhās* are used during the hot weather. The most beautiful French furniture was to be bought in Calcutta of M. de Bast, at whose shop marble tables, fine mirrors, and luxurious couches were in abundance. Very excellent furniture was also to be had at the Europe shops, made by native workmen under the superintendence of European cabinet and furniture makers; and furniture of an inferior description in the native bazaars.

On arriving in Calcutta, I was charmed with the climate; the weather was delicious; and nothing could exceed the kindness we experienced from our friends. I thought India a most delightful country, and could I have gathered around me the dear ones I had left in England, my happiness would have been complete. The number of servants necessary to an establishment in India is most surprising to a person fresh from Europe: it appeared the commencement of ruin. Their wages are not high, and they find themselves in food; nevertheless, from their number, the expense is very great.

The Sircār

A very useful but expensive person in an establishment is a *sircār*; the man attends every morning early to receive orders, he then proceeds to the bazaars, or to the Europe shops, and brings back for inspection and approval, furniture, books, dresses, or whatever may have been ordered: his profit is a heavy percentage on all he purchases for the family.

One morning our *sircār*, in answer to my having observed that the articles purchased were highly priced, said, 'You are my father and my mother, and I am your poor little child: I have only taken two annas in the rupee *dasturi*.'

This man's language was a strong specimen of Eastern hyperbole: one day he said to me, 'You are my mother, and my father, and *my God!*' With great disgust, I reproved him severely for using such terms, when he explained, 'you are my protector and my support, therefore you are to me as my God.' The offence was never repeated. They dress themselves with the utmost care and most scrupulous neatness in white muslin; and the turban often consists of twenty-one yards of fine Indian muslin, by fourteen inches in breadth, most carefully folded and arranged in small plaits; his reed pen is behind his ear, and the roll of paper in his hand is in readiness for the orders of the sāhib. The shoes are of common leather; sometimes they wear them most elaborately embroidered in gold and silver thread and coloured beads. All men in India wear moustaches; they look on the bare faces of the English with amazement and contempt. The *sircār* is an Hindu, as shown by the opening of the vest on the *right* side, and the white dot, the mark of his caste, between his eyes.

Dasturi is an absolute tax. The *darwān* will turn from the gate the *boxwallas*, people who bring articles for sale in boxes, unless he gets *dasturi* for admittance. If the sāhib buy any article, his *sirdār*-bearer will demand *dasturi*. If the memsāhib purchase finery, the *ayah* must have her *dasturi* – which, of course, is added by the *boxwalla* to the price the gentleman is compelled to pay.

Dasturi is from two to four pice in the rupee; one anna, or one sixteenth of the rupee is, I imagine, generally taken. But all these contending interests are abolished if the *sircār* purchase the article: he takes the lion's share. The servants hold him in great respect, as he is generally the person who answers for their characters, and places them in service.

It appeared curious to be surrounded by servants who, with the exception of the tailor, could not speak one word of English; and I was forced to learn to speak Hindustani.

To a *griffin*, as a new-comer is called for the first year, India is a most interesting country; everything appears on so vast a scale, and the novelty is so great.

In December, the climate was so delightful, it rendered the country preferable to any place under the sun; could it always have continued the same, I should have advised all people to flee unto the East.

My husband gave me a beautiful Arab, Azor by name, but as the *sā'is* always persisted in calling him Aurora, or a Roarer, we were obliged to change his name to Rajah. I felt very happy cantering my beautiful high-caste Arab on the race course at six o'clock or, in the evening, on the well-watered drive in front of the Government House. Large birds, called adjutants, stalk about the Maidān in numbers; and on the heads of the lions that crown the entrance arches to the Government House, you are sure to see this bird (the *hargila* or gigantic crane) in the most picturesque attitudes, looking as if a part of the building itself.

The arrival of the 16th Lancers, and the approaching departure of the Governor-General, rendered Calcutta extremely gay. Dinner parties and fancy balls were numerous; at the latter, the costumes were excellent and superb.

December 16th – The Marquis of Hastings gave a ball at the Government House, to the gentlemen of the Civil and Military Services, and the inhabitants of Calcutta; the variety of costume displayed by Nawābs, Rajahs, Mahrattas, Greeks, Turks, Armenians, Musulmāns, and Hindus, and the gay attire of the military, rendered it a very interesting spectacle. Going to the ball was a service of danger, on account of the thickness of one of those remarkable fogs so common an annoyance during the cold season at the Presidency. It was impossible to see the road, although the carriage had lights and two *mashalchis*, with torches in their hands, preceded the horses; but the glare of the *mashals*, and the shouts of the men, prevented our meeting with any accident in the dense cloud by which we were surrounded .

Palanquins were novel objects; the bearers go at a good rate; the pace is neither walking nor running, it is the amble of the biped, in the style of the amble taught the native horses, accompanied by a grunting noise that enables them to keep time. Well-trained bearers do not shake the *pālkee*. *Bilees*, *hackeries*, and *khraunchies*, came in also for their share of wonder.

The Sircār

So few of the gentry in England can afford to keep riding-horses for their wives and daughters that I was surprised, on my arrival in Calcutta, to see almost every lady on horseback; and that not on hired hacks, but on their own good steeds. My astonishment was great one morning on beholding a lady galloping away, on a fiery horse, only three weeks after her confinement. What nerves the woman must have had!

December 16th – The Civil Service, the military, and the inhabitants of Calcutta gave a farewell ball to the Marquis and Marchioness of Hastings, after which the Governor-General quitted India.

On Christmas Day the servants adorned the gateways with chaplets (*hārs*) and garlands of fresh flowers. The bearers and *dhobees* brought in trays of fruit, cakes, and sweetmeats, with garlands of flowers upon them, and requested *bakhshish*, probably the origin of our Christmas-boxes. We accepted the sweet-meats, and gave some rupees in return.

They say that, next to the Chinese, the people of India are the most dexter-ous thieves in the world; we kept a porter (*darwān*) at the gate, two watchmen (*chaukidārs*), and the compound (ground surrounding the house) was encom-passed by a high wall.

January 12th 1832 – There was much talking below amongst the bearers; during the night the shout of the *chaukidārs* was frequent, to show they were on the alert; nevertheless, the next morning a friend who was staying with us found that his desk, with gold mohurs and valuables in it, had been carried off from his room, together with some clothes and his military cloak. We could not prove the theft, but had reason to believe it was perpetrated by a head table-servant (*khānsāmān*) whom we had discharged, connived at by the *darwān* and *chaukidārs*.

March 20th – I have now been four months in India, and my idea of the climate has altered considerably; the hot winds are blowing; it is very oppres-sive; if you go out during the day, I can compare it to nothing but the hot blast you would receive in your face were you suddenly to open the door of an oven.

The evenings are cool and refreshing; we drive out late; and the moonlit evenings at present are beautiful; when darkness comes on, the fireflies illumi-nate the trees, which appear full of flitting sparks of fire; these little insects are in swarms; they are very small and ugly, with a light like the glow-worm's in the tail, which, as they fly, appears and suddenly disappears: how beautifully the trees in the adjoining grounds are illuminated at night, by these little dazzling sparks of fire!

The first sight of a *pankhā* is a novelty to a griffin. It is a monstrous fan, a wooden frame covered with cloth, some ten, twenty, thirty, or more feet long, suspended from the ceiling of a room, and moved to and fro by a man outside by means of a rope and pulleys, and a hole in the wall through which the rope passes; the invention is a native one; they are the greatest luxuries, and are also handsome, some being painted and gilt, the ropes covered with silk, and so shaped or scooped as to admit their vibratory motion without touching the chandeliers, suspended in the same line with the *pankhā*, and when at rest, occupying the space scooped out. In the up-country, the *pankhā* is always pulled during the night over the *chārpāī* or bed.

The weather is very uncertain; sometimes very hot, then suddenly comes a northwester, blowing open every door in the house, attended with a deluge of heavy rain, falling straight down in immense drops: the other evening it was dark as night, the lightning blazed for a second or two with the blue sulphurous light you see represented on the stage; the effect was beautiful; the forked lightning was remarkably strong; I did not envy the ships in the bay.

The foliage of the trees, so luxuriously beautiful and so novel, is to me a source of constant admiration. When we girls used to laugh at the odd trees on the screens, we wronged the Chinese in imagining they were the productions of fancy; the whole nation was never before accused of having had a fanciful idea, and those trees were copied from nature, as I have found from seeing the same in my drives and rides around Calcutta. The country is quite flat, but the foliage very fine and rich. The idleness of the natives is excessive; for instance, my *ayah* will dress me, after which she will go to her house, eat her dinner, and then returning, will sleep in one corner of my room on the floor for the whole day. The bearers also do nothing but eat and sleep, when they are not pulling the *pankhās*.

Some of the natives are remarkably handsome, but appear far from being strong men. It is *impossible* to do with a few servants, you *must* have many; their customs and prejudices are inviolable; a servant will do such and such things, and nothing more. They are great plagues; much more troublesome than English servants. I knew not before the oppressive power of the hot winds, and find myself as listless as any Indian lady is universally considered to be; I can now excuse what I before condemned as indolence and want of energy – so much for experience. The greatest annoyance are the mosquito bites; it is almost impossible not to scratch them, which causes them to inflame, and they are then often very difficult to cure: they are to me much worse than the heat itself; my irritable constitution cannot endure them.

The elephantiasis is very common amongst the natives, it causes one or both legs to swell to an enormous size, making the leg at the ankle as large as it is above the knee; there are some deplorable objects of this sort, with legs like those of the elephant – whence the name. Leprosy is very common; we see lepers continually. The insects are of monstrous growth. Such spiders! And the small-lizards are numerous on the walls of the rooms, darting out from behind pictures, etc. Curtains are not used in Calcutta, they would harbour mosquitoes, scorpions, and lizards.

The Chŭrŭk Pooja

The other day, hearing it was a *Burra Din* (day of festival in honour of the goddess Kālee, whose temple is about a mile and a half from Calcutta), I drove down in the evening to Kālee Ghaut, where, had not the novelty of the scene excited my curiosity, disgust would have made me sick. Thousands of people were on the road, dressed in all their gayest attire, to do honour to the festival of the *Chŭrŭk Pooja*, the swinging by hooks. Amongst the crowd, the most remarkable objects were several Voiragee mendicants; their bodies were covered with ashes, their hair clotted with mud and twisted round their head; they were naked all but a shred of cloth. One man had held up both arms over his head until they had withered and were immoveable, the nails of the clenched fists had penetrated through the back of the hands, and came out on the other side like the claws of a bird. To fulfil some vow to Vishna this agony is endured, not as a penance for sin, but as an act of extraordinary merit. At first the pain must be great, but it ceases as the arms become benumbed. A man of this description is reckoned remarkably holy, having perfect dependence upon god for support, being unable, his arms having become immoveable, to carry food to his mouth or assist himself. Two or three other mendicants who were present had only one withered arm raised above their heads. Some Hindus of low caste, either for their sins or for money, had cut three or four gashes in the muscular part of the arm, and through these gashes they kept running a sword, dancing violently all the time to hideous music; others ran bamboos as thick as three fingers through the holes in the arm, dancing in the same manner. One man passed a spit up and down through the holes, another a dagger, and a third had a skewer through his tongue.

A little further on were three swinging posts erected in this fashion, a post some thirty feet in height was crossed at the top by a horizontal bamboo, from one end of which a man was swinging, suspended by a rope, from the other end another rope was fastened to a horizontal pole below, which was turned by men running round like horses in a mill. The man swung in a circle of perhaps thirty feet diameter, supported by four iron hooks, two through the flesh of his back, and two in that of his chest, by which, and a small bit of cloth across the breast, he was entirely supported: he carried a bag in one hand, from which he

The Chŭrŭk Pooja

threw sweetmeats and flowers to the populace below. Some men swing with four hooks in the back and four on the chest without any cloth, eight hooks being considered sufficient to support the body. The man I saw swinging looked very wild, from the quantity of opium and *bengh* he had taken to deaden the sense of pain. *Bengh* is an intoxicating liquor, which is prepared with the leaves of the Gánja plant (*Cannabis Indica*).

Hindus of the lower castes are very fond of this amusement, accidental deaths occasioned by it are reckoned about three per cent. Sometimes four men swing together for half an hour; some in penance for their own sins; some for those of others, richer men, who reward their deputies and thus do penance by proxy.

Khraunchies full of *nách* girls were there in all their gaily-coloured dresses and ornaments, as well as a number of respectable men of good caste.

I was much disgusted, but greatly interested.

Sentries from the Calcutta militia were stationed round the swings to keep off the crowd.

CHAPTER IV

Residence in Calcutta

i.e. A man in debt is always at the mercy of his creditors,
as a woman at her husband's.

MAY 1823 – The other evening we went to a party given by Ramohun Roy, a rich Bengali *baboo*; the grounds, which are extensive, were well illuminated, and excellent fireworks displayed.

In various rooms of the house *nāch* girls were dancing and singing. They wear a petticoat measuring, *on dit*, one hundred yards in width, of fine white or coloured muslin, trimmed with deep borders of gold and silver; full satin trousers cover the feet; the *dupatta*, or large veil, highly embroidered, is worn over the head, and various ornaments of native jewellery adorn the person.

They dance, or rather move in a circle, attitudinising and making the small brass bells fastened to their ankles sound in unison with their movements. Several men attended the women, playing on divers curiously-shaped native instruments.

The style of singing was curious; at times the tones proceeded finely from their noses; some of the airs were very pretty; one of the women was Nickee, the Catalani of the East. Indian jugglers were introduced after supper, who played various tricks, swallowed swords, and breathed out fire and smoke. One man stood on his right foot, and putting his left leg behind his back, hooked his left foot on the top of his right shoulder; just try the attitude *pour passer le temps*. The house was very handsomely furnished, everything in European style, with the exception of the owner.

The children of Europeans in India have a pale sickly hue, even when they are in the best of health; very different from the chubby brats of England.

All the Indian fruits appear very large, and a new comer thinks them inferior in point of flavour to the European; as for the far-famed mangoes, I was disgusted with them, all those to be had at that time in Calcutta being stringy, with a strong taste of turpentine.

The fort is spacious and handsome, but very hot from the ramparts that surround it. The 44th Queen's have lost three officers by death, nine more have returned to England on sick certificate, and three hundred of the privates are in hospital; this in six months! The mortality amongst the privates has been dreadful owing, I believe, to the cheapness of spirituous liquors, and exposure to the sun.

Port or sherry is seldom seen on table during the hot weather; Madeira is not much used; Burgundy, Claret and light French wines are very rationally preferred.

Where the climate is so oppressive, what are luxuries indeed at home are here necessary to health and existence; to walk is impossible, even the most petty Europe shopkeeper in Calcutta has his buggy, to enable him to drive out in the cool of the evening.

June 1st – This is the first day of the month; the morning has been very hot, but at this moment the rain is descending as if the windows of heaven were again opened to deluge the earth; the thunder rolls awfully, and the forked lightning is very vivid. I never heard such peals of thunder in Europe. No one here appears to think about it; all the houses have conductors, and as the storm cools the air, it is always welcomed with pleasure by those on shore.

[...]

Lord Amherst arrived, and we attended a party given to those over whom he has come to reign.

[...]

At this time we became anxious for an appointment up the country, at a cooler and healthier station than Calcutta, far removed from the damp, low, swampy country of Bengal Proper.

August 29th – The Governor-General and Lady Amherst are great favourites in Calcutta; the latter renders herself particularly agreeable to her guests at the Government House. The new Governor-General is so economical he has discharged a number of servants, quenched a number of lamps; *on dit*, he intends to plant potatoes in the park at Barrackpore; people are so unaccustomed to anything of the sort in India, that all this European economy produces considerable surprise.

It happens that in India, as in other places, they have an absurd custom of demanding a certain portion of the precious metals in exchange for the necessaries and luxuries of life, to procure which, if you have them not, you are forced to borrow from agents, the richest dogs in Calcutta: and why? Because, forsooth, they merely require *now* eight per cent (formerly ten), added to which, after your debt reaches a certain amount, they oblige you to ensure your life, and in this ticklish country the rate of insurance is very high.

In the third place, which to us is the *argumentum ad hominem*, many and many are the lives that have been sacrificed, because poor miserable invalids have been unable from their debts to leave India. Interest – horrible interest – soon doubles the original sum, and a man is thus obliged to pay the debt three or four times over, and after that he may put by a fortune to support him in his native land.

Do not suppose I am *painting;* this is the plain fact, of which almost every month furnishes an example.

A man on first arrival (a griffin) cannot or will not comprehend that 'one and one make eleven'.

September 7th – Since our arrival we have been annoyed with constant robbery in the house. Seventy rupees were stolen one day, and now they have carried off about eighteen silver covers that are used to put over tumblers and wineglasses to keep out the flies; in consequence we have discharged our Ooriah bearers, who we suspect are the thieves, and have taken a set of up-country men.

October 1st – We have had a singular visitor, Shahzadah Zahangeer Zaman Jamh o Deen Mahomud, Prince of Mysore, the son of Tippoo Sāhib, and one of the two hostages.

He resides in a house near us, and sent us word he would honour us with a visit. The next morning he called, and sat two hours. He had studied English for twelve months. Seeing a bird in a cage, he said, 'Pretty bird that, little yellow bird, what you call?' 'A canary bird.' 'Yes, canary bird, pretty bird, make fine noise, they not *grow here.'* In this style we conversed, and I thought my visitor would never depart. I was ignorant of the oriental saying, 'Coming is voluntary, but departing depends upon permission;' his *politesse* made him remain awaiting my permission for his departure, whilst I was doubting if the visit would ever terminate. At last he arose, saying, 'I take leave now, come *gen* soon.' The next day he sent three decanters full of sweetmeats, very like the hats and caps that used to be given me in my childish days, mixed with caraway comfits, and accompanied by this note: 'Some sweetmeats for Missess — with respectful thanks of P. Jamh o Deen.' I suppose my visitor Prince Jamh o Deen did not understand the difference between compliments and thanks. I did not comprehend why the sweetmeats had been sent, until I was informed it was the custom of the natives to send some little valueless offering after paying a visit, and that it would be considered an insult to refuse it.

October 13th – We went to a *nāch* at the house of a wealthy *baboo* during the festival of the *Doorga Pooja* or *Dasera*, held in honour of the goddess Doorga. The house was a four-sided building, leaving an area in the middle; on one side of the area was the image of the goddess raised on a throne, and some Brahmins were in attendance on the steps of the platform. This image has ten arms, in one of her right hands is a spear with which she pierced a giant, with one of the left she holds the tail of a serpent and the hair of the giant, whose breast the serpent is biting; her other hands are all stretched behind her head, and are filled with different instruments of war. Against her right leg leans a lion, and against her left leg the above giant. In the rooms on one side the area a handsome supper was laid out, in the European style, supplied by Messrs Gunter and Hooper, where ices and French wines were in plenty for the European guests. In the rooms on the other sides of the square, and in the area, were groups of *nách* women dancing and singing, and crowds of European and native gentlemen sitting on sofas or on chairs listening to Hindustani airs. 'The bright half of the month Ashwina, the first of the *Hindu* lunar year, is peculiarly devoted to Doorga. The first nine nights are allotted to her decoration; on the sixth she is awakened; on the seventh she is invited to a bower formed of the leaves of nine plants, of which the *Bilwa* (or *Bilva*, *Crataeva Marmelos* Linn.) is the chief. The seventh, eighth and ninth are the great days, on the last of which the victims are immolated to her honour, and must be killed by one blow only of a sharp sword or axe. The next day the goddess is reverently dismissed, and her image is cast into the river, which finishes the festival of the *Dasera*.

'On the fifteenth day, that of the full moon, her devotees pass the night in sports and merriment, and games of various sorts: it is unlucky to sleep; for on this night the fiend Nicumbha led his army against Doorga, and Lakshmi, the goddess of prosperity, descended, promising wealth to those who were awake.' (Moor's *Hindu Pantheon*)

A short time before this festival, the *sircārs* employed in Calcutta generally return home to enjoy a holiday of some weeks.

Immense sums are expended by the wealthy *baboos* during the *Doorga Pooja*.

December 2nd – Would you believe that we sit at this time of the year without *pankhās*, with closed windows, and our floors carpeted! In some houses, fires are adopted. We have not yet come to this, though I occasionally have found it cold enough to desire one. The mornings are delightful, and the nights so colds I sleep under a silk counterpane quilted with cotton, called a *rezāi*.

The natives form images in clay; the countenances are excellent; the eyes, eyelids, and lips move remarkably well; they are very brittle; they represent servants, *fakirs*, and natives of all castes: the best, perhaps, are to be procured in or near Calcutta. They are attired according to the fashion of the country, and cost from eight annas to one rupee each.

We are in the midst of our gaieties, balls, plays, and parties, agreeably varied. Our first meeting (the races) is held during this month; for we have our Derby, and Oaks, and Riddlesworth. The Riddlesworth is with us a very interesting race, all the riders being gentlemen, and sometimes ten or twelve horses starting. From the stand, of a clear morning, there is a good view of the horses during the whole of their course.

We have just received from China two magnificent screens, of eight panels each; they are exceedingly handsome, and keep out the glare by day and the air by night: I think I may say they are magnificent.

Amongst the ornaments of the household, let Crab the terrier be also mentioned; he is much like unto a tinker's dog, but is humorous and good-tempered, plays about, chases cats and kills rats, not only in the stable, but house, and serves us in the place of a *parvulus Aeneas.*

CHAPTER V

RESIDENCE IN CALCUTTA

JANUARY 1824 – The advantages of a residence in Calcutta are these: you are under the eye of the Government, not likely to be overlooked, and are ready for any appointment falling vacant; you get the latest news from England, and have the best medical attendance. On the other hand, you have to pay high house rent; the necessary expenses are great; and the temptations to squander away money in gratifying your fancies more numerous than in the *mofussil*.

A friend, now high in the Civil Service, contracted, on his arrival here about eighteen years ago, a debt of Rs 15,000, about £1500 or £1800. Interest was then at twelve per cent. To give security, he insured his life which, with his agent's commission of one per cent, made the sum total of interest sixteen per cent. After paying the original debt five times, he hoped his agents upon the last payment would not suffer the interest to continue accumulating. He received for answer, 'that interest never slept, it was awake night and day'; and he is now employed in saving enough to settle the balance.

I wish much that those who exclaim against our extravagances here knew how essential to a man's comfort, to his quiet, and to his health it is to have everything good about him – a good house, good furniture, good carriages, good horses, good wine for his friends, good humour; good servants and a good quantity of them, good credit, and a good appointment: they would then be less virulent in their philippics against oriental extravagance.

January 15th – The Governor-General has a country residence, with a fine park, at Barrackpore; during the races the Calcutta world assembles there; we went over for a week; it was delightful to be again in the country. Lady Amherst rendered the Government House gay with quadrilles and displays of fireworks but I most enjoyed a party we made to see the ruins of an ancient fort, near Cairipoor, belonging to the Rajah of Burdwan, about five miles from Barrackpore, and thought them beautiful.

The road was very bad, therefore I quitted the buggy and mounted an elephant for the first time, feeling half-frightened but very much pleased. I ascended by a ladder placed against the side of the kneeling elephant; when he rose up, it was like a house making unto itself legs and walking therewith.

We went straight across the country, over hedges and ditches, and through the cultivated fields, the elephant with his great feet crushing down the corn, which certainly did not 'rise elastic from his airy tread.' The fields are divided by ridges of earth like those in salterns at home; these ridges are narrow, and in general, to prevent injury to the crops, the *mahout* guides the elephant along the ridge: it is curious to observe how firmly he treads on the narrow raised path.

By the side of the road was a remarkable object: 'The appearance of a *fakir* is his petition in itself.' In a small hole in the earth lay a *fakir*, or religious mendicant; the fragment of a straw mat was over him, and a bit of cloth covered his loins. He was very ill and quite helpless, the most worn emaciated being I ever beheld; he had lain in that hole day and night for five years and refused to live in a village, his only comfort, a small fire of charcoal, was kindled near his head during the night. Having been forcibly deprived of the property he possessed in the upper provinces, he came to Calcutta to seek redress, but being unsuccessful he had, in despair, betaken himself to that hole in the earth. An old woman was kindling the fire; it is a marvel the jackals do not put an end to his misery. The natives say, 'It is his pleasure to be there, what can *we* do?' and they pass on with their usual indifference: the hole was just big enough for his body, in a cold swampy soil.

There is a menagerie in the park at Barrackpore, in which are some remarkably fine tigers and cheetahs. My *ayah* requested to be allowed to go with me, particularly wishing to see an hyena. While she was looking at the beast I said, 'Why did you wish to see an hyena?' Laughing and crying hysterically, she answered, 'My husband and I were asleep, our child was between us, an hyena stole the child, and ran off with it to the jungle; we roused the villagers, who pursued the beast; when they returned, they brought me half the mangled body of my infant daughter – that is why I wished to see an hyena.'

Before we quitted Calcutta, we placed the plate in a large iron treasure chest. A friend, during his absence from home, having left his plate in a large oaken chest clamped with iron found, on his return, that the bearers had set fire to the chest to get at the plate, being unable to open it, and had melted the greater part of the silver!

It appears as if the plan of communicating with India by steamboats will not end in smoke: a very large bonus has been voted to the first *regular company* who bring it about, and the sum is so considerable, that I have no doubt some will be bold enough to attempt it.

In Calcutta, as in every place, it is difficult to suit yourself with a residence. Our first house was very ill defended from the hot winds; the situation of the second we thought low and swampy, and the cause of fever in our household. My husband, having quitted college, was gazetted to an appointment in Calcutta, and we again changed our residence for one in Chowringhee Road.

Prince Jamh o Deen, hearing me express a wish to see what was considered a good *nāch*, invited me to one. I could not, however, admire the dancing; some of the airs the women sang were very pretty.

Calcutta was gay in those days, parties numerous at the Government House, and dinners and fancy balls amongst the inhabitants.

A friend sent me a mouse deer, which I keep in a cage in the verandah; it is a curious and most delicate little animal, but not so pretty as the young pet fawns running about the compound with the spotted deer. The cows' milk generally sold in Calcutta is poor, that of goats is principally used: a good Bengali goat, when in full milk, will give a quart every morning; they are small-sized, short-legged, and well-bred. The servants milk the goats near the window of the morning room, and bring the bowl full and foaming to the breakfast table.

February 27th – My husband put into one of the smaller lotteries in Calcutta, and won thirteen and a half tickets, each worth Rs 100: he sent them to his agents, with the exception of one, which he presented to me. My ticket came up a prize of Rs 5000. The next day we bought a fine, high caste fiery Arab, whom we called Orelio, and a pair of grey Persian horses.

February 28th – Trial by Rice – The other day some friends dined with us: my husband left his watch on the drawing-room table when we went to dinner: the watch was stolen, the theft was immediately discovered, and we sent to the police. The *moonshee* assembled all who were present, took down their names, and appointed that day seven days hence for a trial by rice, unless, during the time, the watch should be restored, stolen property being often replaced from the dread the natives entertain of the ordeal by rice. On the appointed day the police *moonshee* returned, and the servants, whom he had ordered to appear fasting, were summoned before him, and by his desire were seated on the ground in a row.

The natives have great faith in the square *akbarābādee* rupee which they prefer to, and use on such occasions in lieu of, the circular rupee.

The *moonshee*, having soaked 2lb. weight of rice in cold water, carefully dried it in the sun: he then weighed rice equal to the weight of the square rupee in a pair of scales, and, calling one of the servants to him, made him take a solemn oath that he had not taken the watch, did not know who had taken it, where it was, or anything about it or the person who stole it. When the oath had been taken, the *moonshee* put the weighed rice into the man's hand to hold during the time every servant in the room was served in like manner. There were thirty-five present. When each had taken the oath, and received the rice in his hand, they all sat down on the ground, and a bit of plantain leaf was placed before each person. The *moonshee* then said 'Some person or persons amongst you have taken a false oath; God is in the midst of us; let every man put his portion of rice into his mouth, and having chewed it, let him spit it out upon the plantain leaf before him; he who is the thief, or knows aught concerning the theft, from his mouth it shall come forth as dry as it was put in; from the mouths of those who are innocent, it will come forth wet and well chewed.'

Every man chewed his rice, and spat it out like so much milk and water, with the exception of three persons, from whose mouths it came forth as dry and as fine as powder. Of these men, one had secreted two-thirds of the rice, hoping to chew the smaller quantity, but all to no purpose; it came *perfectly dry* from his mouth from the effect of fear, although it was ground to dust. The *moonshee* said, 'Those are the guilty men, one of them will probably inform against the others' and he carried them off to the police. It is a fact, that a person under great alarm will find it utterly impossible to chew and put forth rice in a moistened state, whilst one who fears not will find it as impossible to chew and to spit it out perfectly dry and ground to dust. An *harkāra*, in the service of one of our guests, was one of the men whom the *moonshee* pronounced guilty; about a fortnight before, a silver saucepan had been stolen from his master's house, by one of his own servants.

Against another, one of our own men, we have gained some very suspicious intelligence, and although we never expect the watch to be restored, we shall get rid of the thieves. So much for the ordeal by rice, in which I have firm faith.

May 4th – The weather is tremendously hot. A gentleman came in yesterday, and said, 'this room is delightful, it is cold as a well.' We have discovered, however, that it is infested below with rats and muskrats, three or four of which my little Scotch terrier kills daily; the latter make him foam at the mouth with disgust. My little dog Crab, you are the most delightful Scotch terrier that ever came to seek his fortune in the East!

Some friends have sent to us for garden-seeds. But, oh! observe how nature is degenerated in this country – they have sent alone for vegetable-seeds – the feast of roses being here thought inferior to the feast of marrowfat peas!

[...]

July 17th – On this day, having discovered a young friend ill in the Writer's Buildings, we brought him to our house. Two days afterwards I was seized with the fever, from which I did not recover for thirteen days. My husband nursed me with great care, until he fell ill himself; and eleven of our servants were laid up with the same disorder.

The people in Calcutta have all had it; I suppose, out of the whole population, European and native, not two hundred persons have escaped; and what is singular, it has not occasioned one death amongst the adults. I was so well and strong – over night we were talking of the best means of escaping the epidemic – in the morning it came and remained thirty-six hours, then quitted me; a strong eruption came out, like the measles, and left me weak and thin. My husband's fever left him in thirty-six hours, but he was unable to quit the house for nine days: the rash was the same. Some faces were covered with spots like those on a leopard's skin. It was so prevalent that the Courts of Justice, the Custom House, the Lottery Office and almost every public department in Calcutta were closed in consequence of the sickness. In the course of three days, three different physicians attended me, one after the other having fallen ill. It is wonderful that a fever producing so much pain in the head and limbs, leaving the patient weak, reduced, and covered with a violent eruption, should have been so harmless; after three weeks, nobody appeared to have suffered, with the exception of two or three children whom it attacked more violently than it did grown-up people, and carried them off.

The politicians at home have anticipated us in reckoning upon the probability of a Burmese war. We have hitherto been altogether successful. I saw yesterday a gold and a silver sword, and a very murderous looking weapon resembling a butcher's knife, but on a larger scale. A necklace (so called from its circling the neck, for it was composed of plates of gold hammered on a silken string), and some little squab images, gods perhaps, taken from a chief, whom Major Sale of H. M. 13th dispatched in an attack upon a stockade, leaving the chief in exchange part of the blade of his own sword, which was broken in his skull by the force of the blow that felled him.

It is an unlucky business: the Company certainly do not require at present more territory on that side of India, and the expense to which Government is put by this elegant little mill, as Pierce Egan might call it, is more than the worthies in Leadenhall Street suppose.

I see Lord Hastings is made Civil Governor of Malta! 'To what base uses we may return!' I observe the motion to prevent the necessity of parents sending their sons to Haileybury has been lost. The grand object of the students should be the acquisition of the oriental languages; here nothing else tells.

If a young man gets out of college in three or four months after his arrival which, if he crams at college in England, he may easily effect, he is considered forthwith as a brilliant character and is sealed with the seal of genius. Likewise pockets medals and moneys and this he may do without knowing anything else.

To a person fresh from England, the number of servants attending at table is remarkable. We had only a small party of eight to dinner yesterday, including ourselves; three-and-twenty servants were in attendance! Each gentleman takes his own servant or servants, in number from one to six, and each lady her attendant or attendants, as it pleases her fancy. The *huqqa* was very commonly smoked at that time in Calcutta: before dinner was finished, every man's pipe was behind his chair. The tobacco was generally so well prepared that the odour was not unpleasant, unless by chance you sat next to a man from the *mofussil*, when the fume of the spices used by the up-country *huqqa bardārs* preparing the tobacco, rendered it oppressive and disagreeable.

September 1st – The fever has quitted Calcutta, and travelled up the country stage by stage. It was amusing to see, upon your return to the Course, the whole of the company stamped, like yourself, with the marks of the leech upon the temples. Its origin has been attributed to many causes, and it has been called by many names. The gentlemen of the lancet are greatly divided in their opinions; some attribute it to the want of rain, others to the scarcity of thunder and lightning this season. There was an instance of the same general fever prevailing in the time of Warren Hastings. Not a single instance has been heard of its having proved mortal to adults.

CHAPTER VI

Residence in Calcutta ·

JANUARY 1825 – The cold weather is delightful, and a Persian carpet pleasant over the Indian matting, but a fire is not required – indeed, few houses in Calcutta have a fireplace. Ice is sent from Hoogly, and is procurable in the bazaar during the cold weather; it is preserved in pits for the hot season.

March 23rd – I will describe a day at this time of the year. At six o'clock it is so cold that a good gallop in a cloth habit will just keep you warm. At nine o'clock – a fine breeze – very pleasant – windows open – no *pankhā*. Three o'clock – blue linen blinds lowered to keep off the glare of the sunshine, which is distressing to the eyes; every Venetian shut, the *pankhā* in full swing, the very mosquitoes asleep on the walls, yourself asleep on a sofa, not a breath of air – a dead silence around you. Four o'clock – a heavy thunderstorm, with the rain descending in torrents; you stop the *pankhā*, rejoice in the *fraicheur*, and are only prevented from taking a walk in the grounds by the falling rain. Five o'clock – you mount your Arab, and enjoy the coolness for the remainder of the day – such is today.

April 11th – The hot winds are blowing for the first time this year.

We understand that after twenty-five years' service, and twenty-two of actual residence in India, we of the Civil Service are to retire upon an annuity of £1,000 a year, for which we are to pay Rs 50,000, or about £5,000. This, on first appearance, looks well for us and generous in the Company; but I should like first to know, how many will be able to serve their full time of bondage? Secondly, what the life of a man, an annuitant, is then worth, who has lingered two and twenty years in a tropical climate.

May 9th – The heat is intense – very oppressive. I dare not go to church for fear of its bringing on fits, which might disturb the congregation; you have little idea of the heat of a collection of many assembled in such a climate – even at home, with all appliances and means to boot for reducing the temperature, the heat is sickening. You in England imagine a lady in India has nothing to do. For myself, I superintend the household, and find it difficult at times to write even letters, there is so much to which it is necessary to attend. At this moment I would willingly be quiet, but am continually interrupted. The coachman, making his salam, 'Memsāhib, Atlas is very ill, I cannot wait for the sāhib's return; I have brought the horse to the door, will you give your orders?' The gatekeeper (*darwān*), 'Memsāhib, the deer have jumped over the wall and have run away.' The *sirdār*-bearer, 'Memsāhib, will you advance me some rupees to make a great feast? My wife is dead.' The *mate*-bearer then presented his petition, 'Will the memsāhib give me a plaister? The rats have gnawed my fingers and toes.' It is a fact that the lower part of the house is overrun with enormous rats, they bite the fingers and feet of the men when they are asleep on the ground.

The other evening I was with my beautiful and charming friend Mrs F—, she had put her infant on a mat, where it was quietly sleeping in the room where we were sitting. The evening darkened, a sharp cry from the child startled us – a bandicoot rat had bitten one of its little feet!

It is reported the Burmese war is nearly finished. I hope it may be true; it is a horrible sacrifice of human life, a war in such a climate! I hear much of all the hardships of fighting against the climate endured by the military, from friends who return to Calcutta on sick leave.

When we arrived in Calcutta the only drive was on the Course, which was well-watered; a fine broad road has since been made along the side of the river, about two miles in length; it is a delightful drive in the evening, close to the ships.

The Course is deserted for the Strand.

[...]

October – Lord Combermere intends to render the cold weather gay with balls and dinner parties. His staff are quite a relief to the eye, looking so well dressed, so fresh and European. They express themselves horrified at beholding the fishy hue of the faces on the Course; wonder how they are ever to stay at home during the heat of the day, and sigh for gaiety and variety. Speaking of the ladies in the East, one of them said, 'Amongst the womankind, there are some few worth the trouble of running away with; but then the exertion would be too much for the hot season; and in the cold, we shall have something else to think about!'

December 1st – We changed our residence for one in Middletonrow, Chowringhee, having taken a dislike to the house in which we were residing, from its vicinity to tanks and native huts.

The house has a good ground floor and two stories above, with verandahs to each; the rent Rs 325 per month; the third story consists of bedrooms. The deep fogs in Calcutta rise thick and heavy as high as the first floor; from the verandah of the second you may look down on the white fog below your feet, whilst the stars are bright above, and the atmosphere clear around you. The spotted deer play about the compound, and the mouse deer runs about my dressing-room, doing infinite mischief.

The Barā bazaar, the great mart where shawls are bought, is worth visiting. It is also interesting to watch the dexterity with which seed pearls are bored by the natives. This operation being one of difficulty, they tell me seed pearls are sent from England to be pierced in Calcutta.

CHAPTER VII

Departure from the Presidency

MARCH 1826 – In a climate so oppressive as this, billiards are a great resource in a private house; the table keeps one from going to sleep during the heat of the day, or from visiting Europe shops.

April 17th – The perusal of Lady Mary Wortley Montagu's work has rendered me very anxious to visit a *zenāna*, and to become acquainted with the ladies of the East. I have now been nearly four years in India, and have never beheld any women but those in attendance as servants in European families, the low caste wives of petty shopkeepers, and *nāch* women.

I was invited to a *nāch* at the house of an opulent Hindu in Calcutta, and was much amused with an excellent set of jugglers; their feats with swords were curious: at the conclusion, the *baboo* asked me if I should like to visit his wives and female relatives. He led me before a large curtain, which having passed I found myself in almost utter darkness: two females took hold of my hands and led me up a long flight of stairs to a well-lighted room, where I was received by the wives and relatives. Two of the ladies were pretty; on beholding their attire I was no longer surprised that no other men than their husbands were permitted to enter the *zenāna*. The dress consisted of one long strip of Benares gauze of thin texture, with a gold border, passing twice round the limbs, with the end thrown over the shoulder. The dress was rather transparent, almost useless as a veil: their necks and arms were covered with jewels. The complexion of some of the ladies was of a pale mahogany, and some of the female attendants were of a very dark colour, almost black. Passing from the lighted room, we entered a dark balcony, in front of which were fine bamboo screens, impervious to the eye from without, but from the interior we could look down upon the guests in the hall below, and distinguish perfectly all that passed. The ladies of the *zenāna* appeared to know all the gentlemen by sight, and told me their names. They were very inquisitive, requested me to point out my husband, inquired how many children I had, and asked a thousand questions. I was glad to have seen a *zenāna*, but much disappointed: the women were not ladylike; but, be it remembered, it was only at the house of a rich Calcutta native gentleman. I soon quitted the apartments and the *nāch*.

April – We heard, with sorrow, the death of Bishop Heber, from my sister at Cuddalore, whose house he had just quitted for Trichinopoly; after preaching twice in one day, he went into a bath and was there found dead. It was supposed that bathing, after the fatigue he had undergone, sent the blood to the head and occasioned apoplexy.

May 18th – Killed a scorpion in my bathing-room, a good fat old fellow; prepared him with arsenical soap, and added him to the collection of curiosities in my museum.

My Italian master praises me for application: he says, the heat is killing him, and complains greatly of the want of rain. When I told him we had had a little during the last two days, he replied, 'You are the favoured of God in Chowringhee, we have had none in Calcutta.' The natives suffer dreadfully. Cholera and the heat are carrying off three and sometimes five hundred a day.

An eclipse has produced a change in the weather, and the sickness has ceased in the bazaars.

August – A gloom has been thrown over Calcutta; and Lord Amherst's family are in the deepest affliction, caused by the death of Captain Amherst which took place a short time ago. His lordship, his son, and his nephew were seized with fever at the same time; Captain Amherst's became typhus, and carried him off. The family have proceeded up the country. All those who have the pleasure of their acquaintance sympathise most deeply in their affliction; they are much respected.

October 18th – My husband having received an acting appointment at Allahabad, we prepared to quit Calcutta. The distance by the river being eight hundred miles, and by land five hundred, we determined to march up stage by stage, sending the heavy baggage by water.

On quitting the Presidency, a great part of our furniture, horses, etc. were sold. I had refused Rs 2,000 for my beautiful Arab; but determined, as economy was the order of the day, to fix his price at Rs 2,500. The pair of greys, Atlas and Mercury, carriage-horses, sold for Rs 2,200, Rs 300 less than they cost; they, as well as Scamp, were too valuable to march up the country. This will give you some idea of the price of good horses in Calcutta. One morning a note was sent, which I opened (having received instructions to that effect), requesting to know if the grey Arab was for sale. I answered it, and mentioned the price. The gentleman enclosed the amount, Rs 2,500, about £250, in a note to me, requesting me to keep and ride the horse during the remainder of my stay in Calcutta, and on my departure to send him to his stables. For this charming proof of Indian *politesse*, I returned thanks, but declined the offer. I felt so sorry to part with my beautiful horse, I could not bear the sight of him

A Bengali Woman

when he was no longer my own: it was my own act; my husband blamed me for having sold a creature in which I took so much delight, and was not satisfied until he had replaced him by a milk-white Arab, with a silken mane and long tail. Mootee, the name of my new acquisition, was very gay at first, not comprehending the petticoat, but on becoming used to it carried me most agreeably. A fine Scotch terrier was given me to bear me company on the journey, but he was stolen from us ere we quitted Calcutta.

The people in Calcutta abused the Upper Provinces so much, we felt little inclination to quit the city, although we had applied for an appointment in the *mofussil*. Imagining the march would be very fatiguing, I went on board several pinnaces; they did not please me; then I crossed the river to see the first *dāk* bungalow, and brought back a good account.

November 22nd – We quitted Calcutta, crossed the river to the bungalow, on the New Road, stayed there one day to muster our forces, and commenced our journey the next.

Our marching establishment consisted of two good mares for the Stanhope, two fine saddle Arabs for ourselves, two ponies, and nine *hackeries*, which contained supplies and clothes, also a number of goats, and two Arabs, which we had taken charge of for a friend. We travelled by the Grand Military road, riding the first part of the stage, and finishing it in the buggy.

November 30th – I now write from Bancoorah, some hundred miles from the Presidency. Thus far we have proceeded into the bowels of the *mofussil* very much to our satisfaction. The change of air, and change of scene, have wrought wonders in us both. My husband has never felt so well in health or so *désennuyé* since he left England. I am as strong as a Diana Vernon, and ride my eight or ten miles before breakfast without fatigue. We have still some four hundred miles to march; but the country is to improve daily, and when we arrive at the hills, I hear we are to be carried back, in imagination, to the highlands of Scotland. I have never been there; *n'importe*, I can fancy as well as others. We rejoiced in having passed Bengal Proper, the first one hundred miles; the country was extremely flat, and, for the greater part, under water, said water being stagnant: the road was raised of mud, high enough to keep it above the swamp; a disagreeable road on a flyaway horse like my new purchase; low, marshy fields of paddy (rice) were on either side: sometimes we came to a bridge, surrounded by water, so that instead of being able to cross it, you had to ford the *nālā* (stream) lower down. No marvel, Calcutta is unhealthy, and that fevers prevail there; the wind flowing over these marshes must be charged with malaria.

Bancoorah has a bad name. It is remarkable that almost all the horses that are any time at the station go weak in the loins.

December 2nd – We reached Rogonautpoor, a very pretty spot, where there are some peculiar hills. Here we found Sir A. B— and his daughters; we accompanied them in a ramble over the hills in the evening. Sir A. took his *sipahi* guard with him, having heard the hills were infested with bears, but we found none.

At Chass, quail and partridge, snipe and pigeons were abundant. I generally accompanied my husband on his sporting expeditions in the evening, either on foot or on a pony, and enjoyed it very much.

At Hazāree Bāgh I became possessed of the first pellet bow I had seen, and found it difficult to use. We travelled from bungalow to bungalow. They are built by government, and are all on the same plan; at each a *khidmatgar* and a bearer are in attendance. At Khutkumsandy we were on the hills. Partridges were in plenty by the *nālā*.

At one of the stages the bearer of the *dāk* bungalow stole a large silver spoon off the breakfast-table. Happening, from his defending himself with great vehemence, to suspect him of the theft, we sent for the police, to whom he confessed he had hidden the spoon in the thatch of his own house. They carried him on a prisoner.

The country from this place, through Ranachitty to Dunghye, is most beautiful; fine hills, from the tops of which you have a noble and extensive view. Sometimes I was reminded of my own dear forest, which in parts it much resembles. The weak Calcutta bullocks finding it hard work, we were obliged to hire six more *hackeries*. We rode the whole of this stage. The road was too bad, and the hills too steep, for the buggy; but as it was nearly shaded the whole distance by high trees, the heat of the sun did not affect us. Tigers are found in this pass; and when Mootee my Arab snorted, and drew back apparently alarmed, I expected a *sortie* from the jungle. At this stage a horse ran away in a buggy, alarmed by a bear sleeping in the road.

At the Dunghye bungalow some travellers had been extremely poetical:

> Dunghye! Dunghye! With hills so high,
> A sorry place art thou;
> Thou boasts not e'en a blade of grass,
> Enough to feed an hungry ass,
> Or e'en a half-starved cow.

Nevertheless, we saw fine jungle and grass in plenty on every side, and were told partridge and jungle fowl were abundant.

En route were several parties of *fakirs*, who said they were going to Jaganāth. These rascals had some capital tattoos with them. Several of these men had one withered arm raised straight, with the long nails growing through the back of the hand. These people are said to be great thieves; and when any of them were encamped near us on the march, we directed the *chaukidārs* (watchmen) to keep a good look out, on our horses as well as our chattels. The adage says of the *fakir*, 'Externally he is a saint, but internally a devil'.

At Sherghāttee we delivered the stealer of the spoon over to the magistrate. In the evening I went out with the gentlemen on an elephant; they had some sport with their guns.

At Baroon we bought some uncut Soane pebbles, which turned out remarkably good when cut and polished. We rode across the Soane river, which was three miles in breadth, and had two large sandbanks in the middle of the stream. Wading through the water was most troublesome work on horseback. Twice we were obliged to put the horses into boats, they struggled, and kicked, and gave so much trouble. The Arab, Rajah, jumped fairly out of the boat into the stream. The mares worked hard getting the buggy across the deep sand; they went into and came out of the boats very steadily.

On our arrival at Sahseram, a native gentleman, Shāh Kubbeeroo-deen Ahmud, called upon us. At tiffin-time he sent us some *ready-dressed* native dishes; I was much surprised at it, but the natives told me it was his usual custom. In the evening, some fireworks, sent by the same gentleman, were displayed, particularly for my amusement. The town is very ancient, and there are numerous remains of former magnificence rapidly falling into decay. The tombs are well worth a visit.

December 23rd – We arrived at Nobutpoor, a very pretty place. The bungalow is on a high bank, just above the Curamnassa river. To the right you have a view of a suspension-bridge, built of bamboo and rope; on the left is a *sati*-ground, to me a most interesting sight. I had heard a great deal regarding *satis* in Calcutta, but had never seen one; here was a spot to which it was customary to bring the widows to be burned alive, on the banks of the Curamnassa, a river considered holy by the Hindus.

In the sketch I took of the place are seven *sati* mounds, raised of earth, one of which is kept in good repair, and there are several more in the mango tope to the left. The people said no *sati* had taken place there for twenty years, but that the family who owned the large mound kept it in repair, and were very proud of the glory reflected on their house by one of the females having become *sati*. A fine stone bridge had been begun some years before by a Mahratta lady, but was never finished; the remains are in the river. The touch of its waters is a dire misfortune to an Hindu; they carefully cross the suspension-bridge.

The next stage took us to the Mogul Serai; and, some rain having fallen, we felt the difference between the cold of the up-country and the fogs of Calcutta.

December 25th – Arrived at Benares; and here, again, crossing the Ganges was a great difficulty. The Arab, Rajah, was so extremely violent in the boat that we were obliged to swim him over. At length we reached the house of a friend in the civil service, and were well pleased to rest from our labours. Rising and being on horseback by four o'clock daily, is hard work when continued for a month.

My husband, finding it necessary to reach Allahabad by December 30th, left me at Benares to discharge the Calcutta *hackeries*, to get others, and to continue my journey. During my stay, our friend took me into the holy city, and showed me a great deal of what was most remarkable. Long as I had lived in Calcutta, I had seen very little of native life or the forms of *pooja*. The most holy city of Benares is the high place of superstition. I went into a Hindu temple in which *pooja* was being performed, and thought the organ of gullibility must be very strongly developed in the Hindus.

It was the early morning, and before the people went to their daily avocations, they came to perform worship before the idols. Each man brought a little vessel of brass, containing oil, another containing boiled rice, another Ganges' water and freshly-gathered flowers. Each worshipper, on coming into the temple, poured his offering on the head of the idol, and laid the flowers before it; prayed with his face to the earth, then struck a small bell three times, and departed. The Hindu women follow the same custom.

There were numerous uncouth idols in the temple. A black bull and a white bull, both carved in stone, attracted many worshippers; whilst two *living* bulls stood by the side, who were regarded as most holy, and fed with flowers.

If an Hindu wishes to perform an act of devotion, he purchases a young bull without blemish, and presents him to the Brāhmans, who stamp a particular mark upon him; he is then turned loose, as a Brāhmani bull, and allowed to roam at pleasure. To kill this animal would be sacrilege. When they get savage they become very dangerous. The Brahmani bulls roam at pleasure through the bazaars, taking a feed whenever they encounter a grain shop.

We ascended the minarets, and looked down upon the city and the Ganges. Young men prefer ascending them at early dawn, having then a chance of seeing the females of some *zenāna*, who often sleep on the flat roof of the house, which is surrounded by a high wall. From the height of the minarets you overlook the walls. I thought of Hadji Baba and the unfortunate Zeenab, whom he first saw spreading tobacco on the roof to dry. The shops of the *kimkhwāb* and turban manufacturers, as also of those who prepare the silver and gold wire used in the fabric of the brocade worked in gold and silver flowers, are well worth visiting.

Beetle wings are procurable at Benares, and are used there for ornamenting *kimkhwāb* and native dresses. In Calcutta and Madras, they embroider gowns for European ladies with three wings, edged with gold; the effect is beautiful. The wings are cheap at Benares, expensive at other places.

I was carried in a *tanjan* through Benares. In many parts, in the narrow streets, I could touch the houses on both sides of the street with my hands. The houses are from six to seven storeys high.

In one of these narrow passages it is not agreeable to meet a Brahmani bull. Four armed men, *barkandāzes*, ran on before the *tanjan* to clear the road. I procured a number of the brazen vessels that are used in *pooja*. On my return we will have it in grand style; the baby shall represent the idol, and we will pour oil and flowers over his curly head.

The cattle live on the ground-floor; and to enter a gay Hindu house, you must first pass through a place filled with cows and calves; then you encounter a heavy door, the entrance to a narrow, dark passage; and after ascending a flight of steps, you arrive at the inhabited part of the house, which is painted with all sorts of curious devices. I visited one of these houses; it was furnished, but uninhabited.

The contents of the thirteen small *hackeries* were stowed away upon four of the large *hackeries* of Benares, which started on their march with the buggy and horses. For myself, a *dāk* was hired. Our friend drove me the first stage, and then put me into my palanquin. I overtook the *hackeries*, and could not resist getting out and looking into the horses' tents. There they were, warm and comfortable, well littered down, with their *sā'ises* asleep at their sides; much more comfortable than myself during the coldness of the night, in the *pālkee*. The bearers broke open one of my *bahangīs*, and stole some articles.

I reached Rāj Ghāt early, and crossed the river. The fort, with its long line of ramparts washed by the river, and the beauty of a *dhrumsālā*, or Hindu alms-house, on the opposite bank, under one of the arches of which was an enormous image of Ganesh, greatly attracted my attention. I watched the worshippers for some time, and promised myself to return and sketch it.

The carriage of a friend was in waiting at this spot, and took me to Papamhow, where I rejoined my husband. Notwithstanding the difficulties, which according to report we expected, we made good progress, and arrived at Allahabad on the 1st of January, after a very pleasant trip. Indeed, this short time we agreed was the most approaching to delightful that we had passed in India; the constant change of scenery, and the country very beautiful in some parts, with the daily exercise, kept us all, horses included, in high health and spirits. We travelled at the rate of about fifteen miles a day, making use of the staging bungalows that have been erected for the accommodation of travellers, as far as Benares; thence we travelled by *dāk* to Prāg, the distance being only ninety miles. So much for our journey which, considering our inexperience, I think we performed with much credit to ourselves.

A friend received us at Papamhow with the utmost kindness, housed and fed us, and assisted us in arranging our new residence which, by the by, has one great beauty, that of being rent free: no small consideration where the expense of an unfurnished house is equal to that of a small income in England. Said house is very prettily situated on the banks of the Jumna, a little beyond the Fort. We like our new situation, and do not regret the gaiety of the City of Palaces; indeed, it now appears to me most wonderful how we could have remained there so long: in climate there is no comparison, and as to expense, if we can but commence the good work of economy, we may return on furlough ere long.

The peaceful termination of the war with Ava was one of the happy events of this year.

CHAPTER VIII

LIFE IN THE MOFUSSIL

PLANT A TREE, DIG A WELL, WRITE A BOOK AND GO TO HEAVEN

JANUARY 1827 – It is usual in India for those newly arrived to call upon the resident families of the station; the gentleman makes his call, which is returned by the resident and his family; after which the lady returns the visit with her husband. An invitation is then received to a dinner-party given in honour of the strangers, the lady being always handed to dinner by the host, and made the queen of the day, whether or not entitled to it by rank.

Our début in the *mofussil* was at the house of the judge, where we met almost all the station, and were much pleased that destiny had brought us to Prāg. Prāg was named Allahabad when the old Hindu city was conquered by the Mahomedans. We were very fortunate in bringing up our horses and baggage uninjured, and in not having been robbed *en route*. Lord Amherst has lost two horses, and his aide-de-camp three: guards are stationed around the Governor-General's horse-tents and baggage night and day, nevertheless native robbers have carried off those five animals. His lordship is at present at Lucknow.

We have spent the last three weeks most delightfully at Papamhow. Every sort of scientific amusement was going forward. Painting in oil and water colours, sketching from nature, turning, making curious articles in silver and brass, constructing Aeolian harps, amusing ourselves with archery, trying the rockets on the sands of an evening, chemical experiments, botany, gardening; in fact, the day was never half long enough for our employment in the work-shop and the grounds.

Papamhow is five miles from our own house, standing on higher ground and in a better situation, on the Ganges; when we can make holiday, we go up and stay at *our country house*, as our neighbours call it.

The old *moonshee* is cutting out my name in the Persian character, on the bottom of a Burmese idol, to answer as a seal. What an excellent picture the old man, with his long grey beard, would make! I have caught two beautiful little squirrels, with bushy tails and three white stripes on their backs; they run about the table, come to my shoulder, and feed from my hand.

May – Our friend at Papamhow is gunpowder agent to the Government, and manager of the rocket manufactory; his services are likely to be fully exerted, as it is reported that Runjeet Singh is not expected to live four months, being in the last stage of a liver complaint, and that his son, it is thought, will hoist the standard of rebellion. What gives foundation for this is that Lord Combermere is about to make the tour of the Upper Provinces, and that a concentration of forces is to take place on the frontier, under the pretext of a grand military inspection and review. There is no doubt as to who will go to the wall.

We have just received news of the death of Lord Hastings, and learn from the same papers that Lord Amherst has been created an earl, and Lord Combermere a viscount.

We have been occupied in planting a small avenue of *neem* trees in front of the house; unlike the air around the tamarind, that near a *neem* tree is reckoned wholesome – according to the Gujerāti proverb, we had made no advance on our heavenward road until the avenue was planted, which carried us on one-third of the journey. No sooner were the trees in the ground, than the servants requested to be allowed to marry a *neem* to a young peepal tree (*Ficus religiosa*), which marriage was accordingly celebrated by planting a peepal and *neem* together, and entwining their branches. Some *pooja* was performed at the same time which, with the ceremony of the marriage, was sure to bring good fortune to the newly-planted avenue.

The *neem* is a large and beautiful tree, common in most parts of India (*Melia azadirachta* or margosa tree); its flowers are fragrant – a strong decoction of the leaves is used as a cure for strains.

Oil is prepared from the berry of the *neem*, (*neem cowrie*, as they call it,) which is esteemed excellent, and used as a liniment in violent headaches brought on by exposure to the sun, and in rheumatic and spasmodic affections. The flowers are fragrant: anything remarkably bitter is compared to the *neem* tree; '*yeh duwa kurwee hy jyse neem*': this medicine is bitter as *neem*.

The bacäin, or māhā nimba (*Melia sempervivens*), a variety of the *neem* tree, is remarkably beautiful. 'The *neem* tree will not become sweet though watered with syrup and clarified butter'.

My pearl of the desert, my milk-white Arab, Mootee, is useless; laid up with an inflammation and swelling in his forelegs; he looks like a creature afflicted with elephantiasis – they tell us to keep him cool – we cannot reduce the heat of the stable below 120°!

I feel the want of daily exercise: here it is very difficult to procure a good Arab; the native horses are vicious, and utterly unfit for a lady; and I am too much the spoiled child of my mother to mount an indifferent horse.

August 28th – Last week we made our salam to the Earl of Arracan and his lady, who stopped at Allahabad, *en route*, and were graciously received.

The society is good and the station pretty and well-ordered; the roads the best in India, no small source of gratification to those whose enjoyment consists in a morning and evening drive: a course is also in progress, round which we are to gallop next cold weather when we have, indeed, the finest of climates, of which you, living in your dusty, damp, dull, foggy, fuliginous *England*, have no idea.

About the middle of April the hot winds set in, when we are confined to the house, rendered cool by artificial means; after this come four months of the rains, generally a very pleasant time; then a pause of a month, and then the cold weather.

September 20th – I have just received a most charming present, a white Arab, from Koordistān: he is a beautiful creature, and from having been educated in the tents of the Koords, is as tame as a pet lamb. His colour grey, his mane long and dark; his long white tail touches his heels; such a beautiful little head! He looks like a younger brother of Scamp, the Arab I sold on quitting Calcutta. I hear that when a lady was riding Scamp the other day, he threw her, and nearly fractured her skull. She was for some time in danger, but has recovered.

December 1st – For the last three weeks I have been gadding about the country, the gayest of the gay. A friend at Lucknow invited me to pay her a visit, at the time Lord Combermere was to stay at the residency. Having a great desire to see a native court, and elephant and tiger fights, I accepted the invitation with pleasure.

Accompanied by an aide-de-camp who was going to see the *tamāshā*, I reached Lucknow after a run of three nights. Mr Mordaunt Ricketts received me with great kindness; I spent a few days at the residency, and the rest with my friend.

On the arrival at Lucknow of his excellency the commander-in-chief, the King of Oude, Nusseer-ood-Deen Hyder, as a compliment to that nobleman, sent his son, Prince Kywan Jah, with the deputation appointed to receive his lordship, by whom the prince was treated as the *wali-ahd*, or heir-apparent.

The first day, Lord Combermere and the resident breakfasted with the King of Oude; the party was very numerous. We retired afterwards to another room, where trays of presents were arranged upon the floor, ticketed with the names of the persons for whom they were intended, and differing in their number and value according to the rank of the guests. Two trays were presented to me, the first containing several pairs of cashmere shawls, and a pile of India muslin and *kimkhwāb*, or cloth of gold. The other tray contained strings of pearl, precious stones, bracelets, and other beautiful native jewellery. I was desired to make my salam in honour of the bounty of his majesty. As soon as the ceremony had finished, the trays were carried off and placed in the Company's treasury, an order having arrived directing that all presents made to the servants of the Company should be accepted – but for the benefit of the state.

That night his majesty dined at the residency, and took his departure at ten o'clock, when quadrilles immediately commenced. The ladies were not allowed to dance while his majesty was present, as, on one occasion, he said, 'that will do, let them leave off'; thinking the ladies were quadrilling for his amusement, like *nāch* women. The second day, the king breakfasted with Lord Combermere, and we dined at the palace.

During dinner a favourite *nāch* woman attitudinised a little behind and to the right of his majesty's chair; at times he cast an approving glance at her performance. Sometimes she sang and moved about, and sometimes she bent her body *backwards*, until her head touched the ground; a marvellously supple, but not a graceful action.

The mornings were devoted to sports, and quadrilles passed away the evenings. I saw some very good elephant fights, some indifferent tiger fights, a rhinoceros against three wild buffaloes, in short, battles of every sort; some were very cruel, and the poor animals had not fair play.

The best fight was seen after breakfast at the palace. Two quails (*battaire*) were placed on the table; a hen bird was put near them; they set to instantly, and fought valiantly. One of the quails was driven back by his adversary, until the little bird, who fought every inch of his forced retreat, fell off the table into my lap. I picked him up and placed him upon the table again; he flew at his adversary instantly. They fight, unless separated, until they die. His majesty was delighted with the amusement. The saying is, 'Cocks fight for fighting's sake, quails for food, and the Lalls for love'. It appeared to me the quails were animated by the same passion as the Lalls:

> *Deux coqs vivaient en paix: une poule survint,*
> *Et voila la guerre allumée.*
> *Amour, tu perdis Troie!*

On quitting the presence of his majesty, a necklace of silver and gold tissue (*harrh*), very beautifully made, was placed around the neck of each of the guests, and *atr* of roses put on their hands.

The resident having sent me a fine English horse, I used to take my morning canter, return to cantonments, dress, and drive to the presidency to breakfast by eight o'clock. The horse, a magnificent fellow, had but one fault – a trick of walking almost upright on his hind legs. It was a contest between us; he liked to have his own way, and I was determined to have mine.

The dinners, balls, and breakfasts were frequent. Lord Combermere was in high good humour. His visit lasted about eight days, during which time he was entertained by the resident in Oriental style.

My journey having been delayed for want of bearers for my palanquin from Cawnpore, I arrived at Lucknow too late to see the ladies of the royal *zenāna*. The lady of the resident had been invited to visit their apartments the day before my arrival. She told me they were very fine, at least the *dupatta* (veil) was gay in gold and silver, but the rest of the attire very dirty. They appeared to have been taken by surprise, as they were not so highly ornamented as they usually are on a day of parade. I felt disappointed in being unable to see the *begums*; they would have interested me more than the elephant fights, which, of all the sights I beheld at Lucknow, pleased me the most.

I returned home at the end of December. The resident had the kindness to give me an escort of Skinner's horse to protect my palanquin, and see me safely out of the kingdom of Oude as far as Cawnpore, which, being in the Company's territories, was considered out of danger; and during the rest of the journey I was accompanied by two gentlemen.

Colonel Luard thus speaks of Skinner's horse: 'This is a most effective irregular corps, taking its name from its gallant colonel. An extraordinary feat is performed with the lance: a tent-peg is driven into the ground, nearly up to the head; and the lancer, starting at speed some distance from the peg, passes it on the near side, at his utmost pace, and, while passing, with considerable force drives his lance into the tent-peg, allowing the lance instantly to pass through his hand, or the shock would unhorse him; then, by a dexterous turn of the wrist, forces the peg out of the ground at the point of his lance, and bears the prize in triumph over his shoulder.'

In my vanity I had flattered myself dullness would have reigned triumphant at Prāg; nevertheless, I found my husband had killed the fatted calf, and 'lighted the lamp of *ghee*' i.e. made merry.

I sent a little seal, on which this motto was engraved, '*Toom ghee ka dhye jalāo*', to a lady in England, telling her *ghee* is clarified butter. When a native gives a feast, he lights a number of small lamps with *ghee*. If he say to a friend 'Will you come to my feast?' the answer may be, 'Light thou the lamp of *ghee*', which means, 'Be you merry, I will be there.' Therefore if you accept an invitation, you may use this seal with propriety.

CHAPTER IX

RESIDENCE AT ALLAHABAD

JANUARY 1828 – Leap Year – I before mentioned we had accomplished one-third of our way to heaven, by planting an avenue; we now performed another portion of the journey, by sinking a well. As soon as the work was completed, the servants lighted it up with numerous little lamps, and strewed flowers upon its margin, to bring a blessing upon the newly-raised water. From Hissar we received six cows and a bull, very handsome animals, with remarkably fine humps, such as are sold in England under the denomination of buffalo humps, which are, in reality, the humps of Indian cows and oxen.

Tame buffaloes are numerous at Prāg. The milk is strong, and not generally used for making butter, but is made into *ghee* (clarified butter), useful for culinary purposes. Some most beautiful Barbary goats arrived with the cows; they were spotted brown and white or black and white and almost as beautiful as deer. The Bengali goats yield a much larger portion of milk. I had also a Jumnapār goat, an enormous fellow, with very broad, long, thin, and silky ears, as soft as velvet. The Jumnapār are the best adapted for marching. Unless they can go into the jungle and browse, they become thin and lose their milk.

These goats, bred on the banks of the Jumna, thence called 'Jumnapār', are remarkably fine, and of a large size.

We had a Doomba ram at Prāg. The Doomba sheep are difficult to keep alive in this climate. Their enormous tails are reckoned delicacies; the lambs are particularly fine flavoured.

January – Our garden was now in good order; we had vegetables in abundance, marrowfat peas as fine as in England, and the water-cresses, planted close to the new well, were pearls beyond price. Allahabad is famous for the growth of the finest carrots in India. At this time of the year we gave our horses twelve seer each daily; it kept them in high health, and *French-polished* their coats. The geraniums grew luxuriantly during this delightful time; and I could be out in the garden all day, when protected by an enormous *chatr*, carried by a bearer. The up-country *chatr* is a very large umbrella, in shape like a large flat mushroom, covered with doubled cloth, with a deep circle of fringe. Great people have them made of silk, and highly ornamented. The pole is very long, and it is full employment for one man to carry the *chatr* properly.

The oleander (*kaner*), the beautiful sweet-scented oleander, was in pro-fusion – deep red, pure white, pink, and variegated, with single and double blossoms. I rooted up many clusters of this beautiful shrub in the grounds, fearing the horses and cows might eat the leaves, which are poisonous. Hindu women, when tormented by jealousy, have recourse to this poison for self-destruction.

The Ice-pits

January 22nd – My husband has the management of the ice concern this year. It is now in full work, the weather bitterly cold, and we are making ice by evaporation almost every night. I may here remark, the work continued until the 19th of February, when the pit was closed with 3000 mann – a mann is about 80lb. weight. There are two ice-pits; over each a house is erected; the walls, built of mud, are low, thick, and circular; the roof is thickly thatched; there is only one entrance, by a small door, which, when closed, is defended from the sun and air by a *jhamp*, or framework of bamboo covered with straw.
   [...]

It is amusing to see the old *ābdār* who has charge of the ice concern, walking up and down of an evening, watching the weather, and calculating if there be a chance of making ice. This is a grand point to decide, as the expense of filling the pans is great, and not to be incurred without a fair prospect of a crop of ice (*barf*) the next morning. He looks in the wind's eye, and if the breeze be fresh, and likely to increase, the old man draws his warm garment around him, and returning to his own habitation – a hut close to the pits – resigns himself to fate and his hubble-bubble. But should there be a crisp frosty feeling in the air, he prepares for action at about six or seven o'clock, by beating a tom-tom (a native hand-drum), a signal well known to the *coolies* in the bazaar, who hasten to the pits. By the aid of the little cup fastened to the long sticks, they fill all the *rukābees* with the water from the jars in the pathway. Many hundred *coolies*, men, women, and children, are thus employed until every little pan is filled.

If the night be frosty, without wind, the ice will form perhaps an inch and a half in thickness in the pans. If a breeze should blow, it will often prevent the freezing of the water, except in those parts of the grounds that are sheltered from the wind.

About three o'clock the *ābdār*, carefully muffled in some yards of English red or yellow broad cloth, would be seen emerging from his hut; and if the

The ice-pits

formation of ice was sufficiently thick, his tom-tom was heard, and the shivering *coolies* would collect, wrapped up in black bazaar blankets, and shaking with cold. Sometimes it was extremely difficult to rouse them to their work, and the increased noise of the tom-toms – discordant native instruments – disturbed us and our neighbours with the pleasing notice of more ice for the pits. Each *cooly*, armed with a spud, knocked the ice out of the little pans into a basket, which having filled, he placed it on his head, ran with it to the ice-house, and threw it down the great pit.

When all the pans had been emptied, the people assembled around the old *ābdār*, who kept an account of the number at work on a roll of paper or a book. From a great bag full of *pice* (copper coins) and cowrie-shells, he paid each man his hire.

About ten men were retained, on extra pay, to finish the work. Each man having been supplied with a blanket, shoes, and a heavy wooden mallet, four at a time descended into the pit by a ladder, and beat down the ice collected there into a hard flat mass; these men were constantly relieved by a fresh set, the cold being too great for them to remain long at the bottom of the pit.

When the ice was all firmly beaten down, it was covered in with mats, over which a quantity of straw was piled, and the door of the ice-house locked. The pits are usually opened on the 1st of May, but it is better to open them on the 1st of April. We had ice this year until the 20th of August. Each subscriber's allowance is twelve ser (24 lb.) every other day. A bearer, or a *cooly* is sent with an ice-basket, a large bazaar blanket, a cotton cloth, and a wooden mallet, at four o'clock, to bring the ice from the pit. The *ābdār*, having weighed the ice, puts it into the cloth, and ties it up tightly with a string; the *cooly* then beats it all round into the smallest compass possible, ties it afresh, and, having placed it in the blanket within the ice-basket, he returns home. The gentleman's *ābdār*, on his arrival at his master's house, re-weighs the ice, as the *coolies* often stop in the bazaars, and sell a quantity of it to natives, who are particularly fond of it, the man pretending it has melted away *en route*.

The natives make ice for themselves, and sell it at two annas a seer; they do not preserve it for the hot winds, but give a good price for the ice stolen from the *sāhib loge* (European gentleman).

[. . .]

As the *ābdārs* generally dislike rising early to weigh the ice, the *cooly* may generally steal it with impunity. The ice baskets are made of strips of bamboo covered inside and out with *namdā*, a thick coarse woollen wadding. The interior is lined with *dosootee* (white cotton cloth), and the exterior covered with *ghuwā kopra*, a coarse red cloth that rots less than any other from moisture. The basket should be placed on a wooden stool, with a pan below to catch the dripping water.

Calcutta was supplied, in 1833, with fine clear ice from America, sent in enormous blocks, which sold at two annas a seer, about twopence per pound: this ice is greatly superior to that made in India, which is beaten up when collected into a mass, and dissolves more rapidly than the block ice. It is not as an article of luxury only that ice is delightful in this climate, medicinally it is of great use: there is much virtue in an iced nightcap to a feverish head. The American ice has not yet penetrated to the up-country; we shall have ice from Calcutta when the railroads are established. No climate under the sun can be more delightful than this during the cold weather, at which time we enjoy fires very much, and burn excellent coal, which is brought by water from Calcutta. The coal mines are at Burdwan, a hundred miles from the presidency. In Calcutta it costs eight annas a mann; here, if procurable, it is one rupee: this year we had fires until the 29th of February.

After a good gallop round the Mahratta Bund on Master George, a remark-ably fine Arab, with what zest we and our friends partook of Hunter's beef and brawn! – as good as that of Oxford; the table drawn close to the fire, and the bright blaze not exceeding in cheerfulness the gaiety of the party!

March 31st – How fearful are fevers in India! On this day my husband was attacked; a medical man was instantly called in, medicine was of no avail, the illness increased hourly. On the 9th of April, the aid of the superintending surgeon was requested; a long consultation took place, and a debate as to which was to be employed, the lancet, or a bottle of claret; it terminated in favour of the latter, and claret to the extent of a bottle a day was given him: his head was enveloped in three bladders of ice, and iced towels were around his neck. On the 17th day for the first time since the commencement of the attack, he tasted food; that is, he ate half a small bun; before that, he had been supported solely on claret and fresh strawberries, being unable to take broth or arrowroot.

Not daring to leave him a moment night or day, I got two European artillerymen from the fort to assist me in nursing him. On the 23rd, the anxiety I had suffered, and over exertion, brought on fever, which confined me to my *chārpāis* for seven days; all this time my husband was too ill to quit his bed; so we lay on two *chārpāis*, under the same *pankhā*, two artillerymen for our nurses, applying iced towels to our heads while my two women, with true native apathy, lay on the ground by the side of my bed, seldom attending to me, and only thinking how soon they could get away to eat and smoke. The attention and kindness of the medical men, and of our friends at the station, were beyond praise. Thanks to good doctoring, good nursing, and good claret, at the end of the month we began to recover health and strength.

May 18th – The ice-pits were opened, and every subscriber received twenty-four pounds weight of ice every other day – perfectly invaluable with a thermometer at 93°. Our friends had kindly allowed them to be opened before, during our fevers. It is impossible to describe the comfort of ice to the head, or of iced-soda water to a parched and tasteless palate, and an exhausted frame.

April – Lord Amherst was requested by the directors to remain here until the arrival of Lord William Bentinck; and such was his intention, I believe, had he not been prevented by the dangerous illness of Lady Sarah; and by this time, it is possible the family are on their way home. Mr Bayley is Viceroy, and will reign longer than he expected as Lord William Bentinck does not sail before January.

Our politicians are all on the *qui vive* at the *mêlée* between the Russians and Persians, and the old story of an invasion of India is again agitated – we are not alarmed.

June 7th – The weather is more oppressive than we have ever found it; the heat intolerable; the thermometer in my room 93° in spite of *tattis* and *pankhās*. Allahabad may boast of being the oven of India; and the flat stone roof of our house renders it much hotter than if it were thatched.

We were most fortunate in quitting Calcutta; this past year the cholera has raged there most severely, the Europeans have suffered much; many from perfect health have been carried to their graves in a few hours.

A novel and a sofa is all one is equal to during such intense heat, which renders life scarcely endurable.

Ice is our greatest luxury; and our ice, made from the cream of our own cows and Gunter's jam, is as good as any in England. My thoughts flow heavily and stupidly under such intolerable heat: when the thermometer *is only 82°*, *we rejoice* in the coolness of the season; today it is 92°, and will be hotter as the day advances; the wind *will* not blow. If a breeze would but spring up, we could be comfortable, as the air is cooled passing through the wet *khas-khas*: what would I not give for a fresh sea-breeze! Let me not think of it.

Horses at this season of the year are almost useless; it is too hot to ride, and even a man feels that he has scarcely nerve enough to mount his horse with pleasure: in the buggy it is very oppressive, the fiery wind is so overpowering; and a carriage is too hot to be borne. I speak not of the middle of the day, but of the hours between seven o'clock at night to six o'clock in the morning – the *cool* hours as we call them!

From Madras they write the thermometer is at 96°! How can they breathe!

Here at 93° it is fearfully hot – if they have a sea-breeze to render the nights cool, it is a blessing; here the heat at night is scarcely endurable, and to sleep almost impossible.

I had a very large farmyard. The heat has killed all the guinea-fowls, turkeys, and pigeons, half the fowls, and half the rabbits.

June 12th – We have had a most miserable time of it for the last two months; this has been one of the hottest seasons in recollection, and Allahabad has well sustained its *sobriquet* of Chōtā Jahannum! which, being interpreted, is Hell the Little. Within these two days the state of affairs has been changed; we are now enjoying the freshness of the rains, whose very fall is music to our ears: another such season would tempt us to quit this station, in spite of its other recommendations.

Lord William Bentinck arrived July 3rd. The new Bishop of Calcutta is gone home, obliged to fly the country for his life; indeed, he was so ill, that a report of his death having come up here, some of his friends are in mourning for him; but I trust, poor man, he is going on well at sea at this minute.

September 8th – My verandah presents an interesting scene: at present, at one end, two carpenters are making a wardrobe; near them is a man polishing steel. Two silversmiths are busy making me some ornaments after the Hindustani patterns; the tailors are finishing a gown, and the *ayah* is polishing silk stockings with a large cowrie shell. The horses are standing near, in a row, eating lucerne grass, and the *jamadār* is making a report on their health, which is the custom at twelve noon, when they come round for their tiffin.

Yesterday a mad pariah dog ran into the drawing-room; I closed the doors instantly, and the servants shot the animal: dogs are numerous and dangerous at some seasons.

Exchanged a little mare – who could sing 'I'm sweet fifteen, and one year more' – for a stud-bred Arab, named Trelawny; the latter being too impetuous to please his master.

Our friend Major D— is anxious to tempt us to Nagpur, if we could get a good appointment there. 'He rides a steed of air;' and we have indulged in building *chateaux d'Espagne*, or castles in Ayrshire.

August 21st – It is thought the gentleman for whom my husband now officiates will not rejoin this appointment; should he be disappointed of his hope of reigning in his stead, he will apply for something else rather than return to Calcutta, which we do not wish to see till the year of furlough, 1833–4. Meantime we must make it out as well as we can and live upon hope, with the assurance that *if* we live, we shall *not* die fasting.

I wish the intermediate years would pass by as quickly as the river Jumna before our house, which is in such a furious hurry, that it is quite awful to see the velocity with which the boats fly along. Both the Ganges and the Jumna have this year been unusually high, and much mischief to the villages on the banks has been the consequence. There was a report the day before yesterday that the Ganges, about a mile from this, had burst its banks. Luckily it was false; but it was a very near thing. Since then the river has sunk nearly twenty feet, so that we have no fear at present. The Jumna was within six feet of our garden bank.

Of the climate we cannot form a fair opinion, but it is certainly very superior to any they have in Bengal. This year has been most unnatural; no regular hot winds, unexpected storms, and the rains delayed beyond their proper season. Allahabad is called the oven of India, therefore I expect to become a *jolie brune,* and the sāhib well baked.

We have just received telegraphic intelligence of the bishop's death at the Sandheads where he was sent on account of severe illness, which terminated fatally on the 13th instant. It is said that *three* bishops are to be imported, the late consumption having been so great. They ought to make bishops of the clergy who have passed their lives in India, and not send out old men who cannot stand the climate.

We have the use of a native steam-bath, which is most refreshing when the skin feels dry and uncomfortable. There are three rooms – the temperature of the first is moderate; that of the second, warmer; and the third, which contains the steam, is heated to about 100°. There you sit, until the perspiration starts in great drops from every pore; the women are then admitted, who rub you with *besun* (the flour or meal of pulse, particularly of *chana* (*Cicer arietinum*)) and native hand-rubbers (*khisas*) and pour hot water over you until the surface peels off; and you come out a new creature, like the snake that has cast its skin. One feels fresh and elastic, and the joints supple: the steam-bath is a fine invention.

October 1st – The first steamer arrived at Allahabad in twenty-six days from Calcutta; the natives came down in crowds to view it from the banks of the Jumna; it was to them a cause of great astonishment.

CHAPTER X

LIFE IN THE ZENĀNA

OCTOBER 1823 – A letter just received from a lady, a friend of mine, at Lucknow is so amusing and so novel, I must make an extract: 'The other day, (October 18th) was the anniversary of the King of Oude's coronation; and I went to see the ceremony, one I had never witnessed before, and with which I was much gratified. But the greatest treat was a visit to the *begum*'s afterwards, when the whole of the wives, aunts, cousins, etc., were assembled in state to receive us.

'The old *begum* (the king's mother) was the *great lady,* of course, and in her palace were we received; the others being considered her guests, as well as ourselves. It was a most amusing sight, as I had never witnessed the interior of a *zenāna* before, and so many women assembled at once I had never beheld. I suppose from first to last we saw some thousands. *Women bearers* carried our *tanjans*; a regiment of female gold and silver-sticks, dressed in male costume, were drawn up before the entrance; and those men, chiefly *Africans,* who were employed inside the *zenāna* (and there were abundance of these frightful creatures), were all of the same class as the celebrated Velluti. The old *begum* was without jewels or ornaments, likewise a very pretty and favourite wife of the late king, their state of widowhood precluding their wearing them. But the present king's wives were most superbly dressed, and looked like creatures of the Arabian tales. Indeed, one was so beautiful that I could think of nothing but Lalla Rookh in her bridal attire.

'I never saw anyone so lovely, either black or white. Her features were perfect; and such eyes and eyelashes I never beheld before. She is the favourite queen at present, and has only been married a month or two: her age about fourteen; and such a little creature, with the smallest hands and feet, and the most *timid, modest* look imaginable. You would have been charmed with her, she was so graceful and fawnlike. Her dress was of gold and scarlet brocade, and her hair was literally strewed with pearls, which hung down upon her neck in long single strings, terminating in large pearls, which mixed with and hung *as low* as her hair, which was curled on each side her head in long ringlets, like Charles II's beauties.

'On her forehead she wore a small gold circlet, from which depended (and hung halfway down her forehead) large pear-shaped pearls, interspersed with emeralds. Above this was a paradise plume, from which strings of pearls were carried over to the head, as we turn *our hair.*

'I fear you will not understand me. Her earrings were immense gold-rings, with pearls and emeralds suspended all round in long strings, the pearls increasing in size. She had a nose-ring also, with large round pearls and emeralds; and her necklaces, etc., were too numerous to be described. She wore long sleeves, open at the elbow; and her dress was a full petticoat, some dozen yards wide, with a tight body attached, and only open at the throat. She had several persons to bear her train when she walked; and her women stood behind her couch to arrange her headdress, when in moving her pearls got entangled in the immense *dupatta* of scarlet and gold she had thrown around her. How I wished for you when we were seated! You would have been delighted with the whole scene. This beautiful creature is the envy of all the other wives, and the favourite, at present, of the king and his mother, both of whom have given her titles – the king's is after the favourite wife of one of the celebrated kings of Delhi, "Tājmahul", and Nourmahul herself could not have been more lovely.

'The other newly-made queen is nearly *European,* but not a whit fairer than Tājmahul. She is, in my opinion, plain, but is considered by the native ladies very handsome; and she was the king's favourite until he saw Tājmahul.

'She was more splendidly dressed than even Tājmahul; her headdress was a coronet of diamonds, with a fine crescent and plume of the same. She is the daughter of an European merchant, and is accomplished for an inhabitant of a *zenāna,* as she writes and speaks Persian fluently, as well as Hindustani, and it is said she is teaching the king *English;* though when we spoke to her in English she said she had forgotten it, and could not reply. She was, I fancy, afraid of the old *begum,* as she evidently understood us; and when asked if she liked being in the *zenāna,* she shook her head and looked quite melancholy. Jealousy of the new favourite, however, appeared the cause of her discontent as, though they sat on the same couch, they never addressed each other. And now you must be as tired of the *begums,* as I am of writing about them.

'The mother of the king's children, Mulka Zumanee, did not visit us at the old queen's, but we went to see her at her own palace: she is, *after all,* the person of the most political consequence, being the mother of the heir-apparent; and she has great power over her royal husband, whose ears she boxes occasionally.

'The Delhi princess, to whom the king was betrothed and married by his father, we did not see; she is in disgrace, and confined to her own palace. The old *begum* talked away to us, but appeared surprised I should admire Tājmahul more than the English *begum*, as she is called – *my country-woman* as they styled her!

'Poor thing, I felt ashamed of the circumstance, when I saw her chewing *pān* with all the gusto of a regular Hindustani.'

The above letter contains so charming an account of Lucknow, that I cannot refrain from adding an extract from another of the same lady.

'At the residency, on such a day as this, the thermometer is seldom short of 100°!

'Did you ever hear of Colonel Gardner? He is married to a native princess. The other day he paid Lucknow a visit. His son's wife is sister to the *legal* queen of our present worthy sovereign of Oude. Colonel Gardner came on a visit to the *begum*'s father, Mirza Suliman Sheko, a prince of the house of Delhi, blessed with fifty-two children, twelve sons and forty daughters! Did you ever hear of such enormity? The poor papa is without a rupee, his pension from government of Rs 5,000 a month is mortgaged to his numerous creditors. He has quarrelled with his illustrious son-in-law, the King of Oude; and Colonel Gardner has come over with the laudable purpose of removing his family from Oude to Delhi, where they will have a better chance of being provided for.

'Indeed, the other day, seventeen of the daughters were betrothed to seventeen princes of Delhi: this is disposing of one's daughters by wholesale! is it not? Colonel Gardner, who is a very gentlemanlike person, I hear, of the old school, was educated in France some fifty years ago. He gave a description of his sojourn amongst this *small family* in the city, in these words – "I slept every night with the thermometer at 100° and surrounded by five hundred females!"

'What a situation! I do not know which would be the most overpowering, the extreme heat or the incessant clack of the forty princesses and their attendants. It reminds me of the old fairy tale of the "Ogre's forty daughters with golden crowns on their heads".'

On dit the English *begum* was the daughter of a half-caste and an English officer; her mother afterwards married a native *baniyā* (shopkeeper). She had a sister; both the girls lived with the mother, and employed themselves in embroidering saddle-cloths for the horses of the rich natives. They were both very plain; nevertheless, one of them sent her picture to his majesty who, charmed with the portrait, married the lady. She had money in profusion at her command: she made her father-in law her treasurer, and pensioned her mother and sister.

The Sati

A rich *baniyā*, a corn chandler, whose house was near the gate of our grounds, departed this life; he was an Hindu. On the 7th of November, the natives in the bazaar were making a great noise with their tom toms, drums, and other discordant musical instruments, rejoicing that his widow had determined to perform *sati*, i.e. to burn on his funeral-pile.

The magistrate sent for the woman, used every argument to dissuade her, and offered her money. Her only answer was dashing her head on the floor, and saying, 'If you will not let me burn with my husband, I will hang myself in your court of justice.' The *shāstras* say, 'The prayers and imprecations of a *sati* are never uttered in vain; the great gods themselves cannot listen to them unmoved.'

If a widow touch either food or water from the time her husband expires until she ascend the pile, she cannot, by Hindu law, be burned with the body; therefore the magistrate kept the corpse *forty-eight* hours, in the hope that hunger would compel the woman to eat. Guards were set over her, but she never touched anything. My husband accompanied the magistrate to see the *sati*: about five thousand people were collected together on the banks of the Ganges: the pile was then built, and the putrid body placed upon it; the magistrate stationed guards to prevent the people from approaching it. After having bathed in the river, the widow lighted a brand, walked round the pile, set it on fire, and then mounted cheerfully: the flame caught and blazed up instantly; she sat down, placing the head of the corpse on her lap, and repeated several times the usual form, '*Rām, Rām, sati; Rām, Rām, sati;*' i.e. 'God, God, I am chaste.'

As the wind drove the fierce fire upon her, she shook her arms and limbs as if in agony; at length she started up and approached the side to escape. An Hindu, one of the police who had been placed near the pile to see she had fair play, and should not be burned by force, raised his sword to strike her, and the poor wretch shrank back into the flames. The magistrate seized and committed him to prison. The woman again approached the side of the blazing pile, sprang fairly out, and ran into the Ganges, which was within a few yards. When the crowd and the brothers of the dead man saw this, they called out, 'Cut her down, knock her on the head with a bamboo; tie her hands and feet, and throw her in again' and rushed down to execute their murderous intentions, when the gentlemen and the police drove them back.

The woman drank some water, and having extinguished the fire on her red garment, said she would mount the pile again and be burned.

The magistrate placed his hand on her shoulder (which rendered her impure), and said, 'By your own law, having once quitted the pile you cannot ascend again; I forbid it. You are now an outcast from the Hindus, but I will take charge of you, the Company will protect you, and you shall never want food or clothing.'

He then sent her, in a palanquin, under a guard, to the hospital. The crowd made way, shrinking from her with signs of horror, but returned peaceably to their homes: the Hindus annoyed at her escape, and the Musulmāns saying, 'It was better that she should escape, but it was a pity we should have lost the *tamāshā* (amusement) of seeing her burnt to death.'

Had not the magistrate and the English gentlemen been present, the Hindus would have cut her down when she attempted to quit the fire; or had she leapt out, would have thrown her in again, and have said, 'She performed *sati* of *her own accord*, how could *we* make her? It was the will of God.' As a specimen of their religion the woman said, 'I have transmigrated six times, and have been burned six times with six different husbands; if I do not burn the seventh time, it will prove unlucky for me!' 'What good will burning do you?' asked a bystander. She replied, 'The women of my husband's family have all been *satis*, why should I bring disgrace upon them? I shall go to heaven, and afterwards reappear on earth, and be married to a very rich man.' She was about twenty or twenty-five years of age, and possessed of some property, for the sake of which her relatives wished to put her out of the world.

If every *sati* were conducted in this way, very few would take place in India. The woman was not much burned, with the exception of some parts on her arms and legs. Had she performed *sati*, they would have raised a little cenotaph, or a mound of earth by the side of the river, and every Hindu who passed the place returning from bathing would have made salam to it; a high honour to the family. While we were in Calcutta, many *satis* took place; but as they were generally on the other side of the river, we only heard of them after they had occurred. Here the people passed in procession, flags flying, and drums beating, close by our door. I saw them from the verandah; the widow, dressed in a red garment, was walking in the midst. My servants all ran to me, begging to be allowed to go and see the *tamāshā* (fun, sport), and having obtained permission, they all started off; except one man, who was pulling the *pankhā*, and he looked greatly vexed at being obliged to remain. The sāhib said, the woman appeared so perfectly determined, he did not think she would have quitted the fire. Having performed *sati* according to her own account six times before, one would have thought from her miraculous incombustibility, she had become asbestos, only purified and not consumed by fire. I was glad the poor creature was not murdered, but she will be an outcast. No Hindu will eat with her, enter her house, or give her assistance; and when she appears they will point at her and give her abuse. Her own and her husband's family would lose caste if they were to speak to her: but, as an example, it will prevent a number of women from becoming *satis*, and do infinite good: fortunately, she has no children. And these are the people called in Europe the 'mild inoffensive Hindus!'

The woman was mistress of a good house and about Rs 800; the brothers of her deceased husband would, after her destruction, have inherited the property.

The burning of the widow is not commanded by the *shāstra*: to perform *sati* is a proof of devotion to the husband. The mountain Himalaya, being personified, is represented as a powerful monarch: his wife, Mena; their daughter is called Parvatī, or mountain-born, and Doorga, or difficult of access. She is said to have been married to Shiva in a *pre-existing* state when she was called Sati. After the marriage, Shiva on a certain occasion offended his father-in-law, King Dukshu, by refusing to make salam to him as he entered the circle in which the king was sitting.

To be revenged, the monarch refused to invite Shiva to a sacrifice which he was about to perform. Sati, the king's daughter, however, was resolved to go, though uninvited and forbidden by her husband. On her arrival, Dukshu poured a torrent of abuse on Shiva, which affected Sati so much that she died.

In memory of this proof of great affection, a Hindu widow burning with her husband on the funeral-pile, is called a *sati*.

[...]

The *sati* took place on the banks of the Ganges, under the Bund between the Fort and Raj Ghāt, a spot reckoned very holy and fortunate for the performance of the rite.

Several of our friends requested me, in case another *sati* occurred, to send them timely notice. Five days afterwards, I was informed that a *rānee* (Hindu queen or princess) was to be burned. Accordingly I sent word to all my friends. Eight thousand people were assembled on the *sati*-mound, who waited from midday to sunset: then a cry arose – 'The memsāhib sent us here! The memsāhib said it was to take place today! See, the sun has set, there can now be no *sati*!' The people dispersed. My informant told me what he himself believed, and I mystified some eight thousand people most unintentionally.

Temple of Bhawāni and satis, Alopee Bagh

In Alopee Bagh, in the centre of a large plantation of mango trees, is a small temple dedicated to Bhawāni; there is no image in it, merely a raised altar, on which victims were, I suppose, formerly sacrificed. Each of the small buildings on the right contains the ashes of a *sati*; there are seven *sati*-graves of masonry on this, and six of earth on the other side, near the temple, in the mango tope. The largest *sati*-tomb contains the ashes of a woman who was burnt in 1825, i.e. six years ago. The ashes are always buried near a temple sacred to Bhawāni, and *never* by any other. Families too poor to raise a tomb of masonry in memory of the burnt-sacrifice are contented to raise a mound of earth, and place a *kulsa* of red earthenware to mark the spot.

The temple of Bhawāni is shaded by a most beautiful peepal tree, from the centre of which a *fakir*'s flag was flying; it stands in a plantation of mango trees. I desired an Hindu, who was present when I sketched the temple, to count the *sati* graves around it. As he counted them, he repeatedly made salam to each mound.

[...]

November – My beautiful Arab, Mootee, after taking a most marvellous quantity of blue vitriol and opium, has recovered, but will be unfit for my riding; the sinews of his foreleg are injured; besides which he is rather too playful; he knocked down his *sā'is* yesterday, tore his clothes to pieces, bit two bits of flesh out of his back, and would perhaps have killed him, had not the people in the bazaar interfered and rescued the man. It was an odd freak, he is such a sweet tempered animal, and I never knew him behave incorrectly before.

We spent the month of December, our hunting season, at Papamhow, and purchased several couple of the Berkeley hounds, from the Calcutta kennel, for the pack at Allahabad. I received a present of an excellent little black horse with a long tail and, mounted on him, used to go out every day after the jackals and foxes. I am rich in riding-horses, and the dark brown stud-Arab Trelawny bids fair to rival Mootee in my affections. Returning from chasing a jackal one evening it was very dark, and as Captain A. S— was cantering his Arab across the parade-ground, the animal put his foot into a deep hole, and fell; our friend thought nothing of it, and refused to be bled; a few days afterwards the regiment quitted Allahabad, and he died the second day, on the march to Benares. He was an ill-fated animal, that little horse of his: they called him an Arab pony, but no good caste animal would have been so vicious; he had one fault, a trick of biting at the foot of his rider – he bit off the toe of his former master, mortification ensued, and the man died. I often wished to mount him, but they would never allow me: the creature was very handsome, and remarkably well formed. Doubtless a native would have found unlucky marks upon him – at that time I was ignorant respecting *samāt*, or unlucky marks on horses.

CHAPTER XI

RESIDENCE AT PRĀG

I KEEP WRITING ON UPON THE PRINCIPLE OF A GOOD ECONOMIST,
THAT IT IS A PITY SO MUCH PAPER SHOULD BE LOST, WHICH,
LIKE THE QUEER LITTLE OLD MAN IN THE SONG, 'HAS A LONG WAY TO GO'

WHAT RELIANCE IS THERE IN LIFE

HE WHO HAS ILL-LUCK FOR HIS COMPANION WILL BE BITTEN BY A DOG
ALTHOUGH MOUNTED ON A CAMEL

JANUARY 1829 – In the beginning of this month, having promised to meet Captain A. S— at the races at Ghazipur, we started by land, having sent tents and provisions by water to await our arrival. A violent headache preventing me from mounting my horse, I proceeded in a *pālkee* much against medical advice, and slept halfway to Benares in our tents.

Rising late the next day, we had a hot ride before reaching the Stanhope, where we learnt that our pitaras had been stolen. My husband rode forward in pursuit of the thieves, leaving me seated by the side of the road; the sun becoming very hot, I got into the buggy overcome from my recent illness, the *sā'is* holding the horse. I was startled from a doze by the sound of the bells of a native cart passing with flags flying; the horse alarmed sprang from the *sā'is's* hands, pulling away the reins, which fell to the ground; away galloped the horse, a strong animal fifteen hands high; he looked down the steep ditch on one side the raised road, turned round, looked over the ditch on the other side, made one more sudden turn in alarm, and upset the buggy. I was thrown head foremost through the opening in the back, my limbs remaining under the buggy-hood, which was broken to pieces; the horse fairly kicked himself out of the shafts, and galloped off; I was glad when I found he was free, and knew he could not break my legs, which were still under the hood: at length I dragged them out, with my long habit-skirt, and made an attempt to go after the horse, but was obliged to sit down – blue and yellow suns, stars, and bright objects floated before my eyes – I was unable to stand: my dressing-case having been thrown out of the buggy, I drank some *sal volatile*, which took off the giddiness. My husband returned at this moment, and an officer from some tents near at hand came to our assistance. The Stanhope was carried forward by *coolies*; we had a Calcutta buggy also with us, in which we proceeded. The road was covered with the finest sand, rendering it impossible to see the deep holes in every direction. The horse, a powerful English imported creature, was going very fast, when he put both his fore feet into a deep hole, and came down; the high Calcutta buggy swung forwards with such force I was pitched out over the wheel on my head, and remained insensible for a few seconds. My husband was not thrown out. He was unable to leave the frightened horse; it was a relief when he heard a voice from the dust, saying, 'I am not hurt;' a voice he feared he should never hear again. The bruises I had before received, united with this blow on my head, which cut through my riding hat, made me very nervous; and when at the last stage we had to drive a runaway mare, laid for us by a friend, I really sat in fear and trembling. At last we arrived at Benares. I was carried upstairs to bed, my limbs being stiff and painful. For ten days I could scarcely move, so much was my body bruised by the iron rail and hood of the buggy and my right arm was greatly swollen.

My recovery was brought about by having four women to shampoo me for five hours daily, and by going into a vapour-bath belonging to the Rajah of Benares. In the bath the women shampooed, and twisted, and pinched my limbs, until I could walk without assistance – that vapour bath was a great relief.

One morning the rajah sent me a bouquet of flowers, they were beautifully made of *ubruk* (talc, mica) and coloured wax, the first I had seen well executed.

My husband at the billiard-table, said: 'I am uncertain respecting that stroke, I wish A. S— was here.' 'Do you not know he is dead?' said his opponent, 'he died in consequence of his fall with that Arab pony at Papamhow.' We were greatly shocked.

January 29th – We quitted our kind friends at Benares to return home: ill-luck pursued us – the first stage the horse fell lame and we reached our tent with difficulty. During the night a heavy storm came on; the tent being old was soon saturated, and the water poured in on our *chārpāis*. The horses picketed outside were drenched, they neighed and shook their chains; the *sā'ises* crept under the corners of the *rāwti*, and we had the floorcloth put over us, to protect us from the rain and cold.

The next day we galloped to our second tent, which we found soaked through from the rain of the night. There was the tent, and nothing else. One of the camels having fallen lame, the servants had made it a pretext for not continuing their march, and we were *planté* in the jungle without food, bedding, or warm clothing! A camel driver caught a chicken, and drawing out a long queer crooked blade, killed it and dressed an excellent curry in a few minutes; having had no food all day, and much exercise, we devoured it to the last grain of rice. I thought of the saying, 'If you ask a hungry man how much two and two make – he answers, "Four loaves".' The night was miserable, the wind blowing through the wet canvass; we could not even borrow a blanket from the horses, everything was drenched. A *pukka* ague and fever was the consequence, which lasted seven or eight days, and returned regularly once every four weeks for three months.

Nor did our misfortunes end here. Much to the surprise of my husband his Arab, Rajah, whom he had had for seven years, threw him over his right shoulder. Rajah was particularly pleased; for having looked at him, he cocked his tail and went off at his best pace towards home. Monsieur was not hurt, and received only a few bruises for his carelessness which, considering he now weighs fourteen stone, shows that like Caesar he has much respect for his person and can fall in proper form.

Another *malheur*! A box from England on its way up the river was stolen at Patna; it contained letters and presents for me, amongst the rest a veritable *tête montée à la Giraffe*, a serious loss, *qui pourrait bien faire monter la tête* – but I bear the misfortune bravely.

The arrival of a friend from England has pleased us greatly. What pleasure reminiscences Etonian and Harrovian give him and the sāhib! "Economy, *esperanza*, and 1833,' is our motto. 'In five years,' says an old Harrovian, 'we may hear the bell and going up – sounds worth listening to.'

Cicer arietinum (chick pea), is called *arietinum* because the young seed bears a very curious resemblance to a ram's horn. The crops being favourable this year, this chick pea (*chāna* or *gram*) was sold in the city one mun twenty-two ser per rupee; and in the district, one mun thirty-five ser for the same.

March 8th – At this time my husband was attacked with ague and fever, the consequence of our expedition to Benares.

There is a rumour of a central government being established, the location to be hereabouts, so that Allahabad may again become a city of repute.

We have had much annoyance of late from the servants stealing all sorts of little things, as also wine. Two of the *khidmatgārs* were the culprits: one has been retained, and put in irons to work on the road; we could not punish the other, but it was a pleasure to get him out of the house. In India, amongst so many servants, it is very difficult to discover the thief:

May 31st – How I rejoice this month is over! – this vile month! It appears almost wicked to abuse the merry merry month of May, so delightful at home, but so hot in India. Mr M— started from Calcutta to come up *dāk* on the 7th instant, and died in his *pālkee* of brain-fever only three days afterwards, in consequence of the intense heat! We spare no expense to keep the house cool, and have fourteen men whose sole business night and day is to throw water on *tattis* to cool the rooms; unless the wind blows, the *tattis* are useless. The heat makes you as sick as if you were to shut your head up in an oven.

A young bullock was standing in the stable today by the side of three horses. A snake bit the animal, and it died in a few minutes. The horses escaped – and so did the snake, much to my sorrow.

July 19th – The other evening Major P— was with us when Rām Din, a favourite Hindu servant, brought into the room a piece of cotton cloth containing Rs 150 tightly tied up in it; the man placed it on the table by my side, and retired. Major P—, who thought the cloth looked dirty, took it up and saying 'Oh the vile rupees!' let it drop upon the ground between his chair and mine. We took tea and I retired to rest, entirely forgetting the bag of rupees. When I looked for it the following morning, of course it had disappeared. By the advice of the *jamadār* of the office we sent for a *gosāin*, a holy personage, who lived in a most remarkable temple on the ruins of an old well by the side of the Jumna, close to our house. The *gosāin* came. He collected the Hindus together, and made *pooja*. Having anointed a sacred piece of wood (*acacia arabica* or *babool*) with oil and turmeric and placed it in a hut, he closed the door; and coming forth, said: 'To show you that I am able to point out the thief, I have now left a gold ring in front of the idol in that house; go in and worship, every man of you. Each man must put his hand upon the idol. Let one amongst you take the ring, I will point out the man.'

The Hindus looked at him with reverence; they all separately entered the dwelling, and did as they were ordered. The *jamadār* performed the same ceremony, although he was a Musulmān. On their appearing before the *gosāin*, he desired them all to show their hands, and having examined them with much attention, he exclaimed, looking at the hands of the *jamadār*, 'You are the thief!' The man held up his hands to heaven, exclaiming, 'God is great, and you are a wonderful man!' A Musulmān did not believe in your power; your words are words of truth; I took the ring, here it is: if it be your pleasure you can, doubtless, point out the man who stole the rupees.'

The *gosāin* then told the people, that unless the money were forthcoming the next day, he would come and point out the thief. That evening the *jamadār* roamed around the house, calling out in the most dismal voice imaginable 'You had better put back the rupees, you had better put back the rupees.' The police came, and wished to carry off Rām Din to prison, because he was the servant who had put the money by my side. The man looked at me. 'Is it your will? I am a Rajpoot, and shall lose caste; I have served you faithfully, I am present.'

'Who will be security that you will not run away?' said the *barkandāz*. I replied, 'I will be his security: Rām Din will remain with us, and when the magistrate sends for him, I will answer for it he will be present.' The man's eyes filled with tears: it was the greatest compliment I could pay him: he made a deep salam, saying, 'Memsāhib! Memsāhib!' in an agitated and grateful tone. The next morning the *jamadār* informed me that a bag was on the top of the wardrobe in my dressing-room, and none of the servants would touch it. I went to the spot, and desired Rām Din to take it down.

'This is the cloth that contained the rupees,' said the man, 'and it has never been opened; I know it by a peculiar knot that I always tie.' He opened the bag, and found the whole of the money.

We had reason to believe one of the under-bearers committed the theft. The Hindus have such faith in their *gosāins*, and their influence over them is so great, they dare not do otherwise than as they are ordered by the holy men. I got back the £15, and gave £4 to those who had exerted themselves to find it.

[...]

THE DIVER WHO THINKS ON THE JAWS OF THE CROCODILE WILL NEVER GATHER PRECIOUS PEARLS.

CHAPTER XII

SKETCHES OF ALLAHABAD

OCTOBER 1829 – Snakes are very numerous in our garden; the *cobra de capello*, and the black snake, whose bite is just as mortal. This morning I turned over some tiles with my foot when a cobra I had disturbed glided into the centre of the heap, where we killed him.

[...]

Several were in the stable and henhouse. A snake-charmer came, who offered to fascinate and catch the snakes for me at one rupee a head. He caught one, for which I gave him a rupee; but as I had it killed, he never returned – the charm was broken. It was a tame fangless snake, which he had tried to pass off as the wild one.

We killed three scorpions in the dining-room, of rather large dimensions. Our friend and neighbour had much compassion on frogs. Many an enormous bullfrog he rescued alive from the jaws of the snakes he killed in his garden. The poor frogs lost their defender on his return to England, and we an excellent friend.

[...]

October 29th – We drove to the Parade-ground, to view the celebration of the Rām Leela festival. Rām the warrior god is particularly revered by the *sipahis*. An annual *tamāshā* is held in his honour, and that of Seeta his consort. A figure of Rawan the giant, as large as a windmill, was erected on the Parade-ground: the interior of the monster was filled with fireworks. This giant was destroyed by Rām. All sorts of games are played by the *sipahis*, on the Parade. Mock fights and wrestling matches take place, and fireworks are let off. Two young natives, about ten or twelve years old, are often attired to represent Rām and Seeta; and men with long tails figure as the army of monkeys, headed by their leader Hanumān.

On dit, that the children who personate Rām and Seeta, the handsomest they can select, never live more than a year after the festival. For this I vouch not – it is said they are poisoned.

One ceremony was very remarkable: each native regiment took out its colours and made *pooja* to the standards, offering them sweetmeats, flowers, rice and *pān*, as they do to a god! At Cawnpore I saw the men of the third cavalry riding round the image of the giant, with their colours flying, after having made *pooja* to them.

At the conclusion of the *tamāshā*, the figure of Rawan is blown up by the conqueror Rām.

[…]

Rāj Ghat is on the banks of the Ganges, about a mile and a half above the Fort of Allahabad, and the village of Daraganj extends along the side of the Mahratta Bund above for some distance. To the right of the spot where travellers land on coming from Benares is a fine building, called a *dhrumsālā*, or place to distribute alms; it is dedicated to a form of Māhadēo, which stands in the *shiwālā*, or little temple, above: the form of this octagonal temple, as well as that of a similar one, which stands at the other side of the building, is very beautiful. On the left are the remains of a very large and curious old well.

After sketching this *dhrumsālā*, we ascended the bank to Daraganj, to see the inner court, and found it filled with elephants, *tattoos*, cows, and natives. It is used as a *sarāe*, or abode for travellers. I saw there a most beautiful and exceedingly small *gynee* (a dwarf cow), with two bars of silver round each of her little legs; she looked so pretty, and was quite tame. Through the doorways of this court you look into the little octagonal temples, and, through their arches, on a fine expanse of the Ganges which flows below.

You cannot roam in India as in Europe, or go into places crowded with natives, without a gentleman; they think it so incorrect and so marvellous, that they collect in crowds to see a memsāhib who is indecent enough to appear unveiled. A riding-habit and hat, also, creates much surprise in unfrequented bazaars, where such a thing is a novelty.

We proceeded through the *basti* (village) on foot, and up a dirty alley, through which I could scarcely pass, to the Temple of Hanumān, the black-faced and deified monkey, and found there an enormous image of the god painted red and white, and made either of mud or stone. A great number of worshippers were present. The bearers hold Hanumān in the greatest reverence.

In another apartment were forty or fifty large and small figures, representing Rām and Seeta his consort, with his brother Lutchnlan, Hanumān, and all his army of monkeys. Seeta was carried off by the giant Ravana, Hanumān fought for and restored her to Rām, therefore they are worshipped together.

These figures were decorated with coloured cloth and tinsel, much in the same manner in which the saints are clothed in the churches in France. I had never but once before seen idols in India, tricked out after this fashion. Many lamps were burning before the shrine. We were allowed to behold them from the door, but not to enter the apartment.

[. . .]

At this time the plain in front of the fort, by the avenue on the side of the Jumna, was exceedingly picturesque. It was covered by an encampment awaiting the arrival of the Governor-General. There were assembled two hundred elephants, one thousand camels, horses and *hackeries*, servants and natives without number. A double set of new tents for the Governor-General were pitched on the plain; the tents which were new the year before, and which cost a lac, having been discarded. These new tents, the elephants, camels, horses, and thousands of servants, will cost the Company more than half *batta* saves in the course of a year.

News has just arrived that the Directors have rendered all this encampment useless, by sending orders to Lord William Bentinck not to proceed up the country at *their* expense; in consequence Lord William has discharged the people. I am glad they are going away. Last night a friend of ours, who is in tents in our grounds, had his gun and dressing-case stolen, no doubt by thieves from the encampment.

December 20th – The ashes of a rajah were brought to Prāg this morning to be thrown into the Ganges at the holy junction; they were accompanied by the servants of the rajah, bearing presents to be given, as is the custom, to the Brahmans, amongst which were two remarkably fine Persian horses. One of these horses, a flea-bitten grey from Bokhara, was bought by us from the Brahman to whom it had been presented. On Christmas Day my husband gave me this horse, making my own particular riding-stud amount to a fair number – Mootee, Black Poney, Trelawney, Bokhāra. Are ladies in England as fond of their horses as I am? They cannot make pets of them in that country as we can in India.

December 25th – How many presents I received this day – and such odd ones – the Bokhara grey, a sketch of Lord William Bentinck, Martin's *Deluge*, a proof-print, a bag of walnuts, a diamond ring, a hill-shawl, two jars of jam, and two bottles of hill-honey! All farewell gifts from friends bound to England. We spent the evening around the horseshoe-table, the coal fire blazing brightly as we cracked the hill-walnuts and enjoyed the society of our friends. Of all the offerings of that day, the most welcome was a packet of letters from the beloved and absent ones in England. 'A letter is half an interview.'

CHAPTER XIII

Removal to Cawnpore – Confessions
of a Thug

WHAT VARIETY OF HERBS SOEVER ARE SHUFFLED TOGETHER IN A DISH, YET
THE WHOLE MASS IS SWALLOWED UP IN ONE NAME OF SALLET. IN LIKE MANNER
I WILL MAKE A HODGE-PODGE OF DIFFERING ARTICLES.

JANUARY 1830 – The failure of Messrs Palmer and Co., early in this month, caused the greatest consternation in India, and fell most severely on the widows and orphans of military men, who, having left their little portions in Palmer's house, had returned to England.

January 9th – My husband gave over charge of his office to Mr N—, who had returned from the Cape, and we began to speculate as to our destiny.

March 1st – My husband, having applied to remain up the country, was informed he might proceed to Cawnpore as acting-collector for eight months, on condition that he consented to give up the deputation-allowance to which he was entitled by the rules of the Civil Service. The conditions were hard, although offered as a personal favour, and were accepted in preference to returning to Calcutta.

Cawnpore, 150 miles from Allahabad, and 50 from Lucknow, a large station, is on a bleak, dreary, sandy, dusty, treeless plain, cut into ravines by torrents of rain; if possible, the place is considered hotter than Prāg.

Like the patriarchs of old we travelled with our flocks and herds or, rather, we sent them on in advance, and followed *dāk*.

March 27th – We quitted Allahabad, and drove the first stage to Alamchand, where we were kindly received by friends. At this place I first remarked the mowa tree (*Bassia longifolia*).

The fruit was falling and the natives were collecting it to make bazaar *srāb* (ardent spirits). The fruit, which is white, only falls during the daytime; when dried, it is given to cows as cheap food – from it the butter takes a fine yellow colour.

In the evening we proceeded *dāk*, and arrived the next morning at the house of the judge of Fatehpur. Just before entering his compound I stopped my palanquin, and desired a bearer to draw me a *lota* full of water from a well at the road side. The man took the brass vessel, which was fastened to a very long string, and threw it into the well; then drawing it up, he poured the contents on the ground, saying, 'A thuggee has been committed, you cannot drink that water. Did you not hear the *lota* – bump – bump upon a dead body in the well?' I reported the circumstance on my arrival, and not having before heard of the Thugs, was very much interested in the following account of *The Confessions of a Thug*. These fellows, it appears, roam about the country in gangs strangling people for their money; it is their only employment. During the three weeks of my stay at Futtehpore, the bodies of three men were found in the neighbouring wells – *thugged* – that is, strangled. Some years ago the Thugs were in great force, but they were well looked after by the police, and a *thuggee* was seldom committed: within a few months they have become very daring, especially around Cawnpore, Humeerpore, and Fatehpur.

A Kutcherry or Kachahri

A copy of *The Confessions of a Thug*, from a circular dated August, 1829, was sent by the Governor-General to the judges of the different stations on this subject. The reason for the Governor-General sending this circular to all the judges and magistrates, was to induce them to be on the alert after Thugs, in consequence of a party of them having been seized up the country by Captain Borthwick, four of whom turned evidence against the others. They were examined separately, and their confessions compared.

The following is the confession and statement of the principal witness:

'My father was a cultivator of land in Buraicha and other neighbouring villages, and I followed the same occupation until I entered my thirtieth year, when I joined the Thugs, with whom I have been more or less connected ever since, a period of upwards of thirty years.

'During this time, however, I have not accompanied them on every excursion; but, on the contrary, for intervals of two, three, and even six years, have remained at home and earned a subsistence by cultivating land, so that I have been engaged in only six predatory excursions: four under a leader, since dead, called Oo-dey Singh, and two under my present chief and fellow-prisoner, Mokhun Jemadar.

[...]

'Oo-dey Singh, my former leader was, at the period of my joining his gang, beyond the prime of life, although, at the same time, active and enterprising; but gradually becoming unfit for the exertion required of him by his situation, and his son Roman being seized with other Thugs and cast into prison at Jubbalpore, he abandoned his former course of life and shortly after died.

'At the time I was serving under Oo-dey Singh, tranquillity had not been established throughout the country, and our excursions were neither carried to so great a distance, nor were they so lucrative or certain as they have since been; for in those days travellers, particularly those possessed of much property, seldom ventured from one place to another unless in large parties, or under a strong escort; and we ourselves held the Pindaries and other armed plunderers in as much dread as other travellers.

'About three months after I had joined Mokhun's gang, which consisted of forty men, we set out from Bundelkand for the Dekkan, this was in the month of Phalgun, 1883 (about March, 1826). We proceeded by regular stages, and crossed the Narbada at the Chepanair Ghāt, where we fell in with Chotee Jamadār (a Brahman), who joined us with his gang, the strength of which was about the same as our own.

'We then continued our course towards Mallygaow, and at Thokur, near that cantonment, celebrated the Hooly; after which we resumed our route and reached Mallygaow, where we struck off by the Nassuk road, intending to turn from Nassuk to Poona and Aurangabad.

'After proceeding a coss or two on this road we met a relation of Mokhun's, belonging to Oomrao and Ruttyram's gangs, who informed us that these two leaders with their gangs were near at hand on the Poona road, engaged in the pursuit of some *angriahs* with treasure. It was proposed that Mokhun should join them with some of his men, in order to be entitled to a share of the spoil. Mokhun at first thought of going himself, but recollecting that Oomrao and himself were not on good terms, he sent twenty-five men with Chotee Jamadar. On the day following we heard the business was effected, and that they intended to proceed with Oomrao and Ruttyram to Bhoorampore, at which place they requested us to meet them. We accordingly proceeded to that quarter, and found Chotee Jemadar and his party at Bhoorampore, Oomrao and Ruttyram having returned to their homes.

'Here we learnt that the *angriahs* had been attacked and murdered near Koker (the place where we had celebrated the Hooly), and that no less a sum than Rs 22,000 was found on their persons in gold, bullion, mohurs and pootlies. Of this Rs 6000 had been received as the share of our two gangs, and was disposed of in the following manner.

'Mokhun received one-third for himself and his gang, a third was given to Chotee Jamadar for himself and his gang, and the remainder was reserved for the mutual expenses of the two gangs. Mokhun and Chotee despatched the two-thirds above mentioned to their homes that sent by the latter reached its destination safely; but one of Mokhun's men in charge of our share having got drunk at Jansy, blabbed that he was a Thug and returning with others with a large amount of treasure; he was consequently seized by the *sirdār* of the place, and the money taken from him. We now quitted Bhoorampore, and proceeded to Aurangabad but, meeting with little or no success, we returned by Dhoolia and Bhopāl to Bundelkand, and reached our several homes before the rains set in. Our next excursion was towards Gujerat, but in this nothing occurred worthy of note.

'I have never, during my connection with the Thugs, known a single instance of their committing a robbery without the previous destruction of life, which is almost invariably accomplished by strangulation. This is effected either by means of a *roomal* (handkerchief) or shred of cloth well twisted and wetted, or merely by the hands, though the latter is rarely practised and only had recourse to from accidental failure in the former and usual mode.

'A preconcerted signal being given, the victim or victims are instantly overpowered and death, either by the *roomal* or hands, is the act of a moment. In perpetrating murder it is an invariable rule with the Thugs never, if possible, to spill the blood of their victims, in order that no traces of murder may appear, to awaken suspicion of the deed in the minds of those who may happen to pass the spot, and detection be the consequence. In the hurry in which it is sometimes necessary to dispose of the bodies, holes cannot be dug sufficiently large to contain them in an entire state, particularly when the number of them is great; the bodies are then cut in pieces and packed therein.

'When these holes are near the roadside, and especially in an exposed spot, it is usual, after covering them with earth, to burn fires over them, to do away with the appearance of the earth having been newly turned. Murders, in the manner just described, are perpetrated as frequently and with equal facility and certainty, whilst the victims are walking along the road, as when they have been enticed to our places of encampment and, unconscious of what is to befall them, are sitting amongst us with everything carefully and leisurely arranged for their destruction.

'These murders frequently take place near villages where we encamp, and usually during twilight; and always, whilst the business is going on, the hand-drum is beaten and singing commenced, to drown any noise that might be made by the victims.

'The several persons actually engaged commence their operations simultaneously at a preconcerted signal given.

'The signal is an arbitrary one; generally a common, coarse expression is used, not likely to strike the attention of the victims, such as *"Tumbakoo lao"* (bring tobacco).

'I have never seen the *phansy* (or noose) made of cord employed for strangling, though I am fully aware of the general supposition, that it is with it that we strangle people; but if such has ever been employed, which I greatly doubt, it has long since been laid aside, for the obvious reason that if a Thug were seized having it about his person it would inevitably lead to his detection.

'A direct understanding with the local authorities in Bundelkand is constantly kept up by Oormtao, Mokhun, and all the other leaders and *jamadārs*, who on their return from their excursions reside in that part of the country, and these authorities are conciliated and their favour gained by suitable presents.

'Assistance and support from the English authorities being likewise indispensable, are obtained through artifice. This is effected by means of their emissaries who, by misrepresentation and falsehood, frequently contrive to extricate them from the difficulties in which persons of our habits are constantly involved. A relation of Oomrao's, Motee by name, and Lala Hajain, an inhabitant of Sikandra, render important services in this way. Motee, who was himself a Thug formerly, has for some years past discontinued going on predatory excursions. He first brought himself into notice with European gentlemen by informing against a gang which was seized in consequence, and confined at Jabalpur, where the greater part still remain.

'Since then Motee has advanced in favour with these gentlemen, who are led to suppose he acts as a check upon the Thugs and other plunderers; at least, he persuades us that such is the case, the consequence of which is that he exercises great influence over us, making us pay well for his connivance, and the good offices he no doubt frequently performs in our behalf.

[...]

'Few of us carry arms, indeed, amongst fifteen or twenty persons not more than two or three swords may be found.

'When Thugs, though strangers to each other, meet, there is something in their manner which discovers itself; and, to make "assurance doubly sure", one exclaims "Alee khān!" which being repeated by the other party recognition takes place, but is never followed by a disclosure of past acts.

'In the division of plunder the *jamadārs* receive seven and a half per cent, besides sharing equally with the rest of the gang; but, before any division is made, a certain portion is devoted to Bhawāni, our tutelar deity. This applies only to money in gold or silver; for when the plunder consists of diamonds and pearls, the leader draws blood from his hand, and having sprinkled a little over them, the sanction of the goddess to a division is thereby obtained without any other alienation. But the omission of this ceremony, or neglecting, when success attends us, to propitiate a continuance of Bhawāni's favour by laying aside a part of our acquisitions for her service, would, we firmly believe, bring heavy misfortune upon us.

'The office of strangler is never allowed to be self-assumed, but is conferred with due ceremony, after the fitness of the candidate in point of firmness, activity and bodily strength has been ascertained, and a sufficient degree of expertness in the use of the *roomal* has been acquired by long sham practice amongst ourselves.

'When thus qualified, the person on whom the office is to be conferred proceeds to the fields, conducted by his guru (spiritual guide), previously selected, who carries with him the *roomal*, and anxiously looking out for some favourable omen, such as the chirping of certain birds, or their flight past the right hand, knots the *roomal* at each end the moment that either occurs and delivers it to the candidate, imploring success upon him.

'After this they return, when the ceremony is closed by a feast, or distribution of sweetmeats. The seniors only confer this office, generally old Thugs held in some estimation but who from infirmity or age have ceased to accompany the gangs in their expeditions, and whose chief support is received from the voluntary contributions of those on whom they have conferred the privilege of using the *roomal*.

[...]

This is the end of *The Thug's Confession*.

The other men, on their examination, acknowledged having murdered a bearer, on whom they found four rupees. They also met with twelve seapoys; eight of the soldiers took one road, and the other four another. The Thugs, therefore, divided into two parties, overtook the seapoys, and killed them all.

One Thug said that on a certain day eleven men were killed and buried. The other Thug said that on the same day only seven were strangled: on re-examination he replied, 'Yes, it is true I only mentioned seven – there might have been eleven or more, I cannot remember; we strangled people so constantly, that I took little account of the numbers buried. I only know on that day about seven or eleven were buried.'

The Thugs never attack Europeans.

CHAPTER XIV

RESIDENCE AT CAWNPORE

[…]

MARCH 29TH – My husband proceeded *dāk* to Cawnpore, to take charge of his appointment and to engage a house, leaving me with my friends. On one stage of the road he had such a set of *coolies*, instead of bearers, to his *pālkee*, that they could not continue to carry it – at last, setting it down, they all ran away, and he had to wait six hours on the road until other bearers came: as this happened during the night, it was of no further consequence than making the latter part of his *dāk* very hot, as he did not reach his destination until eleven o'clock. The bearers on this road are proverbially bad.

Here I saw the first thermantidote (window fan), and took a sketch of it, in order to make one for myself. Here also, I saw the first alligator, a snub-nosed fellow, which was caught in the Jumna, and sent up on a *chārpāi*. Mr W— had the kindness to give me skulls of alligators, crocodiles, hyenas, and tigers, beautifully prepared, to add to my cabinet of curiosities.

Collecting Persian and Hindustani proverbs and sayings, and having them cut on seals, was another of my amusements.

April 19th – This day brought a letter saying a good bungalow had at length been procured, and I started *dāk* the next day. The judge, that I might meet with no adventures on the road, gave me a guard, which was relieved at the different *chaukis*, police stations.

A *barkandāz* (policeman) and two *chaukidārs* (watchmen) ran by the side of my palanquin all the way; in consequence I was not detained one moment more than necessary on the road. One of the *barkandāz* was armed with two swords and a great bamboo!

The journey was very unpleasant, very hot, and not a breath of air.

The dust from the trampling of the bearers' feet rolled up in clouds, filling my eyes and mouth and powdering my hair; and my little terrier, Fairy Poppus, as the natives call her, in imitation of my 'Fury, pup, pup', was very troublesome in the *pālkee*.

I arrived at Cawnpore at seven in the morning, and was glad to take shelter in my new house, which I found very cool and pleasant after a hot drive during the last stage in a buggy.

The house, or rather bungalow, properly Bangla, for it is tiled over a thatch, is situated in the centre of the station, near the theatre; it stands on a platform of stone rising out of the Ganges, which flows below and washes the walls. The station is a very large one: besides the gentlemen of the Civil Service, there are the artillery, the eleventh dragoons, the fourth cavalry, and three or four regiments of infantry.

The work of this day began by what is really an operation in India, and constantly repeated, that is, washing the hair. My *ayah* understood it remarkably well.

June 9th—The deaths are numerous in our farmyard; in such weather it is a matter of surprise that any thing can exist. At four o'clock the thermometer outside the verandah, in the sun, stood at 130°; in the shade, at 110°! From this time to the end of August we lost two hundred and eighty guinea fowls from vertigo, and three calves also died.

A storm is raging: it arose in clouds of dust, which, sweeping over the river from the Lucknow side, blow directly on the windows of the drawing-room; they are all fastened, and a man at every one of them, or the violence of the wind would burst them open; my mouth and eyes are full of the sand; I can scarcely write – not a drop of rain, only the high wind, and the clouds of dust so thick we cannot see across the verandah. I feel rather afraid lest some part of the house, which is not in good repair, should give way if it continue to blow in such gusts. This bay-windowed room feels the whole force of the *tufān*, which is the heaviest I have seen. In Calcutta we had severe storms, with thunder and lightning; here, nothing but clouds of sand – reaching from earth to heaven – with a hot yellow tinge, shutting out the view entirely. The storm has blown for an hour, and is beginning to clear off; I can just see the little white-crested waves on the river beneath the verandah.

In the open air the thermometer stands at 130°; in the drawing-room, with three *tattis* up, at 88°. The heat is too oppressive to admit of an evening drive.

A high caste and religious native gentleman, Shāh Kubbeer-oo-deen Ahmud, requested to be allowed to play at chess with me; the natives are passionately fond of the game, which is remarkable, as chess was one of the games forbidden by the prophet. On the arrival of my opponent, I recognised the native gentleman who had entertained me with fireworks at Sahseram. I have spoken of him as of *high caste* – that term is only correct when applied to an Hindu, Musulmāns have no distinction of caste.

June 14th – A *tufān*, a sand storm, or rather a storm of sand and dust, is now blowing; indeed, a little while ago the darkness was so great from that cause, I was obliged to leave off writing, being unable to distinguish the letters.

The Barkandāz

The Ganges opposite Cawnpore is about three miles in breadth; and, at this season, the water being low, the natives cultivate melons, cucumbers, wheat, etc., on the islands in the centre of the stream; some of the melons are delicious, remarkably fragrant and very cheap. During the rains the islands are entirely under water, and the river, when there is a breeze, swells into waves like a little sea.

If a house has a flat roof covered with flagstones and mortar, it is called a pukka house; if the roof be raised and it be thatched, it is called a bungalow; the latter are generally supposed to be cooler than the pukka houses. The rooms of our house are lofty and good; the dining-room forty feet by twenty-eight, the swimming-bath thirty feet by twenty-one, and all the other rooms on a suitable scale. There is a fine garden belonging to and surrounding the house, having two good wells, coach-house, stables, cow-house, etc. In India the kitchen and all the servants' offices are detached from the dwelling on account of the heat. We pay Rs 150 a month, about 150 guineas per annum, a heavy rent for an up-country house: the houses are always let unfurnished.

Very fine white grapes are now selling at fourpence-halfpenny per pound. Cawnpore is famous for its fruit-gardens.

[. . .]

Women have more influence over men in India than in any other country. All outdoor amusements are nearly denied to the latter by the climate, unless before sunrise or after sunset; therefore the whole time of military men, generally speaking, is spent in the house, devoted either to music or drawing, which of course they prefer in the society of ladies, or in the study of the languages or in gaming. The young officers at this station play exceedingly high, ruinously so – two-guinea points at short whist and one hundred guineas on the rubber is not unusual amongst the young men.

Happily the gentlemen in the Civil Service have too much employment to admit of their devoting their time to gambling.

If you ask a native – 'Where is your master gone?' if the gentleman be from home, you are sure to receive the answer – 'Howā khānā-ke-wāste' (to eat the air); this chameleon-like propensity of eating the air is always the object during the early morning ride and the evening drive.

Our servants at present only amount to fifty-four, and I find it quite difficult enough to keep them in order; they quarrel amongst themselves, and when they become quite outrageous, they demand their discharge.

My *ayah* and the *ābdār* had a laughable quarrel. She was making herself a pair of Europe chintz pyjamas (trousers) such as they usually wear, made very full round the body, and quite tight from the knee to the ankle.

Musulmān women never wear a petticoat when amongst themselves, it is the badge of servitude, and put on to please European ladies; the moment an *ayah* gets into her own house, she takes off her full petticoat and the large white mantle (*chādar*) that covers her head and the upper part of her body, and walks about in the curiously shaped trousers I have described, with a sort of loose jacket of muslin over the upper part, beneath which is the *angiya*.

The *ayah* was sitting on her *chārpāi* (native bed) working away with great eagerness, when her friend the *ābdār* advised her to make the trousers full to the ankle; and she came to me to give warning to quit my service, vowing revenge upon the *ābdār*, because *nāch* women wear trousers of that description. The old *ābdār*, Sheik-jee, was sitting down very quietly making *chapāties* (flour-cakes), and smoking his *narjil* (coconut shell *huqqa*) at intervals, enjoying the *ayah*'s anger until she stood up and, screaming with passion, gave him *gālee* (abuse); he then flew into a rage, and I had some trouble to restore peace and quietness. Natives seldom, indeed hardly ever, come to blows, but they will go on for hours abusing each other in the grossest language, screaming out their words from passion.

A *darzee* (tailor) is an Indian luxury: they work beautifully – as strongly and finely as the French milliners; they have great patience – because they are paid by the month, and not by the piece. In Calcutta I found my tailors great thieves – knives, scissors, seals – they would steal anything. One man carried off a present I had just received, a necklace and bracelets of a very curious pattern, and a box full of polished pebbles, in sets, from the Soane river.

[...]

In Calcutta, the tank water being unwholesome to drink, it is necessary to catch rain water, and preserve it in great jars, sixty jars full will last a year in our family. It is purified with alum, and a heated iron is put into it. Here we drink the Ganges water, reckoned the most wholesome in India; it is purified in jars in the same manner. The water of the Jumna is considered unwholesome, and in some parts, my old *ābdār* declares it is absolutely poisonous.

We were glad to quit Allahabad, the smallpox having commenced its ravages at that station. On our arrival at Cawnpore, we found it raging still worse; the magistrate took it and died in three days. Hundreds of children are ill of this disease in the bazaar; and the government, in their humanity, have done away with the vaccine department here. Surely it is a cruel act, where there are so many regiments and so many European children who cannot now be vaccinated. It is very severe and numbers of adults have been attacked.

In India wax candles are always burned. A bearer will not touch a mould because they say it is made of pig's fat. We burn spermaceti generally. The first time the bearers saw them, they would not touch the spermaceti, and I had great difficulty in persuading them the candles were made from the fat of a great fish. Some bearers in Calcutta will not snuff a candle if it be on the dinner-table, but a *khidmatgār* having put it on the ground, the bearer will snuff it when the other man replaces it. In the Upper Provinces they are not so particular.

[...]

People think of nothing but converting the Hindus; and religion is often used as a cloak by the greatest schemers after good appointments. Religious meetings are held continually in Calcutta, frequented by people to pray themselves into high salaries, who never thought of praying before.

In India we use no bells to call servants; but as the *chaprāsis* are always in attendance just without the door, if you want one, you say 'Qui hy?' i.e. 'is there any one?' – or 'Kon hy?' – 'who is there?' when a servant appears. For this reason old Indians are called Qui hys.

August 7th – The plagues of Egypt were not worse than the plagues of India. Last night the dinner-table was covered with white ants, having wings: these ants, at a certain period after a shower, rise from the earth with four large wings. They fly to the lights, and your lamps are put out in a few minutes by swarms of them: they fall into your plate at dinner and over your book when reading, being most troublesome. Last night heavy rain fell and the rooms were swarming with winged-ants which flew in; their wings fell off almost immediately, verifying the proverb: 'When ants get wings they die.'

Tonight we are suffering under a more disagreeable infliction; a quantity of winged-bugs flew in just as dinner was put on the table, the bamboo screens having been let down rather too late. They are odious; they fly upon your face and arms, and into your plate; if you brush them away, they emit such terrible effluvia it is sickening, and yet one cannot bear them to crawl over one's body, as one is at this minute doing on my ear, without pushing them off.

[...]

August 22nd – They tell me the people in Calcutta are dying fast from a fever resembling the yellow fever. The European soldiers, here are also going to their graves very quickly; three days ago, six men died; two days ago, six more expired; and one hundred and sixty are in the hospital. The fever, which rages, tinges the skin and eyes yellow; perhaps only the severe bilious fever of India brought on by drinking brandy and *arak*, a bazaar spirit extremely injurious, to say nothing of exposure to the sun. Almost every evening we meet the two elephants belonging to the hospital carrying each about ten sick men, who are sufficiently recovered to be able to go out 'to eat the air', and for exercise; the poor fellows look so wan and ghastly.

The Darwān

[...]

What can be more wretched than the life of a private soldier in the East? His profession employs but little of his time. During the heat of the day, he is forced to remain within the intensely hot barrack-rooms; heat produces thirst, and idleness discontent. He drinks *arak* like a fish, and soon finds life a burden, almost insupportable. To the man weary of the burden of existence, to escape from it, transportation appears a blessing. The great source of all this misery is the cheapness of *arak* mixed with datura, and the restlessness arising from the want of occupation; although a library is generally provided for the privates by the regiment.

You at home, who sleep in gay beds of carved mahogany with handsome curtains, would be surprised at sight of the beds used by us during the hot winds. Four small posts, and a frame, on which very broad tape (*nawār*) is plaited and strained very tight, over this a *sītal-pātā*, a sort of fine cool Manilla mat, then the sheets, and for warmth, either an Indian shawl, or a *rezai*, which is of silk quilted with cotton, and very light. We use no mosquito curtains, for each *chārpāi* is placed just before an open window, with the east wind blowing on it, and a *pankhā*, with a deep double frill, is in full swing over the beds all night, pulled by a string which passes through a hole in the wall – the wind it creates drives off the mosquitoes, and the man who pulls the pankhā is relieved every two hours.

[...]

The Governor-General left Calcutta on the 11th inst., and proposes to be at Benares on the 10th December. Lady William Bentinck accompanies him in his tour. They say that she is dreadfully nervous about him. His unpopularity is increasing and some ill-regulated person, in a moment of disappointment and frenzy, might perhaps cause a scene. The events of the last few years, since Mr Canning's death, have been astounding. I wonder if there is more room for amazement. I hope his Grace the Duke will not take us under his charge. We are satisfied with King Log, provided he stands in the way of King Stork.

Lord William has been doing away with all the good appointments in the Civil Service; and the army have been cruelly treated, with respect to the half-*batta*. Perhaps, when the renewal of the charter is concluded, the directors will again be enabled to treat those living under their command with the generosity which has ever distinguished them, and which has rendered their service one of the finest in the world.

CHAPTER XV

THE THUG'S DICE – EXECUTION OF ELEVEN THUGS

OCTOBER 16TH 1830 – In the Government Gazette of this evening is an account of the execution of eleven Thugs in a letter from a man up the country to the editor. The account is so interesting, I cannot refrain from copying it.

'SIR – I was yesterday present at the execution of eleven Thugs, who had been seized in the neighbourhood of Bhilsa, convicted of the murder of thirty-five travellers (whose bodies were disinterred as evidence against them at the different places along the lines of road between Bhopāl and Saugor, where they had been strangled and buried), and sentenced to death by the agent to the Governor-General, Mr Smith.

'As the sun rose, the eleven men were brought out from the jail, decorated with chaplets of flowers, and marched up to the front of the drop, where they arranged themselves in line with infinite self-possession.

'When arranged, each opposite the noose that best pleased him, they lifted up their hands and shouted, "*Bindachul ka jae! Bhawāni ka jae!*" i.e. Glory to Bindachul! Bhawāni's glory! Everyone making use of precisely the same invocation, though four were Mahomedans, one a Brahman, and the rest Rajpoots, and other castes of Hindus; they all ascended the steps, and took their position upon the platform with great composure, then, taking the noose in both hands, made same invocation to Bhawāni, after which they placed them over their heads and adjusted them to their necks; some of the younger ones laughing at the observations of the crowd around them.

'One of the youngest, a Mohammedan, impatient of the delay, stooped down so as to tighten the rope, and, stepping deliberately over the platform, hanged himself as coolly as one would step over a rock to take a swim in the sea! This man was known to have assisted in strangling a party of six travellers at Omurpatan, in the Rewah Rajah's territories in December last, and closely pursued to have gone off, joined another gang, and, in less than a month, to have assisted in strangling thirty more in Bhopāl; he was taken at Bhilsa, the last scene of his murders. Omurpatan is one hundred miles east of Jabalpur, and the place in which the Thug assisted in strangling in the Bhopāl territories, a month afterwards, is two hundred miles west of Jabalpore. Such is the rapidity with which these murderers change the scene of their operations, when conscious of keen pursuit! He was taken at Bhilsa by the very man whom he found upon his trail at Omurpatan, three hundred miles distant.

'On being asked whether they had any wish to express to the magistrate, they prayed that for every man hanged, *five convicts might be released from jail*, and that they might have a little money to be distributed in charity.

'Their invocation of Bhawāni at the drop was a confession of their guilt, for no one in such a situation invokes Bhawāni but a Thug, and he invokes no other deity in any situation, whatever may be his religion or sect. She is worshipped under her four names, Devi, Kālee, Doorga, and Bhawānī, and her temple at Bindachun, a few miles west of Mirzapur on the Ganges, is constantly filled with murderers from every quarter of India, who go there to offer up a share of the booty acquired from their strangled victims in their annual excursions.

'This accounts for the invocation – "*Jae Bindachul!*" made use of by these men in approaching and ascending the drop. These pilgrimages to the temple are made generally at the latter end of the rainy season, and whilst on the road from their homes to the temple, nothing can ever tempt them to commit a robbery. They are not, however, so scrupulous on their way back.

'The priests promise the Thugs impunity and wealth, provided a due share be offered to the goddess. If they die by the sword in the execution of murders, she promises them paradise in all its most exquisite delights; if taken and executed, it must arise from her displeasure, incurred by some neglect of the duties they owe her and they must, as disturbed spirits, inhabit midair until her wrath be appeased. After they have propitiated the goddess by offering up a share of the preceding year, and received the priest's suggestions on the subject, they prepare for the next year's expedition.

'The different members who form the gang assemble at the village of the leader at a certain day and, after determining the scene of operations, they proceed to consecrate their *kodalee*, or small pickaxe, which they use to dig the graves of their victims and which they consider as their standard. They believe that no spirit can ever rise to trouble their repose from a grave dug by this instrument, provided it be duly consecrated, and they are fearfully scrupulous in the observance of every ceremony enjoined in the consecration, and never allow the earth to be turned with any other instrument. It is a neatly made pickaxe of about four or five pounds' weight, six or eight inches long, and with one point.

'They sacrifice a goat and offer it up, with a coconut, to Bhawānī; they then make a mixture of sandal and other scented woods, spirits, sugar, flour, and butter, and boil it in a cauldron.

'The *kodalee*, having been carefully washed, is put upon a spot cleared away for the purpose, and plastered with cow dung, and the mixture is poured over it with certain prayers and ceremonies.

'It is now wiped and folded in a clean white cloth by the priest, and the whole gang proceed some distance from the village upon the road they intend to take and stand until they hear a partridge call, the priest having in his mind someone as the bearer of the sacred deposit. If the partridge calls on their right, he places it in the hands of that individual, and in a solemn manner impresses upon him the responsibility of the charge. If a partridge calls on the left, or one does not call until the sun is high, they all return and wait until the next morning, when they proceed to another spot, and the priest fixes his mind upon some other individual; and so every morning, until the deity has signified her approbation of the choice by the calling of the partridge on the right.

'If the *kodalee* should fall to the ground at any time, the gang consider it as an evil omen, leave that part of the country without delay, and select another standard-bearer. If no accident happen, the man first elected bears it the whole season; but a new election must take place for the next. The man who bears it carries it in his waistband, but never sleeps with it on his person, nor lets any man see where he conceals it during the night, or whilst he takes his rest.

'All oaths of the members of the gang are administered upon this instrument, folded in a clean white cloth, and placed on ground cleared away and plastered with cow dung: I have heard the oldest of them declare, that they believe any man who should make a false oath upon it would be immediately punished by some fatal disease. If any man be suspected of treachery, they make him swear in this manner.

'The standard-bearer, immediately after his election, proceeds across the first running stream in the direction of the country to which the gang intend to proceed, accompanied by only one witness, to wait for a favourable omen. When they come to the Narbada, Jumna, or any other river of this class, the whole gang must accompany him. A deer on the right of the road is a good omen, especially if single, according to the verse –

> Leela Mirga daena – Suda daena Tas.
> Kishunrut hark doo, bhule kure Bhugwan.

'If a wolf is seen to cross the road, either before or behind them, they must return, and take another road. If they hear a jackal call during the day, or a partridge during the night, they leave that part of the country forthwith. An old man once told me, in proof of the faith to be placed in these signs, that he was, in his youth, one of a gang of fifty who were sleeping under some date trees between Indore and Ojeya, when a partridge was heard to call out of one of them about two in the morning. They got up in great alarm, moved off instantly, but about daylight met a party of horse going from Ojeya to Indore. Some dispute took place between them, and they were taken back to Indore.

'They had murdered the guru (or chief priest) of the Holcar family and his followers; and their leader, taking a liking to a parrot of his, had brought it with them.

'On arriving at Indore the parrot began to talk, and was almost immediately recognised by one of Holcar's family as the parrot of the guru who had gone off for Ojeya some days before. One of the youngest of them was immediately tied up and flogged, and after a couple of dozen, he confessed the robbery and murder. The bodies were taken up and recognised, and five-and-forty Thugs were blown off at once from the mouths of cannon. He was one of the five who were pardoned on account of their youth and taken into service.

[...]

'In the territories of the native chiefs of Bundelkand, and those of Scindia and Holkar, a Thug feels just as independent and free as an Englishman in a tavern, and they will probably begin to feel themselves just as much so in those of Nagpur now that European superintendency has been withdrawn. But they are not confined to the territories of the native chiefs; they are becoming numerous in our own, and are often found most securely and comfortably situated in the very seats of our principal judicial establishments; and of late years they are known to have formed some settlements to the east of the Ganges, in parts that they formerly used merely to visit in the course of their annual excursions.

'I should mention that the cow being a form of Doorga, or Bhawāni, the Mahomedans must forego the use of beef the moment they enlist themselves under her banners; and though they may read their Qur'an, they are not suffered to invoke the name of Mahommed.

'The Qur'an is still their civil code and they are governed by its laws in all matters of inheritance, marriage, etc.

'Your obedient servant,

'H'*

I have been greatly interested in the above account: there are numerous

---

* From the *Calcutta Literary Gazette*, inserted in the *Government Gazette* of October 7th 1830.

Thugs in and around Cawnpore; they never attack Europeans; but the natives are afraid of travelling alone, as a poor bearer with one month's wages of four rupees has quite sufficient to attract them. They seldom bury them in these parts, but having strangled and robbed their victim, then throw him down a well, wells being numerous by the side of the high roads.

CHAPTER XVI

RESIDENCE AT CAWNPORE – THE DEWALI

OCTOBER 1830 – Mooatummud-ood-Dowlah, generally known as Aghā Meer, the deposed Prime Minister to the King of Oude, Ghazee-ood-Deen Hyder, is coming over to Cawnpore; his *zenāna*, treasures, two lacs of shawls, etc. etc., have arrived on the other bank of the Ganges, escorted by the military. The ex-minister has not yet arrived, and a large detachment of the military from this station has been sent to escort him in safety to the Company's territories.

This morning, from the verandah, I was watching what appeared to be a number of buffaloes floating down the stream, with their drivers; but, as they approached, found them to be sixteen of Aghā Meer's elephants swimming over.

The distance from the Camp on the opposite side the river to our garden, under which they landed, must be four miles, or more. Elephants swim very low, and put down their trunks occasionally to ascertain if they are in deep water. Their heads are almost invisible at times, and the *mahouts* strike them with the goad (*ānkus*) to guide them.

On reaching the bank just below our verandah, they set up a loud *bellowing*, which was answered by those still struggling to get to land, a work rather difficult to accomplish on account of the rapidity of the river.

What would not the people at home give to see sixteen fine elephants swimming four miles over a rapid river, with their *mahouts* on their backs, the men hallooing with all their might, and the elephants every now and then roaring in concert! It was an interesting sight, and my first view of their power in the water.

October 2nd – A friend, just returned from the hills, brought down with him some forty cashmere goats; the shawl goats, such as are found in the hills: they die very fast on quitting the cold regions; he has lost all but three females, which he has given to me; they will scarcely live in this burning Cawnpore.

Report says the Governor-General has put off his journey for a month longer; it is supposed he will, if possible, avoid this large military station; the soldiers are in so discontented a state, he may perchance receive a bullet on parade. The privates here have several times attempted the lives of their officers, by shooting and cutting them down, sometimes upon the slightest cause of complaint and often without having any to provoke such conduct.

October 7th – I have just returned from calling on a friend of mine, and overheard the remarks of a gentleman who was speaking of her to another; they amused me.

'Really that is a noble creature, she has a neck like an Arab, her head is so well set on!'

Buffaloes from Cawnpore swim off in the early morning in herds to the bank in the centre of the river, where they feed; they return in the evening of their own accord. The other evening I thought a shoal of porpoises were beneath the verandah – but they were buffaloes trying to find a landing-place; they swim so deeply, their black heads are only partly visible, and at a little distance they may easily be mistaken for porpoises.

Sometimes I see a native drive his cow into the river; when he wishes to cross it, he takes hold of the animal by the tail, and holding, on, easily crosses over with her; sometimes he aids the cow by using one hand in swimming.

'What is that going down the river?' exclaimed a gentleman. On applying a telescope, we found fifty or sixty buffaloes all in a heap were coming down with the stream, whilst ten natives swimming with them kept thrashing them with long bamboos to make them exert themselves, and keep all together: the natives shouting and urging on the animals and the buffaloes bellowing at every blow they received. At what a rate they come down! The stream flows with such rapidity during the rains! This is the first time I have seen such a large herd driven in this curious fashion.

Methodism is gaining ground very fast in Cawnpore; young ladies sometimes profess to believe it highly incorrect to go to balls, plays, races, or to any party where it is possible there may be a quadrille. A number of the officers also profess these opinions, and set themselves up as New Lights.

October 9th – I was remarking to an officer today I thought it very unlikely anyone would attempt the life of the Governor-General. He replied: 'The danger is to be feared from the discharged *sipahis*, who are in a most turbulent and discontented state. Squadrons of them are gone over to Runjeet Singh who is most happy to receive well-disciplined troops into his service.'

I have just learned how to tell the age of a stud-bred horse. All stud horses are marked on the flank, when they are one year old, with the first letter of the stud and the last figure of the year. Our little mare, Lakshmi, is marked K O, therefore she was foaled at Kharuntadee in 1819, and marked in 1820 – making her age now eleven years.

October 10th – I see in the papers – 'A member in the House of Commons expressed his satisfaction that so abominable a practice as that of *sati* should have been abolished without convulsion or bloodshed. Great credit was due to the noble lord at the head of the Government there and to the missionaries, to whom much of the credit was owing.'

How very absurd all this is was proved to me by what came to my knowledge at the time of the *sati* at Allahabad. If Government at that time had issued the order to forbid *sati*, not one word would have been said. The missionaries had nothing to do with it; the rite might have been abolished long before without danger.

Women in all countries are considered such dust in the balance, when their interests are pitted against those of the men, that I rejoice no more widows are to be grilled to ensure the whole of the property passing to the sons of the deceased.

The Government interferes with native superstition where rupees are in question – witness the tax they levy on pilgrims at the junction of the Ganges and Jumna. Every man, even the veriest beggar, is obliged to give one rupee for liberty to bathe at the holy spot; and if you consider that one rupee is sufficient to keep that man in comfort for one month, the tax is severe.

The Dewālī

October 16th – This is the great day of the *Dewālī*, celebrated by the Hindus in honour of Kālī, also called Kālī-*pooja*. This evening, happening to go down to the river just below the verandah to look at a large toon-wood tree lying in a boat which some people had brought in hopes we should purchase it, my attention was attracted to a vast quantity of lamps burning on Sirsya Ghāt, and I desired the boatmen to row to the place; I had never been on the river before, nor had I seen this *ghāt*, although only a stone's throw from our bungalow, it being hidden by a point of land.

On reaching the *ghāt*, I was quite delighted with the beauty of a scene resembling fairyland. Along the side of the Ganges, for the distance of a quarter of a mile are, I should think, about fifty small *ghāts* built with steps low down into the river which flows over the lower portion of them. Above these *ghāts* are, I should imagine, fifteen small Hindu temples, mixed with native houses; and some beautifully picturesque trees overshadow the whole.

The spot must be particularly interesting by daylight – but imagine its beauty at the time I saw it, at the Festival of Lights.

On every temple, on every *ghāt*, and on the steps down to the river's side, thousands of small lamps were placed, from the foundation to the highest pinnacle, tracing the architecture in lines of light.

The evening was very dark and the whole scene was reflected in the Ganges. Hundreds of Hindus were worshipping before the images of Māhadeo and Ganésha: some men on the *ghāts* standing within circles of light were prostrating themselves on the pavement; others doing *pooja* standing in the river; others bathing. The Brahmans before the idols were tolling their bells, whilst the worshippers poured Ganges water, rice, oil, and flowers over the images of the gods.

Numbers of people were sending off little paper boats, each containing a lamp, which, floating down the river, added to the beauty of the scene. I saw some women sending off these little firefly boats in which they had adventured their happiness, earnestly watching them as they floated down the stream: if at the moment the paper boat disappeared in the distance the lamp was still burning, the wish of the votary would be crowned with success; but if the lamp was extinguished, the hope for which the offering was made was doomed to disappointment. With what eagerness did many a mother watch the little light to know if her child would or would not recover from sickness! The river was covered with fleets of these little lamps, hurried along by the rapid stream.

The stone *ghāts* are of all shapes and sizes, built by the Cawnpore merchants according to their wealth. Some are large and handsome – some not a yard in diameter. A good one, with arches facing the water, is put aside for the sole use of the women; and all were most brilliantly lighted. The houses in the city were also gaily illuminated. But to see the *Dewālī* in perfection, you must float past the temples during the dark hours on Ganga-ji. I was greatly pleased: so Eastern, so fairylike a scene I had not witnessed since my arrival in India; nor could I have imagined that the dreary-looking station of Cawnpore contained so much of beauty.

The goddess Kālee, to whom this festival is dedicated, is the black goddess to whom human sacrifices are offered. This evening beholding the pretty and fanciful adorations of the Hindus, offering rice and flowers and sending off their floating lamps upon the river, I could scarcely believe the worship could be in honour of Kālee.

I have seen no temples dedicated to her up the country. Her celebrated shrine is at Kālee Ghāt, near Calcutta. A Hindu often makes a vow, generally to Kālee, that if she will grant his prayer he will not cut off a particular lock of his hair for so many years; at the end of that time he goes to the shrine, makes *pooja*, and shaves the lock: at particular times of the year, they say, piles of hair are shaved off at Kālee Ghāt.

When we were residing in Chowringhee, we heard of the body of a man who had been sacrificed to the goddess having been found before the image at Kālee

Ghāt. It was supposed he was some poor wanderer or devotee, possessing no friends to make inquiries concerning his fate. When a victim is sacrificed it is considered necessary to cut off the head at one blow with a broad heavy axe.

At Benares I purchased thirty-two paintings of the Hindu deities for one rupee and amongst them was a sketch of the goddess Kālee.

Phŭlŭ-Hurēē

A figure of Kālee, exactly similar to the one purchased at Benares, and attired in the same manner, I saw worshipped at Prāg under the name of Phŭlŭ-hŭrēē (she who receives much fruit). She is worshipped at the total wane of the moon, in the month Jaystha – or any other month, at the pleasure of the worshipper. Her offerings are fruits especially. Animals are sacrificed in her honour, and Jack-fruit and mangoes are presented to her in that particular month.

The day after the worship the people carried the goddess in state down to the river Jumna, and sank her in its deep waters: the procession was accompanied by the discordant music of tom-toms, etc., and all the rabble of Kydganj. The image, about three feet in height, dressed and painted, was borne on a sort of platform.

The goddess is represented as a black female with four arms standing on the breast of Shiva. In one hand she carries a scimitar; in two others the heads of giants, which she holds by the hair; and the fourth hand supports giants' heads.

'She wears two dead bodies for earrings, and a necklace of skulls. Her tongue hangs down to her chin. The heads of giants are hung as a girdle around her loins, and her jet black hair falls to her heels. Having drunk the blood of the giants she slew, her eyebrows are bloody, and the blood is falling in a stream down her breast. Her eyes are red, like those of a drunkard. She stands with one leg on the breast of her husband Shiva, and rests the other on his thigh.'

Men are pointed out amongst *other animals* as a proper sacrifice to Kālee: the blood of a tiger pleases her for one hundred years; the blood of a lion, a reindeer, or a man, for one thousand years. By the sacrifice of three men she is pleased for one hundred thousand years.

Kālee had a contest with the giant Ravana, which lasted ten years; having conquered him, she became mad with joy and her dancing shook the earth to its centre. To restore the peace of the world Shiva, her husband, threw himself amongst the dead bodies at her feet. She continued her dancing and trampled upon him. When she discovered her husband she stood still, horror-struck and ashamed, and threw out her tongue to an uncommon length. By this means

Shiva stopped her frantic dancing and saved the universe. When the Hindu women are shocked or ashamed at anything, they put out their tongues as a mode of expressing their feelings. Nor is this practice confined to the women of the East alone, it is common amongst the lower orders of the English.

October 18th – Aghā Meer, the ex-minister of Oude, has come over. His train consisted of fifty-six elephants covered with crimson clothing deeply embroidered with gold, and forty *garees* (carts) filled with gold mohurs and rupees.

His *zenāna* came over some days ago, consisting of nearly four hundred palanquins; how much I should like to pay the ladies a visit and see if there are any remarkably handsome women amongst them!

[...]

October 20th – In the evening I went with Mr A— to Sirsya Ghāt; whilst we were sketching the *mut'hs* (Hindu temples), about fifty women came down, two by two, to the *ghāt*. After having burnt the corpse of a Hindu by the side of the Ganges, they came in procession, to lament, bathe and put on clean garments; one woman walked in front, reciting a monotonous chant in which the others every now and then joined in chorus, beating their breasts and foreheads in time to the monotonous singing.

They assembled on the steps of the *ghāt*. Each woman wore a white *chador* (in shape like a sheet), which was wrapped so closely around her that it covered her body and head entirely, the eyes alone being visible. Standing on the steps of the *ghāt*, they renewed their lament, beating their breasts, foreheads, and limbs and chanting their lament all the time; then they all sat down, and beat their knees with their hands in time to the dirge; afterwards, they descended into the river to bathe and change their clothes; such an assortment of ugly limbs I never beheld! A native woman thinks no more of displaying her form as high as the knee, or some inches above it, than we do of showing our faces. This being rather too great an exhibition, I proposed to my companion to proceed a little further that the lovely damsels might bathe undisturbed.

October 25th – I have been more disgusted today than I can express: the cause is too truly Indian not to have a place in my journal. I fancied I saw the corpse of a European floating down the Ganges just now, but, on looking through the telescope, I beheld the most disgusting object imaginable.

When a rich Hindu dies, his body is burned, and the ashes are thrown into the Ganges; when a poor man is burned, they will not go to the expense of wood sufficient to consume the body. The corpse I saw floating down had been put on a pile, covered with *ghee* (clarified butter) and fire enough had been allowed just to take off all the skin from the body and head, giving it a white appearance; anything so ghastly and horrible as the limbs from the effect of the fire was never beheld, and it floated almost entirely out of the water, whilst the crows that were perched upon it tore the eyes out. In some parts, where the stream forms a little bay, numbers of these dreadful objects are collected together by the eddy, and render the air pestiferous until a strong current carries them onwards. The poorer Hindus think they have paid all due honour to their relatives when they have thus skinned them on the funeral pile and thrown them, like dead dogs, into the Ganges.

The Musulmāns bury their dead – generally under the shade of trees – and erect tombs to their memory, which they keep in repair; they burn lights upon the graves every Thursday (*Jumarāt*) and adorn the tomb with flowers.

October 27th – As we floated down the stream this evening, I observed the first *ghāt* was lighted up, and looked very brilliant, with hundreds of little lamps; the *dāndis* said it was not on account of any particular festival, but merely the merchant, to whom the *ghāt* and temple belonged, offering lamps to Ganga-ji.

November 8th – My husband received an order to return to Allahabad; this gave us much satisfaction.

[...]

November 18th – Today, our Mug cook died suddenly after a short illness; the corpse will be burned, and the ashes thrown into the Ganges; the man came from Ava. The Mugs are reckoned better cooks than the Musulmāns. He was an excellent *artiste* and a good servant; we shall replace him with difficulty. He professed himself a Hindu, and during their festivals would give money and worship according to their fashion.

During the Muharram he called himself a follower of the prophet; he gave forty rupees to assist in building a *taziya*, performed all the ceremonies peculiar to the faithful, and was allowed to be considered a Musulmān for the time; at the conclusion, when the *taziya* was thrown into the river, he became a Mug again.

November 22nd – With a westerly wind, and the thermometer at 65°, we Indians find it very cold, the contrast to the hot winds is so great. I have worn a shawl all the morning and tonight, for the first time this year, we have begun fires; and have had the horseshoe table placed in front of the fireplace, that we may enjoy the warmth during dinner-time. The room looks so cheerful, it puts me into good humour and good spirits; I feel so *English,* without lassitude, so strong and well. My husband has just sallied out in his great coat to take a very long walk; and the little terrier is lying under the table, watching a musk rat which has taken refuge in a hole under the grate.

November 26th – I have just heard of an occurrence at Lucknow which is

in true native style. The Nawāb Hakīm Menhdi Ali Khān, the present minister, poisoned the King of Oude's ear against one of his people by declaring
that the man betrayed some state secrets and intrigues; the king accordingly,
without judge or jury, ordered the man's head to be fixed and a heavy weight
to be fastened on his tongue until the tongue should be so wrenched from the
roots that it should ever after hang out of his mouth. This brutal punishment
was inflicted some two or three months ago and the poor creature's life has
been preserved by pouring liquids down his throat as, of course, he is unable
to eat at present. They have now discovered the man is innocent! But what
does it avail him? His accuser, the Nawāb Hukīm Menhdi, is rich; money is
power. The king is displeased with the minister, I understand, for his misrep-
resentations; he is also on bad terms with the resident – they do not speak.

Any lady having a horror of the plagues of Egypt would not admire what is
going on at this moment; several lizards are peering about, as they hang on the
window frames with their bright round eyes; a great fat frog or toad, I know
not which, is jumping across the floor under the dinner table; and a wild cat
from the jungles, having come in, has made her exit through the window,
breaking a pane of glass; a muskrat is squeaking in the next room, I must go
and prevent the little terrier from catching it: I do not like to see the dog foam
at the mouth, which she always does after killing this sort of rat.

December 1st – A marriage has taken place this day, between the widow of
the Mug cook, a low caste Hindu, old and ugly, and one of our *khidmātgars*, a
Mahommedan. On account of her caste the man cannot eat with her without
pollution; therefore, having taken her to a mosque, and the *Qur'an* having
been read before her, she declares herself a convert. The Musulmān servants
have dined with her; she is now a follower of the prophet. They are very fond of
making converts, but the Hindus never attempt to convert anyone; in fact, they
will not admit converts to their faith, nor will they embrace any other religion;
here and there a woman becomes a Musulmān on her marriage with a man of
that faith.

December 5th – Today's news is that the Governor-General met the 3rd
cavalry at Allahabad, on their march from Cawnpore to Benares. His lordship
reviewed the regiment and asked the officers to dinner an invitation they all
refused. This annoyed his lordship very much, being the first display of *resent-
ment* manifested towards him on his march by the army, and he *ordered* them
to dine with him on pain of forfeiting their rank, pay, and allowances, pending
a reference to the Court of Directors. Of course the officers obeyed *the order*;
they were obliged to do so. What an agreeable party the Governor-General
must have had, with guests whom he had forced to partake of the feast!

[...]

December 13th – I accompanied some ladies to the riding-school of the 11th dragoons and, being much pleased, requested to be allowed to take lessons with them; afterwards, riding there during those hours that the school was unoccupied by the dragoons formed one of our greatest amusements. As for the corporal, the rough rider of the 11th dragoons who attends in the riding-school, his affections are quite divided between my horse Trelawny and myself; I heard him say the other day, speaking of the former, 'I like that little chap, he looks so *innicent.*'

My *sā'is* cannot accomplish putting me on my horse after the English fashion; therefore, he kneels down on one knee, holding the horse in his left hand, and the stirrup in the right; I step from his knee to the stirrup, and take my seat on the saddle; rather a good method, and one of his own invention.

Christmas Day – The house is gaily decorated with plantain trees, roses, and chaplets of gaudy flowers, but no holly; we miss the holly and mistletoe of an English Christmas. The servants are all coming in with their offerings – trays of apples, grapes, *kishmish*, walnuts, sugar, almonds in the shell, oranges, etc. The saddler, who is also a servant, has brought five trays in honour of *kissmiss* (Christmas); these presents are rather expensive to the receiver, who returns *kissmiss bakhshish* (Christmas boxes) in rupees; the apples *au naturel*, brought down at this time of the year by the Arab merchants [Pathans] from Kabul, are rather insipid, yet the sight is very grateful to the eye; they are large, fine, and of a roseate hue. The grapes, which are in small round boxes, are picked off the bunch, and placed in layers of cotton. The dates are excellent. *Kishmish* are small raisins without stones, which have an agreeable acidity; they are known in England as sultana raisins. These Arab merchants bring *pattu, pashmina*, cashmere gloves and socks, curiously illuminated old Persian books, swords and daggers, *sāleb misree* and Persian cats, saffron, and various other incongruous articles which are all laden on camels, which they bring in strings in large numbers. The men are fine, hardy, picturesque-looking personages, independent in their bearing; and some of the younger ones have a colour on their cheeks like the bright red on their apples. Their complexions are much fairer than any I have seen in India.

CHAPTER XVII

Scenes in Oude

JANUARY 1ST 1831 – New Year's Day was celebrated with all due honour at home, the party separating at four o'clock; punch *à la Romaine* and fine ices making men forget the lapse of time. The people here are ice-making mad; I flatter myself I understand the mystery of ice-ification better than anyone in India.

January 5th – The view from our verandah is remarkably good; the King of Oude, Ghazee-ood-Deen Hyder, has pitched his tent on the opposite side of the Ganges and has constructed a bridge of boats across the river. In attendance upon him, they say, there are two thousand elephants, camels and men in proportionate number; the sides of the river swarm with troops, animals, and tents.

Early on the morning of the 6th, the Governor-General, Lord William Bentinck, arrived at Cawnpore; and her Ladyship received the station. We paid our *devoirs*; and, in conversation with Lady William on the subject of the *zenāna* of the King of Oude, I excited her curiosity so much by my account of Tājmahul, that I feel convinced she will pay her a visit on her arrival at Lucknow.

January 7th – We were invited to breakfast with the Governor-General, with whom the King of Oude was to breakfast in state. We rode to the tents – but let me commence the narrative from the dawn of day. Long before sunrise the guns and drums in the king's encampment announced that all were in preparation to cross the bridge of boats. About seven o'clock an enormous train of elephants, camels and troops crossed over, brilliantly decorated, and proceeded to the camp of the Governor-General. We then cantered off – I on the Bokhara grey who became very impetuous; but, although surrounded with elephants, camels, galloping horses and guns firing, I never lost my courage for an instant: nevertheless, I will play no such game again, it is too hazardous.

Lord William met the king halfway, and having been invited to enter the royal *howdah*, he took his seat on the king's elephant and they proceeded together to the breakfast-tent through a street of dragoons, infantry, etc. Lady William, with all her visitors assembled around her, was in the tent awaiting the entrance of the great people; on their arrival, after the usual embracings and forms were over, we proceeded to breakfast.

The whole scene was one of extreme beauty. The magnificent dresses of the natives, the superb elephants covered with crimson velvet embroidered with gold, the English troops, the happy faces and the brilliant day rendered it delightful.

After breakfast Lord William received all visitors who asked for a private audience in a separate tent: my husband made his salam, and requested permission to visit Lucknow in his Lordship's train; having received a kind affirmative, we returned home.

January 8th – The Governor-General returned the king's visit and, crossing the bridge of boats, breakfasted with his majesty on the territories of Oude.

January 10th – Lady William gave a ball to the station.

January 11th – His lordship was invited to dinner – and dined with the eleventh dragoons, he being their colonel; the next day the Governor-General's party commenced their march to Lucknow, the king having quitted the day before.

January 18th – Having sent on our camels and tents beforehand, we started for Lucknow, intending to drive the whole distance in one day, for which purpose we had laid eight buggy horses on the road, the distance being only fifty-five miles.

Going over the sandy bed of the Ganges, the horse being unable to drag the Stanhope, we mounted an elephant which took us some miles; being obliged to return the elephant, we got into a native cart drawn by bullocks, and so arrived at the spot where the second horse was laid. But the horses found it almost impossible to get through the sand, the country had been so much cut up from the multitudes that had crossed and recrossed it. In consequence night overtook us in the middle of Oude without a tent or food, and a dark night in prospect; whilst debating where to find shelter, we espied a tent in the distance which proved to be an empty one belonging to a friend of ours, and there we took up our quarters.

A boy came forward and saying, 'I Christian,' offered to procure a chicken and give us a curry, which we ate off red earthen dishes, with two bits of bamboo as a knife and fork, after the style of chopsticks. I must not forget to mention that after our repast Christian came forward and repeated the Creed and the Lord's Prayer in Hindustanī; he repeated them like a parrot, but, judging from his answers when questioned, did not appear at all to comprehend his newly-acquired religion.

The *sutrāengī*, the cotton carpet of the tent, served to defend us from the cold during the night; and the next morning we recommenced our journey, but did not reach Lucknow in time to join the dinner-party at the Residency to which we were invited to meet Lady William Bentinck.

January 18th – The Governor-General breakfasted with the king. The whole party quitted the Residency on elephants most beautifully clothed and were met halfway by his majesty. The scene was magnificent. The elephants, the camels, the crowds of picturesque natives, the horsemen and the English troops formed a *tout ensemble* that was quite inspiring. The Governor-General got into the king's *howdah* and proceeded to the palace, where breakfast was laid in a fine service of gold and silver. After breakfast we proceeded to a verandah to see various fights and, having taken our seats, the order was given to commence the *tamāshā*.

The Elephant Fights

The river Goomtee runs in front of the verandah; and on the opposite side were collected a number of elephants paired for the combat. The animals exhibited at first no inclination to fight, although urged on by their respective *mahouts*, and we began to imagine this native sport would prove a failure.

At length two elephants, equally matched, were guided by the *mahouts* on their backs to some distance from each other and a female elephant was placed midway. As soon as the elephants turned and saw the female they became angry, and set off at a long swinging trot to meet each other; they attacked with their long tusks, and appeared to be pressing against each other with all their might. One elephant caught the leg of the other in his trunk, and strove to throw his adversary or break his foreleg. But the most dangerous part appeared to be when they seized one another by their long trunks and interlaced them; then the combat began in good earnest. When they grew very fierce, and there was danger of their injuring themselves, fireworks were thrown in their faces which alarmed and separated them, and small rockets were also let off for that purpose.

The situation of a *mahout* during the fight is one of danger. The year before, the shock of the combat having thrown the *mahout* to the ground, the elephant opposed to him took a step to one side and, putting his great foot upon him, quietly crushed the man to death!

Sometimes the elephant will put up his trunk to seize his opponent's *mahout* and pull him off: skill and activity are requisite to avoid the danger.

The second pair of elephants that were brought in front of the verandah hung back, as if unwilling to fight, for some time; several natives, both on horseback and on foot, touched them up every now and then with long spears to rouse their anger. One of the elephants was a long time ere he could be induced to combat but, when once excited, he fought bravely; he was a powerful animal, too much for his adversary for having placed his tusks against the flank of his opponents, he drove him before him step-by-step across the plain to the edge of the river, and fairly rolled him over into the Goomtee. Sometimes a defeated elephant will take to the water and his adversary will pursue him across the river.

The animals are rendered furious by giving them balls to eat made of the wax of the human ear, which the barbers collect for that purpose!

The hair on the tail of an elephant is reckoned of such importance that the price of the animal rises or falls according to the quantity and length of the hair on the tail. It is sometimes made into bracelets for English ladies.

A great number of elephants fought in pairs during the morning, but to have a good view of the combat one ought to be on the plain on the other side the river, nearer to the combatants. The verandah from which we viewed the scene is rather too distant.

When the elephant fights were over, two rhinoceros were brought before us and an amusing fight took place between them; they fought like pigs.

The plain was covered by natives in thousands, on foot or on horseback. When the rhinoceros grew fierce they charged the crowd, and it was beautiful to see the mass of people flying before them.

On the Goomtee, in front of the verandah, a large pleasure-boat belonging to his Majesty was sailing up and down. The boat was made in the shape of a fish, and the golden scales glittered in the sun.

The scene was picturesque, animated, and full of novelty.

In an enclosed court, the walls of which we overlooked, seven or eight fine wild buffaloes were confined: two tigers, one hyena and three bears were turned loose upon them. I expected to see the tigers spring upon the buffaloes, instead of which they slunk round and round the walls of the court, apparently only anxious to escape. The tigers had not a fair chance and were sadly injured, being thrown into the air by the buffaloes, and were received again when falling on their enormous horns. The buffaloes attacked them three or four together, advancing in line with their heads to the ground. I observed that when the buffaloes came up to the tiger, who was generally lying on the ground, and presented their horns close to him – if the animal raised his paw and struck one of them, he was tossed in a moment; if he remained quiet, they sometimes retreated without molesting him.

The bears fought well, but in a most laughable style. The scene was a cruel one and I was glad when it was over. None of the animals, however, were killed.

A fight was to have taken place between a country horse and two tigers, but

Lady William Bentinck broke up the party and retired. I was anxious to see the animal, he is such a vicious beast; the other day he killed two tigers that were turned loose upon him.

Combats also took place between rams. The creatures attacked each other fiercely – the jar and the noise were surprising as head met head in full tilt. Well might they be called battering rams!

January 21st – We visited Constantia, a beautiful and most singular house built by General Martin it would take pages to describe it; the house is constructed to suit the climate; ventilation is carried up through the walls from the ground floor to the top of the building, and the marble hall is a luxurious apartment. The king having refused to give General Martin the price he asked for Constantia, the latter declared his tomb should be handsomer than any palace in his Majesty's dominions. He therefore built a vault for himself under the house, and there he lies buried; this has desecrated the place, no Musulmān can inhabit a tomb.

The monument stands in the vault; a bust of the general adorns it. Lights are constantly burned before the tomb. The figures of four *sipahis*, large as life with their arms reversed, stand in niches at the sides of the monument. In the centre of the vault, on a long plain slab, is this inscription:

HERE LIES MAJOR-GENERAL CLAUDE MARTIN,

BORN AT LYONS, 1735;

ARRIVED IN INDIA A COMMON SOLDIER,

AND DIED AT LUCKNOW, THE 13TH DECEMBER, 1801.

PRAY FOR HIS SOUL.

Claude Martin was a native of the city of Lyons. He was originally a common soldier, and fought under Count Lally; he afterwards entered the service of the East India Company and rose to the rank of a Major-general. He died possessed of enormous wealth, and endowed a noble charity in Calcutta, called La Martinière.

The house is a large and very singular building; a motto fronts the whole – '*Labore et Constantia*' – hence the name of the house.

Returning from this interesting place, we proceeded on elephants to see the Roomee Durwāza, a gateway built at the entrance of the city, on the Delhi road, by Ussuf-ood-Dowla; it is most beautiful and elegant, a copy of a gate at Constantinople.

Near this spot is the Imām-Bārā, a building almost too delicate and elegant to be described; it contains the tomb of Ussuf-ood Dowla, the second king of this family. Within the court is a beautiful mosque.

We were delighted with the place and the scene altogether – the time being evening and the streets crowded with natives.

January 22nd – The Governor-General quitted Lucknow at daybreak. On account of some points of etiquette respecting the queen mother and the king's favourite wife, Gosseina, Lady William Bentinck did not visit the royal *zenāna*.

This day we visited a palace called Padshān-i-Takht, containing the king's throne and the banqueting-rooms, a delightful place; on quitting it we crossed the river to a new house and garden, built by the present king, called Padshāh Bāgh, of which I must give a description, it being the most luxurious palace I have seen in India.

A large space has been enclosed as a garden within a high wall; it contains three houses and two gateways; the first house is a most delightful one, all you can wish for in such a climate as this; beautiful rooms, with six fountains playing in them, and everything in fairyland style; then such an *hammām* or steam baths, containing rooms heated to different temperatures, the heat of each increasing until you arrive at the steam bath itself.

The apartments are built of white variegated marble, and the roofs arched; the rooms were so delightful, we felt every inclination to remain in the *hammām*, the temperature was so luxurious.

Crossing from this palace to the centre of the garden, we entered another elegant building, supported on white marble pillars, beautifully finished, and adorned and furnished with crimson and gold.

On the left of the garden is a third palace, sacred to the ladies of the *zenāna*; this house is built of marble, and covered with flower-work of pounded *tālk* (talc), which has exactly the appearance of silver, giving an eastern style to the place. There are two handsome gateways, a steam-engine to supply the fountains, and a superb tiger in a cage. Every luxury of life may be contained within the walls of this garden; it is at present scarcely finished, but displays great taste and beauty.

On our return we visited the king's stables and saw two hundred horses, amongst which were some very fine Arabs. His Majesty has five hundred horses in his private stables. This day was one of much fatigue; we were on elephants, and exposed to the sun throughout the whole day.

January 23rd – Mr M— invited us to quit our tents and come into the Residency, giving us the apartments vacated by the Governor-General, which are delightful; and here we are installed with some most agreeable people. First and foremost, our kind host the Resident; Mr G—, the Resident of Nagpur; Mr H—, the Resident of Delhi; and Colonel Gardner, a most charming old gentleman – but he will require pages to himself, he is one of *many* thousand.

But I can write no more – my aide-de-camp, a young Bhopāl chieftain, is in attendance to invite me to ride with the Resident. This little native chief is a fine intelligent boy about fourteen years of age; he rides well, on a small horse covered with silver ornaments; and his own dress, with two and sometimes three swords at his waist, is so curious, I should like to have his picture taken. The young chief with his followers often attends me on horseback to do my bidding.

The king has a charming park near Lucknow, called Dil-Kushā, or 'Heart's Delight', filled with game: deer, *nilgāi*, antelopes, bears, tigers, peacocks and game of all sorts. The drive through it is most agreeable, the road being kept constantly watered: the house is good, and very convenient. His Majesty visits the place often for shooting.

Just beyond the park is a second park called Beebeepore, formerly the residence of Mr Cherry, who was murdered at Benares.

January 24th – I took a steam bath in true oriental style, which was very delightful; when the pleasing fatigue was over I joined a party and proceeded to Daulat Khāna, a palace built by Ussuf-ood-Dowla, but now uninhabited, except by some of the ladies and attendants of the old king's *zenāna*.

We went there to see a picture painted in oil by Zoffani, an Italian artist, of a match of cocks between the Nawāb Ussuf-ood-Dowla and the Resident, Colonel Mordaunt; the whole of the figures are portraits; the picture excellent, but fast falling into decay.

The next place visited was the country-house of one of the richest merchants in India, a place called Govinda Bāgh. It is one of the handsomest houses I have entered, and beautifully furnished with fine mirrors and lustres; its painted ceilings are remarkably well done and have a very rich effect; the pillars also in imitation of porphyry look extremely well. The owner, Govind Lal, lives in a mean dirty house in one of the meanest *galīs* (lanes) in the city, that his wealth may not attract robbers or cause jealousy.

January 25th – My husband accompanied the Resident and a party to breakfast with the King, and I called on my charming friend, Mrs F—, in cantonments.

In the evening I accompanied the Resident, in his barouche drawn by four fine horses, round the grounds of Dil-Kushā. The carriage was attended by an escort on horseback; when it passed the guards, arms were presented, and trumpets blown: and sometimes men with baskets of birds running by the side of the carriage let them fly whenever they caught his eye, in the hope of some reward being thrown to them for having liberated their captives in compliment to the great man.

To release captive birds propitiates the favour of heaven. A great man will release prisoners from jail when he is anxious for the recovery of a relative from illness, or to procure an heir!

The Jānwar Khāna, a menagerie filled with wild beasts, animals of every sort and birds in profusion, next attracted my attention. You may talk of Le Jardin des Plantes, but the Jānwar Khāna at Lucknow is far better worth visiting. There was an immense Doomba sheep, with *four* horns, and such a tail! Perfectly enormous.

We paid a visit to the tomb of Saadut Ulee Khān, the king's grandfather, a beautiful building, near which is the tomb of the *begum*, both worth seeing.

January 20th – I rode with the Resident to his country-house, a short distance from Lucknow, situated in the midst of delightful gardens; there are about twenty of these gardens, filled with fine tanks, wells, and beautiful trees; the Resident contemplates turning them into a park.

January 28th – We went over a *zenāna* garden; the house, dedicated to the ladies, was a good one, situated in a large garden surrounded by a high stone wall. The orthodox height for the four walls of a *zenāna* garden is that no man standing on an elephant can overlook them. The building is surrounded with fine trees; and a fountain played before it, in which gold and silver fish were swimming. Near it was an avenue in which was a swing, the invariable accompaniment of a *zenāna* garden. The season in which the ladies more particularly delight to swing in the open air is during the rains. I cantered back to the Residency at ten o'clock; the sun was warm, but I thought not of his beams.

After breakfast, I retired to write my journal (knowing how much pleasure it would give her for whom it was kept), although I had that delightful man, Colonel Gardner, to converse with; such a high caste gentleman! How I wish I had his picture! He is married to a native princess, and his granddaughter is betrothed to one of the princes of Delhi. The *begum*, his wife, is in Lucknow, but so ill that I have been unable to pay my respects to her. Colonel Gardner has promised me, if we will visit Agra or Delhi next year which we hope to do, he will give me letters of introduction to some of the ladies of the palace, under which circumstances I shall have the opportunity of seeing Delhi to the greatest advantage.

A very fine corps of men, called Gardner's Horse, were raised by him; single-handed nothing can resist them, such masters are they of their horses and weapons. I told him I was anxious to see good native riding, and feats of horsemanship; he said, 'An old servant of mine is now in Lucknow, in the king's service; he is the finest horseman in India. I gave that man Rs 150 a month (about £150 per annum) for the pleasure of seeing him ride. He could cut his way through thousands. All men who know anything of native horse-manship, know that man: he has just sent me word he cannot pay his respects to me, for if he were to do so, the king would turn him out of service.' I asked why? He answered, 'There is such a jealousy of the English at court: as for the king, he is a poor creature and can neither like nor dislike. Hakīm Menhdi the minister rules him entirely, and he abhors the English.'

It is a curious circumstance that many of the palaces in Lucknow have fronts in imitation of the palaces in Naples and Rome, etc.; and the real native palace is beyond in an enclosed space.

Being tired with writing, I will go down and talk to Colonel Gardner. Should no men be in the room, he will converse respecting the *zenāna*, but the moment a man enters, it is a forbidden subject.

Lucknow is a very beautiful city; and the view from the roof of the Residency particularly good.

I am fatigued with my ride through the sun; nevertheless, I will go out on an elephant this evening, and view all the old part of the city. I like this *barā sāhib* life; this living *en prince*; in a climate so fine as this is at present it is delightful.

The subjects of his Majesty of Oude are by no means desirous of participating in the blessings of British rule. They are a richer, sleeker and merrier race than the natives in the territories of the Company.

What a delightful companion is this Colonel Gardner! I have had most interesting conversation with him which has been interrupted by his being obliged to attend his poor sick wife, as he calls the *begum*. She is very ill, and her mind is as much affected as her body: he cannot persuade her to call in the aid of medicine. A short time ago she lost her son, Allan Gardner, aged twenty-nine years: then she lost a daughter and a grandson; afterwards a favourite daughter; and now another young, grandson is dangerously ill. These misfortunes have broken her spirit and she refuses all medical aid. That dear old man has made me weep like a child. I could not bear the recital of his sorrows and sufferings. He said, 'You often see me talking and apparently cheerful at the Resident's table, when my heart is bleeding.'

We have had a long conversation respecting his own life, and I have been trying to persuade him to write it. He says, 'If I were to write it, you would scarcely believe it; it would appear fiction.' He is gone to the sick *begum*. How I long for another *tête à tête*, in the hope of learning his private history!

He must have been, and is, very handsome; such a high caste man! How he came to marry the *begum* I know not. What a romance his love must have been! I wish I had his portrait, just as he now appears, so dignified and interesting. His partiality flatters me greatly.

CHAPTER XVIII

REVELATIONS OF LIFE IN THE ZENĀNA

JANUARY 29TH 1831 – We drove to Barouda, a palace built in the French style; I saw there nothing worthy of remark, but two marble tables, inlaid in the most delicate and beautiful manner with flowers of the convolvulus.

January 20th – The Resident and all his party breakfasted with the King on the anniversary of his coronation, which takes place in any month, and on any day, according to his Majesty's pleasure.

During breakfast my attention was deeply engrossed by the prime minister, the Nawāb Moontuzim-ul-Dowla, Menhdi Ulee Khān Bahadur, commonly called Nawāb Hakim Menhdi. I conversed with him at times and eyed him well as he was seated next to me and opposite the King, telling his beads the whole time, for good luck perhaps; his rosary was composed of enormous pearls.

His majesty's *huqqa* was presented to the Nawāb; Lord William Bentinck and the Resident were honoured with the same: it is a great distinction; no subject can smoke, unless by permission, in the royal presence. *Huqqas* are only presented to the Governor-General, the Commander-in-chief, the Resident, and the Bishop of Calcutta – if he likes a pipe.

Numerous histories respecting the prime minister were current in the bazaar, far too romantic and extraordinary to be believed, of which the following is a specimen: 'The truth or falsehood of the story rests on the head of the narrator.'

The *hakim* (physician or learned man) was formerly employed on a salary of about twenty rupees a month. The commencement of his enormous fortune began thus: he was in tents in the district; a very rich Hindu was with him within the canvas walls (*kanats*), with which tents are surrounded. This man was said to have died during the night; his corpse was given to his relations, who were in the camp, to be burned according to Hindu custom. There were two black marks round the neck of the corpse. It is a custom amongst Hindus to put sweetmeats into the mouth of a dead body. When they opened the mouth of the corpse for this purpose, within it was found a finger, bitten off at the second joint. On that very night the *confidential servant* of the *hakim* lost his finger! The *hakim* seized the man's treasure, which laid the foundation of his fortune. He next took into pay a number of thieves and murderers who made excursions and shared the booty with the *hakim*. They say the man's art is such that he keeps in favour both with natives and Europeans, in spite of his crimes.

Having been unable to bring the Resident over to his views, he is his sworn enemy and would give thousands to any one who would poison him. Many of the servants now standing behind the Resident's chair know the reward they might obtain. They would not poison any dish from which many might eat, the most likely thing in which it would be administered would be coffee or ice!

After breakfast, the King went into the next apartment where the Resident, with all due form, having taken off the King's turban, placed the crown upon his head and he ascended the *masnad*.

Khema-jah, the eldest boy, about fourteen years of age, is an ill-looking low caste wretch, with long, straight, lank hair, coarse, falling lips, and bad teeth. The manners and looks of the boy proclaim his caste. He was the first person presented to his Majesty, and received four or five dresses of honour, made of thick Benares gold and silver *kinkhwāb*, which were *all* put upon his person one over the other. A jewelled turban was put on his head, and a necklace of pearls and precious stones round his neck; and over all these dresses of honour were placed four or five pairs of cashmere shawls. A sword, dagger and shield were given him; an elephant, a horse, and a palanquin. Having made his salam to his majesty and offered some gold mohurs, he retired.

The younger boy, Feredooa Buckht, a bold and independent child, then came forward and received the same presents in the same style.

The dresses of honour (*khil'ats*) are sometimes given away to dependants on the same day; this, if known, would be considered an insult.

Then appeared the minister, the Nawāb Hakīm Menhdi: when the first dress of honour was put on him, it being too small, he could only put in one arm; and there he stood shaking, perhaps from an idea of its being a bad omen. The Nawāb prostrated himself before the King, and took off his own turban; His Majesty himself immediately placed a jewelled one on the uncovered head of the minister. Imagine the old man, sinking beneath the weight of years, his head totally bald and his person overwhelmed with dresses of honour, shawls, and presents, like those before given to the young princes. He trembled so much, the elephant-goad fell from his hand, a sign of his own fall; and the gold mohurs he attempted to retain in his hands fell at the foot of the throne. The people say there is a prophecy he will come to an untimely end next February: 'A bad omen ought not to be mentioned .'

When Mossem-ood-Dowla (the true heir) approached, he was coldly received, and a deep cloud for some time darkened his countenance. Mossem-ood-Dowla is a fine, handsome man with a keen eye and a very intelligent, good-natured countenance. It was a painful sight to see him do homage to one who had no right to the throne, but through the power of an unjust law.

I was standing next to the Resident and the Prime Minister when, during a part of the ceremony, a shower of precious stones was thrown over us; I looked at the Resident, and saw him move his arm to allow the valuables that had fallen upon him to drop to the ground; I imitated his example by moving my scarf, on which some were caught; it would have been *infra dig.* to have retained them; they fell to the ground, and were scrambled for by the natives; the shower consisted of emeralds, rubies, pearls, etc., etc.

A *magnifique* style of largesse!

After all the dresses of honour had been presented to the different persons, a *hār*, a necklace of gold and silver tinsel, very elegantly made, was placed around the neck of each of the visitors; *atr* of roses was put on my hands, and on the hands of some other visitors, in compliment to the Resident, by his Majesty himself. *Pān* was presented, and rose water was sprinkled over us; after which ceremonies, we all made our *bohut bohut ādāb* salam (most respectful reverence) to the King of Oude, and took our departure. The gold and silver tinsel *hārs* have been substituted for strings of pearl, which it was customary to present to visitors until an order of government, promulgated four years ago, forbade the acceptance of presents.

The Zenāna

The following account of the *begums* was given me by one whose life would have paid the forfeit had it been known he had revealed the secrets of the *zenāna*; he desired me not to mention it at the time, or he should be murdered on quitting Oude.

Sultana Boa

'The Queen is the daughter of his Royal Highness Mirza Muhammad Sulimān Shekō, the own brother of the present Emperor of Delhi, Akbar Shāh.

'From the first day after marriage, neglected and ill-treated, she was only allowed, until lately, Rs 20 rupees a day; she has now Rs 2000 a month, but is not permitted to leave her apartments; the servants of her family have all been discharged and she is in fact a prisoner. Neither the King nor any of his family ever visit her, and no other person is permitted to approach her apartments.

'The lady of the Resident told me, 'She is a great beauty, the handsomest woman she ever saw.' I have seen her sister, and can easily believe she has not exaggerated. The Queen is now about sixteen or seventeen years old (1830) and has been married, I believe, about five years.

'Mirza Sulimān Shekō, the father, lived at Lucknow since the time of Ussuf-ood-Dowla and was forced by the late King of Oude to give him his daughter in marriage. The dower (*mehr*) of the Princess was settled at five crores (a crore is ten million rupees) and the father had a grant of Rs 5000 a month, which is not paid; and in June 1828 the Prince was insulted, and obliged to quit Lucknow with every sort of indignity.'

Mulka Zumanee

'The second *begum* is the wife of Ramzanee, a *cherkut* or elephant servant, who is now pensioned on thirty rupees a month, and kept in surveillance at Sandee; some time after her marriage the lady proved naughty and was next acknowledged as the *chère amie* of an itinerant barber; she left him, and took service with Mirza Jewad Ali Beg's family as a servant-of-all-work, on eight anās a month and her food. She was next heard of as a *gram*-grinder at – serai, where her eldest son, by name Tillooah, was born; her next child was a daughter.

'At this time Moonah Jāh (Feredooa Buckht) was born in the palace; and, amongst others who sought the situation of nurse, Ramzanee's wife attended; she was approved of by the *hākims* and was installed nurse to the heir-apparent.

'Her age was then near forty, her size immoderate, her complexion the darkest; but she soon obtained such influence over the King that he married her and gave her the title of (the daughter of the Emperor Furrukshere, and the wife of the Emperor Mohummud Shāh,) – Mulka Zumanee! Well may she exclaim, "Oh Father! I have got into a strange difficulty, I have left off picking up cow-dung, and am employed in embroidery!".

'She has a *jagir* of Rs 50,000 a month, and the power of expending Rs 50,000 more from the treasury monthly. Her son Tillooah was about three years of age when she was entertained as nurse, but such was her power that his Majesty publicly declared himself the father of the boy, and he was in consequence recognised as heir to the crown, with the title of Khema Jāh!'

The King has five queens, although by Mohammedan law he ought only to have four. His Majesty of Oude possesses, to a considerable extent, that peculiarly masculine faculty of retaining the *passion* and changing the *object*.

He heeds not the proverb, 'Do not put your beard into the hands of another.'

As far as I recollect the history of his last and favourite wife it is this: the Nawāb Hakīm Menhdi, finding his influence less than usual, adopted a *nāch* girl as his daughter because the King admired her, and induced his Majesty to marry her. Her name is Gosseina; she is not pretty, but possesses great influence over her royal lover. This girl, some fourteen months ago, was dancing at the Residency for twenty-five rupees a night: and a woman of such low caste not even a *sā'is* would have married her. The King now calls the *hakīm* his father-in-law, and says, 'I have married your daughter, but you have not married her mother; I insist on your marrying her mother.' The *hakīm* tries to fight off and says he is too old; but the King often annoys him by asking when the marriage is to take place.

'There is no bird like a man,' i.e. so volatile and unsteady.

The beautiful Tājmahul; whom I mentioned in Chapter x, is entirely superseded by this Gosseina, the present reigning favourite; Tājmahul has taken to drinking, and all the King's drunken bouts are held at her house.

When he marched to Cawnpore he took Tājmahul and Gosseina with him, and their retinue was immense. It is said that the beautiful Timoorian, Sultana Boa, the Princess of Delhi, was so much disgusted at her father's being forced to give her in marriage to Nusseer-ood-Deen Hydur, and looked upon him as a man of such low caste in comparison with herself, that she never allowed him to enter her palace – a virgin queen.

Her sister, Mulka Begum, married her first cousin, Mirza Selim, the son of the emperor, Akbār Shāh; from whom she eloped with Mr James Gardner, and to the latter she was afterwards married. This elopement was the cause of the greatest annoyance and distress to Colonel Gardner, nor did he grant his forgiveness to his son for years afterwards.

Affairs being in so unpleasant a state at the Court of Lucknow was the cause of Lady William Bentinck's being unable to visit the *zenāna*; and after her ladyship's departure, I was prevented going there by the same reason.

One cannot be surprised at a Musulmān taking advantage of the permission given him by his lawgiver with respect to a plurality of wives.

The Prophet himself did not set the best possible example in his own domestic circle, having had eighteen wives! Nevertheless, his code of laws respecting marriage restricted his followers to four wives, besides concubines.

In a book published in England, it is observed, 'there are some instances of remarkable generosity in the conduct of good wives which would hardly gain credit with females differently educated.' This, being interpreted, means, a good wife provides new wives for her husband!

The King is very anxious the Resident should patronise Khema Jāh, his adopted son, and is much annoyed he can gain no control over so independent and noble-minded a man.

CHAPTER XIX

The Return to Allahabad –
Execution of twenty-five Thugs

WHO HAS SEEN TOMORROW

i.e. Enjoy today, no one knows what will happen tomorrow.

FEBRUARY 1ST 1832 – We quitted the Residency at Lucknow, feeling greatly gratified by the kindness we had experienced from the Resident, and returned to Cawnpore.

We now prepared for our removal to Allahabad. The horses and carriages having been dispatched by land, the furniture, etc. was put into six great country boats, one of which, an immense 900 man *pataila*, contained cows, sheep, goats, besides a number of fowls, guinea-fowls, turkeys, etc.; and on the top of all was a great thermantidote (window fan).

February 17th – We quitted Cawnpore, and commenced our voyage down the Ganges.

February 18th – The low sandbanks in the river swarm with crocodiles; ten are basking on a bank to the left of our boat, and five or six are just ahead. The sāhib has fired at them several times, but they are beyond the reach of pistol shot. They are timid animals; as soon as you approach them they dive down into the river. We have only seen the long-nosed crocodiles, none of the snub-nosed alligators. What a monster there is very near us, and such a winsome wee one by its side! I want a baby crocodile very much for my cabinet.

At Sheorajpore our friends tried to tempt us to remain with them, showing us a *nilgāi*, a wild boar, hares, black partridges and the common grey partridges that they had shot; and offering us an elephant to enable us to join the sportsmen the next day.

How much I enjoy the quietude of floating down the river, and admiring the picturesque *ghāts* and temples on its banks! This is the country of the picturesque, and the banks of the river in parts are beautiful.

On the morning of our quitting Lucknow, my aide-de-camp, the young Bhopāl chieftain, was made quite happy by being allowed to make his salam to his Majesty, who gave him a dress of honour.

I can write no more; the sāhib's vessel has *lugoed*, that is, has made fast to the bank; I must go out shooting with him and mark the game.

February 19th – We slept off Nobusta; the wind was very high, it blew a gale, but the high bank afforded us protection. Our boats are large, flat-bottomed, shallow and broad country boats, on each of which a great house is built of bamboo and mats, and the roof is thatched. The interior is fitted up with coloured chintz, like that used for tents. Such unwieldy vessels are very likely to be upset in a storm. The great *patailā*, which contains the cows, etc., has given us much trouble; she has been aground several times being, from her height and bulk, almost unmanageable in a strong wind.

It is very cold, the rain is falling fast; all the servants and the crew look so deplorable and keep their shoulders to their ears. The horses on their march will be exposed to it; they are merely sheltered by a tree at night – a cold berth for animals accustomed to warm stables.

February 20th – This has been a day of rain and contrary wind; we have made but little way, and being unable to reach Mirzapur, have *lugoed* off a sandbank.

February 21st – We breakfasted at Mirzapur and reached Kurrah at night, where we moored our little fleet under an old fort built by Aurangzeb. No sooner had we made fast than a heavy storm came on, accompanied by thunder and lightning, hail and rain; the latter was so heavy, it soaked through the thatch of the bamboo houses on the boats and rendered us very uncomfortable. The large *patailā* was missing, but came in the next day with her cargo of cows and sheep; from her height she must have been in danger, as she had not gained the land when the storm came on.

We have moored just below Aurangzeb's fort, over which I have roamed; it is an excellent subject for a sketch; the view from the height is beautiful.

On the other side is an old well, built of the very small Hindustani bricks; the river has washed away all the bank in which the well was originally sunk, and it now stands naked on the sand – a remarkable object.

February 24th – We arrived at Allahabad, and my husband took charge of his appointment. Then commenced dinner-parties given in honour of our return by our old friends at the station.

Am I not happy once more in dear old Prāg? We have no troubles as at Cawnpore; no one poisons our horses; all the people around us appear pleased at our return and eager to serve us; our neighbours here are friends interested in our welfare. My old carpenters, the saddler, the ironsmith, the painter, the stonecutter and the sealing-wax-maker are all in their old nooks in the verandah.

March 1st – It was so cold we had fires of an evening, which were not discontinued until the 5th of the month.

Our friend Captain B— is going home; he will tell those we love of our goings out and comings in, and will be as a connecting link to those betwixt whom and us this great gulf of distance is fixed. It really requires an exile from home to be able to enjoy its blessings. He will or ought to run about almost demented for the first year. Heaven prosper the good country! I hope to turn Hampshire hog myself, either here or hereafter, after the Pythagorean system.

The weather is becoming very hot; we are making our house look cool and comfortable, colouring it with French grey, and hanging *pankhās* in preparation for the hot winds. We hope to feel cool by the aid of a thermantidote, for which we are building a terrace and verandah.

The thermantidote is a structure awful to behold; but we shall benefit from its good effect; and, like a steamboat, shall be able to do without wind which, with the *tattis* commonly in use, is the *sine qua non* for *fraîcheur*.

A thermantidote is an enormous machine for forcing cool air into the house; it is made of *amrā* (mango wood), or of *sākoo* (*Shorea robusta*): the wheels and axle are of iron. In height, it is about seven feet, in breadth four or five, and some nine or ten or twelve feet in length.

There is a little machine sold in England, under the name of a fire-blower, which is on the same principle, and is almost a miniature thermantidote. It also resembles in some respects a machine for winnowing corn, but on a larger scale.

The thermantidote, which is hollow and of circular form, has a projecting funnel, which is put through and fixed into a window of the house, from the machine which stands in the verandah.

In the interior, four large fans are affixed to an iron axle, which, passing through the centre of the machine, is turned round by two men on the outside; by which means the fans revolve, and force the air out of the thermantidote through the funnel into the house.

To render the outer air cool, which is thus driven into the house, a circle of about four feet in diameter is cut out in the planks which form the two broad sides of the thermantidote; and beyond these circles *khas-khas tattis* are affixed; so that the vacuum produced by forcing the air out of the machine is supplied by air passing through the *tattis*.

On each side of the thermantidote, on the outside at the top, a long trough is fixed, perforated with small holes in its bottom. Water is constantly poured into these troughs which, dropping through the holes upon the *tattis* placed below them, keeps them constantly wetted. This water is received below in two similar troughs and, passing through a little spout at the side, is collected in tubs, or in large high earthen pans. *Coolies* are constantly employed in handing up this water, in earthen waterpots (*thiliyas*), to other *coolies* on the top of the thermantidote, whose business it is to keep the *tattis* constantly dripping wet. By this means all the air that passes into the body of the machine through the wetted *khas-khas* is rendered cool, and fit to be forced into the house by the action of the fans in their circular course.

The thermantidote stands upon four small wheels, which facilitate the movement of so cumbersome and ponderous a machine.

Khas-khas was put on the thermantidote today; you have no idea how fragrant, delicious and refreshing is the scent of the fresh *khas-khas*, which is the root of a high jungle grass, called *gandar* (*Andropogon muricatum*). These fibrous roots are thinly worked into bamboo frames, which fit exactly into the thermantidote, or into windows. These frames are kept constantly watered, for the purpose of cooling the hot wind which, passing through the wetted roots, is lowered many degrees in temperature, owing to the evaporation that is produced.

Our station is about to be increased by the addition of two Boards; one of Revenue, and one of Criminal and Civil Justice. The station is already sufficiently large for quiet society.

We have received the news of a Chinese revolution; or rather the old squabble, but of a more violent sort, between the Factory and the Hong merchants. Trade is stopped and the papers here are talking of the necessity of fitting out an expedition to chastise the celestials. The mob broke into the factory and, amongst other extravagancies, amused themselves with spitting at the King's picture and then turning it with its face to the wall!

The Arabs [Pathans] bring down a sort of coarse shawl, called *puttuah* or *pattū*. It is extremely light and remarkably soft and warm. I was examining some, intending to purchase it: 'This is not a good piece,' said I. 'The name of God is better than this!' exclaimed the man, with indignation; meaning, nothing is superior to it but the name of God.

Execution of twenty-five Thugs

May 9th.—The inhabitants at Jabalpur were this morning assembled to witness the execution of twenty-five Thugs, who were all hanged at the same time, arrangements having been previously made. It would be impossible to find in any country a set of men who meet death with more indifference than these wretches; and, had it been in a better cause, they would have excited universal sympathy.

As it was, there was something dreadful in the thought that men who had so often imbrued their hands in blood should meet their death with such carelessness. I believe they had previously requested to be allowed to fasten the cord around their necks with their own hands; certain it is that each individual, as soon as he had adjusted the noose, jumped off the beam and launched himself into eternity; and those who first mounted the ladder selected their ropes, rejecting such as did not please them. One of them, who had leaped off the beam and had been hanging for more than three seconds, put his hand up and pulled his cap over his face. This is the second execution of Thugs that has taken place here, but no accident happened this time, nor did a single rope break.

[...]

Too much credit cannot be given to the principal assistants of this district, who have succeeded in capturing so many of them; and Capt. S— has the satisfaction of knowing that by his endeavours these men have been seized.

The extent of murder committed by the Thugs exceeds belief; and some time since a sergeant-major was murdered by a party of them. One of the principal assistants, some time ago, when marching in the district, received information that some bodies which had been strangled were under his tent, and upon digging, he discovered a great many!

One of the men who was executed this morning was a *chaprāsi*, who had been sent towards Nagpur to seize the party, but who joined himself with them and by his presence protected them.

A guard of a company of *sipahis*, under the command of Lieut. G—, was in attendance; but there was not the slightest disturbance, nor did the natives betray the slightest emotion of any kind, except one Nujeeb, who fainted.

May 18th – The thermantidote has been put up in our verandah. The rooms are ten degrees cooler than when we had only *tattis*. For the first time I have been laid up with a strong attack of rheumatism and lumbago. My medical man says, 'The thermantidote pours forth such a volume of cold air that if you have fallen asleep near it, it has caused all these aches and pains. "*Nulla rosa senza spine.*" '

[...]

The Arabian Leprosy (Koostum)

Happily this dreadful disease is not as common as the other forms of leprosy: but once I beheld a dreadful specimen of its virulence; going into the verandah at seven o'clock, where the carpenters were all at work, a close and most disagreeable effluvium annoyed me – the cause could not be discovered.

Just beyond, in the garden, lay a lump under a black blanket. 'What is this?' said Lutchman, the carpenter, 'the smell proceeds from this lump.' He raised the blanket, beneath it was a leper. Lutchman desired the man to quit the grounds. The poor wretch held up his hands and showed his feet; the fingers and toes of which were festering and rotten from the black Arabian leprosy!

I desired he might be carried to the hospital. 'We will not touch him,' said the servants; 'let him go to the leper hospital.' I sent the man a rupee. 'What is the use of a rupee?' said Lutchman, 'he cannot enter the bazaar; how can he change it?' I sent him some copper coins. 'Perhaps someone of low caste will bring him food and take the ānnās,' said the carpenter. The poor wretch raised himself; made salam for the money, and crawled away on his knees and elbows. The next day he was found dead in a field: some of the copper coins had been expended, the remainder and the rupee were on his person.

The man had come up from Calcutta on a boat, had been put ashore under our garden bank and had crawled up; he had not a cowrie. 'There was not even left a sigh in his heart'.'

He was totally destitute: but of this I was ignorant until the next day. The effluvium was so bad, and the danger of infection so fearful, it was necessary to remove him at once from the garden.

There is a pink leprosy very common: I have often seen a man – once I saw two men – bathing amongst a multitude of men and women, their skins were pink, like the pink of salmon; the disease is not catching, I understand, and they are not avoided.

Another leprosy shows itself in white spots on their dark skins. I was practising archery one morning early; suddenly from behind a tree, a woman came to me and throwing herself on the ground, laid hold of my foot with both hands and bent her head upon it saying, 'Mercy, mercy, Bibi Sāhiba! May you bathe in milk, and be fruitful in children!' A gentleman present caught me by the shoulder and pulled me back, at the same time speaking angrily to the woman. 'Do you not see,' said he, 'she is a leper? She is covered with spots, come away, I am very sorry she touched you.' I gave her some ānnās, and told her to go to the hospital – one established by the contributions of the gentlemen at the station and supported by subscription. There is, also, an asylum for the blind, supported in the same manner.

[...]

June 1st – Finding myself ill for want of exercise, I commenced rising early; dressing by candlelight, going out by moonlight and mounting my horse at half-past three! What an unnatural life! The buggy is always sent forward to await my arrival at a certain spot; I never draw my horse's rein until I arrive at the place, the heat is so much greater when you walk your horse. I return in the buggy at six o'clock, go to bed for a couple of hours, bathe, and appear at breakfast.

How often 'Chār vajr, bari fajr,' i.e. four o'clock in the early dawn, sleepy and unwilling to exert myself, have I thought of the proverb: 'Oh, thou who art so fond of sleep, why don't you die at once?'

Today the heat is dreadful; 89° even at the mouth of the thermantidote, and in the other parts of the house six degrees higher! After my early canter, I did not quit my chārpāi until three o'clock, so completely was I exhausted by the heat.

Although by nature not inclined to the melting mood, I felt as if I should dissolve, such streams from my forehead, such thirst and lassitude; I really 'thaw, and resolve myself into a dew'. The call all day is soda-water, soda-water.

To the 21st of June, this oppressive weather held its sway; our only consolation grapes, iced-water, and the thermantidote, which answers admirably, almost too well, as on the 22nd I was laid up with rheumatic fever and lumbago occasioned, they tell me, by standing or sleeping before it after coming in from a canter before sunrise.

June 22nd – Heavy rain fell, the thermantidote was stopped, and the tattis taken down; nor were they replaced as the rain poured down almost night and day from that time until the end of the month.

June 30th – We had a party at home: the thermometer during the day 88°; after dinner it rose to 91° in consequence of the numerous lamps in the rooms and the little multitude of servants in attendance.

A list of servants in a private family

	Wages in rupees per month
A khānsāmān, or head man; a Musalmān servant who purchases the provisions, makes the confectionary, and superintends the table	Rs 12
The ābdār, or water-cooler; cools the water, ices the wines, and attends with them at table	Rs 8
The head khidmatgār; he takes charge of the plate chest, and waits at table	Rs 7
A second khidmatgār, who waits at table	Rs 6
A bāwarchi, or cook	Rs 12
Mate bāwarchi	Rs 4
Mashalchī; dishwasher and torchbearer	Rs 4
Dhobee, or washerman	Rs 8
Istree wālā, washerman for ironing	Rs 8
A darzee, or tailor	Rs 8
A second tailor	Rs 6

An *ayah*, or lady's maid   Rs 10
An under woman
A *doriya*; a sweeper, who also attends to the dogs   Rs 4
Sirdār-bearer, a Hindu servant, the head of the bearers, and the keeper
   of the sāhib's wardrobe; the keys of which are always
    carried in his cummerbund, the folds of cloth around his waist   Rs 8
The mate-bearer; assists as valet, and attends to the lamps   Rs 6
Six bearers to pull the *punkahs*, and dust the furniture, etc.,
   at Rs4 each   Rs 24
A *gwala*, or cowherd   Rs 4
A *bher-i-wālā*, or shepherd   Rs 5
A *murgh-i-wālā*, to take care of the fowls, wild-ducks, quail,
   rabbits, guinea-fowls and pigeons   Rs 4
A *mālee*, or gardener   Rs 5
A mate *mālee*   Rs 3
Another mate, or a *cooly*   Rs 2
A *gram*-grinder, generally a woman who grinds the *chanā*
   for the horses   Rs 2
A coachman   Rs 10
Eight *sā'ises*, or (grooms), at Rs 5 each, for eight horses   Rs 40
Eight grass-cutters, at Rs 3 each, for the above   Rs 24
A *bihishti*, or water-carrier   Rs 5
A mate *bihishti*   Rs 4
A *Barha'i mistree*, a carpenter   Rs 8
Another carpenter   Rs 7
Two *coolies*, to throw water on the *tattis*, at Rs 2 each   Rs 4
Two *chaukidārs*, or watchmen, at Rs 4 each   Rs 8
A *darwān*, or gatekeeper   Rs 4
Two *chaprāsis*, or running footmen, to carry notes, and be in
   attendance in the verandah, at Rs 5 each   Rs 10

               Total for the 57 servants per month Rs 290
                    or about £290 per annum

During the hot winds, a number of extra *coolies*, twelve or fourteen, are necessary if you have more than one thermantidote, or if you keep it going all night as well as during the day; these men, as well as an extra *bihishti*, are discharged when the rains set in.

We, as quiet people, find these servants necessary. Some gentlemen for state add an *assa burdar*, the bearer of a long silver staff; and a *sonta burdar*, or *chob-dar*, who carries a silver club with a grim head on the top of it. The business of these people is to announce the arrival of company.

If many dogs are kept, an extra *doriya* will be required.

The above is a list of our own domestics, and the rate of their wages.

The heat of the climate, added to the customs and prejudices of the natives, oblige you to keep a number of servants; but you do not find them in food as in England. One man will not do the work of another, but says, 'I shall lose caste', which caste, by the by, may be regained by the expenditure of a few rupees in a dinner to their friends and relatives. The Mohammedan servants pretend they shall lose caste; but, in fact, they have none: the term is only applicable to the Hindus.

If your *khānsāmān* and *sirdār*-bearer are good and honest servants, you have little or no trouble with an Indian household; but, unless you are fortunate with your head servants, there is great trouble in keeping between fifty or sixty domestics in order.

CHAPTER XX

Scenes at Allahabad

JULY 6TH 1831 – I study the customs and superstitions of the Hindus so eagerly that my friends laugh and say, 'We expect some day to see you at *pooja* in the river!'

[. . .]

The Peepal Tree (Ficus religiosa)

A peepal tree grows on the banks of the Jumna, just in front of our house; the fine old tree moans in the wind, and the rustling of the leaves sounds like the falling of rain; this is accounted for by the almost constant trembling of its beautiful and sacred leaves, which is occasioned by the great length and delicacy of the foot stalks; whence it is called *Chalada*, or the tree with tremulous leaves. The leaves are of a beautiful bright glossy green, heart-shaped, scalloped, and *daggered*; from their stalks, when gathered, a milky juice pours out; on wounding the bark of the trunk this milk is also poured out, with which the natives prepare a kind of birdlime.

There is a remarkable similarity between the Ancient Britons and the Hindus: on the sixth day of the moon's age, which is called Aranya-Shashti, 'women walk in the forests, with a fan in one hand, and eat certain vegetables, in hope of beautiful children. See the account, given by Pliny, of the Druidical mistletoe, or viscum, which was to be gathered when the moon was six days old as a preservative from sterility' (Moor's *Pantheon*).' The Hindu women eat the fruit of the peepal tree and believe it to have the same wondrous qualities. There is another similarity between the hill tribes and the Ancient Britons, which will be mentioned hereafter. The peepal is sacred to Vishnu, one of the Hindu Triad; they believe a god resides in every leaf, who delights in the music of their rustling and their tremulous motion.

During the festival of the Muharram, the followers of the Prophet suspend lamps in the air, and in their houses, made of the skeleton leaves of the peepal tree, on which they paint figures; some of these lamps are beautifully made; no other leaves will form such fine and delicate transparencies; I have tried the large leaf of the teak tree, but could not succeed as well with it as with that of the *ficus religiosa*. The Chinese paint beautifully on these leaves, first putting a transparent varnish over them. At Schwalbach, in Germany, I purchased skeleton leaves of the plane, in the centre of which the figure of Frederick the Great was preserved in the green of the leaf, whilst all around the skeleton fibres were perfect; how this is accomplished, I know not. The skeleton leaves are very beautiful, and easily prepared.

The peepal is universally sacred; the Hindu women, and the men also, are often seen in the early morning putting flowers in *pooja* at the foot of the tree and pouring water on its roots. They place their idols of stone beneath this tree and the *bér* (banyan), and worship them constantly; nor will they cut a branch, unless to benefit the tree.

The native *panchāyats* (courts of justice) are often held beneath it. The accused first invokes the god in his sylvan throne above him, to destroy him and his (as he himself could crush a leaf in his hand), if he speak anything but the truth; then gathering and crushing a leaf, he makes his deposition.

The Hindus suspend lamps in the air on bamboos in the month Kartika, in honour of their gods; these lamps are generally formed of *ubruk* (talc). Sometimes they are formed of clay, pierced through with fretwork in remarkably pretty patterns. This offering to all the gods in this month procures many benefits, in their belief, to the giver; and the offering of lamps to particular gods, or to Ganga-ji, is also esteemed an act of merit.

Speaking of *ubruk* reminds me of the many uses to which it is applied. The costumes of native servants, *nāch* women and their attendants, the procession of the Muharram, the trades, etc., are painted upon it by native artists, and sold in sets; the best are executed at Benares. By the aid of *ubruk*, drawings can be very correctly copied; they are speedily done, and look well. We also used *ubruk* in lieu of glass for the windows of the *hammām*.

It was a source of great pleasure to me at Allahabad to ride out long distances in the early morning, hunting for rare plants and flowers; on my return I took off the impressions in a book of Chinese paper, and added to it the history of the tree or plant, its medicinal virtues, its sacred qualities and all the legends attached to it, that I could collect.

From the Calcutta John Bull, *July 26th, 1831*

'The Governor-General has sold the beautiful piece of architecture, called the Mootee Masjid, at Agra, for Rs 125,000 (about £12,500), and it is now being pulled down! The Tāj has also been offered for sale! but the price required has not been obtained. Two lacs, however, have been offered for it. Should the Tāj be pulled down, it is rumoured that disturbances may take place amongst the natives.'

If this be true, is it not shameful? The present king might as well sell the chapel of Henry VII in Westminster Abbey for the paltry sum of £12,500: for any sum the impropriety of the act would be the same. By what authority does the Governor-General offer the Tāj for sale? Has he any right to molest the dead? To sell the tomb raised over an empress, which from its extraordinary beauty is the wonder of the world? It is impossible the Court of Directors can sanction the sale of the tomb for the sake of its marble and gems. They say that a Hindu wishes to buy the Tāj to carry away the marble and erect a temple to his own idols at Bindrabund!

The crows are a pest; they will pounce upon meat carried on a plate, and bear it off: they infest the door of the cook room (*bawarchī khānā*) and annoy the servants, who retaliate on a poor *kawwā*, if they can catch one, by dressing it up in an officer's uniform, and letting it go to frighten the others. The poor bird looks so absurd hopping about. Sometimes they drill a hole through the beak and passing a wire through it, string thereon five cowries; this bears the poor crow's head to the ground, and must torture it. Such cruelty I have forbidden. The crow is a bird of ill omen.

[...]

My *ayah* is ill with cholera: there is no hope of her recovery. The disease came across the Jumna, about four miles higher up than our house, and is regularly marching across the country to the Ganges: as it proceeds no fresh cases occur in the villages it leaves behind.

The old peepal moans and rustles in the wind so much that, deceived by the sound, we have often gone into the verandah joyously exclaiming 'There is the rain!' To our sorrow it was only the leaves of the tree agitated by the wind.

In such a climate and during the hot winds, you cannot imagine how delightful the noise of the wind (like rain) in the old peepal appeared to us, or the lullaby it formed. It is a holy tree, every leaf being the seat of a god. They do not listen to the music of its rustling with greater pleasure than I experience; indeed, my *penchant* for the tree is so great, I am half inclined to believe in its miraculous powers.

August 31st – The ice has lasted four months and fifteen days, which we consider particularly fortunate. It was opened the 15th of April.

October – We are collecting grass and making hay for use during the hot winds. The people cut the grass in the jungles, and bring it home on camels. We have one stack of hay just finished, and one of straw.

'Bring me the silver tankard.' 'I have it not, I know not where it is,' said the *khidmatgār*. The plate-chest was searched. It was gone.

It was the parting gift of a friend; we would not have lost it for fifty times its value. The servants held a *panchāyat* and examined the man who had charge of the plate. When it was over, he came to me, saying, 'I had charge of the tankard – it is gone – the keys were in my hands; allow me to remain in your service; cut four rupees a month from my pay and let another silver cup be made.' The old man lived with us many years, and only quitted us when he thought his age entitled him to retire on the money he had earned honestly and fairly in service.

My tame squirrel has acquired a vile habit of getting up the windows and eating all the flies; if he would kill the mosquitoes, it would be a very good employment, but he prefers the great fat flies – a little brute. The little squirrel is the only animal unaffected by the heat; he is as impudent as ever, and as cunning as possible.

October 24th – A slight earthquake has just taken place – this instant. I did not know what was the matter; there was a rumbling noise for some time, as if a carriage were driving over the roof of the house. My chair shook under me, and the table on which I am writing shook also. I became very sick and giddy, so much so that I fancied I had fallen ill suddenly. When the noise and trembling ceased, I found I was quite well and the giddy sickness went off. I never felt the earth quake before. Every one in the house was sensible of it. At the Circuit bungalow, nearly three miles off, it was felt as much as on the banks of the Jumna.

In a native family, if a person be ill, one of the relations takes a small earthen pan, filled with water, flowers, and rice, and places it in the middle of the road or street, in front of the house of the sick person, believing that if any one *en passant* should touch the offering, either by chance or design, the illness would quit the sufferer and cleave to the person who had touched the flowers or the little pan containing the offering. A native carefully steps aside and avoids coming in contact with the flowers.

Today, a man was punished for perjury in this manner; he was mounted on a donkey, with his face to the tail of the animal; one half of his face was painted black, the other white, and around his neck was hung a necklace of old shoes and old bones. Surrounded by a mob of natives, with hideous music and shouts, he was paraded by the police all through the town! An excellent punishment.

[. . .]

November 7th – We took the hounds to Papamhow and soon found a jackal in the grounds: he took shelter in a field of *jwār* or millet (*Andropogon sorghum*), from which he could not again be started. Hounds in this country are extremely expensive; it is scarcely possible to keep them alive. Out of eight couple brought from England and added to the pack at Allahabad a few months ago, only three couple are alive. We rode over the grounds: how deserted they looked! The flowers dead, the fountain dry.

> 'Twas sweet of yore to see it play
> And chase the sultriness of day;
> As springing high, the silver dew
> In whirls fantastically flew,
> And spread luxurious coolness round
> The air, and verdure on the ground.

'Demons take possession of an empty house. The place is a wilderness. The old Brahman, who lives at a picturesque temple in the grounds by the side of the Ganges, did not remember me; he spoke in the warmest terms of the agent for gunpowder to the Government, who formerly lived here; and said he prayed to Mahadēo to send him back to Papamhow, as the natives had never had so good a master, either before or since.

A fair is annually held in these grounds, at which period the old Brahman reaps a plentiful harvest of *paisa*. The people who attend the fair make *pooja* at his little temple. The old man had an idiot son who, having a great dislike to clothes, constantly tore all his attire to pieces. The poor boy was speechless, but not dumb, for he could utter the most horrible sounds: and when enraged at his father's attempting to clothe him, he would howl, make angry gestures, and tear off the obnoxious attire. During the time of the fair the groups of natives, of horses, and odd-looking conveyances are very picturesque beneath the spreading branches of the great Adansonia trees.

Our friend was not only agent for gunpowder but also, by the order of Government, he had established a manufactory for rockets at Papamhow, in consequence of the congreve rockets sent from England having proved unserviceable. He was obliged to make many experiments to suit the composition to our burning climate, and to test the result of exposure to the sun. When the trials were to be made and the rockets proved, I often went down upon the white sands in the bed of the river to see the experiments.

The Ganges is from forty to forty-five feet deeper during the rains than during the dry season; and banks of the finest white sand, of immense extent, are left dry for many months in the bed of the river when the rains have passed away. The sands extended three or four miles and being without cultivation or inhabitants were exactly suited to the purpose. When the rockets were laid upon the sands and fired, it was beautiful to see them rushing along, leaving a train of fire and smoke behind them; the roar of the large rockets was very fine – quite magnificent.

When the rockets were fired from an iron tube at an elevation, it was surprising to see them ranging through the air for a mile and a half or two miles before they came to the sands, where, a certain distance being marked by range pegs at every fifty yards, the extent of their ranges was accurately ascertained: one of the large rockets ranged 3,700 yards, upwards of two miles. I should think they would prove most formidable weapons in warfare.

November 14th – Some natives have just brought a lynx to the door – such a savage beast! It was caught in the grounds of the Circuit bungalow; the first animal of the sort I have beheld. At Papamhow we found a wolf and had a long chase, until the hounds lost him in an immense plantation of sugar-cane, from which there were too few dogs to dislodge him.

November 15th – This is delightful weather; we ride from six to eight o'clock, and take a drive at four in the evening, returning to dinner at six, at which time a coal fire is agreeable. I am in stronger health than I ever before enjoyed in India, which I attribute to the cold weather and great exercise.

CHAPTER XXI

LIFE IN THE ZENĀNA

FEBRUARY 2ND 1832 – I went to the Bura Mela, the great annual fair on the sands of the Ganges, and purchased bows and arrows, some curious Indian ornaments, and a few fine pearls. On the sands were a number of devotees, of whom the most holy person had made a vow that for fourteen years he would spend every night up to his neck in the Ganges; nine years he has kept his vow: at sunset he enters the river, is taken out at sunrise, rubbed into warmth, and placed by a fire; he was sitting, when I saw him, by a great log of burning wood, is apparently about thirty years of age, very fat and jovial, and does not appear to suffer in the slightest degree from his penance. Another religious mendicant lies all day on his back on the ground, his face encrusted with the mud of the Ganges. The Hindus throw flowers over them and feed them, paying the holy men divine honours.

The fair this year is thinly attended, the people not amounting to a *lakh*, in consequence of the very heavy rain which fell throughout December last and prevented many of those from attending who had to come from a very great distance.

February 25th – I went with my husband into tents near Alamchand, for the sake of shooting; and used to accompany him on an elephant, or on my little black horse, to mark the game. Quail were in abundance, and particularly fine; common grey partridge, plentiful; a few black partridges, most beautiful birds; and some hares. Instead of dogs, we took twenty men with us armed with long bamboos, to beat up the game; as for dogs in such high plantations, they are useless and invisible.

March 14th – During the cold weather we collect wild ducks and keep them for the hot winds. We have just finished a new brick house for the birds, consisting of a sleeping apartment with a tank in front, in which they have a fine supply of running water; the whole surrounded by lattice work, covered with an immense climber, the *gāo pāt*, or elephant creeper (*Convolvulus speciosus* Linn.), of which the large velvet-like leaves shade the birds from prying eyes. Unfortunately, by some mischance or other, a jackal got into the place at night and killed fifty out of one hundred: very unlucky, as the season for collecting them is nearly over, and we require wild ducks and teal during the hot winds when beef and mutton are disagreeable even to see on table; fowls, turkeys, rabbits, wild fowl, game and fish are the only things to tempt one's appetite in the grilling season, when curries and anchovies are in requisition.

Speaking of wild ducks; we used to send out men into the jungle to catch them, which was performed in a singular manner. The man, when he got near water on which the wild fowl were floating, would wade into the stream up to his neck with a kedgeree pot upon his head; beneath this mask of pottery the birds would allow him to approach them without taking alarm, they being used to the sight of these earthen pots (*thiliyas*) which are constantly to be seen floating down the stream, thrown away by the natives. When close to a bird, the man puts up his hand, catches its legs, pulls it instantly under water, and fastens it to his girdle. Having caught a few, he quits the river and secures them in a basket. The wild ducks are in beautiful condition and very fine when first brought in. They pine and waste away in confinement for the first fortnight; then resigning themselves with all due philosophy to their fate, they devour barley with great glee and swim about in the tank, eating principally at night. They must be surrounded by mats to keep them quiet and composed: in a short time they again become fat and are most excellent. As soon as the rains commence, the wild ducks lose all their flavour; it is then better to open the door and let the survivors escape. They are good for nothing if kept for the next season. The teal are as good, if not superior, to the wild ducks.

[...]

We hunt jackals in the grounds at Papamhow, and sometimes have a canter after a wolf in the ravines. The gentlemen have a pack of hounds: ten English imported dogs were added to the pack last year. It is disheartening to see those fine dogs die daily. The price now asked in Calcutta for English hounds is considered too high, even by us Indians, being fifty guineas a couple! Of the ten bought last year, two only are alive. Perhaps accidents have occurred; from ignorance at the time that castor-oil, when not cold-drawn, is certain death to dogs. The natives have a great objection to using castor-oil medicinally when the seeds have been heated before putting them into the mill.

March 19th – The arrival of Colonel Gardner pleased us greatly: his boats were anchored in the Jumna, under our bank. He came down from Lucknow to visit the quarries, in order to build a bridge for the King of Oude; and after having spent nine days with us, he departed for Benares. He is a great favourite at present, both with the king and the minister at Lucknow; and if he is allowed to retain the *jagir* he now holds upon the same terms for a few years, he will be a rich man. He deserves it all; we found him the same kind, mild, gentlemanly, polished, entertaining companion I have before described him. He was looking ill; but now that his fatigues are over and he is once more at rest, he will soon recover. I requested him to inform me how native ladies amuse themselves within a *zenāna*, and he gave me the following account:

'They have ponies to ride upon within the four walls of the *zenāna* grounds. Archery is a favourite amusement; my son, James Gardner, who is a very fine marksman, was taught by a woman.

'A silver swing is the great object of ambition; and it is *the fashion* to swing in the rains, when it is thought charming to come in dripping wet. The swings are hung between two high posts in the garden.

'Fashion is as much regarded by the Musulmān ladies as by the English; they will not do this or that, because it is not the fashion.

'It is general amongst the higher and the middle classes of females in Hindustān to be able to read the Qur'an in Arabic (it is not allowed to be translated), and the Commentary in Persian.

'The ladies are very fond of eating fresh whole roasted coffee. When a number of women are sitting on the ground, all eating the dry roasted coffee, the noise puts me in mind of a flock of sheep at the gram trough.

'The most correct hour for dinner is eleven or twelve at night: they smoke their *huqqas* all through the night, and sleep during the day.

'Nothing can exceed the quarrels that go on in the *zenāna*, or the complaints the *begums* make against each other. A common complaint is, "Such an one has been practising witchcraft against me". If the husband make a present to one wife, even if it be only a basket of mangoes, he must make the same exactly to all the other wives to keep the peace. A wife, when in a rage with her husband, if on account of jealousy often says, "I wish I were married to a grass-cutter", i.e. because a grass-cutter is so poor he can only afford to have one wife.

'My having been married some thirty or forty years and never having taken another wife, surprises the Musulmān very much, and the ladies all look upon me as a pattern: they do not admire a system of having three or four rivals, however well pleased the gentlemen may be with the custom.'

Colonel Gardner admired the game of 'La Grace'. I requested him to take a set of sticks and hoops for the ladies of his *zenāna*: he told me afterwards they never took any pleasure in the game, because it was not the *dasturi*, the custom.

The account of the style in which affairs are conducted amused us exceedingly.

[...]

Colonel Gardner tells me that the two boys, Khema Jāh and Feredooa Buckht, whom I saw at Lucknow, and whom the King declared to be his heirs,

The Gram Grinder

are now out of favour and are not allowed to enter the palace; I am glad that low-caste boy has no chance of being raised to the throne. The King has taken another wife; his taste is certainly curious, she is an ugly low caste woman. The old Nawāb Hakīm Menhdi has the whole power in his hands; the King amuses himself sitting up all night and sleeping all day, leaving the cares of state to the Hakīm. The revenue, under his superintendence, has increased very considerably; the Hakīm's passion is saving money, and he appears to take as much pleasure in saving it for the King as for himself.

Colonel Gardner gave us some instructions in archery, for which we have a great *penchant*; nor could I resist going continually into the verandah to take a shot at the targets, in spite of the heat – 84°, or the annoyance of an ague and fever from which I was suffering. Archery, as practised in India, is very different from that in England; the arm is raised over the head, and the bow drawn in that manner: native bowmen throw up the elbow, and depress the right hand in a most extraordinary style, instead of drawing to the ear, as practised by the English. A very fine bow was given me, which was one of the presents made by Runjeet Singh to Lord William Bentinck; it is formed of strips of buffalo horn, and adorned with bareilly work; when strung, it resembles the outline of a well-formed upper lip, Cupid's bow.

During the rains, the natives unstring their bows and, bending them backwards until they curl round almost into a circle, fix them between two slips of bamboo until the rains are over, when they re-string them: the string of this bow is of thick silk. To bring back the bow to its proper form is a difficult affair; they warm it over a charcoal fire, and bend it back by fixing two iron chains upon it; after this it is usually strung by taking one end of the bow in the left hand, passing it behind the left leg, and over the shin bone of the right, then bending it by forcing, the upper end round towards the opposite side, when the string, which has been previously secured on the lower horn, is slipped into its place by the right hand.

The quiver, which is of crimson velvet embroidered with gold, is very handsome. The arrows are steel-headed and bound with brass rings to render the pile more secure; the shafts are made of beautifully smooth, straight, hard reeds; the heads are either plain, or of a fish-hook shape; and the whole are highly ornamented with bareilly work.

The natives do not draw the bow with two or three fingers, as practised in Europe; they make use of a thumb-ring, of which I have seen two kinds.

Whistling arrows are reeds on which, in lieu of a pile of steel, a hollow bit of wood is affixed, in form not unlike a small egg; when shot perpendicularly into the air they produce a shrill whistling sound. Sometimes a slip of paper is rolled up and put into the hole in the head, when the arrow is shot into a *zenāna* garden, over the high wall, or into a fortress.

[...]

Sorcery is practised with a charmed bow. At a *sati*, bamboo levers are often brought down over the whole pile, to hold down the woman, and the corpse of her husband; and several persons are employed to keep down the levers, whilst others throw water upon them that the wood may not be scorched.

A person sometimes takes one of these bamboo levers after the bodies are burnt; and, making a bow and arrow with it, repeats incantations over it. He then makes an image of some enemy with clay, and lets fly the arrow at it. The person whose image is thus pierced is said to be immediately seized with a pain in his breast.

April 1st – What would the people at home think of being up at five o'clock, and in church by six o'clock! This is the usual hour for divine service at this time of the year. To us Indians accustomed to early rising, it is no fatigue.

April 7th – This morning I cantered down to see our fields of oats by the side of the Ganges, which they have just begun to cut; such a fine crop! When they are stacked, we shall have three or four large ricks.

CHAPTER XXII

ADVENTURES IN THE EAST

MAY 1832 – Allahabad is now one of the gayest and is, as it always has been, one of the prettiest stations in India. We have dinner-parties more than enough; balls occasionally; a book society; some five or six billiard-tables; a pack of dogs, some amongst them hounds, and (how could I have forgotten!) fourteen spinsters!

May 2nd – Colonel Gardner has sent us twelve jars of the most delicious Lucknow chutnee, the very *beau ideal* of mixtures of sharp, bitter, sour, sweet, hot and cold!

This station, which in former days was thought one of the least to-be-coveted positions, has now become what from the first we always pronounced it to be, one of the most desirable. We have a kind neighbourly society, as much or even more of gaiety than we sober folks require, and, *mirabile*, no squabbling. I hope his lordship will not disturb our coterie by moving the Boards of Revenue and of Criminal and Civil Justice higher up the country, which some think not improbable.

[...]

June 19th – We drove into the Fort to call on a fair friend at five o'clock. No sooner had I entered the house, than we saw clouds of locusts in the air: immediately afterwards a heavy storm of rain fell, and the locusts were beaten down by it in great numbers to the ground. The native servants immediately ran out and caught them by handfuls, delighted to get them to make a curry; for which purpose they may, perhaps, be as delicate as prawns, which are most excellent. I took some to preserve with arsenical soap: they look like very large grasshoppers. I never saw a flight of locusts before; on our return home the air was full of them.

The food of St John in the wilderness was locusts and wild honey: very luxurious fare, according to the natives, who say either in a curry or fried in clarified butter, they are excellent. I believe they divest them of their wings, and dress them after the fashion of woodcocks.

Some assert that St John did not live upon locusts, but upon the bean of a tree called by the Arabs Kharroùb, the locust tree of Scripture (the carob tree,

St John's Bread, *Ceratonia siliqua*) – a point too difficult to be decided by a poor *hāji* (pilgrim) in search of the picturesque.

May 20th – At five o'clock I rode out with a friend and met the hounds under the Mahratta Bund; no other persons were present, and we had not gone twenty yards before two jackals crossed the road just before the dogs: away they went in the prettiest style imaginable. Mr B— galloped off across a ploughed field: the horse had scarcely gone ten yards when his legs sunk into a deep soft hole; the creature could not recover himself; over he went, falling on his back, with his rider under him; and there the horse lay, kicking with all four legs in the air for a short time, ere the gentleman had the power to extricate himself from under the animal. I was not five yards behind and, jumping off my horse, went to his assistance. The blood was pouring from his mouth and nose, and his right shoulder was dislocated. Two natives came up. Leaving the fainting man in their care, I galloped off for a surgeon. During my absence, a medical man fortunately arrived at the spot: he found the gentleman senseless. Having set his shoulder and bled him, he put him into a palanquin and sent him home. My search for a surgeon was unsuccessful for a length of time: at last I rode into the court of the Hospital at Kydganj, in search of Dr S—, when the first object I beheld was the corpse of a man being carried out, marked with blood on the head; it made me shudder: the medical man was just on the point of opening the head of a European who had died suddenly. This was rather a nervous adventure and a frightful sight. My friend was so much stunned by the blow and the dislocation of his arm, he could make but feeble efforts to extricate himself from his horse. I thought at first he was killed by the way in which the two streams of blood poured from the corners of his mouth when I raised his head. It was unfortunate being alone at such a moment.

The rats during the harvest-time collect grain in holes; and the poor people dig wherever they think they may chance to find a rat's store, for the sake of the grain: sometimes on one spot they find 20lb. weight secreted by these provident animals, generally in the midst of the fields. The natives steal the grain, and leave the holes open, which are very dangerous for horses. The place into which Mr B—'s horse fell was an opening of the sort, filled by the rain of the day before with light mould, therefore he could not see he was upon treacherous ground. I escaped from being five yards in the rear of his horse; had he passed over I should, in all probability, have gone in; the ground appeared perfectly good, instead of being like a quicksand.

The other night, for the first time up the country, I saw a glow-worm; it was very thin, about half an inch in length, and more like a maggot in a cheese than anything else.

August 14th – Last week we were at a ball given by the officers of the 6th Native Infantry to the station; in spite of the heat, the people appeared to enjoy dancing very much, and kept it up until very late. A ballroom in India, with all the windows open and the *pankhās* in full play, is not half so oppressive as a ballroom in London: the heat of pure air is much better than the heat of a number of persons, all crowded together and breathing the same atmosphere over and over again. Balls up the country take place principally during the hot winds and rains; they make a variety at a quiet station. During the cold months the people are dispersed on duty in divers parts of the district.

I amuse myself turning profiles in *rous* wood on my lathe; the likenesses of Bonaparte and the Duke of Wellington are good, because it is less difficult to turn a strong profile. I look at the drawing whilst turning the wood; when finished it is cut open, and the profile, if properly done, is exact.

Snakes are in abundance: I caught a small venomous whip-snake in my dressing-room today and put it into the bottle of horrors. A lady stepped upon the head of one a short time ago; the reptile curled round her leg; when she raised her foot in a fright, it glided off, and was found half killed in the next room.

[...]

Our great Bengal Lion Rajah Rammohun Roy appears to have created no small sensation on the other side of the water. He is one of the few well-educated natives we possess and is, decidedly, a very remarkable person. He holds his title of Rajah from the King of Delhi, the great Mogul, whose ambassador he is to the British Court in a suit versus John Company.

[...]

October 25th – The sale of the property of a friend took place today. Many valuable works in octavo sold for twopence a volume! The furniture went at about one fourth of its value. We took the opportunity of getting rid of extra sofas and chairs; much furniture is a great inconvenience in this climate; it harbours mosquitoes.

Through the stupidity of our servants, some animal got into the quail-house last night and killed seventy-nine fat quail; very provoking – but as this is the season for them it is not of much consequence, we can replace them; had it been during the hot winds, when no quail are to be procured, it would have been a great loss in the eating department.

All my finery coming from England has been totally lost, about twenty days' journey from this place, by the swamping of the boat; all my presents gone 'at one fell swoop', leaving me *sans pompons, sans souliers, sans everything;* my pen is bad, my knife blunt and my new penknife is feeding the fish at the bottom of the Ganges, off Monghir.

[...]

I have received a present that pleases me greatly, a *sitar*, a musical instrument in general use all over India; it was made at Lucknow from a hollow gourd and is very beautifully put together. It has four strings; the first is of steel wire, the two next are of brass wire, and the fourth and smallest of steel. It is played with the first finger of the right hand alone, on which is placed a little steel wire frame, called a *misrāb*, with which the strings are struck; the left hand stops the notes on the frets, but you only stop the notes on the first string; the other three strings produce a sort of pedal sound as the *misrāb* passes over them, from the manner in which they are tuned. The instrument is most elegantly formed.

The *ektāra*, a one-stringed instrument as the name implies, is used by wandering minstrels. A man of this description, the veritable Paganini of the East, appeared before me the other day; he was an Hindu mendicant, carrying an *ektāra* which was formed of a gourd; and on its one string he played in a strange and peculiar style. From the upper end of the *ektāra* two peacock's feathers were displayed. The man's attire was a rope around his waist and a bit of cloth; a black blanket hung over his shoulder; on his forehead, breast, and arms were the sectarial marks, and the brahmanical thread was over his shoulder; three necklaces and one bracelet completed the costume. His hair fell to his shoulders and, like all natives he wore a moustache. My friends laugh at me when I play on the *sitār*, and ask, 'Why do you not put a peacock's feather at the end of it?'

December 1st – We have become great farmers, having sown our crop of oats and are building outhouses to receive some thirty-four dwarf cows and oxen (*gynees*), which are to be fed up for the table and produced after some eight months' stuffing. The *gynee* club consists of eight members, and it gives us better food than we could procure from the bazaar: 'Whose dog am I that I should eat from the bazaar?'

A little distance from the stacks the unmuzzled bullocks are treading out the corn: 'Thou shalt not muzzle the ox that treadeth out the corn'. This patriarchal method breaks and renders the straw soft and friable; the corn is winnowed by taking it up in a basket and pouring it out; the grain falls to the ground, while the west wind blows the chaff into a heap beyond. The corn is deposited in a large pit, which has been duly prepared by having had the walls well dried and hardened from a fire burning in it for many days. These pits are carefully concealed by the natives and their armies have people, called *soonghees* or smellers, whose business it is to find out these underground and secret granaries.

Our friend Colonel Gardner is still at Lucknow which, in all probability, will speedily be taken into the hands of the British government for *its better protection*! The King has lately dismissed a man of great talent who was his prime minister and put in a fool by way of a change. The consequence is already felt in the accounts of the royal treasury. It is said it is impossible to collect the revenue without force, and that where that has been used, his Majesty's forces have been beaten.

A friend writes from England, 'I shall always regret having quitted India without having seen Colonel Gardner and the Tāj.'

He is a very remarkable man; his age nearly seventy, I believe. I had a long letter from him two days since, full of all the playfulness of youth and of all kindness. I never met so entertaining or so instructive a companion; his life, if he would publish it, would be indeed a legacy and shame our modern biography.

December 20th – For the first time this year it has been cold enough to collect ice; during my early ride this morning I saw the *coolies* gathering it into the pits.

CHAPTER XXIII

THE GREAT FAIR AT ALLAHABAD

TALKING TO A MAN WHO IS IN ECSTASY (OR A RELIGIOUS NATURE PRACTISED
OR FEIGNED BY *FAKIRS*) IS LIKE BEATING CURDS WITH A PESTLE

JANUARY 1833 – The *burā melā* at Prāg, or the great fair at Allahabad, is held annually on the sands of the Ganges below the ramparts of the Fort, extending from the Mahratta Bund to the extreme point of the sacred junction of the rivers. The booths extend the whole distance, composed of mud walls, covered with mats or thatched. This fair lasts about two months, and attracts merchants from all parts of India, Calcutta, Delhi, Lucknow, Jaipur, etc. Very good diamonds, pearls, coral, shawls, cloth, woollens, China, furs, etc. are to be purchased. Numerous booths display brass and copper vessels, glittering in the sun with many brazen idols: others are filled with Benares' toys for children. Bows and arrows are displayed, also native caps made of sable, the crowns of which are of the richest gold and silver embroidery.

The pearl merchants offer long strings of large pearls for sale, amongst which some few are fine, round and of a good colour. The natives value size, but are not very particular as to colour, they do not care to have them perfectly round and do not object to an uneven surface. They will allow a purchaser to select the best at pleasure from long strings.

The deep red coral is valued by the natives much more than the pink. I bought some very fine pink coral at the fair: the beads were immense; the price of the largest, Rs 11 per *tola*; i.e. Rs 11 for a rupee's weight of coral. The smallest, Rs 6–4 per *tola*; it was remarkably fine. Some years afterwards the Brija Bāī, a Mahratta lady, a friend of mine, called on me; she observed the long string of fine pink coral around my neck and said, 'I am astonished a memsāhib should wear coral; we only decorate our horses with it: that is pink coral, the colour is not good; look at my horse.' I went to the verandah; her horse was adorned with a necklace of fine deep red coral. She was quite right and I made over mine to my grey steed.

Some of the prettiest things sold at the *melā* are the *tīkas*, an ornament for the forehead for native women. The *tika* is of different sizes and patterns; in gold or silver for the wealthy, tinsel for the poorer classes; and of various shapes. The prettiest are of silver, a little hollow cup like a dewdrop cut in halves: the ornament is stuck with an adhesive mixture on the forehead, just in the centre between the eyebrows. Some *tīkas* are larger, resembling the *ferronière* worn by Europeans ladies.

The Allahabad *hakāks* are famous for their imitation in glass of precious stones. I purchased a number of native ornaments in imitation of the jewellery worn by native ladies, which were remarkably well made and cost only a few rupees. I also bought strings of mock pearls brought from China that are scarcely to be distinguished from real pearls, either in colour or weight.

The toys the rich natives give their children, consisting in imitations of all sorts of animals, are remarkably pretty; they are made in silver and enamelled: others are made of ivory very beautifully carved; and for the poorer classes they are of pewter, moulded into the most marvellous shapes.

At this time of the year *lakhs* and *lakhs* of natives come to bathe at the junction of the Ganges and Jumna; they unite at the extremity of a neck of land, or rather sand, that runs out just below the Fort. On this holy spot the Brahmans and religious mendicants assemble in thousands. Each *fakir* pitches a bamboo from the end of which his flag is displayed, to which those of the same persuasion resort. Here they make *pooja*, shave, give money to the *fakir* and bathe at the junction. The clothes of the bathers are put upon *chārpāis* to be taken care of; for so many *paisa*. Every native, however poor he may be, pays tribute of R. 1 to Government before he is allowed to bathe.

Two boats, by order of Government, are in attendance at this point to prevent persons from drowning themselves or their children. The mere act of bathing in the waters of the Ganges, on a particular day, removes ten sins, however enormous, committed in ten previous births. How much greater must be the efficacy at the junction of the Ganges and Jumna which the Saraswāti, the third sacred river, is supposed to join underground! The benefits arising from bathing at the lucky moment of the conjunction of the moon with a particular star is very great, or at the time of an eclipse of the sun or moon.

The holy waters are convenient for washing away a man's sins, and as efficacious as a pope's bull for this purpose. Groups of natives stand in the river whilst their Brahman reads to them, awaiting the happy moment at which to dip into the sacred and triple waves. They fast until the bathing is over. Suicide committed at the junction is meritorious in persons of a certain caste, but a *sin* for a Brahman!

The holy men prefer the loaves and fishes of this world to the immediate *moksh* or beatitude, without further risk of transmigration, which is awarded to those who die at the sacred junction.

Bathing will remove sins, gain admittance into heaven and the devotee will be reborn on earth in an honourable station.

A married woman without children often vows to Ganges to cast her first-born into the river: this in former times was often done at Prāg, it now rarely occurs. If the infant's life is preserved, the mother cannot take it again.

Religious Mendicants

The most remarkable people at this *melā* are the religious mendicants; they assemble by hundreds and live within enclosures fenced off by sticks, a little distance from the booths. These people are the monks of the East; there are two orders of them; the Gosāins, or followers of Shiva, and the Byragies, disciples of Vishnu. Any Mohammedan may become a *fakir*, and a Hindu of any caste a religious mendicant. The ashes of cow-dung are considered purifying: these people are often rubbed over from head to foot with an ashen mixture and have a strange dirty white, or rather blue appearance. Ganges mud, cow-dung, and ashes of cow-dung form, I believe, the delectable mixture.

The sectarial marks or symbols are painted on their faces according to their caste, with a red, yellow, white or brown pigment, also on their breasts and arms. Their only covering is a bit of rag passed between the legs and tied round the waist by a cord or rope.

One man whom I saw this day at the *melā* was remarkably picturesque, and attracted my admiration. He was a religious mendicant, a disciple of Shiva. In stature he was short and dreadfully lean, almost a skeleton. His long black hair, matted with cow-dung, was twisted like a turban round his head – a filthy *juta* (braided locks)! On his forehead three horizontal lines were drawn with ashes and a circlet beneath them marked in red sanders – his sectarial mark. If possible, they obtain the ashes from the hearth on which a consecrated fire has been lighted. His left arm he had held erect so long that the skin and flesh had withered, and clung round the bones most frightfully; the nails of the hand, which had been kept immoveably clenched, had pierced through the palm and grew out at the back of the hand like the long claws of a bird of prey. His horrible and skeleton-like arm was encircled by a twisted stick, the stem, perhaps, of a thick creeper, the end of which was cut into the shape of the head of the *cobra de capello*, with its hood displayed, and the twisted withy looked like the body of the reptile wreathed around his horrible arm. His only garment, the skin of a tiger thrown over his shoulders, and a bit of rag and rope at his waist. He was of a dirty-white or dirty-ashen colour from mud and paint; perhaps in imitation of Shiva who, when he appeared on earth as a naked mendicant of an ashy colour, was recognised as Mahadēo the great god. This man was considered a very holy person. His right hand contained an empty gourd and a small rosary, and two long rosaries were around his neck of the rough beads called *mundrāsee*. His flag hung from the top of a bamboo, stuck in the ground by the side of a trident, the symbol of his caste, to which hung a sort of drum used by the mendicants. A very small and most beautifully formed little *gynee* (a dwarf cow) was with the man. She was decorated with crimson cloth embroidered with cowrie shells, and a plume of peacock's feathers as a *jika* rose from the top of her head. A brass bell was on her neck, and around her legs were anklets of the same metal. Numbers of *fakirs* come to the sacred junction, each leading one of these little dwarf cows decorated with shells, cowries, coloured worsted tassels, peacock's feathers and bells. Some are very small, about the size of a large European sheep, very fat and sleek, and are considered so sacred that they will not sell them.

Acts of severity towards the body, practised by religious mendicants, are not done as penances for sin but as works of extraordinary merit, promising large rewards in a future state. The Byragee is not a penitent, but a proud ascetic. These people bear the character of being thieves and rascals.

Although the Hindus keep their women *parda-nishin*, that is, veiled and secluded behind the curtain, the *fakirs* have the privilege of entering any house they please and even of going into the *zenāna*; and so great is their influence over the natives that if a religious mendicant enter a habitation leaving his slippers at the door, the husband may not enter his own house. They have the character of being great libertines.

[...]

January 11th – Some natives are at the door with the most beautiful snakes, two of them very large and striped like tigers; the men carry them twisted round their bodies and also round their necks, as a young lady wears a boa; the effect is good. The two tiger-striped ones were greatly admired as a well-matched pair; they are not venomous. A fine cobra, with his great hood spread out, made me shrink away as he came towards me, darting out his forked tongue.

There were also two snakes of a dun yellow colour, spotted with white, which appeared in a half torpid state; the men said they were as dangerous as the cobra. They had a biscobra; the poor reptile was quite lame, the people having broken all its four legs, to prevent its running away. They had a large black scorpion, but not so fine a fellow as that in my bottle of horrors.

The *melā* is very full; such beautiful dresses of real sable as I have seen today brought down by the Moguls for sale! Lined with shawl, they would make magnificent dressing-gowns. I have bought a Persian writing-case and a book beautifully illuminated and written in Persian and Arabic: the Moguls beguile me of my rupees.

We are going to a ball tonight at Mr F—'s, given in honour of Lady William Bentinck, who is expected to arrive this evening. The natives have reported the failure of Messrs Mackintosh & Co. in Calcutta; I do not think it is known amongst the Europeans here; the natives always get the first intelligence. I will not mention it, lest it should throw a shade over the gaiety of the party. An officer who got the *lakh*, and Rs 60,000 also in the lottery last year, passed down the river today to place it in Government security; it is all gone; a note has been despatched to inform him of the failure and save him a useless trip of eight hundred miles; he lost twenty-five thousand only a few weeks ago by Messrs Alexander's failure. Lackshmi abides not in his house.

January 12th – The ball went off very well, in spite of Messrs Mackintosh's failure being known; and people who had lost their all danced as merrily as if the savings of years and years had not been swept away by 'one fell swoop'!

January 20th – It is so cold today I am shivering; the coconut oil in the lamps is frozen slightly; this weather is fit for England. I must get all the bricklayer's work over before the hot winds, that I may be perfectly quiet during the fiery time of the year.

January 21st – This being a great Hindu holiday and bathing day induced me to pay another visit to the fair. Amongst the sport (*tamāshā*) at the *melā*, was a Hindu beggar who was *sitting upon thorns*, up to his waist in water – an agreeable amusement. One man played with his right hand on a curious instrument, called a *been*, while in his left hand he held two pieces of black stone, about the length and thickness of a finger which he jarred together in the most dexterous manner, producing an effect something like castanets, singing at the same time. The passers-by threw cowries, *paisa* (copper coins) and rice to the man.

I purchased two musical instruments called *sarinda*, generally used by the *fakirs*, most curious things; Hindu ornaments, idols, china and some white marble images from Jaipur.

Amongst other remarkable objects of worship which I beheld at the sacred spot was one joint of the backbone of some enormous fish or animal; two great staring circular eyes were painted upon it, and the ends of the bone stood out like the stumps of amputated arms; a bit of *ghuwā* (red cloth) covered the lower part; and this was an image of Jaganāth! It had worshippers around it; rice and cowries were the offerings spread before it.

On platforms raised of mud and sand, some ten or twelve missionaries were preaching; every man had his platform to himself and a crowd of natives surrounded each orator. Seeing one of my own servants, an Hindu, apparently an attentive listener, I asked the man what he had heard. 'How call I tell?' said he; 'the English padre is talking.' I explained to him the subject of the discourse, and received for answer, 'Very well; it is their business to preach, they get *paisa* for so doing; what more is to be said?'

  [...]

CHAPTER XXIV

THE NUT LOG

[. . .]

FEBRUARY 22ND 1833 – Today is the Eed: it is customary for the Musulmāns to put on very gay new clothes on this day and to go to prayers at the Jāmma Masjid, the large mosque on the banks of the Jumna. A camel is often sacrificed on the Buckra Eed, on the idea that the animal will be in readiness to carry the person who offers it over the bridge of Sirraat, safe to heaven. The poorer classes will offer a goat (*buckra*), or a sheep, lambs, or kids. This festival is to commemorate Abraham's sacrifice of Isaac. The Musulmāns contend it was Ishmael not Isaac who was the offering.

I have lost my companion, my horse Trelawny: he was so quiet and good-tempered and good-looking; he was as pretty a boy as Hindu or Musulmān might look on in the Central Provinces. Poor Trelawny, Jumna-ji rolls over my good steed! He died this morning of inflammation, caused by some internal injury he received when we were plunging together in the quicksands on the banks of the Ganges.

[. . .]

The Nut Log

April 19th —Yesterday, some wandering gypsies (Nut Log) came to the door; they were a family of tumblers. Nut is the name of a tribe who are generally jugglers, rope-dancers, etc. There was one girl amongst them whose figure was most beautiful and her attitudes more classic and elegant than any I have ever beheld; Madame Sacci would hide her diminished head before the supple and graceful attitudes of this Indian girl.

A man placed a solid piece of wood, of the shape of an hourglass and about eighteen inches in height, on his head; the girl ran up his back and, standing on one foot on the top of the wood, maintained her balance in the most beautiful attitude whilst the man ran round and round in a small circle; she then sprang off his head to the ground. After this she again ran up his back and kneeling on the hour-glass-like wood on his head, allowed him to run in the circle; then she balanced herself on the small of her back, her hands and feet in the air. After that, she stood on her head, her feet straight in the air, the man performing the circle all the time! The drapery worn by the natives falls in the most beautiful folds and the girl was a fit subject for a statuary: I was delighted.

They placed a brass vessel, with dust in it, behind her back on the ground, whilst she stood erect; she bent backwards, until her forehead touched the dust in the vessel, and took up between her eyelids two bits of iron that looked like bodkins; the brass pan in which they were laid was only about two inches high from the ground! She threw herself into wonderful attitudes with a sword in her hand. A set of drawings illustrating all the graceful positions which she assumed would be very interesting; I had never seen any thing of the kind before, and thought of *Wilhelm Meister*. The Nut Log consisted of five women, one little child and one man, who performed all these extraordinary feats; another man beat a tom-tom to keep time for them and accompanied it with his voice; the poor little child performed wonderfully well. She could not have been more than six years old; the other girl was, I should suppose, about eighteen years of age.

Another exhibition worth seeing is an Hindustanī juggler with his goat, two monkeys and three bits of wood, like the wood used in England to play the devil and two sticks. The first bit of wood is placed on the ground, the goat ascends it and balances herself on the top; the man by degrees places another bit of wood on the upper edge of the former; the goat ascends, and retains her balance; the third piece, in like manner, is placed on top of the former two pieces; the goat ascends from the two former, a monkey is placed on her back, and she still preserves the balance. I have seen this curious performance many times. The man keeps time with a sort of musical instrument, which he holds in his right hand and sings a wild song to aid the goat; without the song and the measured time, they say the goat could not perform the balance.

[...]

May 23rd – Such a disaster in the quail-house! Through the negligence, or rather stupidity, of the *khānsāmān*, one hundred and sixty fat quail have been killed.

June 1st – The Muharram is over; I am glad of it, it unsettles all the servants so much and nothing is ever well done whilst they are thinking of the *taziya*.

[...]

The Great Gun at Agra

'The utmost offer that has yet been made for the metal of the great gun is Rs 16 per maund; it is proposed to put it up now for sale by auction, at the Agra-Kotwallee, in the course of next month; the upset price of the lots to be fourteen ānas per seer.

'The destruction of the Agra gun, our readers are aware, has, for some time past, been entrusted to the executive engineer. As stated in the last *Meerut Observer*, an attempt was made first to saw and afterwards it was intended to break it to pieces. In the mean time, it is lying, like Robinson Crusoe's boat, perfectly impracticable under the fort. Though there is a tradition in the city of its weight being 1600 maunds, it has not been found, on actual measurement, to contain more than 845md. 9s., which, at the rate of 2lb. to the seer, would be equal to 30 tons, 3 cwt, 2 qrs, 18 lb. The analysis of the filings made by the deputy Assay Master in Calcutta was, we understand, as follows:

	Copper	Tin
1	29.7	7.3
2	92.2	7.8
3	88.3	11. 7
Mean	91.06	8.94

The gun, from its size, is naturally regarded by the native population as one of the lions of our city. Of the Hindus, too, many are accustomed to address their adorations to it as they do, indeed, to all the arms of war, as the *roop* of Devee, the Indian Hecate. Beyond this, Hindu tradition has not invested the gun with any character of mythological sanctity. The antiquaries of our city, indeed, say that it was brought here by the Emperor Akbar, perhaps from the fortress of Chittore. We have, however, ourselves been unable to find any mention of it in *tawareek* of that reign, or of any subsequent period. Among its other just claims to be saved from the hands of the *Thatheras*, we must not forget the fact of its having once fired a shot from Agra to Futehpur Sikri, a distance of twenty-four miles. A stone ball now marks the spot where it fell to the student in artillery practice, putting him entirely out of conceit of the vaunted power of Queen Elizabeth's pocket pistol which, we believe, can scarcely carry one-third of that distance. The fellow of the Agra gun is stated to be still embedded in the sands of the Jumna.

'Its destruction seems as unpopular with the natives as it is with the European community. Its doom, however, being, we believe, sealed, we are grateful to think that the proceeds of its sale are to be devoted to the erection of a permanent bridge of boats over the Jumna at this city, the estimate for which the supposed value of the gun, with an advance of one or two years' ferry tolls, is expected to meet. The future surplus funds derived from the bridge will probably, we hear, be expended in forming a new branch road from Rāj-ghāt to Mynpoory, to unite with the grand trunk now making between Allahabad and Delhi, under Captain Drummond. We shall, however, postpone till another opportunity our remarks on this and other plans to improve the means of communication in this quarter.'

'At five o'clock on Wednesday morning, the Great Gun at this place was burst, other means of breaking it up having proved unsuccessful. The gun was buried about twenty feet deep in the ground, and 1000 lb. of gunpowder was employed for the explosion. The report was scarcely heard, but the ground was considerably agitated and a large quantity of the earth was thrown on all sides. As far as we can learn, the chief engineer has at length been completely successful. A large portion of the European community and multitudes of natives were present to witness the novel spectacle. The inhabitants of the city were so alarmed, that a considerable portion abandoned their houses, and that part of the town in the vicinity of the Fort was completely deserted.' –

Mofussil Akhbar, June 29

July 18th – Last night, as I was writing a long description of the *tēz-pāt*, the leaf of the cinnamon tree, which humbly pickles beef, leaving the honour of crowning heroes to the *laurus nobilis*, the servants set up a hue and cry that one of our *sā'ises* had been bitten by a snake. I gave the man a teaspoonful of *eau-de-luce*, which the *khānsāmān* calls 'blue-dee-roo', mixed with a little water. They had confined the snake in a kedgeree-pot, out of which he jumped into the midst of the servants; how they ran! The *sā'is* is not the worse for the fright, the snake not being a poisonous one; but he says the memsāhib has burnt up his interior and blistered his mouth with the medicine. I hope you admire the corruption of *eau de-luce* – blue-dee-roo! Another beautiful corruption of the wine-coolers is soup-tureen for Sauterne! Here is a list of absurdities:

harricot, Harry Cook	butcher, voucher
parsley, Peter Selly	prisoner, bridgeman
mignionette, Major Mint	Champagne, simkin
bubble-and-squeak, Dublin cook	trumpeter, Jan Peter
decree, diggery	Brigade-major, Bridget
Christmas, kiss miss	Knole cole, old kooby

[...]

August 4th – I have just received a present of the first number of Colonel Luard's most beautiful views in India; how true they are! His snake-catchers are the very people themselves. Apropos, we caught a young cobra yesterday in my dressing-room; the natives said, 'Do not kill it; it is forbidden to kill the snake with the holy mark on the back of its head,' – a mark like a horseshoe. However, as it was the most venomous sort of snake, I put it quietly into my

'Bottle of Horrors'. They say snakes come in pairs; we have searched the room and cannot find its companion. It is not pleasant to have so venomous a snake twisting on the Venetian blinds of one's dressing-room.

August 8th – Yesterday, at dinner, our friends were praising the fatted quail and remarking how well we had preserved them. This morning all the remainder are dead, about two hundred; why or wherefore I know not – it is provoking.

We had the most beautiful bouquet on the table last night an enormous bowl full of flowers, in such luxuriant beauty, some few of which you may find in hot-houses and greenhouses at home. With what pleasure I looked at them and how much amusement taking off the impressions, or practising the *black art*, as we call it, will afford me!

CHAPTER XXV

The Cholera

IT WAS HAMMERED UPON MY FOREHEAD *i.e. It was my destiny*

WHERE IS THE USE OF TAKING PRECAUTIONS, SINCE WHAT HAS
BEEN PRE-ORDAINED MUST HAPPEN?

AUGUST 8TH 1833 – The same terrible weather continues, the thermometer 90° and 91° all day; not a drop of rain! They prophesy sickness and famine; the air is unwholesome; the Europeans are all suffering with fever and ague and rheumatism. The natives, in a dreadful state, are dying in numbers daily of cholera; two days ago, seventy-six natives in Allahabad were seized with cholera – of these, forty-eight died that day! The illness is so severe that half an hour after the first attack the man generally dies; if he survive one hour it is reckoned a length of time.

A brickmaker living near our gates, buried four of his family from cholera in one day! Is not this dreadful? The poor people, terror-stricken, are afraid of eating their food, as they say the disease follows a full meal. Since our arrival in India we have never before experienced such severely hot winds, or such unhealthy rains.

[...]

The *moonshee* tells me the panic amongst the natives is so great that they talk of deserting Allahabad until the cholera has passed away.

My *darzee*, a fine healthy young Musulmān, went home at five o'clock apparently quite well; he died of cholera at three o'clock, the next day; he had every care and attention. This evening the under-gardener has been seized; I sent him medicine; he returned it saying, 'I am a Baghut (a Hindu who neither eats meat nor drinks wine), I cannot take your medicine; it were better that I should die.' The cholera came across the Jumna to the city, thence it took its course up *one side* of the road to the Circuit Bungalow, is now in cantonments and will, I trust, pass on to Papamhow, cross the Ganges, and Allahabad will once more be a healthy place.

'Magic is truth, but the magician is an infidel.' My *ayah* said, 'You have told us several times that rain will fall and your words have been true; perhaps you can tell us when the cholera will quit the city?' I told her, 'Rain will fall, in all probability, next Thursday (new moon); and if there be plenty of it, the cholera may quit the city.' She is off to the bazaar with the joyful tidings.

[...]

August 17th – The new moon has appeared, but Prāg is unblessed with rain; if it would but fall! Every night the Hindus *pooja* their gods; the Musulmāns weary Heaven with prayers, at the Jamma Masjid (great mosque) on the riverside, near our house – all to no effect. The clouds hang dark and heavily; the thunder rolls at times; you think, 'Now the rain must come,' but it clears off with scarcely a sprinkling. Amongst the Europeans there is much illness, but no cholera.

August 22nd – These natives are curious people; they have twice sent the cholera over the river, to get rid of it at Allahabad. They proceed after this fashion: they take a bull, and after having repeated divers prayers and ceremonies, they drive him across the Ganges into Oude laden, as they believe, with the cholera. This year this ceremony has been twice performed. When the people drive the bull into the river, he swims across and lands or attempts to land, on the Lucknow side; the Oude people drive the poor beast back again, when he is generally carried down by the current and drowned, as they will not allow him to land on either side.

During the night, my *ayah* came to me three times for cholera mixture; happily the rain was falling and I thought it would do much more good than all the medicine; of course I gave her the latter.

Out of sixty deaths there will be forty Hindus to twenty Musulmāns; more men are carried off than women, eight men to two women; the Musulmāns eat more nourishing food than the Hindus, and the women are less exposed to the sun than the men.

[...]

August 26th – I was sitting in my dressing-room, reading, and thinking of retiring to rest, when the *khānsāman* ran to the door, and cried out, 'Memsāhib, did you feel the earthquake? The dishes and glasses in the almirahs (wardrobes) are all rattling.' I heard the rumbling noise, but did not feel the quaking of the earth. About half-past eleven this evening a very severe shock came on, with a loud and rumbling noise; it sounded at first as if a four-wheeled carriage had driven up to the door, and then the noise appeared to be just under my feet; my chair and the table shook visibly, the mirror of the dressing-glass swung forwards, and two of the doors nearest my chair opened from the shock. The house shook so much, I felt sick and giddy; I thought I should fall if I were to try to walk; I called out many times to my husband, but he was asleep on the sofa in the next room, and heard me not. Not liking it at all, I ran into the next room, and awoke him; as I sat with him on the sofa, it shook very much from another shock, or rather shocks, for there appeared to be many of them; and the table trembled also. My *ayah* came in from the verandah and said, 'The river is all in motion, in waves, as if a great wind were blowing against the stream.' The natives say tiles fell from several houses. A shoeing-horn that was hanging by a string to the side of my dressing-glass, swung backwards and forwards like the pendulum of a clock. The giddy and sick sensation one experiences during the time of an earthquake is not agreeable; we had one in September 1831, but it was nothing in comparison to that we have just experienced. Mr D— and Mr C—, who live nearly three miles off, ran out of their bungalows in alarm.

September 5th – The rain fell in torrents all night; it was delightful to listen to it, sounding as it was caught in the great water jars which are placed all round the house; now and then a badly made jar cracked with a loud report, and out rushed the water, a proof that most of the jars would be full by morning.

From the flat clean *pukkā* roof of the house the water falls pure and fresh; from the thatch of a bungalow it would be impure. Today it is so dark, so damp, so English, not a glimpse of the sun, a heavy atmosphere and rain still falling delightfully. There is but little cholera now left in the city; this rain will carry it all away.

Our friend Mr S— arrived yesterday: he was robbed ere he quitted Jaunpur of almost all he possessed: the thieves carried off all his property from the bungalow, with the exception of his *sola topī*, a great broad-brimmed white hat, made of the pith of the *sola*.

The best *sola* hats are made in Calcutta; they are very light, and an excellent defence from the sun: the root of which the *topī* is formed is like pith; it is cut into thin layers, which are pasted together to form the hat. At Meerut they cover them with the skin of the pelican with all its feathers on, which renders it impervious to sun or rain; and the feathers sticking out beyond the rim of the hat give a demented air to the wearer. The pelicans are shot in the Tarāi.

'Sholā (commonly sola – *Aeschynomene paludosa*), the wood of which, being very light and spongy, is used by fishermen for floating their nets. A variety of toys, such as artificial birds and flowers, are made of it. Garlands of those flowers are used in marriage ceremonies. When charred it answers the purpose of tinder (Shakespear's *Dictionary*).'

How dangerous the banks of the river are at this season! Mr M— *lugoed* his boats under a bank on the Ganges; during the night a great portion of the bank fell in, swamped the dog-boat, and drowned all the dogs. Our friend himself narrowly escaped: his *budjerow* (barge) broke from her moorings, and went off into the middle of the stream.

September 19th – The weather killingly hot! I can do nothing but read novels and take lessons on the *sitar*. I wish you could see my instructor, a native, who is sitting on the ground before me, playing difficult variations, contorting his face and twisting his body into the most laughable attitudes, the man in ecstasies at his own performance!

Consumption of ice

One of the most striking instances of the enterprise of the merchants of the present age is the importation of a cargo of ice into India from the distant shores of America; and it is to be hoped that the experiment having so far succeeded, it will receive sufficient encouragement here to ensure the community in future a constant supply of the luxury. The speculators are Messrs Tudor, Rogers and Austin, the first of whom has been engaged for fifteen or twenty years in furnishing supplies of ice to the southern parts of America and the West Indian islands.

The following particulars will furnish an idea of the plan pursued in this traffic, and of the cost incurred in it:

The ice is cut from the surface of some ponds rented for the purpose in the neighbourhood of Boston and being properly stowed, is then conveyed to an ice-house in the city, where it remains until transported on board the vessel which has to convey it to its destined market. It is always kept packed in non-conducting materials, such as tan, hay and pine boards, and the vessel in which it is freighted has an ice-house built within, for the purpose of securing it from the effects of the atmosphere. The expense to the speculators must be very considerable, when they have to meet the charges of rent for the ponds, wages for superintendents and labourers and agents at the place of sale; erection of ice-houses, transportation of the article from the ponds to the city, thence to the vessel, freight, packing and landing, and the delivery of the article at the ice-house which has been built for it in Calcutta.

The present cargo has arrived without greater wastage than was at first calculated on, and the packing was so well managed to prevent its being affected by the atmosphere that the temperature on board during the voyage was not perceptibly altered. This large importation of ice may probably give rise to experiments to ascertain in what way it may be applied to medicinal uses, as it has already elsewhere been resorted to for such purposes; but the chief interest the community generally will take in it will be the addition it will make to domestic comfort.

September 23rd – Yesterday, at five o'clock, whilst we were at dinner, a flight of locusts came across the Jumna from below the fort. The greater part alighted on our compound: those that did not settle on the ground flew round and round in upper air, while thousands of them descending in streams gave the appearance of a very severe storm of snow falling in large dingy flakes. The air was really darkened; they settled on the thatched roofs of the outhouses, covering them entirely. They were so numerous the whole ground was thickly spread with them. A *chaprāsi* went out with my butterfly net, and running against the stream of descending locusts, at one attempt caught from twenty to thirty in the net; you may therefore imagine how numerous they were. The bearers ran out, beating brass washhand basins (*chilamchis*), while others, with frying-pans and pokers, increased the din in order to drive them away, which was not accomplished for half an hour. All the servants, Musalmān and Hindu, were eager to catch them; the two washermen (*dhobees*) showed the greatest cleverness in the business; holding a sheet spread out between them, they ran against the flight of descending locusts, caught great numbers, folded the sheet quickly up to secure their prizes, and having deposited them in a jar, spread the sheet for more.

My little terrier Fury caught twenty or thirty, if not more, and ate them raw; it was amusing to see her run at the locusts and catch them so cleverly.

The gentlemen rose from table and were well repaid for their trouble, never having seen such a marvellous flight of locusts before.

The *khānsāmān* Suddu Khān said, 'In curry they are very good, like prawns, but roasted whole the moment they are caught, they are delicious!' I desired him to bring some to table, but we had not resolution enough to taste them. Little Fury ate them all most greedily, barking and jumping until she had finished them.

Going for our evening drive, such a smell of roasted locusts issued forth as we passed the stables! The flight consisted of red locusts, but amongst them were some of a bright yellow colour. Brown locusts are the most common; the red as well as the yellow are scarce; the red in dying become nearly quite brown.

[...]

The *khānsāmān* prepared many of the bodies with arsenical soap and filled them with cotton. An enormous death's-head moth flew in at the moment, and experienced the same fate. Moths, locusts, great beetles and cockroaches are prepared like small birds.

They say red locusts predict war, the others famine. The latter prediction is likely to prove true; the little rain that fell made the crops spring up, since which time the sun has killed the greater part of the young plants. All grain is very dear and the people are exclaiming, 'We shall die if the rain does not fall.'

Famine, earthquakes, pestilence! What do these portend? Let us not sit in judgment man on man, or declare 'The hand of God is on the earth, until one third of the wicked are swept away from the face of it (Revelation of St John).'

[...]

A Rājput Rāna of high degree has pitched his tents in Alopee Bāgh: nineteen guns were fired in honour of his arrival. This great man has a numerous retinue: to bathe at the sacred junction of the rivers has brought him to Prāg. I drove a young lady through his encampment the other evening; many of his people came out of their tents and absolutely ran on by the side of our carriage, staring at us as if we were *bāgh-siras* (*Grylli monstrosi*) or animals as wonderful.

Their astonishment was great, occasioned most likely by the sight of un-veiled ladies driving about. Passing through the encampment was a service of danger; it was difficult, in keeping clear of the teeth of the camels, not to run against a number of stalls where cakes and sugar were displayed for sale. No sight do I like better than a native encampment; the groups of strange-looking men, the Arab horses, the camels, elephants, and tents are charming. No country can furnish more or so many picturesque scenes as India

December 5th – People talk of wonderful storms of hail. I have just wit-nessed one so very severe that had I not seen it, I think I should scarcely have believed it. At ten at night a storm, accompanied by thunder and lightning, came on; the hail fell as thick as flakes of snow – I can scarcely call it hail, the pieces were ice-bolts. I brought in some which measured four inches and a half in circumference, and the ground was covered some inches deep; it appeared as if spread with a white sheet, when by the aid of the lightning one could see through the darkness around. The old peepal tree groaned most bitterly, the glass windows were all broken, the tobacco plants cut down, the great leaves from the young banyan tree were cut off and the small twigs from the mango and *neem* trees covered the ground like a green carpet. It was a fearful storm. The next morning for miles round you saw the effect of the hail, and in the bazaar at eight o'clock the children were playing marbles with the hailstones.

December 31st – I trust we have now become *acclimated*, for we have nearly passed through this year – the most fruitful in illness and death I recollect, both among civilians and soldiers – without much sickness. I have had fever and ague. My husband has suffered from acute rheumatism and the little pet terrier Fury has been delicate, but we are all now re-established. I am on horseback every morning rejoicing in the cold breezes, feeling as strong and full of spirit as the long-tailed grey that carries me; and Fury is chasing squirrels and ferrets and putting the farmyard to the rout.

CHAPTER XXVI

The Muharram

[...]

The Muharram

MAY 19TH 1834 – The mourning festival of the Mohammedans in remembrance of their first martyrs, Hassan and Hussein, lasts ten days; on the last day the *taziya*, the model of the tomb of Hussein, is interred.

[...]

The ceremony takes place annually on the first day of the moon (Muharram). Their year has twelve moons only, and they do not add a moon every third year, as some persons suppose.

The Imām-bāra is expressly built for commemorating the Muharram. In this building the *taziya* is placed facing Mecca, with the banners, the sword, the shield and the bow and arrows supposed to have been used in the battle of Karbala. The most magnificent *taziyas* remain in the Imām-bara. The less costly, which are used in the processions on the tenth day, are buried with funeral rites, in cemeteries named Karbala.

Although the *taziya*, the model of their Imām's tomb at Karbala belongs, by right, only to the Shias, it is remarkable that many Sunis have *taziyas*, and also some Hindus. My cook, who was a Mug, used to expend sometimes as much as Rs 40 on a *taziya* of his own; and after having performed all the ceremonies like a good Musulmān returned to his original Hinduism, when he had placed his *taziya* in the burial-ground, accompanied by rice, corn, flowers, cups of water, etc.

But little or no attention is paid to the models of the *taziya*: they are of different forms, and of every variety of material, according to the wealth of the person who sets up this remembrance of Hussein. On the *taziya* is placed a small portion of corn, rice, bread, fruits, flowers, and cups of water; this is in accordance with the Musulmān funerals at which food is invariably conveyed to the tomb with the corpse.

The *taziya* displayed by the King of Oude during the Muharram is composed of green glass with ormolu or brass mouldings. Some are of ivory, ebony, sandalwood, cedar, etc. or of wrought filigree silver: those for the poor are of coloured talc.

In front of the *taziya* two standards are erected, between which are laid strings of the fresh flowers of the sweet-scented jasmine (*bela*); and a *chaunri*, made of the tail of the *yak* fixed in a silver handle, is used to fan away the flies.

When the *taziya* is placed in the Imām-bāra, the face is turned to Mecca. The institution of carrying the *taziya* in procession first took place in the AH 352 at Baghdad, under Noez-od-Dowla Dhelmé, and is never omitted in Persia.

Hussein, on his favourite horse Dhul Dhul, was pierced by arrows without number; the animal shared the same fate, and the Sunni Musulmāns were the extirpators of all the race of Hussein, the son of Ali, with the exception of one infant son and the females of the family. This is the cause of the battles that so often take place between the Shias and the Sunnis (whom the former regard as an accursed race) at the annual celebration of the Muharram.

The usual arrangement of the procession is as follows: In the order of march the elephants first appear on which men are seated, displaying the consecrated banners crowned by the spread hand. The banners are of silk, embroidered in gold or silver. The spread hand on the top of them represents five: Muhammad, Fatima, Ali, Hassan, Hussein; the three fingers, the Caliphas Omar, Osman and Abubekr. The Sunnis favour the latter; the Shias uphold Imām Ali. The ends of the banners are fringed with bullion, and they are tied with cords of gold. Then follows the band, which is always in attendance and is composed of Arab music only.

The *jilādār* or sword-bearer carries a pole, from which two naked swords, each tipped with a lemon, are suspended from a bow reversed. The arrows are fixed in the centre. The sword bearer is generally dressed in green, the mourning colour of the Syuds. The standard-bearers and a band of musicians attend him, carrying the banner of Hassan and Hussein.

Some men, the mourners of the procession, bear long black poles on which are fixed very long streamers of black unspun silk which are intended to represent grief and despair.

The horse Dhul Dhul next appears: in the procession he sometimes bears a *taziya*, at other times he is caparisoned as if in readiness for his master. After the Muharram, the animal and all its attire are given to a poor Syud; the bloody horsecloth and the legs stained red are supposed to represent the sufferings of the animal. The tail and mane are dyed with *mehndi* or *lakh* dye. The horse is attended by a man carrying the *āftāba*, which is a sun embroidered on crimson velvet, affixed to the end of a long staff; and carried in an elevated position, in order to shelter a man of rank on horseback from the rays of the sun. Men with *chaunris* attend to whisk away the flies from the horse: *asā bardārs*, men with long silver sticks, and *sonta bardārs*, with short silver tiger headed staffs, walk at the side, and running footmen (*harkāras*) are in attendance. An embroidered umbrella (*chatr*) is supported over the head of the horse.

In the cavalcade is a chaunter or reader; he repeats affecting passages descriptive of the death of Hussein, during which time the procession halts for a few minutes whilst the Musulmāns give way to the most frantic expressions of grief, beating their breasts with violence, throwing dust upon their heads, and exclaiming 'Hassan! Hussein! Hassan! Hussein!'

The *paik*, a *fakir*, is a remarkable person, wearing the bow, arrows, sword, *pankhā*, and *chaunri* of the martyred Imām. Some men in the procession carry censers, suspended by chains, which they wave about and perfume the air with the incense of a sweet-scented resin; rose-water, for sprinkling, is also carried in long-necked bottles, called *gulāb-pāsh*.

Then follows the *taziya*, attended by its proprietor, his relatives, and friends; it is surrounded by banners and covered by a canopy upheld by poles supported by men.

A *taziya* of shields and swords, each tipped with a lemon or an orange, is carried in procession and on it are suspended written petitions to Hassan and Hussein, and it is adorned with strings of freshly-gathered jasmine flowers.

The model of the tomb of Kāsim is the next object; it is covered with gold brocade and a canopy is supported over it, the poles carried by men. The *palkee* of his bride, Sakeena Koobar, follows the tomb; and her *chandol*, a sort of palanquin.

Then follow trays of *mehndi*, carried on the heads of men with presents, etc. such as are usually sent during the marriage ceremony, with flowers of *ubruk*.

The *charkh-charkhi wālās* are numerous; the charkhī is composed of ebony or any hard wood, about the size of a cricket ball, divided in halves. Each man has a pair; they are beaten in a particular manner on the flat surface so as to produce the sound of horses galloping; and where some fifty or one hundred men are engaged in the performance the imitation is excellent.

The females during the battle were perishing of thirst; Abbās, the brother of Hussein and his standard-bearer, made great efforts to procure water for them, in doing which the former was severely wounded.

Hence the *bihishti* with his *mashk*; and, in remembrance of this event, sherbets are also distributed gratis, in red earthen cups, from temporary sheds; *abdār khānas*, as they call them by the roadside. The awnings of these sheds are reared on poles, and they are lighted by lamps made of *ubruk* or of the skeleton leaves of the peepal tree. The *bihishti* bears the standard of Hassan and Hussein.

The camels carrying the tent equipage and luggage of Hussein represent the style of his march from Medina to Karbala. Sometimes, in pictures, a small *taziya* is drawn on the back of a camel and the animal is represented as issuing from a rocky pass.

Barkandāz attend and fire their matchlocks singly and at intervals during the march.

Great sums are expended in charity during this mourning festival, and food is always distributed by the richer *taziyadārs* during the ten days.

The procession is closed by several elephants and men seated upon them distribute food and money to the poor.

Natives of all ranks, from the highest to the lowest, walk on the tenth day with their heads uncovered, and without slippers, to the Karbala, whatever may be the distance; and they fast until the third watch has passed, refraining from the *huqqa* or from drinking water. At the Karbala the funeral ceremony is performed, and the *taziya* is committed to the grave with a solemnity equal to that which is observed when their dead are deposited in the tomb. The native ladies within the walls of the *zenāna* keep the fast with the greatest strictness, and observe all the ceremonies of the Muharram.

A religious man will neither ride nor wear shoes during the Muharram; and a pious Musulmān will neither eat nor drink out of a silver or a gold vessel.

[...]

The lamps, which are made of *ubruk* (talc), or of the skeleton leaves of the peepal tree, and lighted up in the houses of the faithful at this time, are beautifully made.

[...]

An alligator, seven feet in length, was caught in the Jumna below our house, a few days ago; I had it prepared with arsenical soap, stuffed and set out in the verandah, where it grins in hideous beauty, nailed down upon the carpenter's large table, where it will remain until it stiffens into proper form.

My cabinet of curiosities and fondness of horrors ensured many a strange present from absent friends. A small military party were dispatched to capture a mud fort; on reaching the spot no enemy was to be discovered; they entered with all due precaution against ambush; an enormous tiger in a cage was the sole occupant. The tiger was sent down by boat to me – the first prize of the campaign; on my refusal to accept the animal, he was forwarded to the accoutrement-maker of the officer, in Calcutta, in liquidation of his account! The tiger was sold at length to an American captain for Rs 250, which just or very nearly paid the expenses of boat-hire, servants, meat, etc., contracted on the tiger's account. Such changes in his way of life must have puzzled his philosophy; the capture, the Ganges and sea voyage ending in North America, will give him a queer idea of the best of all possible worlds; but he well deserves it, being a cruel, treacherous, blood-thirsty brute.

My eccentric friend also wrote to say he had at length procured for me an offering after my own heart, an enormous boa constrictor, perfectly tame, so domestic and sweet tempered that at meals it would cross the room, displaying, as it advanced with undulating motion, its bright-striped and spotted skin, until having gained your chair, it would coil its mazy folds around you and, tenderly putting its head over your shoulder, eat from your hand!

I was greatly tempted to accept this unique offering. They tell us mankind has a *natural* antipathy to a snake; an antipathy I never shared. I have killed them as venomous reptiles, but have a great fancy for them as beautiful ones. No child dislikes snakes until it is taught to fear them.

[...]

June 1st – I have scarcely energy enough to write; an easterly wind renders the *tattis* useless; the thermometer at 93°! The damp air renders me so heavy and listless, it is an exertion either to eat or drink and it is almost impossible to sleep, on account of the heat. At seven o'clock I take a drive through the burning air and come in parched and faint, eager for the only comfort during the twenty-four hours, a glass of English home-made blackcurrant wine, well iced, in a tumbler of well-iced soda water; the greatest luxury imaginable.

I have not heard from home for six months, heartsick with hope deferred. These tardy ships! Will the steam communication ever be established?

[...]

CHAPTER XXVII

White Ants and Cold Mornings for Hunting

[...]

AUGUST 1834 – Last month we were unlucky in the farmyard; forty-seven fat sheep and well-fatted lambs died of smallpox; a very great loss, as to fatten sheep on *gram* for two or three years makes them very expensive; it is remarkable that none of the goats, although living in the same house, were attacked.

This morning three musk-deer, prepared and stuffed, were shown to me; they are a present for Runjeet Singh and are now *en route* from Nepal. The men had also a number of musk bags for the Lion of the Punjab. The hair of the musk-deer is curious stuff, like hog's bristles; and their two tusks are like those of the walrus. Buffon gives an admirable description of this animal. Some time ago a musk-bag was given me as a curiosity; the scent is extremely powerful. The musk-deer is rare and very valuable.

August 9th – This is a holiday, the *nāg-panchami*, on which day the Hindus worship a snake to procure blessing on their children; of course, none of the carpenters or the other workmen have made their appearance. The other day, a gentleman who is staying with us went into his bathing-room to take a bath; the evening was very dark and, as he lifted a *ghāra* (an earthen vessel) to pour the water over his head, he heard a hissing sound among the water-pots and, calling for a light, saw a great *cobra de capello*. 'Look at that snake!' said he to his bearer, in a tone of surprise. 'Yes, sāhib,' replied the Hindu, with the utmost apathy, 'he has been there a great many days, and gives us much trouble!'

September 11th – We purchased a very fine pinnace that an officer had brought up the river and named her *Seagull*. She is as large as a very good yacht; it will be pleasant to visit those *ghāts* on the Ganges and Jumna, during the cold weather, that are under the sāhib's control. The vessel is a fine one, and the natives say, 'She goes before the wind like an arrow from a bow.'

The city of Allahabad, considered as a native one, is handsome. There are but few pukka houses. The rich merchants in the East make no display, and generally live under bamboo and straw. The roads through the city are very good, with rows of fine trees on each side; the drives around are numerous and excellent. There is also a very handsome *sarāy* (caravansary), and a *bā'olī*, a large well, worthy a visit. The tomb and garden of Sultān Khusrau are fine; a description of them will be given hereafter. The fort was built by Akbar in 1581, at the junction of the Ganges and Jumna. Within the fort, near the principal gateway, an enormous pillar is prostrate; the unknown characters inscribed upon it are a marvel and a mystery to the learned, who as yet have been unable to translate them. The bazaar at Allahabad is famous for old coins.

[...]

October 7th – Yesterday being the Hindu festival of the Dewalī, a great illumination was made for my amusement; our house, the gardens, the well, the pinnace on the river below the bank of the garden, the old peepal tree and my bower were lighted up with hundreds of little lamps. My bower on the banks of the Junma-ji, which is quite as beautiful as the 'bower of roses by Bendameer's stream', must be described.

It was canopied by the most luxuriant creepers and climbers of all sorts. The *ishk-pecha*, the 'Twinings of Love' (*Ipomaea quamoclit*), overspread it in profusion; as the slender stems catch upon each other and twine over an arbour, the leaves, falling back, lie over one another *en masse*, spreading over a broad surface in the manner in which the feathers of the tail of a peacock spread over one another, and trail upon the ground; the ruby red and star-like flowers start from amidst the rich green of its delicate leaves as bright as sunshine. This climber, the most beautiful and luxuriant imaginable, bears also the name of *kamalāta*, 'Love's Creeper'. Some have flowers of snowy hue, with a delicate fragrance; and one, breathing after sunset, the odour of cloves!

[...]

I wish I had tried the teeth of the white ants by putting up pillars of stone. An orthodox method of killing these little underminers is by strewing sugar on the places frequented by them: the large black ants, the sworn enemies of the white ants, being attracted by the sugar, quickly appear and destroy the white ones. The white ants are sappers and miners; they will come up through the floor into the foot of a wardrobe, make their way through the centre of it into the drawers, and feast on the contents. I once opened a wardrobe which had been filled with tablecloths and napkins: no outward sign of mischief was there; but the linen was one mass of dirt and utterly destroyed. The most remarkable thing is the little beasts always move under cover, and form for themselves a hollow way through which they move unseen, and do their work of destruction at leisure. The hollow way they form is not unlike pipe macaroni in size, and its colour is that of mud. I never saw them in Calcutta; up the country they are a perfect nuisance. The queen ant is a curious creature; one was shown me that had been dug out of an ants' nest: it was nearly four inches long by two in width and looked something like a bit of blubber. The white ants are the vilest little animals on the face of the earth; they eat their way through walls, through beams of wood and are most marvellously trouble-some. They attack the roots of trees and plants and kill them in a day or two. To drive them away it is advisable to have the plants watered with *hing* (*assafoetida*) steeped in water. If a box be allowed to stand a week upon the floor without being moved, it is likely at the end of that time, when you take it up, the bottom may fall out, destroyed by the white ants. Carpets, mats, chintz, such as we put on the floors, all share, more or less, the same fate. I never saw a white ant until I came to India. They resemble the little white maggots in a cheese, with a black dot for a head and a pair of pincers fixed upon it.

The Calcutta matting is little used for rooms in the Upper Provinces, as it is soon destroyed by the ants; in lieu thereof, gaily-coloured chintz, manufactured by the natives after the patterns of Brussels carpets, is put down in the rooms and gives them a handsome appearance, but it is not so cool as the matting. A cloth (called *sallam*), dyed with indigo, ought to be put down under the chintz to keep off the white ants, which dislike the smell of the indigo.

[. . .]

October 1834 – I have just returned from taking a sketch of the Circuit bungalow; it reminds me of very many pleasant mornings, although to an English ear it may not give an idea of pleasure to rise at three in the morning, to take coffee by candlelight, or by the light of the mist in the verandah! – The *buggy* waiting, the lamps lighted, and the horse covered with a blanket, to keep him from taking a chill. A drab coat with many capes, a shawl beneath, and another round the neck, a drive of two or three miles by lamplight. Just as you come up to the dogs, a gentleman comes forward to assist the memsāhib from the *buggy*, saying, 'Very cold! Very cold! One could not be more delightfully cold in England – half-frozen!' Those fine dogs, Jānpeter, Racer, Merrylass, and the rest of them emerge from the palanquin carriage in which they have been brought to Papamhow, 'Much *tāmashā*! many jackals!' Then the canter through the plantations of Urrah, wet with dew – dew so heavy that the *sā'is* wrings out the skirt of the memsāhib's habit; nevertheless, the lady and the black pony are very happy. Master General carries his rider in most *jemmy* style; a gallant grey by his side takes beautiful leaps, and the memsāhib and her black horse scramble up and down ravines over which the others leap, and by little detours and knowledge of the country find much amusement in the course of the morning.

All natives, from the highest to the lowest, sport the moustache and pride themselves upon its blackness. My old *khānsāmān*, Suddu Khān, whose hair, beard and moustache were perfectly white, came before me one morning, and making salam, requested me to allow him some hours' leave of absence to dye his hair. In the evening he was in attendance at table; his hair, beard, and moustache in the most perfect order and jet black! The 16th Lancers, on their arrival in India, wore no moustache; after the lapse of many years, the order that allowed them the decoration arrived in India, and was hailed with delight by the whole corps. The natives regarded them with much greater respect in consequence, and the young dandis of Delhi could no longer twirl their moustaches and think themselves finer fellows than the Lancers. As a warlike appendage it was absolutely necessary; a man without moustaches being reckoned *nā-mard*, unmanly. A dandified native generally travels with a handkerchief bound under his chin and tied on the top of his turban, that the beauty and precision of his beard may not be disarranged on the journey.

CHAPTER XXVIII

PILGRIMAGE TO THE TĀJ

RESOLUTION OVERCOMES GREAT DIFFICULTIES

You will require the patience of an angel, or of a whole heaven of angels, to reach Agra in a pinnace. I was a month in a boat that I built for the very purpose of threading this Meander, to which that of Troy was a *nālā*, as straight as an arrow. I fear your voyage will be much protracted, but as for the wind, you are sure to have it favourable two or three times a day, let it blow from what quarter it will, for you will have your course during the twenty-four hours to every point of the compass, and these cold days too! Here am I shivering in the warmest room in my house!

W. L. G., Khasganj

DECEMBER 1834 – To look forward to the cold season is always a great pleasure in India; and to plan some expedition for that period is an amusement during the hot winds and rains. We had often determined to visit the Tāj Mahal at Agra – the wonder of the world.

Our beautiful pinnace was now in the Jumna, anchored just below the house, but the height of the banks and the lowness of the river only allowed us to see the top of her masts. My husband proposed that I should go up the Jumna in her, as far as Agra, and anchor off the Tāj; and promised, if he could get leave of absence, to join me there to view all that is so well worth seeing at that remarkable place. Accordingly, the pinnace was prepared for the voyage, and a *patelī* was procured as a cook-boat. Books, drawing materials and everything that could render a voyage up the river agreeable were put on board.

December 9th – I quitted Prāg: *Seagull* spread her sails to the breeze and, in spite of the power of the stream, we made good way against it: at night we *lugoed* off Phoolpoor, i.e. made fast to the bank, as is always the custom, the river not being navigable during the darkness.

December 10th – Saw the first crocodile today basking on a sandbank: a great long-nosed fellow, a very Indian looking personage, of whom I felt the greatest fear as at the moment my little terrier Fury, who was running on the shore with the *dāndis*, seeing me on deck swam off to the pinnace. I was much pleased when a *dāndi* caught her in his arms and put her on the cook-boat.

On the commencement of a voyage the men adorn the bows of the vessel with chaplets of fresh flowers (*hārs*), and ask for money: on days of *pooja*, and at the end of the voyage, the same ceremony is repeated and halfway on the voyage they usually petition for a present, a few rupees for good luck.

I must describe *Seagull*. She was built in Calcutta to go to Chittagong and has a deep keel, therefore unfit for river work unless during the rains: two-masted, copper-bottomed and brig-rigged. She requires water up to a man's waist; her crew consist of twenty-two men, one *sarang*, who commands her, four *khalāsis*, who hold the next rank, one *gal'haiya*, forecastle man (from *galahi*, a forecastle), fourteen *dāndis*, one cook and his mate, all Musulmāns; total twenty-two. The crew, particularly good men, came from Calcutta with the pinnace; they cook their own food and eat and sleep on board. My food and that of my servants is prepared in the cook-boat. The food of the *dāndis* usually consists of curry and rice, or thin cakes of flour (unleavened bread) called *chapātis*: the latter they bake on a *tāwa* (iron plate) over the fire on the bank, and eat whilst hot. It is amusing to see how dexterously they pat these cakes into form, between both hands, chucking them each time into the air: they are usually half an inch in thickness and the size of a dessert plate.

When these common *chapātis* are made thin, and allowed to blow out on the fire until they are perfectly hollow, they are delicious food, if eaten quite hot. Thus made they are much better than those generally put on the table of the *sāhib loge* (gentry), which are made of fine flower and milk.

Being unable to find a boat for hire that would answer as a cook-boat, the *jamadār* purchased a *pateli*, a small boat built after the fashion of a large flat-bottomed *patailā*, for which he gave Rs 80; and we proceeded to fit it up by building a large house upon it of mats and bamboo, thickly thatched with straw. This house was for the cook, the servants and the farmyard. On the top of it was a platform of bamboos on which the *dāndis* (sailors) could live and sleep. The crew consisted of seven men, Hindus; therefore they always cooked their food on shore in the evening, it being contrary to the rules of their religion to eat on board. The sheep, goats, fowls, provisions, wine, etc. were all in the cook-boat, and a space was divided off for the *dhobee* (washerman). The number of servants it is necessary to take with one on a river voyage in India is marvellous. We had also a little boat called a dinghy, which was towed astern the pinnace.

This morning we passed Sujawan Deota, a rock rising out of the river crowned with a temple, a remarkably picturesque spot and adorned with trees. A pinnace is towed by one thick towing line, called a *goon*, carried by ten men.

Native boats containing merchandise are generally towed by small lines, each man having his own line to himself. The wind having become contrary, the men were obliged to tow her; the *goon* broke, the vessel swerved round and was carried some distance down the stream; however, she was brought up without damage, and moored off Sehoree.

December 11th – In passing the Burriaree rocks I felt a strange sort of anxious delight in the danger of the passage, there being only room for one vessel to pass through. The *serang*, a Calcutta man, had never been up the Jumna; and as we cut through the narrow pass I stood on deck watching ahead for a sunken rock. Had there been too little water, with what a crash we should have gone on the rocks! The river is full of them; they show their black heads a foot or two above the stream that rushes down fiercely around or over them: just now we ran directly upon one. The vessel swerved right round, but was brought up again soon after.

We track or sail from six o'clock, and moor the boats at seven in the evening. On anchoring off Deeya I received two matchlocks, sent to me by my husband, on account of his having heard that many salt-boats on the Jumna have been plundered lately; the matchlocks are to be fired off of an evening when the watch is set, to show we are on our guard. At night a *chaprāsī* and two *dāndis* hold their watch, armed, on deck; and two *chaukidārs* (watchmen) from the nearest village keep watch on shore. My little fine-eared terrier is on board, and I sleep without a thought of robbery or danger. If you take a guard from the nearest village, you are pretty safe; if not, perhaps the *chaukidārs* themselves will rob you, in revenge for your not employing them.

[...]

December 13th – Aground off Kuttree, again off Shahpoor and, for the third time, off Jumnapoor: *lugoed* off Mowhie.

December 13th – Aground on a sunken rock off Toolseepoor, again off Dampour. During the rains the river is deep; but at this time of the year it is late to undertake a voyage to Agra and I think it not impossible it may be impracticable to take the pinnace so far up the river. Nevertheless, we have come on very well with occasional difficulties, such as going over sunken rocks at times, bump, bump, under the vessel. I have felt half afraid of seeing their black heads through the floor of the cabin. We have grounded on sandbanks four and five times a day in avoiding the rocks. The Jumna is full of them, and the navigation dangerous on that account. The contrary wind has generally obliged us to track, as our course lies right in the teeth of the west wind which is strong, and generally blows pretty steadily at this time of the year. There is one consolation, the river winds and twists so much, the wind must be fair somewhere or other.

Every twelve miles a *dārogha* comes on board to make salaam to the memsāhib, and to ask her orders. I send letters to Prāg by this means; the *dārogha* gives them to our own *chaprāsis*, who run with them from station to station. There is no *dāk* (post) in these parts. The *dāroghas* bring fish, eggs, kids, anything of which I am in need; and I pay for them, although these are brought as presents, it being against the orders of Government to receive the gift even of a cabbage or beetroot from a native. The tracking ground was fine; moored off Bhowna.

December 15th – Strong west wind, very cold: the river broad and deep; the thermometer at nine o'clock is 60°. The *darzee* in the after cabin is at work on a silk gown: the weather is just cold enough to render warm attire necessary. The other day I was on deck in a green velvet travelling cap, with an Indian shawl, put on after the fashion of the men, amusing myself with firing with a pellet-bow at some cotton-boats *en passant* for *tamāshā*. Some natives came on board to make salam, and looked much surprised at seeing a pellet-bow (*ghulel*) in feminine hands. The cotton-boats would not get out of the way, therefore I pelted the steersmen (*manjhis*) of the vessels, to hasten the movements of the great unwieldy lubberly craft. Of whom can I talk but of myself in this my solitude on the Jumna-ji? Now for the telescope to look out for the picturesque.

December 17th – Wind strong, cold, and westerly, the stream broad and deep, anchored off Jerowlee in a jungle: just the place for a sportsman. A quantity of underwood and small trees amongst the ravines and cliffs afford shelter for the game. Here you find *nilgāi*, peacocks, partridge and quail. Several peacocks were quietly feeding on the cliffs; others roosting on the trees. At this place they told me there is a *bura kund*, which is, I believe, a well, or spring, or basin of water, especially consecrated to some holy purpose or person; but I did not visit the spot.

[…]

December 23rd – A wretched day; cold, damp, and miserable, a most power-ful wind directly against us. To add to the discomfort, we sprang a leak which gave sixty buckets of water in twenty-four hours. The leak was found under the rudder. We had to take down a part of the aft-cabin, and to take up some boards before we could get at it: and when found, we had nothing on board fit to stop it. At last it was effectually stopped with towels, torn up and forced in tight, and stiff clay beaten down over that. I thought this might last until our arrival at Kalpee, where proper repairs might take place: moored of Bowlee.

December 25th – Christmas Day was ushered in by rain and hail, the wind high and contrary. At noon the wind decreased and we got on better, tracking along the banks, with fourteen men on the *goon* (track-rope). At seven in the evening, just as we had moored, a storm came on accompanied with the most brilliant forked lightning; and the most violent wind, blowing a gale, united with the strong stream, bearing full down against us. It was really fearful. After a time the wind and forked lightning became sheeted and the rain fell, like a second deluge, in torrents. The peals of thunder shook the cabin windows and all the panes of glass rattled. We had *lugoed* off a dry *nālā* (the bed of a stream); the torrents of rain filled the *nālā* with water, which poured down against the side of the pinnace with great force and noise. Fearing we should be driven from our moorings by the force of the current, I ran on deck to see if the men were on the alert. It was quite dark: some were on shore taking up the *lāwhāsees* by which she was secured to the bank; the rest were on deck, trying with their long bamboos to shove her out of the power of the current from the *nālā*. Having succeeded in this, we were more comfortable. It was out of the question to take rest during such a storm, while there was a chance of being driven from our moorings; and being quite alone was also unpleasant. At length the gale abated and I was glad to hear only the rain for the rest of the night. Daylight closed my weary eyes: on awaking refreshed from a quiet slumber, I found *Seagull* far from Ekouna, near which place we had passed so anxious a night.

December 26th – Moored off Kalpee, famous for its crystalised sugar. Here a large budget of letters was brought to me. I remained the whole day at the station to procure provisions and answer the letters. Nor did I forget to purchase tools and everything necessary for the repair of the leak in the vessel, although we forbore to remove the towels and clay, as she now only made half a bucket in twenty-four hours.

December 28th – Northwest wind very cold: the river most difficult to navigate in parts; rocky, sandy, shallow. Anchored off Palpoor; found a quantity of river shells; they are not very pretty, but some are curious.

December 29th – We were in the midst of great sandbanks, in a complete wilderness; the stream was strong and deep, the tracking-ground good; here and there the rocks appeared above water under the high cliffs. Off Belaspoor, on one sandbank, I saw ten crocodiles basking in the sun, all close together; some turtle and great white birds were on a rock near them; on the river's edge were three enormous alligators, large savage monsters lying with their enormous mouths wide open, eyeing the boats. The men on board shouted with all their might; the alligators took no notice of the shout; the crocodiles, more timid than the former, ran into the water and disappeared immediately. These are the first alligators I have seen in their own domains; they are very savage, and will attack men; the crocodiles will not, if it be possible to avoid them. I would willingly have taken the voyage for this one sight of alligators and crocodiles in their native wildernesses; the scene was so unusual, so wild, so savage. At sunset anchored off Gheetamow and found some shells during my evening ramble.

At the sale of the effects of the late Colonel Gough, in Calcutta, was the head of an alligator (*magar*) of incredible size, caught in the Megna; which, though deficient in not having an underjaw, was a good weight for a man to carry, stooping to it with both hands. The creeks of a bend of the Sunderbunds, not far below Calcutta, are the places frequented, I hear, by the patriarchs of their race.

The next day we entered a most difficult part of the river; it was impossible to tell in which direction to steer the vessel; rocks on every side; the river full of them; a most powerful stream rushing between the rocks; to add to the danger, we had a strong westerly wind directly in our teeth which, united to the force of the stream, made us fear the *goon* might break; in which case we should have been forced most violently against the rocks. We accomplished only one mile in four hours and a half! I desired the *sarang* to anchor the vessel and let the men have some rest; they had been fagging, up to their waists in water all the time, and I wished the wind to abate ere we attempted to proceed further. After the *dāndis* had dined, we pushed off again. At Rurunka a pilot came on board, which pleased me very much as it was impossible to tell on which side of the rocks the passage might be: the pilot took us up with great difficulty through the rocks to the landmark off the bungalow at Badoura; there he requested leave to anchor until the wind might abate; he was afraid to try the stream, it being still stronger higher up. Of course I consented; after which, accompanied by the pilot, I walked some three miles to collect fossil bones; these bones were discovered by the sappers and miners on the riverside at the little village of Badoura; the bones are petrified, but to what animal they belonged is unknown; some cart-loads of them have been taken to Allahabad, to be shown to the scientific; I brought back five or six of the bones we found at the place. A short time ago this part of the river was impassable; the Company sent sappers and miners who, having surrounded each rock with a fence that kept out the water, blew them up and made a passage down the centre of the river; of course this was a work of time; the fences were then removed and the stream flowed unconfined. Large boats can now go up and down in safety, if they know the passage. The next morning the pilot accompanied us as far as Merapool, when he made his salam and returned to the sappers' and miners' bungalow. The river now became good and clear, we encountered no more difficulties and moored quietly off Seholee at six in the evening.

1835, January 1st – New Year's Day was as disagreeable as Christmas Day;

cold, frosty; a wind in our teeth; rocks and crocodiles. My pet terrier was taken ill; with difficulty she was brought through the attack; poor little Poppus – she has a dozen names, all of endearment. Passed Juggermunpoor, where the fair for horses is held.

January 2nd – A fair wind brought us to the Chumbal river. The fort and Hindu temple of Bhurrage are very picturesque objects. This is one of the most difficult passes on the river, on account of the sand banks, and the power of the stream from the junction of the Jumna and Chumbal. I am directed not to stop a moment for anything but letters on my way to Agra; on my return I shall go on shore (DV), and visit all the picturesque places I now behold merely *en passant*. The Chumbal is a beautiful river; never was a stream more brilliant or more clear; the water, where it unites with the Jumna, is of a bright pellucid green.

From the force of the united streams we had great difficulty in passing the junction; the wind dropped and we could not move the pinnace on the towing-rope; we sent a hawser in the dinghy to the opposite shore and then, with the united force of the crews of both vessels, hauled the pinnace across the junction into the quiet waters of the Jumna; it was six o'clock ere this was effected. Whilst the people anchored and got the cook-boat over, I walked to a beautiful Hindu temple close to the river's edge. The fort beyond put me in mind of Conway Castle; the towers are somewhat similar: on my return I must stop and sketch it. A wealthy native has sent to petition *an audience*; he is anxious to make salam to the memsāhib. I have declined seeing him, as we must start at daybreak; but have told him on my return I shall stay a day or two at this picturesque place and shall then be happy to receive his visit.

Nothing is so shocking, so disgusting, as the practice of burning bodies; generally only half-burning them and throwing them into the river. What a horrible sight I saw today! Crowds of vultures, storks, crows and pariah dogs from the village glutting over a dreadful meal; they fiercely stripped the flesh from the swollen body of the half-burned dead which the stream had thrown on a sand bank; and howled and shrieked as they fought over and for their fearful meal!

How little the natives think of death! This morning when I was on deck the body of a woman floated by the pinnace, within the reach of a bamboo; she was apparently dead, her long black hair spread on the stream; by the style of the red dress, she was a Hindu; she must have fallen, or have been thrown, into the river. I desired the men to pull the body to the vessel's side and see if she might not be saved. They refused to touch it even with a bamboo; nobody seemed to think anything about it, further than to prevent the body touching the vessel, should the stream bring it close to the side. One man coolly said, 'I suppose she fell into the river when getting up water in her *ghará* [earthen vessel]!'

How easily a murdered man might be disposed of! On account of the expense of fuel, the poorer Hindus only slightly burn the bodies of the dead and then cast them into the river; by attiring the corpse after the fashion of a body to be burned, and throwing it into the stream, it would never attract attention; any native would say, 'Do not touch it, do not touch it; it is merely a burnt body.'

This life on the river, however solitary, is to me very agreeable; and I would proceed beyond Agra to Delhi, but that I should think there cannot be water enough for the pinnace; with a fair wind there is much to enjoy in the changing scene but tracking against a contrary one is tiresome work.

January 3rd – A most unpleasant day; we were aground many times, contending against the stream and a powerful wind. The new *goon* broke, and we were at last fixed most firmly and unpleasantly on a bank of sand; in that position, finding it impossible to extricate the pinnace, we remained all night.

January 4th – We were obliged to cut our way through the sandbank to the opposite shore, a distance of about a quarter of a mile; this took twelve hours to accomplish; the anchor was carried to a distance with a chain cable and there dropped, and the pinnace was pulled by main force through the sand, where there was not water enough to float her. When out of it we came upon a stream that ran like a torrent, aided by a most powerful and contrary wind. To remain where we were was dangerous; the men carried a thick cable in the dinghy to the shore, made it fast, and were pulling the vessel across: when halfway, just as we thought ourselves in safety, the cable broke, the pinnace whirled round and round like a bubble on the waters and was carried with fearful velocity down the stream. The *sarang* lost all power over the vessel but, at last, her progress was stopped by being brought up fast on a sandbank. By dint of hard work we once more got the cable fastened to the opposite shore and carried her safely to the other side: where, to my great delight, we anchored to await the decrease of the wind that howled through the ropes as though it would tear them from the masts.

Thinking the vessel must have received a violent strain under all the force she had endured, we opened the hold and found she had sprung a leak that bubbled up at a frightful rate; the leak was under planks it was impossible to remove, unless by sawing off two feet from three large planks, if we could procure a saw; such a thing could not be found. I thought of a razor, the orthodox weapon wherewith to saw through six-inch boards and get out of prison; no one would bring forward a razor. At length I remembered the very small, fine saw I make use of for cutting the soapstone and, by very tender and gentle usage, we at length cut off the ends of the planks and laid open the head of the leak, under the rudder, below watermark. Here the rats and white ants had been very busy and had worked away undisturbed at a principal beam so that you could run your fingers some inches into it. With a very gentle hand the tow was stuffed in, but as we stopped the leak in one part, it sprang up in another; all day long we worked incessantly and at night, in despair, filled it up with stiff clay. I went to rest but my sleep was disturbed by dreams of water hissing in mine ears, and that we were going down stern foremost. During the night I called up the men three times to bale the vessel; she gave up quantities of water. We anchored off Mulgong.

January 5th – Detained by the strong and contrary wind; the leak still gave up water, but in a less quantity; and it was agreed to leave it in its present condition until we could get to Etawah. I was not quite comfortable, knowing the state of the rotten wood and the holes the rats had made, through which the water had bubbled up so fast. The next day, not one drop of water came from the leak and the vessel being quite right afterwards. I determined not to have her examined until our arrival at Agra and could never understand why she did not leak.

January 9th – Ever since the 4th we have had the most violent and contrary winds all day; obliged generally to anchor for two hours at noon, it being impossible to stem the stream and struggle against the wind; most disagreeable work; I am quite tired and sick of it. Thus far I have borne all with the patience of a Hindu, the wish to behold the Tāj carrying me on. It is so cold, my hand shakes, I can scarcely guide my pen; the thermometer 50° at ten o'clock this morning with this bitter and strong wind. I dare not light a fire, as I take cold quitting it to go on deck; all the glass windows are closed – I have on a pair of Indian shawls, snow boots, and a velvet cap – still my face and head throb with rheumatism. When on deck, at midday, I wear a *sola topi*, to defend me from the sun.

This river is very picturesque; high cliffs, well covered with wood, rising abruptly from the water: here and there a Hindu temple, with a great peepal tree spreading its fine green branches around it: a ruined native fort: clusters of native huts: beautiful stone *ghāts* jutting into the river: the effect greatly increased by the native women, in their picturesque drapery, carrying their vessels for water up and down the cliffs, poised on their heads. Fishermen are seen with their large nets; and droves of goats and small cows, buffaloes and peacocks come to the riverside to feed. But the most picturesque of all are the different sorts of native vessels; I am quite charmed with the boats. Oh that I were a painter, who could do justice to the scenery! My pinnace, a beautiful vessel so unlike anything else here, must add beauty to the river, especially when under sail.

Aground on a sandbank again! With such a wind and stream it is not pleasant – hardly safe. What a noise! Attempting to force her off the bank; it is terribly hard work; the men, up to their waists in water, are shoving the vessel with their backs whilst the wind and stream throw her back again. Some call on Allah for aid, some on Ganges, some on Jumna-ji, every man shouting at the height of his voice. What a squall! the vessel lies over frightfully. I wish the wind would abate! Forced sideways down on the sandbank by the wind and stream, it is not pleasant. There! There is a howl that ought to succeed in forcing her off; in spite of the *tufān*; such clouds of fine sand blowing about in every direction! Now the vessel rocks, now we are off once more – back we are again! I fancy the wind and stream will have their own way. Patience, memsāhib, you are only eight miles from Etawah: when you may get over those eight miles may be a difficult calculation. The men are fagging, up to their breasts in the river; I must go on deck and make a speech. What a scene! I may now consider myself really in the wilderness, such watery *wastes* are spread before me!

The Memsāhib's speech

'Ari! Ari! What a day is this! Ahi Khudā! What a wind is here! Is not this a *tufān*? Such an ill-starred river never, never did I see! Every moment, every moment, we are on a sandbank. Come, my children, let her remain; it is the will of God – what can we do? Eat your food and when the gale lulls we may get off. Perhaps, by the blessing of God, in twelve months' time we may reach Etawah.'

After this specimen of eloquence, literally translated from the Hindustani in which it was spoken, the *dāndis* gladly wrapped their blankets round them and crept into corners out of the wind to eat *chabeni*, the parched grain of Indian corn, maize. Could you but see the men whom I term my children! They are just what in my youth I ever pictured to myself cannibals must be, so wild and strange-looking, their long, black, shaggy hair matted over their heads and hanging down to their shoulders; their bodies of dark brown, entirely naked with the exception of a cloth round the waist, which passes between the limbs. They jump overboard and swim ashore with a rope between their teeth and their towing-stick in one hand, just like dogs – river dogs; the water is their element more than the land. If they want any clothes on shore they carry them on the top of their heads and swim to the bank in that fashion. The memsāhib's river dogs; they do not drink strong waters; and when I wish to delight them very much, I give them two or three rupees' worth of sweetmeats, cakes of sugar and *ghee* made in the bazaar; like great babies, they are charmed with their *meetai*, as they call it, and work away willingly for a memsāhib who makes presents of sweetmeats and kids.

Saw the first wolf today; I wish we were at Etawah – to anchor here is detestable: if we were there I should be reading my letters and getting in supplies for Agra. How I long to reach the goal of my pilgrimage, and to make my salām to the *Tāj bibi ke rauza*, the mausoleum of the lady of the Tāj!

CHAPTER XXIX

Pilgrimage to the Tāj

HE WHO HAS NOT PATIENCE POSSESSES NOT PHILOSOPHY
WHETHER DOING, SUFFERING, OR FORBEARING,
YOU MAY DO MIRACLES BY PERSEVERING

JANUARY 10TH 1835 – Ours is the slowest possible progress; the wind seems engaged to meet us at every turn of our route. At three o'clock we *lugoed* at Etawah; while I was admiring the *ghāts*, to my great delight a handful of letters and parcels of many kinds were brought to me. In the evening, the *chaprāsi* in charge of my riding horses, with the *sā'ises* and grass-cutters who had marched from Allahabad to meet me, arrived at the *ghāt*. The grey neighed furiously as if in welcome; how glad I was to see them!

In a minute I was on the little black horse; away we went, the black so glad to have a canter, the memsāhib so happy to give him one: through deep ravines, over a road through the dry bed of a torrent, up steep cliffs; away we went like creatures possessed; the horse and rider were a happy pair. After a canter of about four miles it became dark, or rather moonlight, and I turned my horse towards the river, guided by the sight of a great cliff, some one hundred and fifty to two hundred feet high, beneath which we had anchored. I lost my way, but turned down a bridle road in the bed of a ravine, which of course led somewhere to the river. I rode under a cliff so high and overhanging I felt afraid to speak; at last we got out of the cold and dark ravine and came directly upon the pinnace. I had met, during my ride, two gentlemen in a buggy; one of them, after having arrived at his own house, returned to look for me, thinking I might turn down by mistake the very road I had gone, which at night was very unsafe on account of the wolves; but he did not overtake me.

The next morning he called on me and brought me a letter from a relative; therefore we were soon acquainted and agreed to have a canter when the sun should go down. He told me, on his way down the police had brought him a basket, containing half the mangled body of a child; the wolves had seized the poor child and had devoured the other half the night before, in the ravines. It was fortunate I did not encounter a gang of them under the dark cliff, where the black horse could scarcely pick his way over the stones.

January 11th – I rode with Mr G— through the ravines and the Civil Station, and saw many beautiful and picturesque spots. We returned to the pinnace; he came on board and we had a long conference. It was not to be marvelled at that the memsāhib talked a great deal, when it is considered she had not spoken one word of English for thirty-three days; then she did talk! – ye gods! How she did talk! Mr G— offered to send armed men with me if I felt afraid, but I declined taking them; and he promised to forward my letters by horsemen every day to meet the pinnace. Nothing can be greater than the kindness one meets with from utter strangers in India. He gave my husband and me an invitation to pay him a visit on our way back, which I accepted for the absent sāhib.

I was amused by an officer's coming down to the river which he crossed; he then mounted a camel and his servant another; he carried nothing with him but some bedding, that served as a saddle, and a violin! In this fashion he had come down from Sabbatoo, and was going, via Jabalpur, across to Bombay! Thence to sail for England. How charmingly independent! It is unusual for a gentleman to ride a camel; those who *understand* the motion, a long, swinging, trot, say it is pleasant; others complain it makes the back ache, and brings on a pain in the liver. At Etawah everything was to be had that I wished for; peacocks, partridges, fowls, pigeons, beet were brought for sale; *atr* of roses, peacocks' feathers, milk, bread, green tea, sauces; in short, food of every sort. I read and answered my letters and retired to rest perfectly fagged.

January 12th – At daybreak the pinnace started once more for Agra, once more resumed her pilgrimage; it is seventy-two miles by the road from Etawah; how far it may be by this twisting and winding river remains to be proved. For some days two bird-catchers (*chiri-mārs*) have followed the pinnace and have supplied me with peacocks; today they brought a hen and three young ones; they also brought their nets and the snares with them, which I had seen them use on shore. The springs are beautifully made of buffalo-horn and catgut. I bought one hundred and six springs for catching peacocks, cyrus, wild ducks, etc. for four rupees, and shall set them in the first jungle we meet. I set them immediately in the cabin and caught my own two dogs: it was laughable to see the dismay of the dogs, nor could I help laughing at my own folly in being such a child. My head began to throb bitterly and I spent the rest of the day ill in bed.

January 13th – At eight o'clock the thermometer was 46°, by one o'clock 66°, a great difference in five hours. The peacocks, in the evening, were calling from the cliffs and came down to feed by the riverside, looking beautiful; there were four male birds on one spot, quite fearless, not taking any notice of the men on the *goon*. Anchored at Purrier.

January 16th – A good day's tracking; no obstacles; good water, i.e. deep water; anchored late at Dedowlee ke Nuggra.

January 17th – Found a bar of sand directly across the river; about fourteen enormous boats all aground; numbers of vessels arriving hourly; every one going aground, as close as they could lie together; in the midst of the bar was one vessel which had been there four days. The *sarang* of the pinnace came to me and said, 'Until that salt-boat gets off we cannot move; in all probability, we shall be utterly unable to cross the bar.' The whole day, in the dinghy, did the men sound the river; in the evening I went with them to see and satisfy myself of the impossibility of crossing; even the dinghy grounded; where, then, could the pinnace find water?

I determined to send on the servants, the baggage and food in the flat-bottomed cook-boat, to Agra; to write for a *dāk* for myself; and to remain quietly in the pinnace, until its arrival: went to bed out of spirits at the unlucky accident of the bar across the river. In the morning, hearing a great noise, I went on deck; the salt-boat was gone, all the vessels but one were off; and the crew were preparing to pull the pinnace by main force through the bar of sand; remembering the leak, I viewed these preparations with anxiety that leak being only stopped with mud and towels. They pulled her into the place from which the salt-boat had at last extricated herself; a little more exertion and the pretty *Seagull* slipped and slid out of the sandbank into deep water. Such a shout as arose from the crew! We shall see the *Tāj bibi ke Rauza*: it is our destiny; the memsāhib's fate (*kismat*) is good: to be sure, what a number of rupees has not the memsāhib spent on the pinnace! Her luck is good; this her pilgrimage will be accomplished; and the sāhib will be pleased also!'

And the memsāhib was pleased; for we had got over a bar in half an hour, that, the night before, we calculated might take two or three days to cross, with great risk to the vessel. I had determined to give up attempting to take the *Seagull* further, not liking the chance of straining the timbers so severely, the vessel not being a newly-built one. 'Once more upon the waters!' Thank God, we are not upon the sand!

An acquaintance, the Hon. Mrs R—, has just arrived at Allahabad from England; nothing could exceed her astonishment when she heard I had gone up the Jumna alone, on a pilgrimage of perhaps two months or more to see the Tāj, not forced to make the voyage from necessity. I have books and employments of various sorts to beguile the loneliness; and the adventures I meet with give variety and interest to the monotony of life on the river. Could I follow my own inclinations I would proceed to Delhi, thence to the Hills, and on to the source of the Jumna; this would really be a good undertaking. *Capt.*

Skinner's Travels, which I have just read, have given me the most ardent desire to go to the source of the Jumna.

January 18th – Stags, of the *chicara* sort with small straight horns, come down to drink by the riverside. Wild geese and cyrus are in flocks on the sandbanks. A slight but favourable breeze has sprung up, we are going gently and pleasantly before it. Narangee *ghāt* – what a beautiful scene! The river was turned from its channel by the Rajah Buddun Sing, and directed through a pass, cut straight through a very high cliff: the cut is sharp and steep; the cliffs abrupt and bold; some trees; native huts; a temple in the distance; numbers of boats floating down the stream, through the pass; the pinnace and *pateli* in full sail, going up it; ferryboats and passengers; cows and buffaloes swimming the ferry; a little beyond, before the white temple on a sandbank, are six great crocodiles, basking in the sun. Am I not pleased? One of the fairest views I have seen: what a contrast to yesterday, when my eyes only encountered the sand-bank and the fixture of a salt-boat, our particular enemy! Anchored at Hurrier; fagged and ill from over-exertion.

January 19th – We arrived at the city of Betaizor, which is built across the bed where the Jumna formerly flowed. The Rajah Buddun Sing built his *ghāt*, and very beautiful it is; a perfect crowd of beautiful Hindu temples clustered together, each a picture in itself, and the whole reflected in the bright pure waters of the Jumna. I stopped there for an hour to sketch the *ghāt*, and walked on the sands opposite, charmed with the scene – the high cliffs, the trees; no Europeans are there – a place is spoiled by European residence. In the evening we anchored off the little village of Kheil: rambling on the river's bank, I saw five peacocks in the silk-cotton tree (*shimoul*), and called Jinghoo Bearer, who ran off to fetch a matchlock which he loaded with *two* bullets; the birds were so unmolested they showed no fear when I went under the tree with the dogs, and only flew away when Jinghoo fired at them; the report aroused two more peacocks from the next tree; a flock of wild geese and another of wild duck, sprang up from the sands; and the solitary *chakwā* screamed āw! āw! The *shimoul* is a fine high spreading tree, the flower a brilliant one; and the pod contains a sort of silky down, with which mattresses and pillows are often stuffed. The natives object to pillows stuffed with silk-cotton, saying it makes the head ache. The large silk-cotton tree (*Bombax ceiba*) is the seat of the gods who superintend districts and villages; these gods, although minor deities, are greatly feared. *Panchayats*, or native courts of justice, are held beneath the *shimoul*, under the eye of the deity in the branches. There are fields of the common white cotton plant (*Gossypium herbaceum*), on the side of the river; the cotton has just been gathered; a few pods, bursting with snowy down, are hanging here and there, the leavings of the cotton harvest: the plant is an annual. In my garden at Prāg are numerous specimens of the Bourbon cotton, remarkably fine, the down of which is of a brown colour.

I have met hundreds of enormous boats laden with cotton, going down to Calcutta and other parts of the country; they are most remarkably picturesque. I said the report startled the solitary *chakwā*. The *chakwā* is a large sort of reddish-brown wild duck (*Anas caesarca*), very remarkable in its habits. You never see more than two of these birds together; during the day they are never separate – models of constancy; during the night they are invariably apart, always divided by the stream; the female bird flies to the other side of the river at night, remains there all solitary and in the morning returns to her mate, who during the livelong night has been sitting alone and crying āw! āw! The male calls āw! some ten or twelve times successively; at length the female gives a single response, '*nā'ich!*' Leaving the people, some cooking and some eating their dinners, I rambled on alone, as was my custom, to some distance from the boats, listening to and thinking of the *chakwā*. The first man who finished his meal was the *dhobee*, a Hindu, and he started forth to find me. I questioned him respecting the birds, and he spake as follows: 'When the beautiful Seeta was stolen away from the god Rām, he wandered all over the world seeking his love. He asked of the *chakwā* and his mate, "Where is Seeta, where is my love, have you seen her?" The *chakwā* made answer, "I am eating and attending to my own concerns; trouble me not, what do I know of Seeta?' Rām, angry at these words, replied, "Every night henceforth your love shall be taken from you and divided by a stream; *you* shall bemoan her loss the livelong night; during the day she shall be restored."

'He asked of the stars, "Where is Seeta?" the silent stars hid their beams. He asked of the forest, "Where is my beloved?" the forest moaned and sighed, and could give him no intelligence. He asked of the antelope, "Where is she whom I seek, the lost, the beloved?" The antelope replied, "My mate is gone, my heart is bowed with grief, my own cares oppress me. Her whom you seek mine eyes have not beheld." '

It is true the birds invariably live after this fashion. They are great favourites of mine, the *chakwās*; and I never hear their cry but I think of Seeta Rām.

[...]

January 23rd – I could scarcely close my eyes during the night for the cold, and yet my covering consisted of four Indian shawls, a *rezai* of quilted cotton, and a French blanket. A little pan of water having been put on deck, at eight o'clock the *ayah* brought it to me filled with ice. What fine strong ice they must be making at the pits, where every method to produce evaporation is adopted!

I am sitting by the fire for the first time. At eight o'clock the thermometer was 46°; by ten o'clock 54°. The *dāndis* complain bitterly of the cold. Thirteen men on the *goon* are fagging, up to their knees in water, against the stream in this cold wind; this twist in the river will, however, allow of half an hour's sail, and the poor creatures may then warm themselves. I will send each man a red Lascar's cap and a black blanket, their Indian bodies feel the cold so bitterly. When the sails are up my spirits rise; this tracking day by day against wind and stream so many hundred miles is tiresome work. My solitude is agreeable, but the tracking detestable. I must go on deck, there is a breeze, and enjoy the variety of having a sail. At Pukkaghur eight peacocks were by the riverside, where they had come for water; on our approach they moved gently away. They roost on the largest trees they can find at night. I have just desired three pints of oil to be given to the *dāndis*, that they may rub their limbs. The cold wind, and being constantly in and out of the water, makes their skin split, although it is like the hide of the rhinoceros; they do not suffer so much when their legs have been well rubbed with oil. What a noise the men are making! They are all sitting on the deck whilst a bearer, with a great jar of oil, is doling out a *chhāttak* to each shivering *dāndi*.

[...]

January 25th – Was there ever anything so provoking! We are fast in the centre of a sandbank, cutting through it on a chain-cable: it will take the whole day to get through it – perhaps a day or two. There is a fine favourable wind, the first we have had for ages, and we should be at Agra by sunset could we cross this vile sandbank. I go on deck every now and then to see the progress: we advance about *one yard* in an hour! Then we leave off work, the stream loosens the sand, and the work begins again until another yard is accomplished, and then we wait for the stream. It is sadly tiresome work: however, the wind is a warm one, and we have only to contend with the stream and the sandbank.

From seven in the morning till three in the afternoon we worked away on the bank; at last we cut through into deep water. I was delighted to see a *chaprāsi* from Agra, with a packet of letters for me. How little did the dear ones in England imagine their letters would find me all alone in my beautiful pinnace, fast stuck in a sandbank in the middle of the Jumna!

January 26th – This morning from the cliff the white marble dome of the Tāj could just be discerned, and we made salam to it with great pleasure. The pinnace anchored below Kutoobpoor, unable to proceed in consequence of another great sandbank, a quarter of a mile broad. The *sarang* says, 'To attempt to cut through this on a chain-cable would draw every bolt and nail out of her frame.' The Ghāt Mānjhī is of the same opinion. I have been out in the dinghy sounding and, fearless as I am, I dare not attempt cutting through such a bank; it would injure the vessel. There are two more sandbanks besides this ahead. It is folly to injure the pinnace and I have made up my mind to quit her. Is it not provoking, only sixteen miles from Agra, and to be detained here? I have written to the Hon. H. D— to request him to send down my horses; they must have arrived long ago, and a palanquin: his answer I must await with due patience. What a pity I am not a shot! I saw three deer yesterday whilst I was amusing myself in an original fashion, digging porcupines out of their holes, or rather trying to do so for the dogs found the holes; but the men could not get the animals out of them. Picked up a *chilamchi* full of river-shells. Before us are thirteen large boats aground on this sandbank. In the evening I took a long walk to see the state of another shallow ahead, which they say is worse than the one we are off. Six of the great cotton boats have cut through the sand; perhaps they will deepen the channel and we shall be able to pass on tomorrow. There are peacocks in the fields: what a pity my husband is not here, or that I am not a shot!

January 27th – Not being satisfied to quit the pinnace without having inspected the river myself, I went up to Bissowna in the *pateli* this morning and found it would be utter folly to think of taking the *Seagull* further; besides which, it is impossible. I might upset her, but to get her across a bank half a mile in length is out of the question. The water in the deepest parts is only as high as a man's knee and she requires it up to the hipbone. It is very provoking. I am tired of this vile jungle – nothing to look at but the vessels aground; besides which the noise is eternal, night and day, from the shouts of the men trying to force their boats off the sand into deeper water.

January 28th – My riding horses having arrived, I quitted the pinnace, desiring the *sarang* to return to Dharu-ke-Nuggeria, and await further orders.

I sent off the cook-boat and attendants to Agra, and taking my little pet terrier in my arms cantered off on the black horse to meet the palanquin a friend had sent for me. Late at night I arrived at Agra, found a tent that had been pitched for me within the enclosure of the Tāj, in front of the Kālūn Dāwāzā or great gateway, and congratulated myself on having at length accomplished the pilgrimage in a voyage up the Jumna of fifty-one days! Over-exertion brought on illness, and severe pains in my head laid me up for several days.

CHAPTER XXX

THE TĀJ MAHAL

I have paid two visits to Agra since I returned from Lucknow and thought of you and the sāhib whilst admiring the Tāj. Do not, for the sake of all that is elegant, think of going home without paying it a visit. I shall, with great delight, be your cicerone in these regions: if you put it off much longer (if alive), I shall scarce be able to crawl with old age. Do not think of quitting India; it is a country far preferable to the cold climate, and still colder hearts of Europe.   W. L. G., *Khasganj*

JANUARY 1835 – I have seen the Tāj Mahal; but how shall describe its loveliness? Its unearthly style of beauty! It is not its magnitude; but its elegance, its proportions, its exquisite workmanship, and the extreme delicacy of the whole, that render it the admiration of the world. The tomb, a fine building of white marble erected upwards of two centuries ago, is still in a most wonderful state of preservation, as pure and delicate as when first erected. The veins of grey in the marble give it a sort of pearl-like tint that adds to, rather than diminishes, its beauty. It stands on a square terrace of white marble, on each angle of which is a minaret of the same material. The whole is carved externally and internally, and inlaid with ornaments formed of blood-stones, agates, lapis lazuli, etc. etc. representing natural flowers. The inscriptions over all the arches are in the Arabic character, in black marble, inlaid on white. The dome itself, the four smaller domes and the cupolas on the roof, are all of the same white marble carved beautifully and inlaid with flowers in coloured stones.

The dome of the Tāj, like all domes erected by the Mohammedans, is egg-shaped, a form greatly admired; the dome in Hindu architecture is always semicircular; and it is difficult to determine to which style of building should be awarded the palm of beauty.

This magnificent monument was raised by Shāhjahān to the memory of his favourite Sultāna Arzumund Bānoo on whom, when he ascended the throne, he bestowed the title of Momtāza Zumāni (the Most Exalted of the age).

On the death of Shāhjahān, his grandson Alumgeer placed his cenotaph in the Tāj, on the right hand and close to that of Arzumund Bānoo; this is rather a disfigurement, as the building was intended alone for the Lady of the Tāj, whose cenotaph rests in the centre. Formerly, a screen of silver and gold surrounded it; but when Alumgeer erected the tomb of Shāhjahān by the side of that of the Sultana, he removed the screen of gold and silver, and replaced it by an octagonal marble screen, which occupies about half the diameter of the building and encloses the tombs. The open fretwork and mosaic of this screen are most beautiful: each side is divided into three panels, pierced and carved with a delicacy equal to the finest carving in ivory; and bordered with wreaths of flowers inlaid of agate, bloodstone, cornelian, and every variety of pebble. I had the curiosity to count the number contained in one of the flowers and found there were seventy-two; there are fifty flowers of the same pattern. The cenotaphs themselves are inlaid in the same manner; I never saw anything so elegant; the tombs, to be properly appreciated, must be seen, as all the native drawings make them exceedingly gaudy which they are not. The inscriptions on both are of black marble inlaid on white, ornamented with mosaic flowers of precious stones.

The first glance on entering is imposing in the extreme: the dim religious light, the solemn echoes – at first I imagined that priests in the chambers above were offering up prayers for the soul of the departed, and the echo was the murmur of the requiem. When many persons spoke together it was like thunder – such a volume of powerful sounds; the natives compare it to the roar of many elephants. 'Whatever you say to a dome it says to you again.' A prayer repeated over the tomb is echoed and re-echoed above like the peal of an organ, or the distant and solemn chant in a cathedral.

Each arch has a window, the frames of marble, with little panes of glass about three inches square. Underneath the cenotaphs is a vaulted apartment where the remains of the Emperor and the Sultana are buried in two sarcophagi, facsimiles of the cenotaphs above. The crypt is square and of plain marble; the tombs here are also beautifully inlaid, but sadly defaced in parts by plunderers. The small door by which you enter was formerly of solid silver: it is now formed of rough planks of mango wood.

It is customary with Musulmāns to erect the cenotaph in an apartment over the sarcophagus, as may be seen in all the tombs of their celebrated men. The Musulmāns who visit the Tāj lay offerings of money and flowers both on the tombs below and the cenotaphs above; they also distribute money in charity, at the tomb, or at the gate, to the *fakīrs*.

The Sultāna Arzumund Bānoo was the daughter of the vizier, Asaf-jāh; she was married twenty years to Shāhjahān and bore him a child almost every year; she died on the 15th July, 1631, in child-bed, about two hours after the birth of a princess. Though she seldom interfered in public affairs, Shāhjahān owed the empire to her influence with her father: nor was he ungrateful; he loved her living, and lamented her when dead. Calm, engaging and mild in her disposition, she engrossed his whole affection; and though he maintained a number of women for state, they were only the slaves of her pleasure. She was such an enthusiast in Deism that she could scarcely forbear persecuting the Portuguese for their supposed idolatry, and it was only on what concerned that nation she suffered her temper, which was naturally placid, to be ruffled. To express his respect for her memory, the Emperor raised this tomb, which cost in building the amazing sum of £750,000 sterling. The death of the Sultana, in 1631, was followed by public calamities of various kinds. Four sons and four daughters survived her – Dara, Suja, Aurangzeb and Morâd: Aurangzeb succeeded to the throne of his father. The daughters were, the Princess Jahânārā (the Ornament of the World), Roshenrāi Begum (or the Princess of the Enlightened Mind), Suria Bânū (or the Splendid princess), and another whose name is not recorded. Arzumund Bānoo was the enemy of the Portuguese, then the most powerful European nation in India, in consequence of having accompanied Shāhjahān to one of their settlements, when she was enraged beyond measure against them for the worship they paid to images.

Such is the account given of the Most Exalted of the Age; but we have no record of her beauty, nor have we reason to suppose that she was beautiful. She was the niece of one of the most celebrated of women, the Sultana of Jahāngeer, whose titles were Mher-ul-nissa (the Sun of Women), Noor-māhul (the Light of the Empire), and Noorjahān (Light of the World).

Noorjahān was the sister of the Vizier Asaf-jāh and aunt to the lady of the Tāj. Many people, seeing the beauty of the building, confuse the two persons and bestow in their imaginations the beauty of the aunt on the niece. Looking on the tomb of Shāhjahān, one cannot but remember that, either by the dagger or the bowstring, he dispatched all the males of the house of Timur so that he himself and his children only remained of the posterity of Baber, who conquered India.

In former times no Musulmān was allowed to enter the Tāj but with a bandage over his eyes, which was removed at the grave where he made his offerings. The marble floor was covered with three carpets, on which the feet sank deeply, they were so soft and full. Screens (*pardas*) of silk, of fine and beautiful materials, were hung between all the arches. Chandeliers of crystal, set with precious stones, hung from the ceiling of the dome. There was also one chandelier of agate and another of silver: these were carried off by the Jāt Suruj Mul, who came from the Deccan and despoiled Agra.

It was the intention of Shāhjahān to have erected a mausoleum for himself exactly similar to the Tāj on the opposite side of the river; and the two buildings were to have been united by a bridge of marble across the Jumna. The idea was magnificent; but the death of Shāhjahān took place in 1666, while he was a prisoner, and ere he had time to complete his own monument.

The stones were prepared on the opposite side of the Jumna, and were carried off by the Burtpoor Rajah and a building at Deeg has been formed of those stones. A part of the foundation of the second Tāj is still standing, just opposite the Tāj Mahal.

An immense space of ground is enclosed by a magnificent wall around the Tāj, and contains a number of elegant buildings, surrounded by fine old trees and beds of the most beautiful flowers; the wall itself is remarkable, of great height, of red stone and carved both inside and outside.

The Kalān Darwāza, or great gateway, is a line building; the four large and twenty-two smaller domes over the top of the arched entrance are of white marble; the gateway is of red granite, ornamented with white marble, inlaid with precious stones.

From the second story is a fine view of the Tāj itself, to which it is directly opposite. I sat in this superb gateway some time, looking at the *darwān*'s snakes; he keeps, as pets, cobra de capellos, caught in the gardens of the Tāj. There are four rooms in this gateway, in which strangers, who are visitors, sometimes live during the hot weather

A long line of eighty-four fountains runs up through the centre of the garden from this gateway to the tomb itself, eighty of which are in perfect order. Twenty-two play in the centre of the garden; ten are on the sides of the tomb in the courts before the Masjids, and the rest run up in the line from the gate to the tomb. The water is brought across a fine aqueduct from the Jumna. Of an evening, when the fountains are playing, and the odour of exotic flowers is on the air, the fall of the water has a delightful effect both on the eye and ear: it is really an Indian paradise.

February 1st – A fair, the *melā* of the Eed, was held without the great gateway; crowds of gaily-dressed and most picturesque natives were seen in all directions passing through the avenue of fine trees and by the side of the fountains to the tomb: they added great beauty to the scene, whilst the eye of taste turned away pained and annoyed by the vile round hats and stiff attire of the European gentlemen, and the equally ugly bonnets and stiff and graceless dresses of the English ladies. Besides the *melā* at the time of the Eed, a small fair is held every Sunday evening beyond the gates; the fountains play, the band is sent down occasionally, and the people roam about the beautiful garden, in which some of the trees are very large and must be very ancient.

A thunderbolt has broken a piece of marble off the dome of the Tāj. They say during the same storm another bolt fell on the Mootee Masjid in the Fort, and another on the Jamma Masjid at Delhi.

The gardens are kept in fine order; the produce in fruit is very valuable. A great number of persons are in attendance upon, and in charge of, the tomb, the buildings and the garden, on account of the Honourable Company, who also keep up the repairs of the Tāj.

At this season the variety of flowers is not very great; during the rains the flowers must be in high perfection. The *mālī* always presents me with a bouquet on my entering the garden, and generally points out to my notice the wallflower as of my country, and not a native of India.

All the buildings in the gardens on the right are fitted up for the reception of visitors, if strangers: they are too cold at this time of the year, or I would take up my abode in one of the beautiful turrets (*burj*) next to the river.

The two *jāmma khānas* are beautiful buildings on each side of the tomb, of red stone, carved outside and ornamented with white marble and precious stones. One of them is a *masjid*: the domes are of white marble; the interior is ornamented with flowers in white *chūna* and carved red stone. One of the *burj* near the *masjid* contains a fine well (*bā'olī*). The four *burj* at each corner of the enclosure are of the most beautiful architecture, light and graceful; they are of the same fine red stone and the domes are of white marble. From the one generally used as a residence by visitors to the tomb, the view of the Tāj, the gardens, the river and the Fort of Agra beyond is very fine. During the rains the river rises and flows against the outer wall that surrounds the gardens. The view from the river of this frost-work building, the tomb, is beautiful: the fine trees at the back of it, the reflection of its marble walls, and of the two *jāmma khānas*, with that of the elegant bastions or towers in the stream is very lovely.

The fretwork appearance of the Tāj is produced by the quantity of carving on the white marble, which is also ornamented externally with inlaid Arabic characters and precious stones worked into flowers around the arches and the domes. The marble is cleaned every year and kept in a state of perfect purity and repair. Constant attention is requisite to remove the grass and young trees that shoot forth in any moist crevice: the birds carry the seeds of the peepal tree to the roof, and the young trees shoot forth, injuring those buildings that are in repair while they impart great beauty to ruins.

Beyond the Great Gate, but still within the enclosure of the outer wall of the Tāj are the tombs of two *begums*, erected by Shāhjahān. The sarcophagus over the remains of the Fatehpuri Begum is of white marble, carved very beautifully: its pure white marble, without any inlaid work or mosaic, is particularly to be admired. The building which contains it is of the lightest and most beautiful architecture and of carved, red stone; the dome of plain white marble.

On the other side the enclosure, to correspond with this tomb, is that of the Akbarābādee Begum. The building of red carved stone, the dome of white marble; the floor and the sides of the apartment that contains the sarcophagus are of white marble. The latter is beautifully inlaid with precious stones. On the top of the upper slab is a sort of royal coronet of precious stones, inlaid on the marble.

Both these tombs are in tolerable preservation from being within the enclosure of the walls of the Tāj.

In speaking of the red-stone of which the buildings are formed, let it not be supposed it is of a red like the flaming and varnished red in the pictures by the native artists. The red granite is of a sober and dingy reddish colour, and looks very handsome in buildings; the stones are very large, and generally beautifully carved; they are of three sorts: the first is of pure red granite, the second mottled with white spots and the third sort streaked with white; all very handsome in architecture. I brought away a bit of the fallen ornament of red granite from the tomb of the Akbarābādee Begum as a specimen. The same granite is in quantities in the quarries at Fatehpur Sikri. The buildings in the old city of Agra are of the same material and some of them, which must be very ancient, are of this highly-carved red freestone.

I laid an offering of rupees and roses on the cenotaph of Arzumund Banoo, which purchased me favour in the eyes of the attendants. They are very civil and bring me bouquets of beautiful flowers. I have stolen away many times alone to wander during the evening in the beautiful garden which surrounds it. The other day, long after the usual hour, they allowed the fountains to play until I quitted the gardens.

Can you imagine anything so detestable? European ladies and gentlemen have the band to play on the marble terrace, and dance quadrilles in front of the tomb! It was over the parapet of this terrace a lady fell a few months ago, the depth of twenty feet, to the inlaid pavement below. Her husband beheld this dreadful accident from the top of the minaret he had just ascended.

I cannot enter the Tāj without feelings of deep devotion: the sacredness of the place, the remembrance of the fallen grandeur of the family of the Emperor and that of Asaf Jāh, the father of Arzumund Banoo, the solemn echoes, the dim light, the beautiful architecture, the exquisite finish and delicacy of the whole, the deep devotion with which the natives prostrate themselves when they make their offerings of money and flowers at the tomb, all produce deep and sacred feelings; and I could no more jest or indulge in levity beneath the dome of the Tāj, than I could in my prayers.

[…]

The erection of the Tāj was the most delicate and elegant tribute and the highest compliment ever paid to woman.

And now adieu! – beautiful Tāj – adieu! In the far, far West I shall rejoice that I have gazed upon your beauty; nor will the memory depart until the lowly tomb of an English gentlewoman closes on my remains.

CHAPTER XXXI

PLEASANT DAYS AT AGRA

[...]

FEBRUARY 3RD 1835 – The palace in the Fort contains magnificent buildings, which are all of white marble, and were erected by Shāhjahān. The *denāni-khas* or hall of private audience, is a noble structure; the arches are beautiful; so is the building, which is of the same material, inlaid with coloured stones. In the interior, the roof and sides are beautifully and delicately ornamented with the representations of various flowers, beautifully combined, and formed of precious stones; the whole of the ornaments are also richly gilt. The apartments of the *zenāna*, which adjoin this building, are of white marble, exquisitely carved and inlaid with precious stones, in the style of the mosaic work at the Tāj. These apartments were converted into a prison for Shāhjahān, during the latter part of his reign. The central room is a fountain which plays in and also falls into a basin of white marble inlaid with the most beautiful designs, so that the water appears to fall upon brilliant flowers.

The Noorjahān *burj*, or turret of Noorjahān, is of the same exquisitely carved marble, inlaid in a similar manner. In an apartment on the opposite side of the court the same style is preserved; the water here falls over an inlaid marble slab, which is placed slanting in the side of the wall and, being caught, springs up in a fountain.

Some wretches of European officers – to their disgrace be it said – made this beautiful room a cook-room! and the ceiling, the fine marbles and the inlaid work, are all one mass of blackness and defilement! Perhaps they cooked the *sū'ar*, the hog, the unclean beast, within the sleeping apartments of Noorjahān – the proud, the beautiful Sultana!

In this turret I took refuge for some time from the heat of the noonday sun. What visions of former times passed through my brain! How I pictured to myself the beautiful Empress, until her portrait was clear and well defined in my imagination: still, it bore an European impress. I had never entered the private apartments of any native lady of rank and I longed to behold one of those women of whose beauty I had heard so much; I had seen two paintings of native women, who were very beautiful; but the very fact that these women had been beheld by European gentlemen degraded them to a class respecting which

I had no curiosity. I was now in the deserted *zenāna* of the most beautiful woman recorded in history; and one whose talents and whose power over the Emperor made her, in fact, the actual sovereign; she governed the empire from behind the *parda*. The descendants of Jahāngeer, in their fallen greatness, were still at Delhi; and I determined, if possible, to visit the ladies of the royal *zenāna* now in existence.

The *zenāna masjid*, a gem of beauty, is a small mosque, sacred to the ladies of the *zenāna*, of pure white marble, beautifully carved, with three domes of the same white marble.

[...]

I have just returned from an expedition that has taken a marvellous hold of my fancy. Yesterday Mr C— said that if I would promise to pay the Shīsha-Mahal a visit, he would have it lighted up: the apartments are usually only lighted up to satisfy the curiosity of the Governor-General. I went with pleasure; the place was illuminated with hundreds of little lamps: there was not time to have the water raised from the river or we should have seen the effect of the sheets of water pouring over and beyond the rows of lights in the marble niches. After viewing the Shīsha-Mahal, the effect of which was not as good as I had imagined it would be, Mr C— asked me if I should like to see the apartments under ground in which the *pādshāh* and his family used to reside during the hot winds. We descended to view these *tykkanahs* and the steam-baths belonging to them. Thence we went by the aid of lighted torches to view a place that made me shudder. An officer examining these subterranean passages some time ago observed that he was within the *half* of a vault of an octagon shape, the other half was blocked up by a strong, but hastily formed wall. Tradition amongst the natives asserted that within the underground passages in the Fort, was a vault in which people had been hanged and buried, but no one could say where this vault was to be found.

The officer above-mentioned, with great toil and difficulty, cut through a wall *eight feet in thickness* and found himself in an inner vault of large dimensions, built of stone, with a high and arched roof. Across this roof was a thick and carved beam of wood with a hole in its centre and a hook, such as is used for hanging people. Below and directly under this hole in the beam, and in the centre of the vault, was a grave; this grave he opened and found the bangles (ornaments for the arms) of a woman. Such is the place I have just visited. My blood ran cold as I descended the steps, the torches burning dimly from the foulness of the air and I thought of the poor creatures who might have entered these dismal passages, never to revisit the light of day. I crept from the passage through the hole which had been opened in the thick wall and stood on the ransacked grave, or perhaps graves of secret murder. Close to this vault is another of similar appearance; the thickness of the wall has baffled the patience of some person who has attempted to cut through it; however, the officers who were with me this evening say they will open it, as well as a place which they suppose leads to passages under the city. An old sergeant who has been here thirty years says he once went through those passages, but the entrance has subsequently been bricked up and he cannot discover it: the place which it is supposed is the blocked-up entrance through which he passed will, they say, be opened tomorrow. Having seen this spot of secret murder and burial, I can believe any of the horrible histories recorded in the annals of the *pādshāhs*: only imagine the entrance having been blocked up by a wall eight feet in thickness!

Quitting the Fort, we drove to the Tāj: the moon was at the full, adding beauty to the beautiful; the Tāj looked like fairy frost-work, yet so stately and majestic. And this superb building – this wonder of the world – is the grave of a woman, whilst only a short distance from it is the vault of secret murder – the grave also of a woman! What a contrast! How different the destiny of those two beings! The grave of the unknown and murdered one only just discovered amidst the dismal subterraneous passages in the Fort: the grave of the other bright and pure and beautiful in the calm moonlight. The damp, unwholesome air of the vaults is still in my throat; we were some time exploring and hunting for the passage which, they say, leads to the temple of an Hindu who lives in the Tripolia; he will suffer no one to enter his temple and declares the devil is there *in propria persona*.

When I retired to rest on my *chārpāi*, I found it difficult to drive away the fancies that surrounded me.

The walls of the Fort, and those buildings within it that are of carved red freestone, were built by Akbar: the marble buildings were erected by Shāhjahān.

The seat of the *pādshāh* is an immense slab of black marble, the largest perhaps ever beheld; it was broken in two by an earthquake. A Burā Bahādur, (illustrious officer) from this throne of the *pādshāh*, exclaimed, 'I have come not to succeed Lord Auckland, but Akbar!' The convulsion of the earth that split in two the throne of black marble could not have astonished it more than this modest speech – Allāhu Akbar!

In front, and on the other side of the court, is the seat of the vizier; a slab of white marble. The seat on which the *pādshāh* used to sit to view the fights of the wild beasts in the court below is one of great beauty; the pillars and arches of the most elegant workmanship are beautifully carved; the whole plain and light.

The steam-baths are octagonal rooms below, with arched roofs; three of these rooms are of white marble, with inlaid marble pavements; and there is a fountain, from which hot water springs up from a marble basin. The baths in the apartments below the palace, which most probably belonged to the *zenāna*, were broken up by the Marquis of Hastings: he committed this sacrilege on the past to worship the rising sun; for he sent the most beautiful of the marble baths, with all its fretwork and inlaid flowers, to the Prince Regent, afterwards George IV.

Having thus destroyed the beauty of the baths of the palace, the remaining marble was afterwards sold on account of Government; most happily, the auction brought so small a sum it put a stop to further depredations.

At sunrise from the Bridge of Boats nothing can be more beautiful than the view up and down the river: there are an hundred domed bastions jutting out from the banks amid the gardens and residences of the nobles of former days: the Fort, with its marble buildings peeping over the ramparts; the custom house, and many other prominent objects, form a magnificent *tout ensemble*.

[*An entire chapter is omitted here*]

CHAPTER XXXII

Revelations of Life in the Zenāna

WHOEVER HATH GIVEN HIS HEART TO A BELOVED OBJECT, HATH
PUT HIS BEARD INTO THE HANDS OF ANOTHER

FEBRUARY 1835 – Khasganj, the residence of my friend Colonel
Gardner, is sixty miles from Agra: he wrote to me expressing a wish that I
should visit him and regretting he was too unwell to meet me at Agra and
conduct me to his house. I was delighted to accept the invitation, particularly
at this time, as he informed me a marriage was to take place in his family which
might interest me.

His granddaughter, Susan Gardner, was on the eve of marriage with one of
the princes of Delhi and he wished me to witness the ceremony. I was also
invited to pay a visit *en route* to his son, Mr James Gardner, who was married
to a niece of the reigning emperor, Akbar Shāh.

Was not this delightful? All my dreams in the Turret of Noor-mahal were to
be turned into reality. I was to have an opportunity of viewing life in the
zenāna, of seeing the native ladies of the East, women of high rank, in the
seclusion of their own apartments, in private life: and although the emperors
of Delhi have fallen from their high estate, they and their descendants are
nevertheless Timoorians and descendants of Akbar Shāh.

I know of no European lady but myself, with the exception of one, who has
ever had an opportunity of becoming intimate with native ladies of rank; and
as she had also an invitation to the wedding we agreed to go together.

February 21st – We started *dāk* for Kutchowra, the residence of Mr James
Gardner. This is not *that* Kutchowra which yearly used to bring such treasure
into the Company's coffers in boatloads of cotton; but that Kutchowra which
stopped and fought Lord Lake, and killed the famous Major Nairn of tiger-
killing memory.

We arrived at noon the next day; Mr James Gardner, whom I had never
seen before, received us with much pleasure; his countenance reminded me of
his father whom, in manner, he greatly resembled; he was dressed in handsome native attire, a costume he usually wore.

His grounds contain two houses; the outer one, in which he receives visitors and transacts business and the second, within four walls, which is sacred to the *begum*, and has its entrance guarded night and day.

Mr James Gardner married Nawāb Mulka Humanee Begum, the niece of the emperor Akbar Shāh and daughter of Mirza Sulimān Shekō (the brother of the present emperor), who lives at Agra.

I was taken to the *zenāna* gates when three very fine children, the two sons and a daughter of Mr James Gardner, and the princess in their gay native dresses of silk and satin embroidered in gold and silver, ran out to see the new arrival. They were elegant little creatures and gave promise of being remarkably handsome. I was surprised to see the little girl at liberty, but was informed that girls are not shut up until they are about six years old, until which time they are allowed to run about, play with the boys and enjoy their freedom. Quitting the palanquins, we walked across the court to the entrance of the *zenāna*; there we took off our shoes and left them, it being a point of etiquette not to appear in shoes in the presence of a superior; so much so, that Mr Gardner himself was never guilty of the indecorum of wearing shoes or slippers in the presence of his wife.

The *begum* was sitting on a *chārpāi* when we entered the apartment; when Mrs B— presented me as the friend of Colonel Gardner, she shook hands with me and said, 'How do you do, kurow?' – this was all the English she could speak. The *begum* appeared ill and languid: perhaps the languor was the effect of opium. I had heard so much of Mulka's wonderful beauty that I felt disappointed: her long black and shining hair, divided in front, hung down on both sides of her face as low as her bosom, while the rest of her hair, plaited behind, hung down her back in a long tail.

Her dress consisted of silk full trousers (*pājāmas*) over which she wore a pair of Indian shawls, and ornaments of jewellery were on her hands and arms. *En passant*, be it said that *ladies* in the East never wear petticoats, but full *pājāmas*: the *ayahs*, who attend on English ladies in the capacity of ladies' maids, wear the petticoat; but it is a sign of servitude, and only worn to satisfy the ideal delicacy of English ladies, who dislike to see a female servant without a petticoat. The moment an *ayah* quits her mistress and goes into her own house, she pulls off the petticoat as a useless encumbrance and appears in the native trousers which she always wears beneath it.

The room in which the *begum* received us was the one in which she usually slept; the floor was covered with a white cloth. She was sitting on a native bed (*chārpāi*); and as the natives never use furniture, of course there was none in the room.

Two or three female attendants stood by her side, fanning her with large feather fans; the others drove away the mosquitoes and flies with *chaunris* made of peacocks' feathers, which are appendages of royalty.

Some opium was brought to her; she took a great bit of it herself and put a small bit, the size of half a pea, into the mouth of each of her young children; she eats much opium daily and gives it to her children until they are about six years old.

Native ladies, when questioned on the subject, say 'It keeps them from taking cold; it is the custom; that is enough, it is the custom.'

If a native lady wishes to keep up her reputation for beauty, she should not allow herself to be seen under the effect of opium by daylight.

When the Princess dismissed us from her presence, she invited us to pay her a visit in the evening; Mrs B—, with whom she was very intimate and to whom she was very partial, said 'I trust, Mulka Begum, since we are to obey your commands and pay you a visit this evening, you will put on all your ornaments and make yourself look beautiful.' The *begum* laughed, and said she would do so. On our quitting the apartments, she exclaimed, 'Ah! you English ladies with your white faces, you run about where you will, like dolls, and are so happy!' From which speech I conjecture the princess dislikes the confinement of the four walls. She always spoke Urdū, the court language, which is Hindustani intermixed largely with Persian; her manners were very pleasing and very ladylike. So much for the first sight of the Princess Mulka Begum.

The history I heard in the *zenāna* is as follows: Mulka Begum, the wife of Mirza Selīm, the brother of Akbar Shāh, was on a visit to her sister, the beautiful Queen of Oude; his Majesty fell in love with Mulka and detained her against her will in the palace; Colonel Gardner, indignant at the conduct of the King, brought Mulka from Lucknow and placed her in his own *zenāna*, under the care of his own *begum*. Marriages are generally dependant on geographical position; the opportunity Mr James Gardner had of seeing the Princess, added to her extreme beauty and the romance of the affair, was more than he could withstand; he carried her off from the *zenāna*. Colonel Gardner was extremely angry and refused to see or communicate with his son; they lived in the jungle for nearly two years. One day, Mr James Gardner, who had tried every method to induce his father to be reconciled to him in vain, seeing him in a boat swam after him and vowed, unless Colonel Gardner would take him into the boat, he would perish: Colonel Gardner remained unmoved until, seeing his son exhausted and on the point of sinking, paternal feelings triumphed; he put forth his hand and saved him. 'Whatever a man does who is afflicted with love, he is to be excused for it.'

Durd ishk-e kushīdu'um ki m ' purs
Zahir hijree chush'du'um ki m ' purs.

Hum ne dil sunum ko dya
Phir kissee ko kya?

I have felt the pain of love, ask not of whom:
I have felt the pangs of absence, ask not of whom:

I have given my heart to my beloved,
What is that to another?

Mulka was divorced from Mirza Selīm and legally married to her present husband. We dined with Mr Gardner in the outer house; the dinner was of native dishes which were most excellent. During the repast, two dishes were sent over from the *begum*, in compliment to her guests, which I was particularly desired to taste as the Timoorian ladies pride themselves on their cookery and on particular occasions will superintend the making of the dishes themselves; these dishes were so very unlike, and so superior to any food I had ever tasted, that I never failed afterwards to partake of any dish when it was brought to me with the mysterious whisper, 'It came from within. It would be incorrect to say, 'The *begum* has sent it;' 'It came from within,' being perfectly understood by the initiated.

In the evening we returned to the *zenāna*,and were ushered into a long and large apartment, supported down the centre by eight double pillars of handsome native architecture. The floor of the room was covered with white cloth; several lamps of brass (*chirāgh-dāns*) were placed upon the ground, each stand holding, perhaps, one hundred small lamps. In the centre of the room a carpet was spread and upon that the *gaddī* and pillows for the *begum*; the *gaddī* or throne of the sovereign is a long round pillow which is placed behind the back for support, and two smaller at the sides for the knees; they are placed upon a small carpet of velvet, or cloth of gold (*kimkhwāb*); the whole richly embroidered and superbly fringed with gold. Seats of the same description, but plain and unornamented, were provided for the visitors. A short time after our arrival, Mulka Begum entered the room looking like a dazzling apparition; you could not see her face, she having drawn her *dupatta* (veil) over it; her movements were graceful and the magnificence and elegance of her drapery were surprising to the eye of a European.

She seated herself on the *gaddī* and throwing her *dupatta* partly off her face, conversed with us. How beautiful she looked! How very beautiful! Her animated countenance was constantly varying and her dark eyes struck fire when a joyous thought crossed her mind. The languor of the morning had disappeared; by lamplight she was a different creature; and I felt no surprise when I remembered the wondrous tales told by the men of the beauty of Eastern women. Mulka walks very gracefully and is as straight as an arrow. In Europe, how rarely – how very rarely does a woman walk gracefully! Bound up in stays, the body is as stiff as a lobster in its shell; that snake-like, undulating movement – the poetry of motion – is lost, destroyed by the stiffness of the waist and hip, which impedes the free movement of the limbs. A lady in European attire gives me the idea of a German mannikin; an Asiatic, in her flowing drapery, recalls the statues of antiquity.

I had heard of Mulka's beauty long ere I beheld her, and she was described to me as the loveliest creature in existence. Her eyes, which are very long, large and dark, are remarkably fine and appeared still larger from being darkened on the edges of the eyelids with *soorma*: natives compare the shape of a fine eye to a mango when cut open. Her forehead is very fine; her nose delicate and remarkably beautiful – so finely chiselled, her mouth appeared less beautiful, the lips being rather thin. According to the custom of married women in the East her teeth were blackened, and the inside of her lips also, with antimony (*missee*) which has a peculiarly disagreeable appearance to my eye and may therefore have made me think the lower part of her countenance less perfectly lovely than the upper: in the eye of a native, this application of *missee* adds to beauty. Her figure is tall and commanding; her hair jet black, very long and straight; her hands and arms are lovely! Very lovely.

On the cloth before Mulka were many glass dishes filled with sweetmeats, which were offered to the company, with tea and coffee, by her attendants. Mulka partook of the coffee; her *huqqa* was at her side, which she smoked now and then; she offered her own *huqqa* to me, as a mark of favour. A superior or equal has her *huqqa* in attendance, whilst the *bindah khāna* furnishes several for the inferior visitors. Mrs Valentine Gardner, the wife of Colonel Gardner's brother, was of the party; she lives with the *begum*.

Mulka's dress was extremely elegant, the most becoming attire imaginable. A Musulmān wears only four garments:

Firstly, the *angīya*: a bodice, which fits tight to the bosom and has short sleeves; it is made of silk gauze, profusely ornamented.

Secondly, the *kurtī*: a sort of loose body, without sleeves, which comes down to the hips; it is made of net, crêpe or gauze, and highly ornamented.

Thirdly, *pājāmas* of gold or crimson brocade, or richly-figured silk; made tight at the waist, but gradually expanding until they reach the feet, much after the fashion of a fan, where they measure eight yards eight inches! A gold border finishes the trouser.

Fourthly, the *dupatta*: which is the most graceful and purely feminine attire in the world; it is of white transparent gauze, embroidered with gold and trimmed with gold at the ends, which have also a deep fringe of gold and silver.

The *dupatta* is so transparent it hides not; it merely veils the form, adding beauty to the beautiful by its soft and cloudlike folds. The jewellery sparkles beneath it; and the outline of its drapery is continually changing according to the movements or coquetry of the wearer. Such was the attire of the Princess! Her head was covered with pearls and precious stones most gracefully arranged: from the throat to the waist was a succession of strings of large pearls and precious stones; her arms and hands were covered with armlets, bracelets, and rings innumerable. Her delicate and uncovered feet were each decorated with two large circular anklets composed of gold and precious stones and golden rings were on her toes. In her nose she wore a *n'hut*, a large thin gold ring, on which was strung two large pearls with a ruby between them. A nose-ring is a love token, and is always presented by the bridegroom to the bride. No single woman is allowed to wear one.

In her youth Mulka learned to read and write in Persian, but since her marriage has neglected it. Music is considered disgraceful for a lady of rank, dancing the same – such things are left to *nāch* women. Mulka made enquiries concerning the education of young ladies in England; and on hearing how many hours were devoted to the piano, singing, and dancing, she expressed her surprise, considering such *nāch*-like accomplishments degrading.

A native gentleman, describing the points of beauty in a woman, thus expressed himself: '*Barā barā nāk, barā barā ānkh, munh jaisa chānd, khūb bhāari aisa.*' A very very large nose, very very large eyes, a face like the moon; very very portly, thus! – stretching out his arms as if they could not at their fullest extent encircle the mass of beauty he was describing!

When a woman's movements are considered peculiarly graceful, it is often remarked, 'She walks like a goose, or a drunken elephant.'

Mr Gardner has a fine estate at Kutchowra, with an indigo plantation: his establishment is very large, and completely native. I imagine he is greatly assisted in the management of his estate by the advice of the *begum*: with the exception of this, she appears to have little to amuse her. Her women sit round her working and she gives directions for her dresses. Eating opium and sleeping appear to occupy much of her time. Sometimes her slaves will bring the small, silver cauldrons and cooking pots (*degchas* and *hāndis*) to her and, guided by her instructions, will prepare some highly-esteemed dish over charcoal in a little moveable fireplace, called an *angethi*.

Her husband, who is very proud of her, often speaks of her being a descendant of Timur the Tartar. Timurlane, as we call him, which is a corruption of Timurlung, or the lame Timur: he was a shepherd and as he sat on the mountain one day watching his flocks, a *fakir* came up who, striking him on the leg, said 'Arise, and be King of the World.' He did so, but was lame ever after from the blow. The Timoorians are remarkable for their long, large and fine eyes. English dresses are very unbecoming, both to Europeans and Asiatics. A Musulmān lady is a horror in an English dress; but an English woman is greatly improved by wearing a native one, the attire itself is so elegant, so feminine and so graceful.

Mr Gardner gave me a room within the four walls of the *zenāna*, which afforded me an excellent opportunity of seeing native life. At first the strong scent of *atr* of roses was quite overpowering, absolutely disagreeable, until I became reconciled to it by habit.

The Mohammedan, both male and female, are extremely fond of perfumes of every sort and description; and the quantity of *atr* of roses, *atr* of jasmine, *atr* of *khas-khas*, etc. that the ladies in a *zenāna* put upon their garments is quite overpowering.

The prophet approved of scents: 'Next to women he liked horses, and next to horses perfumes.' Ja'bir-bin-Samurah said, 'I performed noonday prayer with his majesty; after that, he came out of the *masjid*; and some children came before him and he rubbed their cheeks in a most kind manner with his blessed hand, one after another. Then his majesty touched my cheek and I smelt so sweet a smell from it, that you might say he had just taken it out of a pot of perfumes.'

Mulka Begum, and all the females in attendance on her, stained their hands and feet with *mehndi*. Ayesha said, 'Verily, a woman said, "O prophet of God! receive my obedience." He said, "I will not receive your profession until you alter the palms of your hands; that is, colour them with hinà; for without it one might say they were the hands of tearing animals." ' Aa'yeshah said, 'A woman from behind a curtain made a sign of having a letter; and his highness drew away his hand and said, "I do not know whether this is the hand of a man or a woman." The woman said, "It is a woman's." His Highness said, "Were you a woman, verily you would change the colour of your nails with hinà." '

To the slave girls I was myself an object of curiosity. They are never allowed to go beyond the four walls and the arrival of an English lady was a novelty. I could never dress myself but half a dozen were slily peeping in from every corner of the screens (*pardas*), and their astonishment at the number and shape of the garments worn by a European was unbounded!

Ladies of rank are accustomed to be put to sleep by a slave who relates some fairy tale. To be able to invent and relate some romantic or hobgoblin adventure in an agreeable manner is a valuable accomplishment. I have often heard the monotonous tone with which women of this description lulled the *begum* to sleep. To invent and relate stories and fables is the only employment of these persons. The male slaves put their masters to sleep in the same fashion.

Native beds (*chārpāi*) are about one foot high from the ground; people of rank have the feet of these couches covered with thick plates of gold or silver, which is handsomely embossed with flowers. A less expensive, but still a very pretty sort, are of Bareilly work, in coloured flowers; some are merely painted red, green, or yellow; and those used by the poor are of plain mango wood. From the highest to the lowest the shape is all the same, the difference is in the material and the workmanship. No posts, no curtains. The seat of the bed is formed of broad cotton tape (*newār*), skilfully interlaced, drawn up tight as a drum head, but perfectly elastic. It is the most luxurious couch imaginable, and a person accustomed to the *chārpāi* of India will spend many a restless night ere he can sleep with comfort on an English bed.

A Musulmān lady will marry an English gentleman, but she will not permit him to be present during the time of meals. Mr Gardner and Mulka have three children, two boys and a girl; they are remarkably handsome, intelligent children, and appeared as gay and happy as possible. They always wore rich native dresses – a most becoming style of attire. The name of the eldest is Suliman, the second is William Linnaeus, and the little girl is called Noshaba Begum.

When I retired to my *charpai*, my dreams were haunted by visions of the splendour of the Timoorians in former days; the palace at Agra, and the beautiful *begum* with whom I had spent the evening.

February 23rd – Mr Gardner proposed a *chitā* or cheetah hunt: he had a fine hunting leopard; we went out to look for antelopes; the day was very hot, we had no success and returned very much fagged; Mrs B— was laid up in consequence with an ague. There was a fine elephant at Kutchowra, a great number of horses and a few dogs.

The next morning I spent an hour with the *begum*, and took leave of her; it is difficult to find her awake, she sleeps so much from opium. If you call on a native lady and she does not wish to receive a visitor the attendants always say, 'The lady is asleep – ' equivalent to 'not at home'. Sometimes she employs herself in needlework and her attendants sit around, and net *kurtis* for her on a sort of embroidery frame.

It may be as well to remark, that the opium given by the *begum* to her children was remarkably fine and pure; grown in her own garden and collected daily from incisions made in the pod of the deep red poppy.

On my departure, the *begum* presented me with a beautifully embroidered a small bag (*batū'ā*) full of spices; it was highly ornamented, and embroidered in gold and silver, interwoven with coloured beads.

She wished me to put on *churis*, which are bracelets made of *sealing-wax* ornamented with beads; they are extremely pretty, but of little value. I consented and the *churis* were put on in this manner: a *churi*, having been cut open with a hot knife, it was heated over a charcoal fire, opened a little – just enough to allow it to pass over the arm; it was then closed, and the two ends were united by being touched with a hot knife. I wore these *churis* until they broke and dropped off; in memory of my first visit to the *zenāna*.

CHAPTER XXXIII

LIFE IN THE ZENĀNA AND CHĪTA HUNTING

TEN DURWESH MAY SLEEP UNDER THE SAME BLANKET,
BUT TWO KINGS CANNOT EXIST IN ONE KINGDOM

A CONTEMPORARY WIFE, THOUGH A HOORI, IS WORSE THAN A SHE-DEVIL

FEBRUARY 1835 – When a woman of rank marries, two female slaves are given with her, who are also the wives of her husband: this is so completely a custom it is never omitted: nevertheless, 'The very voice of a rival wife is intolerable'.

A number of women are considered to add to a man's dignity: they add to his misery most decidedly. This custom being more honoured in the breach than the observance, was not put in force at the marriage of Mr Gardner with Mulka Begum. 'The malice of a fellow-wife is notorious.' It would only be surprising if such were not the case. 'A contemporary wife is intolerable, even in effigy.' In native life the greatest misery is produced from a plurality of wives; they, very naturally, hate each other most cordially and quarrel all day. The children, also, from their cradles are taught to hate the children of the other wives; nevertheless, the following extract proves that *she* is considered a wife worthy of praise who loves the offspring of her husband and another woman:

'A woman may be married by four qualifications; one, on account of her money; another, on account of the nobility of her pedigree; another, on account of her beauty; the fourth on account of her faith: therefore, look out for a religious woman; but if you do it from any other consideration, may your hands be rubbed in dirt.' – 'The world and all things in it are valuable; but the most valuable thing in the world is a virtuous woman.' – 'The best women, that ride on camels, I mean the women of Arabia, are the virtuous of the Koreish; they are the most affectionate to infants, whether they be their own or their husband's by other women; and they are the most careful of their husband's property.' The proverb is at variance with the opinion of the prophet, since the former asserts, 'A contemporary wife may be good, but her child is bad.' As the means of power over their husbands, native women value their children very much and are miserable if they have none.

A *zenāna* is a place of intrigue, and those who live within four walls cannot pursue a straight path: how can it be otherwise, where so many conflicting passions are called forth? If a man make a present to one wife, he must make a similar offering to all the rest to preserve peace and quietness. The wives must have separate houses or apartments; were it not so, they would agree as well as caged tigers. The Qur'an permits a Musulmān to have *four* wives; the proverb says, 'The man is happy who has no she-goat,' Atàa records that the prophet had *nine* wives; and from Safíah, who was the last of them who died, he wished to be divorced; but she said, 'Keep me with your wives and do not divorce me, peradventure I may be of the number of your wives in paradise.'

Some authorities assert that the prophet had eighteen wives: Atàa only mentions nine. To recompense his warlike followers for allowing them only four wives each, he gives them the *mutâ* marriage for any period they may choose with the wives of their enemies taken in battle.

In the beginning of Islam, the followers of the prophet, the *shias*, were allowed to marry for a limited time; this temporary marriage was called *mutâ*. 'Verily the prophet prohibited, on the day of the battle of Khaiber, a *mutâ* marriage, which is for a fixed time, and he forbade the eating of the flesh of the domestic ass.' 'His Highness permitted, in the year in which he went to Awtàs, *mutâ* for three days; after which he forbade it.' At length a revelation came down which rendered every connection of the sort unlawful for the faithful, 'excepting the captives which their right hands possess.'

If a woman of high rank and consequence has no heir, this farce is often played. The lady appears to expect one; she is fattened up in the same curious manner in which they fatten their horses: five or six low caste women, who really expect children about the same time, are secreted in the *zenāna*: when one of them is delivered of a son, the *begum* takes it, the farce of an *accouchement* is acted and the child is produced as the heir; the real mamma has Rs 500 (£50) given her – and perhaps a dose of poison to secure her silence.

The father of Mulka Begum, the Huzūr Mirza Sulimān Shekō, the brother of the present Emperor of Delhi, resides at Agra on a pension from Government; he has children innumerable, all young princes and princesses; there are, it is said, some forty of his children now alive, proud and poor. By Mulka's first marriage with Mirza Selīm, the second son of the present King of Delhi, she had three children. The first wife of the King of Oude is a sister of Mulka's and is reckoned more beautiful than even Mulka herself:

February 24th – We drove over to Khasganj, Colonel Gardner's residence, thirteen miles over roads that were hardly passable. On our arrival, we found our dear friend seated on the steps in front of his house with many gentlemen, both English and native, around him. I thought I had never seen so dignified and graceful a person; he was dressed in a *lubāda* of red figured Indian shawl, the rest of the dress was English, but the style of the *lubāda* was particularly good and suited to an old man; his half brother, Mr Valentine Gardner was with him, also an old *nawāb* from Cambay.

Colonel Gardner has a fine estate at Khasganj; the outer house is dedicated to his friends and English acquaintants; within four high walls is the *barā-deri*, or pavilion, in the centre of the *zenāna* gardens, in which his *begum* resides.

Apartments were given to my husband and me in the outer house, where the English visitors resided. The dinners at first consisted of European as well as native dishes; but the latter were so excellent, I soon found it impossible to partake of dishes dressed after the English fashion; and as all the guests were of the same opinion, Colonel Gardner had the kindness to banish European dishes from the table.

I must not forget to mention the *arwari* fish, the finest and most delicious I ever tasted; the Kālā-naddī is famed for its *arwari*, a sort of mullet; the fish delights to bask in the sun, floating on the surface of the water. Colonel Gardner kept two *shikarees* (native sportsmen), for the purpose of shooting these fish; one man fired and the other instantly plunged into the water and brought out the fish that were killed or stunned. The Musulmāns object to eating fish having no scales; such fish was also forbidden to the Jews.

In the evening, the native mimics came to perform before us; they imitated Europeans very well and mimicked the gentlemen of the party. A *pūtli-nāch* was afterwards brought forward; I was surprised to see the natives, young and old, so eager and fond of this absurdity, until Colonel Gardner said, 'The natives are madly fond of this *pūtli-nāch*; indeed, it is all the English have left them of their former glory. You see, represented by puppets, Shāhjahān and all his Court and Durbar: one puppet is brought forward and the manager, whilst it bows to the audience, relates the whole history of the minister whom it represents; giving a true account of his pedigrees, riches, influence, etc. At this moment, standing behind my chair, at a salary of four rupees a month, is the lineal descendant of one of the first lords in the Court of Shāhjahān. The managers of the show mix up infinite wit with their relation of events, and sarcasms on the English.'

After this explanation I could see the reason of the fondness of the old natives for this puppet-show which before, in my ignorance, I had not comprehended. One by one every puppet is brought forward and its history recounted. This evening fatigued me a good deal; we sat under the verandah to see the sights, the glare of the torches was painful to my eyes and the noise made my head ache.

February 27th – A lynx (the *caracal*), the property of Colonel Gardner, a most extraordinary looking beast, killed a *goa samp*: I was told, the animal catches crows by springing several feet into the air after them as they rise from the ground.

The cheetah, or *chita* (hunting leopard), killed two antelopes. Some *nāch* girls danced and sang in the evening, and thus closed the day.

My husband, who had accompanied me to Khasganj, now took leave of Colonel Gardner and returned to Allahabad, leaving me with our dear friend to witness the Mohammedan marriage ceremonies. My husband quitted us with regret, being obliged to depart on account of the expiration of his leave of absence.

Colonel Gardner married Nawāb Matmunzilool Nissa Begum, of the Cambay family; she resides in the house or pavilion within the four walls, with her relatives, attendants and slaves. This morning the *begum* sent word she would receive visitors in the evening; Colonel Gardner took me over and introduced me to her as his adopted daughter; she rose and embraced me, putting her cheek to mine on each side the face, after the fashion of the French, and her arms around me: having received her guests, she sat down on her *gaddi* of purple velvet, embroidered with gold; and we seated ourselves on plain white *gaddīs* either side.

The *begum* is a very lively little old woman; she was magnificently dressed in pearls, diamonds, and emeralds – as many as it was possible to put on her little body; she wore a *peshwāz*, or very short full gown, with a tight body, made of red and gold Benares tissue; this is a dress of state; *pajāmās* of silk; and, over all, a *dupatta* of red and gold Benares tissue which, as she sat, covered her entirely; and she looked more like a lump of glittering gold and crimson and pearls than a living woman. A golden *huqqa*, with four *nā'echas* (snakes) was placed before her on a *huqqa* carpet of raised flowers, curiously cut out in paper. The room was covered with a carpet, over which white cloths were spread after the usual fashion and the lamps all stood on the ground.

At the other end of the room sat fourteen slave girls belonging to the *begum*, who played on different instruments, whilst one or two of them *nāched* before us.

The ladies of the family were seated on the *begum*'s left hand.

There was Hinga Bibi Sāhiba, the widow of Allan Gardner, the eldest son of Colonel Gardner; her eldest daughter, Hirmooze, married Mr Stuart William Gardner, an officer in the 28th Native Infantry, and son of Admiral Francis Gardner, a relative of Colonel Gardner.

Her second daughter, Susan, generally called Shubbeah Begum, was not present; being engaged to be married to a young Prince of Delhi, she was kept in *parda*. At her feet were the two daughters of James Gardner by a former marriage; the eldest, Alaida (the Morning Star), about fifteen years old, very fair, with a round pretty face; but her great charm was a remarkably sweet and interesting manner; she of them all was the one whom Colonel Gardner best loved; and indeed she was a sweet girl. Her younger sister (the Evening Star) was darker than Alaida, pretty and lively. They, like the *begum*, had Tartar faces, in which the eyes are wide apart; but were both, nevertheless, very pretty and interesting girls.

Two English gentlemen who were fond of native life and fascinated with Khasganj, requested me to mention to Colonel Gardner their wish to become of his family; I did so. Colonel Gardner replied, 'Shubbeah is engaged to the Prince,' but, said I, 'Do you think she likes him?' 'How little you know of the natives!' he replied; 'it would be considered the greatest indelicacy for a girl to prefer one man to another, or to have seen the man to whom she is to be united. Tell Mr — I am flattered by his wish to be of my family, and would willingly give him my granddaughter, but the *begum* is bent on this *grand alliance*, as *she* considers it: I have withheld my consent for years; "The house may be filled with the falling of drops;" i.e. continual dripping wears away stones. She has carried the point. I have been happy in my marriage but I would not advise a European gentleman to marry a native lady. With respect to the proposals of the other gentleman, in a worldly point of view it would be a good match; but I do not like the man; I cannot bestow upon him the Morning Star!'

Bānoo Bibi Sāhiba was also there; in her younger days she must have been pretty; her liveliness she still retained.

The guests smoked the *huqqa*, and ate *pān*; some very delicate *pān* was prepared for me of which I partook for the first time, and rather liked it.

At the end of the evening, the *begum* gave her guests liberty to depart; *pān* and *atr* of roses were presented to us; rose-water was sprinkled over us; we made salam in due form and returned to the outer house.

The *begum* has a guard of honour of forty men who live at the entrance of the *zenāna*, and guard the gateway night and day.

I must not forget the old Nawāb of Cambay, the uncle of the *begum*; he is quite a character and a very singular one; he has visited England; he used to dine at the table with us and would take sherry with the guests. When a lady was at table he would take sherry; if gentlemen only were present, the sherry was discarded for brandy: one day I observed he drank some white spirit and found it was a strong spirit he himself distilled from different flowers: to my surprise, he used also to play backgammon. Natives have names and titles innumerable, of which his are a good specimen: Fakhr-ul-dawla Moomtaj ul Moolk Nawāb Meer Momun Khān Bahadur Delme Delawor Jung.

Colonel Gardner's name is William Linnaeus, so called after his godfather, the great botanist; he is himself an excellent botanist and pursues the study with much ardour. His garden at Khasganj is a very extensive and a most delightful one, full of fine trees and rare plants, beautiful flowers and shrubs, with fruit in abundance and perfection; no expense is spared to embellish the garden: in the centre is a delightful pavilion under the shade of fine trees. It is one of the pleasures of the *begum* and her attendants to spend the day in that garden: guards are then stationed around it to prevent intrusion. She is herself extremely fond of flowers and, although not a botanist after the European fashion, she knows the medicinal qualities of all the Indian plants and the dyes that can be produced from them; and this knowledge is of daily account in the *zenāna*.

March 1st – Took a gallop on a fine English horse, Rattler by name; being accustomed to ride Arabs, this great monster appeared like a frisky mountain under me.

March 2nd – Mr James Gardner invited us to return to his house at Kutchowra, that we might enjoy *chita* hunting. We drove over and in the evening some *nāch* women exhibited before us for our amusement.

March 3rd – In the early morning I mounted a white pony and we all rode out eight miles to breakfast in a tent which had been sent out over night. After breakfast the party got into the buggies.

We went directly across the country; there were no roads, over banks and through ditches, where it appeared a miracle we were not upset. We came to a deep, narrow, stone watercourse, my companion said, 'If you will get out of the buggy, I will leap the mare over; if I attempt to walk her over, she will be sure to get her foot in and break her leg.' I got out accordingly; away went the mare; she took a leap at the drain and carried the buggy over in excellent style. Buggies in India have the remarkable faculty of leaping, being accustomed to such freaks.

We arrived at the estate of a native gentleman called Petumber where, on the plain, we saw a herd of about three hundred antelopes, bounding, running and playing in the sunshine; and a severe sun it was, enough to give one a brain fever, in spite of the leather hood of the buggy. The antelopes are so timid, they will not allow a buggy to come very near the herd; therefore being determined to see the hunt, we got out of the carriage and mounted upon the *hackery* (cart) on which the *chita* was carried without even an umbrella, lest it should frighten the deer. The *chīta* had a hood over his eyes and a rope round his loins and two natives, his keepers, were with him.

I sat down by accident on the animal's tail: O–o–o–wh, growled the *chīta*. I did not wait for another growl, but released his tail instantly. The bullock *hackery* was driven into the midst of the herd. The bandage was removed from the eyes of the *chīta*, and the cord from his body: he dropped from the cart and bounded, with the most surprising bounds, towards an immense black buck, seized him by the throat, flung him on the ground, and held him there. The keepers went up, they cut the buck's throat and then they cut off the haunch of the hind leg and, dipping a wooden spoon into the cavity, offered it full of blood to the *chīta*. Nothing but this would have induced the *chīta* to quit the throat of the buck. He followed the men to the cart, jumped upon it, drank the blood and the men then put his bandage over his eyes. The haunch was put into the back of the cart, the reward for the animal when the hunting was over. The herd had passed on; we followed, taking care the wind did not betray our approach. The *chīta* was leaning against me in the *hackery* and we proceeded very sociably. Another herd of antelopes went bounding near us, the *chīta*'s eyes were unbound again and the rope removed from his loins; a fine buck passed, we expected he would instantly pursue it as usual, but the animal turned sulky and instead of dropping down from the *hackery*, he put both his forepaws on my lap and stood there two or three seconds with his face and whiskers touching my cheek. O–o–o–wh, O–o–o–wh, growled the *chīta*! – my heart beat faster, but I sat perfectly quiet, as you may well imagine, whilst I thought to myself: 'If he seize my throat, he will never leave it until they cut off my hind quarter, and give him a bowl of blood!' His paws were as light on my lap as those of a cat. How long the few seconds appeared whilst I eyed him askance! Nor was I slightly glad when the *chīta* dropped to the ground, where he crouched down sulkily and would not hunt. He was a very fine-tempered animal but they are all uncertain. I did not like his being quite so near when he was unfastened and *sulky*.

The next time I took care to get off the cart before the creature was freed from restraint. It is painful to witness a *chīta* hunt, the beautiful antelope has so little chance of escape.

During the day, we killed three fine antelopes; the horns of one of them, remarkably large, with five turns on them, I brought to England. We rested under some trees by a well to partake of tiffin when one of the party observed, 'This wood and well are remarkable. Heera Sing, the father of Petumber, was a Thug, and made by Thuggee a large fortune. In this plantation and by the side of this very well his people used to wait for travellers, lure them to the shade and water to refresh themselves, strangle them and cast their bodies into the well.

'After having amassed a fortune, Heera Sing repented and gave orders that life should not be taken on his estate. He would not allow the antelopes to be killed; and his son having followed his example accounts for the large herds of antelopes we have found here: it is an excellent preserve.' We then returned home; I was almost dead with the heat, having been out in such a powerful sun during a drive of about thirty miles.

Mulka Begum sometimes goes out *chita* hunting in a native carriage, drawn by two magnificent bullocks adorned with crimson housings, and their horns covered with plates of gold.

In this manner the princess can behold the sport and enter into the amusement, while she is completely secluded from the profane eye of men.

CHAPTER XXXIV

FATEHPUR SIKRI AND COLONEL GARDNER

MARCH 1835 – The wedding having been deferred for a short time, I took the opportunity of returning *dāk* to Agra, having promised Colonel Gardner to be at Khasganj again in time to witness the ceremony. All this time my pretty pinnace had been awaiting my arrival. I determined to send her back to Allahabad with the cook-boat, and she sailed immediately. I also sent back the carriage and horses, keeping the buggy, Bokhara, the grey and black horse, to accompany me to Khasganj. The *dāk* trip gave me a severe cough and cold and on my reaching Agra I was little fit for exertion.

[...]

Extract from the Asiatic Journal *of October 1844 'Sketches of remarkable characters in India: No. 1 Colonel Gardner – and the Begum Sumroo'*

'A few years ago India presented a wide field for adventure: the distracted state of the country, the ambitious projects and conflicting interests of native princes were highly favourable circumstances to those who brought with them a competent knowledge of the art of war and of military discipline; and who preferred a wild, erratic, roving life amongst the children of the soil, to the regular service of the India Company. There are two individuals still living in the Bengal Residency, and occupying a distinguished, though singular position in society, whose eventful career, if circumstantially related, could not fail to prove highly interesting. The general outlines of the history of the Begum Sumroo and of Colonel Gardner, of Khasganj, are known to every person who has visited the theatre of their exploits, but very few are acquainted with the details; for such is the shifting nature of Anglo-Indian society that it is impossible to gain more than the passing information of the day, in places rendered memorable from circumstances of universal notoriety, but of which nobody can give the particulars.

'Some apology ought, perhaps, to be made for associating the name of so gallant and highly respected an officer as Colonel Gardner with that of the *begum,* and her still more worthless husband; but as those readers of the *Asiatic Journal* who have not been in India are puzzled by the announcement of marriages, or projected marriages, of the daughters of this gentleman with the nephews of the King of Delhi, an explanation of the circumstances which have produced these apparently extraordinary alliances will doubtless prove acceptable. The writer of these pages does not pretend to know more of Colonel Gardner than the tongue of rumour could tell, or a casual meeting in society could afford. But so remarkable a person naturally made a strong impression, and the anecdotes extant concerning him were too singular to be easily forgotten. Colonel Gardner's tall, commanding figure, soldier-like countenance and military air render his appearance very striking. When at his own residence, and associating with natives, it is said that he adopts the Asiatic costume; but while visiting a large military station, in company with the Resident of Lucknow, he wore a blue surtout, resembling the undress uniform of the British army but profusely ornamented with silk lace.

'Colonel Gardner, who is a connection of the noble family bearing that name, came out to India in the King's service, which he soon afterwards quitted; the cause of his resignation is variously related; in the absence of an authentic account it would, perhaps, be wrong to give sanction to any one of the reports afloat concerning it. At this period, it was impossible to foresee that the tide of fortune would bring the British Government of India into actual warfare with the sovereigns of provinces so far beyond the frontier, that human ambition dared not contemplate their subjugation. Many loyal men were, therefore, induced to follow the banners of native princes under the expectation that they never could be called upon to bear arms against their own country; but fate decreed it otherwise and, in the Mahratta war, those officers who had enlisted in Holkar's service found themselves in a very awkward predicament; especially as they were not permitted a choice, or even allowed to remain neutral, their new masters endeavouring to force them, upon pain of death, to commit treason to the land of their birth by fighting in the ranks of a hostile force.

'In some of the native courts, the English were immediately put to death upon the approach of the enemy, or on the slightest suspicion of their fidelity. Upon more than one occasion Colonel Gardner, who, independent of his military skill possessed a thorough knowledge of the native character and very considerable talent, penetrated the designs of his employers and withdrew in time from meditated treachery; but his escape from Holkar was of the most hazardous description, not inferior in picturesque incident and personal jeopardy to that of the renowned Dugald Dalgetty, who was not more successful in all lawful strategy than the subject of this too brief memoir. Anxious to secure the services of so efficient an officer, after all fair means had failed, Holkar tied his prisoner to a gun and threatened him with immediate destruction should he persist in refusing to take the field with his army. The Colonel remained staunch and, perhaps in the hope of tiring him out, the execution was suspended and he was placed under a guard who had orders never to quit him for a single instant. Walking one day along the edge of a bank leading by a precipitous descent to a river, Colonel Gardner suddenly determined to make a bold effort to escape and, perceiving a place fitted to his purpose, he shouted out "Bismillah!" (in the name of God) and flung himself down an abyss some forty or fifty feet deep. None were inclined to follow him; but the guns were fired and an alarm sounded in the town. He recovered his feet and, making for the river, plunged into it. After swimming for some distance, finding that his pursuers gained upon him he took shelter in a friendly covert and, with merely his mouth above the water, waited until they had passed; he then landed on the opposite side and proceeded by unfrequented paths to a town in the neighbourhood which was under the command of a friend who, though a native and a servant of Holkar, he thought would afford him protection. This man proved trustworthy; and, after remaining concealed some time, the Colonel ventured out in the disguise of a grass-cutter and reaching the British outposts in safety was joyously received by his countrymen. He was appointed to the command of a regiment of irregular horse, which he still retains; and his services in the field, at the head of these brave soldiers, have not been more advantageous to the British Government than the accurate acquaintance before mentioned, which his long and intimate association with natives enabled him to obtain of the Asiatic character. It was to his diplomatic skill and knowledge of the best methods of treaty that we owed the capitulation of one of those formidable hill-fortresses (Komalmair in Mewar), whose reduction by arms would have been at the expense of an immense sacrifice of human life. The Commandant of the division despatched to take possession of it, wearied out by the procrastinating and indecisive spirit of the natives, would have stormed the place at every disadvantage had not Colonel Gardner persuaded him to entrust the negotiation to his hands. The result proved that he made a just estimate of his own powers: the garrison agreed to give up the Fortress on the payment of their arrears; and Colonel Tod, in his *Annals of Rajast'han*, mentions the circumstance as one highly honourable to the British character, that, there not being more than Rs 4,000 at the time in the English camp, an order, written by the Commandant for the remainder upon the *shroffs* or bankers in the neighbourhood, was taken without the least hesitation, the natives not having the slightest doubt that it would be paid upon presentation.

'The marriage of Colonel Gardner forms one of the most singular incidents in his romantic story.

'In the midst of his hazardous career, he carried off a Mohammedan princess, the sister of one of the lesser potentates of the Deccan who, though now reduced to comparative insignificance, during the rise and progress of the Mahrattas, were personages of considerable consequence.

> Ever the first to climb a tower,
> As venturous in a lady's bower ,

the sacred recesses of the *zenāna* were penetrated by the enterprising lover who, at the moment in which his life was threatened by the brother's treachery, bore away his prize in triumph and sought an asylum in another court. A European of popular manners and military experience could in those days easily place himself at the head of a formidable body of soldiers, ready to follow his fortunes and trusting to his arrangements with the princes whose cause he supported, for their pay, which was frequently in arrear or dependent upon the capture of some rich province. In the command of such a troop Colonel Gardner was a welcome guest wherever he went; and, until the affair with Holkar, he had always contrived to secure his retreat whenever it was prudent to commence a new career in another quarter.

'It is difficult to say what sort of bridal contract is gone through between a Moslem beauty and a Christian gentleman, but the ceremony is supposed to be binding; at least it is considered so in India, a native female not losing the respect of her associates by forming such a connection. The marriage of Colonel Gardner seems perfectly satisfactory to the people of Hindustan; for the lady has not only continued steadfast to the Mohammedan faith and in the strict observance of all the restrictions prescribed to Asiatic females of rank, but has brought up her daughters in the same religious persuasion and in the same profound seclusion – points seldom conceded by a European father. They are, therefore, eligible to match with the princes of the land, their mother's family connections and high descent atoning for the dis-advantage of foreign ancestry upon the paternal side. Educated according to the most approved fashion of an Oriental court, they are destined to spend the remainder of their lives in the *zenāna*, and this choice for her daughters shows that their mother, at least, does not consider exclusion from the world, in which European women reign and revel, to be any hardship.

'So little of the spirit of adventure is now stirring in India that the Misses Gardner, or the young *begums*, or whatsoever appellation it may be most proper to designate them by, have not attracted the attention of the European community. Doubtless their beauty and accomplishments are blazoned in native society; but, excepting upon the occasion of an announcement like that referred to in the Calcutta periodicals, the existence of these ladies is scarcely known to their father's countrymen residing in India. We are ignorant whether their complexions partake most of the eastern or the northern hue, or whether they have the slightest idea of the privileges from which their mother's adherence to Mohammedan usages has debarred them. Their situation, singular as it may appear in England, excites little or no interest; nobody seems to lament that they were not brought up in the Christian religion, or permitted those advantages which the half-caste offspring of women of lower rank enjoy: and, acquainted with the circumstances of the case, the editors of the aforesaid periodicals do not enter into any explanation of intelligence of the most startling nature to English readers who, in their ignorance of facts, are apt to fancy that European ladies in India are willing to enter into the *zenānas* of native princes.

'Colonel Gardner has, of course, adopted many of the opinions and ideas of the people with whom he has passed so great a portion of his time, and in his mode of living he may be termed half an Asiatic; this, however, does not prevent him from being a most acceptable companion to the European residents, who take the greatest delight in his society whenever he appears among them. His autobiography would be a work of the highest value, affording a picture of Indian manners and Indian policy with which few besides himself have ever had an opportunity of becoming so intimately acquainted. As he is still in the prime and vigour of existence, we may hope that some such employment of these piping times of peace may be suggested to him, and that he may be induced to devote the hours spent in retirement at Khasganj to the writing or the dictation of the incidents of his early life. In looking back upon past events, the Colonel occasionally expresses a regret that he should have been induced to quit the king's service, in which, in all probability, he would have attained the highest rank; but, eminently qualified for the situation in which he has been placed, and more than reconciled to the destiny which binds him to a foreign soil, the station he occupies leaves him little to desire; and he has it in his power to be still farther useful to society by unlocking the stores of a mind fraught with information of the highest interest.'

March 5th 1835 – Two letters having appeared in the *Mofussil Akhbar*, a provincial paper, Colonel Gardner published this answer:

'*To the Editor of the* Mofussil Akhbar.

'Dear Sir – In your paper of the 28th ultimo, just received, I find I have been unwillingly dragged from my obscurity by the author of "Sketches of Living Remarkable Characters in India". This I should not have noticed, but for a mistake or two that it is my duty to correct. In the first place, it was Colonel Casement who ordered me and instructed me in his name to attempt the negotiation for the surrender of the garrison of Komalmair. I obeyed his order successfully, only demurring at the sum demanded, Rs 30,000, which, for so weak a garrison, I considered extravagant: but the resident Colonel Tod arrived at this stage of the business with superior diplomatic power. Colonel Casement was no longer consulted and my poor rushlight was hidden under a bushel. But who can feel anything against the author of such a splendid and correct work as *Rajastan*? The writer of the extract has probably mistaken Komalmair for the Fort of Rampoora where, under the instructions of Colonel Vauzemen, the negotiation for the evacuation was entirely entrusted to me; and, for the sum of Rs 7,000, a siege was prevented at a very advanced season of the year when, as General Ochterlony wrote to me, he would otherwise have been obliged to order the battering-train from Agra.

'When I made my escape, as detailed, by swimming the Taptee, it was from the tender mercies of the gentle Brahman, our late pensioner Emurt Row's force, by whom I was then in close confinement, and not from Holkar.

'I fear I must divest my marriage with her highness the *begum* of a great part of its romantic attraction, by confessing that the young *begum* was only thirteen years of age when I first applied for and received her mother's consent; and which marriage probably saved both their lives. Allow me to assure you, on the *very best authority*, that a Moslem lady's marriage with a Christian is as legal in this country as if the ceremony had been performed by the Bishop of Calcutta; a point lately settled by my son's marriage with the niece of the Emperor, the Nawāb Mulka Humanee Begum; and that the respectability of the females of my family amongst the natives of Hindustan has been settled by the Emperor many years ago, he having adopted my wife as his daughter; a ceremony satisfactorily repeated by the Queen, on a visit to my own house in Delhi. I can assure my partial sketcher that my only daughter died in 1804, and that my granddaughters, by the particular desire of their grandmother, are Christians. It was an act of her own, as by the marriage agreement the daughters were to be brought up in the religion of the mother; the sons in that of your

'Very obedient, humble servant,

'W. L. G .   Khasganj, 5th March, 1835.'

Colonel Tod, in a letter to the editor of the *Asiatic Journal* thus speaks of Colonel Gardner: 'A day or two previous to this number (of your journal) being lent me, an intimate friend of Colonel Gardner's spent the evening with me; and as it is almost impossible that any two men at all acquainted with his diversified life could talk of him without expressing a wish that he would become his own biographer – the subject being started, we mutually agreed that, qualified in every way as he is for the task, the result would be both interesting and instructive. Amongst other remarks, I observed that, although he was well known to me by character, and I had to bear testimony to the brave conduct of a part of his corps attached to me in 1817; the only time I ever had the pleasure of seeing him was the day following the surrender of Komulmér when he dined with me.

'I trust your correspondent will proceed with the "sketches" and that the outline he has now furnished of Colonel Gardner's history may stimulate the original to give, what no other can, his biography in full. Colonel Gardner is one of the many remarkable men who have passed a most extraordinary life, floating, as circumstance or "*nuseeb*" propelled, amidst the chaotic elements of Indian society, during the half-century preceding the halcyon days of 1818; when, by the vigorous mind and measures of the Marquess of Hastings peace, for the first time in its history, reigned from the Himalaya to Cape Comorin. *Aristides was banished Athens!*'

I greatly wished Colonel Gardner would consent to tell me the history of his remarkable life, which I was anxious to write down from his dictation. One evening he said, 'Merā Betee, (my child) when in Holkar's service, I was employed as an envoy to the Company's forces under Lord Lake, with instructions to return within a certain time; my family remained in camp. Suspicion of treachery was caused by my lengthened absence, and accusations were brought forward against me at the *darbār*, held by Holkar on the third day following that on which my presence was expected. I rejoined the camp while the *darbār* was still assembled; on my entrance the Mahārāj, in an angry tone, demanded the reason of the delay; which I gave, pointing out the impossibility of a speedier return. Holkar exclaimed, in great anger, "Had you not returned this day, I would have levelled the *khanāts* of your tents." I drew my sword instantly and attempted to cut his highness down, but was prevented by those around him; and ere they had recovered from the amazement and confusion caused by the attempt, I rushed from the tent, sprang upon my horse and was soon beyond reach of the pursuers.'

To account for Colonel Gardner's indignation, it must be remembered that the *khanāts* are walls of canvas that surround the tents of the ladies of the *zenāna*; to have thrown down those screens, and to have exposed women within *parda* to the gaze of men, would have been an insult for which there could be no atonement. Colonel Gardner's high spirit was as prompt to avenge the threat as it would have been willing to take the life of Holkar had he intruded on the privacy of the *begum*'s apartments.

Through the influence of friends, the Princess and her family were allowed, unmolested, to quit Holkar's dominions and rejoin her husband.

The account Colonel Gardner gave me of his marriage with the *begum* was this: 'When a young man, I was entrusted to negotiate a treaty with one of the native princes of Cambay. *Darbārs* and consultations were continually held; during one of the former, at which I was present, a *parda* curtain near me was gently moved aside and I saw, as I thought, the most beautiful black eyes in the world. It was impossible to think of the treaty; those bright and piercing glances, those beautiful dark eyes, completely bewildered me.

'I felt flattered that a creature so lovely as she of those deep black, loving eyes must be, should venture to gaze upon me; to what danger might not the veiled beauty be exposed, should the movement of the *parda* be seen by any of those at the *darbār*. On quitting the assembly I discovered that the bright-eyed beauty was the daughter of the Prince. At the next *darbār*, my agitation and anxiety were extreme again to behold the bright eyes that had haunted my dreams by night, and my thoughts by day! The *parda* again was gently moved, and my fate was decided.

'I demanded the Princess in marriage; her relations were at first indignant and positively refused my proposal; however, on mature deliberation, the ambassador was considered too influential a person to have a request denied and the hand of the young Princess was promised. The preparations for the marriage were carried forward; "Remember," said I, "it will be useless to attempt to deceive me; I shall know those eyes again, nor will I marry any other."

'On the day of the marriage I raised the veil from the countenance of the bride, and in the mirror that was placed between us beheld the bright eyes that had bewildered me; I smiled – the young *begum* smiled also.'

Such was Colonel Gardner's account of the first time he beheld his bride. Well might she smile when she gazed upon that noble countenance!

The Tomb of Colonel Hessing

March 15th – This beautiful mausoleum is in the Catholic burial ground at Agra and is well worthy a visit. It was built by a native architect, by name Lateef, in imitation of the ancient Mohammedan tombs. The material is the red stone from Fatehpur Sikri, which is highly carved but not inlaid. The tomb is beautiful, very beautiful and in excellent taste. Its cost is estimated at about one lakh of rupees. Lateef's drawings of the Tāj and of all the ancient monuments around Agra are excellent; they cost from Rs 3–40 each. I bought a large collection of them, as well as of marbles and other curiosities. Lateef inlays marble with precious stones, after the style of the work in the Tāj. A chess-table of this sort, with a border of flowers in mosaic, costs from Rs 800–1200, £80–120, and is beautifully executed.

March 16th – My affairs at Agra having come to a conclusion, and the pinnace, carriage and horses being on their way home, I once more turned my steps to Khasganj and arrived there *dāk*, accompanied by a friend, who was extremely anxious to see the marriage ceremony, although all that the eye of a man is permitted to behold is the *tamāshā* that takes place without the four walls. All that passes within is sacred.

On my arrival the whole party at Khasganj were going out to tents by the Ganges to hunt wild boars and otters, to shoot crocodiles, floriken, black partridge and other game. Even for people in good health it was, at that season of the year, a mad expedition and I declined going; I longed indeed to accompany them, but my cold and cough were so severe I was forced to give up the idea.

March 18th – My dear Colonel Gardner, seeing how ill I was, said, 'You will never recover, my child, in the outer house: I will give you a room in the inner one and put you under the care of the *begum*; there you will soon recover.' He took me over to the *zenāna*; the *begum* received me very kindly and appointed four of her slaves to attend upon me and aid my own women. They put me immediately into a steam-bath, shampooed, mulled and half-boiled me; cracked every joint after the most approved fashion, took me out, laid me on a golden-footed bed, gave me sherbet to drink, shampooed me to sleep and, by the time the shooting party returned from the Ganges, I had perfectly recovered and, was able to enter into all the amusement of seeing a Hindustani wedding.

I must here anticipate and remark that Suddu Khān, our excellent little *khānsāmān*, died in June 1841. He had been ill and unable to attend for months. There is a story that being in an *hammām*, he received some injury in the spine while being shampooed and joint-cracked by a barber, who placed his knee to his back and then forcibly brought his two arms backwards. The story says poor Suddu fainted and the barber was so much alarmed, he fled, and has never been seen since at Cawnpore, where the scene took place.

CHAPTER XXXV

THE MARRIAGE

TO DRESS ONE'S OWN DOLL

Spoken of a father who defrays the whole expense of his daughter's marriage, her dress, ornaments, etc. without any charge to the bridegroom or his family.

HE WHO BUILDS A HOUSE AND TAKES A WIFE HEAPS SEVENTY AFFLICTIONS ON HIS HEAD

MARCH 18TH 1835 – Before entering on a description of the marriage ceremonies, it may be as well to explain the singular manner in which Colonel Gardner's family has intermarried with that of the Emperor of Delhi, which the annexed pedigree will exemplify.

William Gardner, Esq., of Coleraine, left a son.

William Gardner, Esq., Lt-Colonel in the 11th regiment of Dragoons. He married Elizabeth, daughter of Valentine Farrington, Esq. and had issue Valentine, born 1739, Allan and other children. Allan was created a baronet and afterwards elevated to the peerage in Ireland in 1800; and created a peer of the United Kingdom, 1806.

Valentine, the eldest son, a Major in the army, married first Alaida, daughter of Robert Livingstone, Esq., by whom he had a son, William Linnaeus, Captain in the army; and, secondly, Frances, daughter of Samuel Holworthy, Esq., by whom he had another son, Valentine.

Colonel William Linnaeus Gardner married Nawāb Matmunzilool Nissa Begum Delmi and by her had two sons, Allan and James, and a daughter; the last mentioned died young.

Allan, the eldest son, married Bibi Sāhiba Hinga and left one son, Mungo, who died young, and two daughters, Hirmoozee and Susan. Hirmoozee married her relative, Stewart William Gardner, Esq., son of Rear-Admiral Francis Gardner, the brother of Allan Hyde Lord Gardner. Susan, the second daughter, or Shubbeah Begum as she is called, is the one whose marriage is on the *tapis*.

James Gardner, the second son of Colonel William Linnaeus Gardner, married first Bibi Sāhiba Banoo, by whom he had one son, Hinga, and two daughters, Alaida, the Morning Star, and the Evening Star. He married,

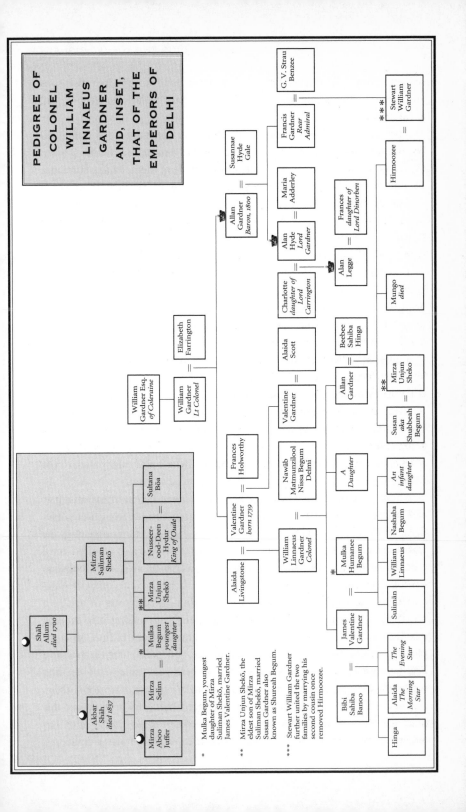

PEDIGREE OF COLONEL WILLIAM LINNAEUS GARDNER AND, INSET, THAT OF THE EMPERORS OF DELHI

Shah Allum *died 1700*

Akbar Shah *died 1837*

Mirza Suliman Shekó

Mirza Aboo Juffier

Mirza Selim

Mulka Begum *youngest daughter*

Mirza Unjun Shekó

Nusseer-ood-Deen Hydur *King of Oude*

Sultana Boa

* Mulka Begum, youngest daughter of Mirza Suliman Shekó, married James Valentine Gardner.

** Mirza Unjun Shekó, the eldest son of Mirza Suliman Shekó, married Susan Gardner also known as Shureah Begum.

*** Stewart William Gardner further united the two families by marrying his second cousin once removed Hirmoozee.

William Gardner Esq. of Coleraine

Elizabeth Farrington

William Gardner *Lt Colonel*

Susannae Hyde Gale

Allan Gardner *Baron, 1800*

Maria Adderley

Francis Gardner *Rear Admiral*

G. V. Strau Benzee

Alan Hyde *Lord Gardner*

Charlotte *daughter of Lord Carrington*

Alaida Scott

Valentine Gardner

Frances Holworthy

Valentine Gardner *born 1759*

Alaida Livingstone

William Linnaeus Gardner *Colonel*

Nawáb Matmunzilool Nissa Begum Delmi

Frances *daughter of Lord Dinorben*

Alan Legge

Stewart William Gardner

Hirmoozee

Mungo *died*

Beebee Sahiba Hinga

Allan Gardner

A Daughter

Mulka Humanee Begum

Susan *aka* Shubbeah Begum

Mirza Unjun Sheko

James Valentine Gardner

Sulimán

William Linnaeus

Nashaba Begum

An infant daughter

Bibi Sahiba Banoo

Alaida *The Morning Star*

The Evening Star

Hinga

secondly, Mulka Humanee Begum and by her had four children, two sons and two daughters: Sulimān and William Linnaeus; Nashaba Begum, and another girl.

Mirza Sulimān Shekō, son of Shāh Allum, the late Emperor of Delhi, and brother of Akbar Shāh, the present Emperor, has a numerous family. Two of the daughters were celebrated for their beauty: one of them, Mulka Humanee Begum, married her cousin, Mirza Selīm, the son of Akbar Shāh, from whom she was divorced: she married, secondly, Mr James Gardner. Sultana Bōa, the other daughter, married Nusseer-ood-Deen Hydur, the King of Oude. Mirza Unjun Shekō, son of Mirza Suliman Shekō and half-brother of Mulka Begum, is engaged to Susan Gardner, as before-mentioned.

Colonel Gardner was exceedingly unwilling to allow of the marriage of his granddaughter with the young prince but the old *begum*, his wife, had set her heart upon it. He would rather have seen her married to a European gentleman; but the *begum*, who is an adopted daughter of the Emperor of Delhi, is delighted with the match – in *her* eyes a fine alliance.

I must describe the bride, Susan Gardner or, as she is called in the *zenāna*, Shubbeah Begum, every lady having her name and title also. She had been cried up by the people at Agra as a great beauty, and Colonel Gardner had received several proposals for her, both from European and native gentlemen. She was also described as very accomplished for the inhabitant of four walls, being able to read, write and keep accounts with *gram*. She is about twenty years of age, very old for a bride in this country, where girls marry at eleven or twelve, and the proverb describes them as 'shrivelled at twenty'.

My surprise was great when I saw her in the *zenāna*. Her complexion is pale and sallow, her face flat, her figure extremely thin and far from pretty. Her flatterers called her 'so fair!' but she has not the fairness of a European or the fine clear brown of some Asiatic ladies: her manners were also admired, but I did not like them, nor did she move stately as an elephant, an epithet applied to a woman having a graceful gait.

Unjun Shekō, the bridegroom, who is about twenty years of age, is a remarkably handsome man; his black curling hair hangs in long locks on each side his face; his eyes very large, long and bright; his features fine; his complexion a clear brown: his figure the middle size; and like all natives, he wore a beard, moustache and whiskers. His three brothers, who came to the wedding with him, are ugly, low-caste looking men. Unjun's manners are good, theirs are cubbish. For four or five years he has been trying to bring about this marriage; but Colonel Gardner opposed it on account of his extravagance. His father, Sulimān Shekō, has refused to give one rupee to the young couple, so that the whole expense of the wedding falls upon Colonel Gardner: he pays for both sides. The young prince has only an allowance of Rs 100 a month! Natives, especially native women, are curious beings; the whole pride of their lives consists in having had a grand wedding: they talk of it and boast of it to the hour of their death. Colonel Gardner said, 'If I were to give Shubbeah the money that will be fooled away in display at this marriage, I should make her miserable; she would think herself disgraced; and although by custom she is not allowed to stir from her room, or to see the sight, still it will charm her to hear the road was lighted up for so many miles, the fireworks were so fine and the procession so grand! She would have this to talk of in preference to the money, even if she were forced to deprive herself of half her food all her life; she is a *pukka* Hindostāni!' They were horrified at my description of an English marriage. A carriage and four, attended by five or six other carriages, made a good wedding; when the ceremony had been performed by the padre, the bride and bridegroom drove away: no procession, no fireworks; the money put in the banker's hands, the parents gave a dinner and ball, and all was finished.

The *begum* was in a perfect agony from morning till night, lest any one thing should be forgotten – lest any, even the smallest gift might be omitted; if it were, the people would say, 'What a shabby wedding!' and, in spite of all the expense, she would lose her good name.

It would be utterly impossible for me to recount the innumerable ceremonies performed at the wedding of a Mohammedan; the following are a few of the most remarkable.

March 12th – The ceremonies began: in the first place, the bridegroom's party, consisting of Mr James Gardner, Mulka Begum, Mrs B— and Mr V—, went into tents four miles distant; while the bride's party, consisting of Colonel Gardner, his *begum*, the bride and myself, remained at Khasganj. We had also, in the outer house, Mr Valentine Gardner, a party of English gentlemen, and the old Nawāb of Cambay. It appeared curious to me to sit down to dinner with these gentlemen, who were all attired in native dresses, and do the honours, at times when my dear Colonel Gardner was too unwell to quit the *zenāna* and join the dinner party in the outer house. The turban is not a necessary appendage to Asiatic attire; in all friendly or familiar intercourse the skull cap is worn – the turban in company; it is disgraceful to uncover the head.

But to return to my story. About three o'clock, Mulka Begum came in procession to bring the bride's dress, which is a present from the bridegroom. The procession consisted of elephants, four-wheeled native carriages drawn by bullocks called *raths*, palanquins, led horses, etc.; and one hundred trays, carried on men's heads, containing the dress for the bride, sweetmeats and *basun* (flour of gram), wherewith to wash the lady. Mulka Begum came in a covered palanquin, screened from the gaze of men.

I, as in duty bound, had made my salam to Shubbeah Begum, and was in attendance in the *zenāna* to receive the bridegroom's party.

'Women of the lower class, on entering·the female assembly, must not say "salam"; if the hostess be a lady of rank, they perform *kudumbosee* (the ceremony of kissing the feet) to her and merely make salam to the rest. When going away they request permission, in the same way as the men in the male assembly, and take their departure.

'*Kudumbosee*, or the ceremony of kissing the feet, is, rather, to touch the feet of the hostess with the right hand and then kiss the latter or, more generally, make salam with it; while her ladyship, scarce allowing it to be done, out of politeness and condescension withdraws her foot; and, taking hold of her hands, says, "Nay, don't do that!" or "Enough!" "Long may you live!" "Come, be seated!" Or, if she be married, "May God render your *sohag* durable!" i.e. May God preserve your husband: if he be dead, "May God cause your end to be happy!"

'The men of the better ranks of society however, when coming in or going away, say, "*Salam, bundugee tuslemat!*" i.e. "My blessing, service or salutation to you!" according to the rank of the lady of the house.

[...]

Speaking of men entering a *zenāna*, the place is considered so sacred that, in a native family, only the nearest male relatives, the father and grandfather, can unrestrainedly obtain admission; the uncles and brothers only on especial occasions. The bride was once allowed to be seen by the brothers of Mirza Selīm, her betrothed husband; but he requested that no other persons but Colonel and Mr James Gardner might behold her and said, after marriage, he should not allow her to be seen even by his own brothers.

The trays containing the presents, brought in procession from the Prince, were received by the female slaves, conveyed by them into the *zenāna* and placed before Colonel Gardner's *begum* and the Princess Mulka. It is a custom never to send back an empty tray; if money be not sent, part of the contents of the tray is left, fruit, flowers, etc. The presents were displayed on the ground before the bride, who was sitting on a *chārpāi*, wrapped in an Indian shawl, hiding her face and sobbing violently; I thought she was really in distress, but found this violent sorrow was only a part of the ceremony. Mulka Begum took a silver bowl, and putting into it sandalwood powder and turmeric and oil, mixed it up, whilst both she and Colonel Gardner's *begum* repeated with great care the names and titles on both sides; it being unlucky if any name be forgotten, as any evil that may chance to befall the bride hereafter would be occasioned by forgetfulness, or mistaking the name over this oily mixture. The bride was well rubbed from head to foot with it; how yellow it made her, the turmeric! The natives say it makes the skin *so beautiful, so yellow*, and so soft: it certainly renders the skin deliciously soft, but the yellow tinge I cannot admire. After this operation was performed, all the mixture was scraped up, put into the bowl and mixed with more oil to be sent to the Prince, that his body might be rubbed with it – this is considered a compliment!

The bridal dress was then put on Shubbeah; it was of yellow gauze, trimmed with silver; the *pājāmas* of red satin and silver. The faces of the attendants were smeared by way of frolic with the oily mixture, and the bridegroom's party returned to their tents. I must not forget to mention that from the moment the bride is rubbed with this turmeric, she is a prisoner for ten days; not allowed to move from her *chārpāi*, on which she sits up or sleeps. Twice a day she is rubbed with almond soap, mixed with turmeric, etc. All this time she is never allowed to bath. She is fed on sweetmeats and not allowed to touch acids or vinegar, etc. Even *pān* is almost denied; but I fancy, without it an Asiatic lady would fret herself to death. And in this horrible state, a girl is kept during all the gaiety of the wedding; never allowed to move; to make her skin soft and yellow and to render her sweet-tempered, I suppose, by feeding her with lumps of sugar!

As soon as the bridegroom's party were gone, Colonel Gardner requested me to go in procession with his pretty granddaughter Alaida (the Morning Star), to the Prince's tents, to escort the dress of the bridegroom, sent as a present by the bride. We went accordingly in full procession, as described before, taking back the oily mixture. Mulka Begum received us at the Prince's tent; he was placed on a silver footstool; Mulka took off his upper dress and rubbed his face and arms with the mixture; she then arrayed him in a dress of yellow and orange muslin, a red turban, and red silk *pājāmas*, in which attire he looked very handsome.

Before him sat three women, the *Domnee*, playing and singing bridal songs; I saw the Prince turn very red; he looked at the women and said something, in a low tone, to Mulka Begum, who answered – 'The memsāhib knows they are singing *gālee* (abuse); but she does not understand Hindustani sufficiently to comprehend their songs.' The language of the songs is complete *slang*. Yellow powder, mixed with water, was then thrown in frolic at all the people; I made my salam, quitted the tent, and finding a gentleman in waiting ready to drive me back, returned to Colonel Gardner's, leaving the rest of the party to play and sing all night. Thus ended the first day of the ceremonies.

At the festival of the Hooli which is particularly dedicated to Krishna, images of the deity are carried about on elephants, horses, in *palkees*, etc. The songs are exclusively in honour of Krishna, and hailing the return of the season, personified under the name of Vasanta, generally pronounced Bessant. Kāma, the god of love, is the son of Krishna.

The Hooli was celebrated by the natives with due glee; they threw *abeer* (red powder) into each other's faces and then squirted orange-coloured water over it; people were also sent on April-fool errands. Colonel Gardner avoided appearing amongst the people during this festival, and I imitated his example. The orange-coloured water is tinged with the flowers of the *dhāk* tree; the *abeer* is flour made from the *singharra* (water nut) and dyed with red sanders; the roots of the *singharra* are loosened by means of ropes fastened between two boats, with several men in each; and iron prongs are used in collecting them.

I mentioned to Colonel Gardner the songs of the women, the *Domnee*, who were in the tent, and the distress of the Prince. He said, 'When marriages are negotiating, in particular, they are of the most unchaste description; they are admitted on occasions, but the *nāch* girls never; the songs of the *Domnee* are indecent beyond the conception of a European.'

Nāch women dance and sing before men and are not allowed to enter *zenānas* of respectability; but in all great establishments, such as Colonel Gardner's and that of his son, the slave girls are formed into sets of dancing girls, to sing and play for the amusement of the *begums*.

Colonel Gardner remarked, 'The songs of the *nāch* girls are never indecent, unless "by particular desire", and then in representing the bearer's dance – a dance which is never performed before ladies.'

[...]

The Sāchak

WHEN THERE IS A MARRIAGE THEY MAY SING ALL NIGHT

March 28th – [...] After the bride and bridegroom had been rubbed a certain number of days with the oily mixture, the time appointed for the second day's ceremonies arrived; which is called the *sāchak*. Mulka Begum and the prince arrived in procession. The bridegroom's party were dressed out in all their bravery. The party of the bride wore their old clothes and looked as deplorable as possible. This was according to custom and therefore strictly observed. On this day it is the fashion for the bride's mother to appear in an undress, and even that soiled! The procession consisted of elephants in all their crimson and gold trappings, led horses, English and Arab; *nalkis*, a sort of litter used by people of rank, palanquins, and *raths*, (native bullock carriages,) etc. A number of men dressed up as horses were prancing about, kicking and playing antics, and two hundred earthen vessels (*gharas*) filled with sweetmeats, which looked very gay from being covered with silver-leaf, were carried on the heads of two hundred men.

The platforms for the *nāch* women were the most curious part of the procession. They are called *takhti-rawān*, a sort of travelling throne, formed of bamboo, square in form, over which was spread an awning ornamented with crimson and gold and silver, and supported by four bamboos, one at each angle of the platform. On each travelling throne sat a native musician playing on a kettledrum, and before him danced two *nāch* women; the girls twirled and *nāched* with all their might and skill. The platforms were *carried on the heads* of a number of men in the procession, and had a curious and singular effect; the situation was a very unsteady one for the dancing girls, one of whom became giddy and tumbled down upon the heads of the crowd of people below. In this fashion ten stands, containing twenty *nāch* girls and ten musicians, were carried on men's heads to the sound of kettledrums. When Mulka had brought in the procession and the company were seated, *atr* of sandalwood was put on each person's face and a necklace of silver tissue around their necks. The same three vile old women began their songs of abuse; abusing the prince, the *begums*, and myself; but as it was the custom, no one could be angry. I could only guess the sort of abuse; I could not understand it, never having heard it before. The prince's yellow dress, now quite dirty, was on him still; according to custom, *over* it was put on a dress of cloth of gold and crimson. In front of his turban the jewelled *jika* was placed, and on his arms valuable *bāzubands* – armlets of precious stones. All this time the poor little bride was kept in her oily attire on her *chārpāi* and not allowed to stir. She only heard the noise and uproar of the procession. Mulka's dress was very elegant.

The Mehndi – the Third Day

March 29th – The *mendhi* is the tree, *Lawsonia inermis*, from the leaves of which the *hinnā* dye is produced: the leaves are gathered and pounded; when put on the hands and feet and allowed to remain an hour or two, it produces a dark brownish red dye, which is permanent for four or five months; the hands and feet, both of men and women, thus dyed are reckoned beautiful. It is remarkable that female mummies have the nails stained with *mendhi*.

A number of trays of this prepared *mendhi* were carried on men's heads, covered with embroidered velvet: they were sent from the bride to dye the bridegroom. This was the grand display on the part of the bride's friends, who all, dressed in all their most costly attire went, at eleven at night, in procession from Khasganj to the Prince's tents. The road was enclosed with bamboo screens, all lighted up with thousands of small lamps; fireworks were let off in profusion and the triumphal arches across the road were all illuminated; five thousand torches were carried by men to light the procession. The *begum* herself was there in her *pālkee*, the curtains all down and fastened; the ladies in a long line of native carriages, called *raths*; the boys in different sorts of native *pālkees*, the men, handsomely dressed, on elephants. I went in an *amāri*, on an elephant; the *amāri* is a litter with two seats, covered by two canopies; when the seat on an elephant is open, without a canopy, it is called a *howdah*. Mr T—, a friend, accompanied me; we sat in the front seat and a native gentleman occupied the seat at the back. The elephant was a very large one; we were a great height from the ground and had a good view, being above the smoke of the blue lights. The native gentleman amused us by his astonishment at Mr T—'s not being a married man; my friend told him he wished to marry, but how could he without seeing the lady? The Asiatic said that was impossible; but could he not depend on his female friends to see and select for him? Mr T— deputed me to select a wife for him; the native gentleman thought him in earnest and said, when every thing was arranged, I might show Mr T— her picture before they were married. In this manner weddings are made up; it would be the height of indelicacy to suppose a girl could have a choice, she marries just anyone whom her friends select. The led horses, in their gay native caparison, looked so well amongst the blue lights; and the handsomest of all was Candidate, an imported English horse, formerly the property of Major P—; Rattler, another English horse, sixteen hands high, whom I had ridden several times was also there. They were so quiet and well-behaved in the crowd and amongst the fireworks, much more quiet than the native horses.

The ten platforms, containing the twenty *nāch* girls and the kettledrum players carried on men's heads, were also there. The effect of the gay dresses of the women, as they twirled and attitudinised, was good by torchlight. Some of the girls, who were horrors by daylight, looked pretty by the artificial light, at a distance. It took two hours to go with the procession the four miles through the village of Khasganj to the tents. All the inhabitants were either on the road or on the roofs of their houses, and we were attended by thousands of people: such a crowd, we could scarcely move forwards. On our arrival at the tents we found Mulka Begum's tent prepared for the reception of the females of our party. It was in utter darkness. In front fine bamboo screens were let down which, inside, were covered with thin white muslin. Through this *parda*, from the inside of the tent, you could see what was going on without, where everything was brilliantly lighted, whilst we were in complete darkness. From without you could not see into the tent in the slightest degree. These screens are called *pardas*, and the women who live within them, *parda nishin*, secluded behind the curtain. In front of the tent was pitched a very large *shamiyāna*, a canopy, supported on every side by high poles; white cloths were spread on the ground. In the centre was seated the young Prince on his *gaddi* (throne of the sovereign), most beautifully dressed and looking very handsome. His four ill-looking brothers were next to him. On a plain *gaddi*, by his side, sat Colonel Gardner and myself; and all the English and native gentlemen were seated on either side. In front, were one hundred *nāch* women, the best to be procured, brought, at an immense expense, from great distances; six or eight of these girls danced at a time and were relieved by another set. Around were countless numbers of natives in all their gayest dresses: and still further back were many elephants, on which people had mounted to get a sight of the *tamāshā*. When the preparations within were ready, Colonel Gardner took me, his son, and the five princes within the tent; a screen (*parda*) was drawn across part of the tent, behind which were some native ladies, whom it would have been improper the men should have seen, they not being their relatives. The Prince was placed on a low silver seat and fed with sugar; the amusement appeared to be, as you offered the sugar and the Prince attempted to take it in his mouth, to snatch away your hand. The ladies behind the *parda* also put forth their hands to feed him with sugar; he tried to catch their hands, and having succeeded in catching the hand of one of the girls who was teasing him, he tried to draw off her ring, and in the struggle she was nearly pulled through the *parda*!

A silver bason was brought, and from it Mulka Begum, Alaida, and her sister, the Evening Star, put the *menhdi* on the Prince's hands and feet, and washed it off with water, which they poured from a silver vessel of the most classical and beautiful shape I almost ever beheld. A turban of green and gold, ornamented with brilliants and precious stones, was placed on his head; he was then dressed in a dress of *kimkhwab* (gold brocade), a red and gold cumerbund, green *pājāmas*, and a ring and armlets of great value and beauty were also put upon him. Sherbet was given to him and all the guests to drink, and their mouths were wiped with a sort of napkin of red and gold cloth by the cup-bearer.

Into the sherbet tray each guest put a gold *mohur*, the perquisite of the girls who had put the *menhdi* on the Prince. Afterwards, a slave-girl brought a silver vessel with water; water was poured over the hands of the guests, each of whom put four or five rupees into the bowl; this was given the *Domnee*, the same three old women who in one corner were singing all the time. Necklaces of the fresh flowers of the yellow jasmine were thrown over the neck of the prince and the guests. After these ceremonies were completed, the Prince and Colonel Gardner quitted the tent. I remained with the *begum*. A ceremony was then performed that surprised me considerably; the native ladies laughed, and appeared to think it high *tamāshā*.

It was now dinner time, being midnight. The inner *pardas* of the tent were let down and lights were brought in. A white cloth was spread on the ground in front of the *begum*'s *gaddī*, upon which eight large round dishes of earthenware were placed. These were filled with boiled rice mixed with almonds and many good things, very pleasant food. These dishes are always prepared at Asiatic weddings, as bride-cake is always an attendant on the same ceremony in Europe. The rice was piled up high, and silvered all over with silver leaf, and a tuft of silver ornamented the top. Silvered food is much used by natives; and in helping a dish, if you wish to pay a compliment, you send as much gold and silver leaf as you can. At weddings the food is served in earthen vessels, instead of the silver vessels commonly used because, when the repast is over, the remainder of it, vessels and all, are given away.

Of course, according to Asiatic custom, we all sat on the ground. The *begum* said, 'What shall we do? we have no knives and forks for the bībīsāhib.' I assured her my fingers were more useful than forks. She sent me a large dish, well filled and well silvered. I bowed over it, saying in an undertone to myself, '*Jupiter omnipotens digitos dedit ante bidentes.*' The *begum* explained to the guests, 'English ladies always say grace before meals.' After holding forth my right hand to have water poured upon it, I boldly dipped my fingers into the dish and contrived to appease my hunger very comfortably, much to the amusement of the Asiatic ladies: but I found I could not get my fingers half so far into my mouth as they contrived to do; certainly the mode is ungraceful, but this may be prejudice. I looked at Mulka Begum, how far she pushed her delicate fingers down her throat – wah! wah!

[. . .]

After the repast silver vessels were handed round and our mouths and fingers underwent ablution. *Besan*, the flour of *gram*, as good for the purpose as almond-paste, was presented to each guest; with it the grease was removed from the fingers, and water was poured over them.

Necklaces most beautifully made of silver tissue were now given to the whole of the company, both within and without the tent; the lights were carried away, a portion of the *parda* was removed and we, unseen, could then observe what was going on without the tent, the *nāching*, and the company. Seeing the *begum* apparently fatigued, I requested she would give me my dismissal which, having received, I made my salam and returned to Colonel Gardner with whom I sat looking at the *nāch* until three o'clock, at which hour the prince, by taking his departure, broke up the assembly. [. . .] I returned to Khasganj in a palanquin, in which I slept all the way home, being fatigued and overcome with the exertions of the day.

It was a sight worth seeing; the thousands of well-dressed natives in picturesque groups and the dancing girls under the brilliantly illuminated trees. I was delighted to sit by my dear Colonel Gardner, and to hear his explanations. In conversation he was most interesting, a man of great intelligence and in mind playful as a child. I often begged him to write his life, or to allow me to write it at his dictation. The description of such varied scenes as those through which he had passed would have been delightful; and he wrote so beautifully, the work would have been invaluable. He used to tell me remarkable incidents in his life, but I never wrote them down, feeling that unless I could remember his language, the histories would be deprived of half their beauty.

I have never described Mr James Gardner, his son. He is a remarkably shrewd, clever, quick man. He has never been in England: he commenced his education at a school in Calcutta; and the remainder he received at home, from Colonel Gardner and his friend Mr B——. Persian he reads and writes as fluently as a native, and transacts all his business in that language. He is very quick and so deep, they say he even outwits the natives. He is very hospitable – expert in all manly exercises – a fine horseman – an excellent swordsman – skilled in the lance exercise – an admirable shot with the bow and arrow – excels in all native games and exercises. I fancy the *begum*, his mother, would never hear of her son's going to England for education; and to induce a native woman to give way to any reasons that are contrary to her own wishes is quite out of the power of mortal man. A man may induce a European wife to be unselfish and make a sacrifice to comply with his wishes, or for the benefit of her children. A native woman would only be violent, enraged and sulky, until the man, tired and weary with the dispute and eternal worry, would give her her own way. Such at least is my opinion from what I have seen of life within the four walls of a *zenāna*. James Gardner is most perfectly suited to the life he leads: the power of the sun does not affect him so much as it does other people: he rides about his estates and farms all day: he has a great number of villages of his own, of which he is lord and master, and is able to conduct his affairs and turn his indigo and farming to profit. In all this he is assisted by the advice of Mulka Begum, to whom the natives look up with the highest respect. She is a clever woman, and her word is regarded as law by her villagers and dependants.

CHAPTER XXXVI

The Barāt

MARCH 30TH 1835 – Colonel Gardner said to me, 'The bridegroom will come tonight to carry away his bride; it is an old Tartar custom for the man to fight for his wife, and carry her away by force of arms; this is still retained. I shall have the doors of the gateway barred at the entrance; and the soldiers on the prince's arrival, after refusing to admit him, will at length allow him to enter, if he give them some gold *mohurs*. We, of the bride's party, are not to join in the procession, but you may go out on an elephant provided you put no gay trappings upon him; and you can look on and say, "What a paltry procession, not half as fine as ours last night!" This is the custom (*dasturi*). I will go in my *tanjan* and stand at one side.' This was the grand day of all: the prince and his party came at night; the village through which they passed was illuminated, as well as the road and the triumphal arches; they were accompanied by bands of music and flags innumerable; at every halt fireworks were let off, while blue lights added a picturesque effect to the scene. The prince rode at the head of the procession on an Arab covered with embroidered trappings; on each side the animal was decorated with the white tails of the yak; and over all was thrown an ornamental armour made of flowers. On the head of the Arab was a *jika*, an ornament from which arose a heron's plume, of which each feather was tipped with gold; his neck, the bridle and the crupper were adorned with ornaments and golden chains. According to etiquette, an attendant on foot by the side of the horse carried an *āftābī*, a sun embroidered on velvet attached to a staff, gaily ornamented and carried in an elevated position: it is used as a protection from the rays of the sun, and also as a point of dignity. Another carried a magnificent *chatr* umbrella of silk, embroidered with gold, a mark of royalty. In Oude the king alone is entitled to the *chatr*, with the exception of the resident and his assistant. Then followed the elephants, friends and attendants on horseback, palanquins and native carriages of many descriptions: the procession was interspersed with the platforms containing dancing girls, carried by men, and a number of horses, English,

Arab and country, were led by their grooms. Innumerable torches flared in every direction, and small lamps fixed on ladders (chirāghs), were carried horizontally by the attendants. Artificial trees made of wax, coloured paper and shola, decorated with gold and silver leaf, mica, and coloured foil, were carried by men in great number, and added a strangely Asiatic effect to the whole, as the blue lights fell upon them.

When the procession arrived at the entrance to Colonel Gardner's estate, the doors of the gateway were found closed and the prince was refused admittance; but after a mock fight, he was allowed to pass through into the grounds. The begum would not have omitted a Timūrian custom for the world. The dress of the bridegroom consisted entirely of cloth of gold; and across his forehead was bound a sort of fillet (sihrā) made of an embroidery of pearls, from which long strings of gold hung down all over his face to his saddle-bow; and to his mouth he kept a red silk handkerchief closely pressed to prevent devils entering his body! In this heavy dress of gold the prince did not look to advantage.

I went out with two gentlemen on a very shabbily-dressed elephant; we stopped by the roadside and had a good view of the procession. One of the party, Mr F—, attired most becomingly in the native fashion, mounted on a handsome white Arab, caparisoned in purple and gold, looked like a picture in a fairy tale, as he rode amongst the blue lights; his plain dress of fine white dacca muslin, with a white muslin turban and a handsome black Indian shawl, put round his waist coxcomically in native style, was in very good taste. We remained about an hour viewing the scene – the effect was excellent; even the old Nawāb of Cambay came out in a tanjan and looked happy and well pleased. On looking for Colonel Gardner, I saw the dear old man seated on the side of a well, in darkness, and quite removed from the crowd, looking on and smiling at the foolery. Perhaps his thoughts reverted to his own marriage, when he had undergone the same ceremonies: I asked him how he could have endured such folly? He answered, 'I was young then; and in love, I would have done or promised anything.'

A very large awnings (shamiyāna) was pitched before Colonel Gardner's house; the ground beneath it was spread with white cloths, on which was placed the Prince's gaddi, of velvet embroidered with gold. An immense number of native gentlemen, wedding guests, were present; they came from their tents, which were all pitched on the estate around the house. During the last two days of the wedding, every man, woman, child, horse, elephant and servant were fed at Colonel Gardner's expense, and an immense outlay it must have been; my jamadār came to me and said, 'For the next two days your horses and servants will be fed by Colonel Gardner; do not object to it, it would bring ill-luck on the wedding; it is the custom (*dasturi*).' It is also the custom to sit up the whole night on this occasion; to beguile the time, a great number of brilliant fireworks (*ātashbāzi*) were let off, which were fixed in the grounds in front of the house. The dancing girls descended from the platforms on which they had been carried, assembled under the *shamiyāna*, and sang and attudinised the whole night, one set relieving the other. The Prince seated himself on his *gaddi*, and the contract of marriage was read to him; it was written in Persian on beautifully illuminated parchment, for which Colonel Gardner paid duty Rs 450, that is £45.

Previous to the signature, it was necessary to gain the formal consent of the bride; for which purpose Mr James Gardner took the *kāzi* (native judge) and two of his native officers, with Mrs B— and myself, into the *zenāna*. We stood in an empty room, adjoining that in which were the bride and the *begum*, her grandmother; between us was the *parda*; we could hear, but not see. The *kāzi* said, 'Is Shubbeah Begum present?' 'Yes.' 'Does Shubbeah Begum give her free consent to marry Mirza Unjun Shekō?' An answer was made, but in so low a tone it was more like a murmur.

Mr Gardner said, 'You are witnesses, and have heard her give her consent.' I replied, 'No; I heard a murmur, but know not what it meant.'

The *begum* then said, 'It is the custom for the bride, from modesty, to be unable to answer; but I, her grandmother, say, "Yes" for her.'

The *kāzi* said, 'Mirza Unjun Shekō will settle seven lakh of rupees upon her.'

The *begum* answered, 'We forgive him two lakh, let him settle five.'

A lady laughed, and whispered to me, 'The young Prince has not five cowries of his own.'

If the bride were to give her consent in words, she would be disgraced for ever as an impudent good-for-nothing; after repeated demands, and sometimes *pinchings*, her voice is heard in a sort of *hem* which, it is taken for granted, means 'Yes.'

A certain number of lumps of sugar were then sent from the bride to the Prince, and we returned to see him sign the contract.

The *kāzi* having taken off the veil of gold tissue and the fillet that were around the head of the bridegroom, requested him to repeat after him, in Arabic, a portion of some of the chapters in the Qur'an, and, having explained the contract, asked him if he consented to it; to which he answered in the affirmative; after which the Qur'an offered up a supplication on behalf of the betrothed pair; and several other ceremonies were performed.

The contract, a most curious document, was then read aloud. The Prince, having listened attentively, signed it; and several English gentlemen added their names as witnesses, to make it as binding as possible.

The dowry is made high as the *only* security the wife has that her husband will not turn her away as soon as he gets tired of her.

Colonel Gardner then took the contract and said, 'I shall keep this in my possession.' I asked him 'Why?' He said, 'It is generally kept by the bride; as long as she has it the husband behaves well; for a few months he treats her kindly, and she becomes fond of him; he coaxes her out of the contract, or he finds out where she hides it and steals it; when once he has got it into his possession he swears she gave it up willingly, and the contract is void.'

During the time we were signing the contract, a different scene was going on within the *zenāna*.

The Prince sent the nose-ring (*n'hut*) to the bride, which is equivalent to putting the wedding-ring on the finger in Europe; it was a large thin hoop of gold, and a ruby between two pearls was strung upon it. On receiving it, the bride was taken from her *chārpāī*, on which she had reposed during all the preceding days of this ceremony, in her yellow dress and oily paste, and was bathed. What a luxury that bath must have been, after so many nights and days of penance! She was then dressed in her handsomest attire, richly embroidered garments and an immense number of jewels; but not one atom of this costume was visible, for *over all* was placed a large square of cloth of silver, and *over that* another large square, formed of cloth of gold, which covered her entirely from head to foot, face and all. Over her forehead was bound the same sort of fillet (*sihrā*) as the Prince wore, composed of strings of pearls and strings of gold, which hung down over the veil so that she could not see and could scarcely breathe.

When the guns fired at the signing of the contract, the Prince ate the lumps of sugar that had been sent him by the bride; he then arose and, quitting the male assembly, went into the *zenāna*, where he was received by the *begum* and her guests! and seated on a *gaddi*. Soon after Mr James Gardner appeared with the bride in his arms; he carried her from her own room, according to custom, and placed her on the *gaddi* by the side of the Prince.

There she sat, looking like a lump of gold; no one could have imagined a human being was under such a covering; with difficulty she was kept from fainting, the heat was so excessive. Her lips and teeth had been blackened for the first time with *misi*, and gold and silver dust had been thrown over her face!

Surma (*collyrium*) also had been applied to her eyelids, at the roots of the lashes, by means of a piece of silver or lead made in the shape of a probe without the knob at the end. The ladies in attendance on the young *begum* then performed innumerable ceremonies; they fed the Prince with sugar-candy and sifted sugar through his hands; they put a lump of sugar on the head of the bride, off which he took it up in his mouth and ate it; sugar was placed on her shoulders, on her hands, on her feet, and it was his duty to eat all this *misri* off all those parts of her body. The bride's slipper was concealed under rich coverings, and the grand art appeared to be to make the Prince eat the sugar-candy off the shoe!

The Qur'an was produced, and some parts of it were read aloud; a large Indian shawl was then spread over the heads of the bride and bridegroom, as they sat on the floor, and the shawl was supported like a canopy by the ladies in attendance. A looking-glass was put into the hands of the Prince, he drew the veil of the bride partly aside, and they beheld each other's faces for the first time in the looking-glass! At this moment, had any false description of the bride been given to the bridegroom, he had the power of saying, 'I have been deceived, the face I see is not the face that was portrayed to me; I will not marry this woman.' However the Prince looked pleased, and so did she, for I saw her smile at this important moment; at which time I particularly observed the expression of their countenances. The Prince took up his bride in his arms – the golden lump I before described – and placing her on a silver *chārpāi*, sat down by her side and fanned her carefully. The poor girl was almost stifled beneath the gold and silver coverings that oppressed but did not adorn her. By this time the light had nearly passed away; the remainder was taken up with tedious and trivial ceremonies; at last morning dawned, and at eleven o'clock the dowry was counted and made ready to carry away.

When the moment arrived for the Prince to carry off his bride, the whole of the women in the *zenāna* came round her and cried and wept with all their might and main; even those who did not regret her departure cried and wept most furiously. Colonel Gardner was sitting there, looking pale and miserable; when he embraced his granddaughter, whom he loved, the old man trembled in every limb, the tears dropped from his eyes and he could scarcely stand. He called the Prince to him and told him that, according to his treatment of his child should be his own conduct towards him; that if he made her happy he should want for nothing; but if he made her unhappy he would make him miserable. Colonel Gardner then said to me 'When I gave her sister to young Gardner I knew she would be happy, but this poor girl, who may prophesy her fate? However, she wished it; her mother and the *begum* had set their hearts upon it; and you know, my *beti* (my child), women will have their own way.'

Although Colonel Gardner always called me his child, and treated me as such, my title in the *zenāna* was 'Fanī Bhua' because his son usually addressed me as '*Sister* of my Father.' When it was announced that the procession was ready, the Prince took the bride up in his arms, in her lump-like position and carried her to her palanquin, the *pardas* of which were then let down and fastened outside with gold and silver cords.

This taking up a girl who is sitting on the floor in your arms, and carrying her away without touching the ground with your knees, and without any assistance from another person, is a difficult affair to accomplish; to fail in doing it would be deemed unlucky. The bridegroom performed it very cleverly.

The Prince, in the dress in which he arrived, attended the palanquin on horseback; and the whole of the bride's dowry followed in procession, carried on the heads of men and displayed to view. One golden-footed bed, and one silver-footed *chārpāī*; a number of large trunks, covered with red cloth, containing cashmere shawls and ready-made clothes, sufficient to last for one year; and unmade clothes and pieces of *kimkhwab*, gold and silver tissues, silks and pieces of India muslin, enough to last for three years. I saw a large pile of *pājāmas* for the bride put into one of the trunks, considered sufficient for the wear of a year; besides which, forty pieces, consisting of coloured silks and gold brocades, for the same article of dress, were sent unmade and deemed sufficient for three years to come. Two elephants, several horses, a very handsome *bilee* for the lady herself, and several *raths* for the ladies in attendance upon her; as also a palanquin. Then came, carried on trays, dishes of various sorts for the household, which were made of pure silver; ewers and *chilamchīs* of the same; also for the cook-room, every article in iron or copper necessary for the establishment of a newly-married couple; and all these things were of the best description. The jewels for the bride, which were very handsome and very valuable, were carried in state, together with a *pāndān* for holding betel, and all the ingredients for *pān*; another box, with partitions for spices, cardamums, etc.; a *misī-dān* for holding *misī* (a powder made of vitriol), with which they tinge the teeth of a black colour; a *surma-dān*, for holding *surma* (the collyrium which they apply to the eyes, to give them a brilliant appearance); an *atr-dān*, a *gulābpāsh* (for sprinkling rose-water); and every article for the toilet of an Asiatic lady. Quilts, mattresses, pillows, carpets, boxes, lamps; in fact, an endless list; besides male and female slaves to attend on the newly-married people. A Qur'an, for the bridegroom, was also carried in procession.

Everything necessary for the use of a native lady is sent on such an occasion and these articles are provided for years: head and heel ropes for the horses, and even wooden pegs to secure them, and the bullocks, are sent with the lady, that nothing may be wanting.

The Prince took his bride to his tents, and a remarkable ceremony was there witnessed by Mr Vigne, which he thus relates:

'I was admitted, as a great favour, to see a custom peculiar, I believe, to the Timūrians, and which perhaps no European ever saw before. Immediately after the marriage ceremony the bridegroom has the bride taken to his home; but before she quitted her palanquin, which was set down close to it, she thrust her bared foot – a very pretty one, and dyed with henna at the extremities – through the sliding doors and the bridegroom touched her great toe with the blood of a goat, which I saw him kill with his own hands, whilst yet in his bridal dress and turban, by then and there cutting its throat. When this was done, the bride withdrew her foot and I made my bow, and the bride and bridegroom retired to their inner apartments.'

By the time the procession had quitted the gates of the *zenāna*, I was very glad to return to my own rooms to bathe preparatory to breakfast. I had eaten nothing during the night but cardamums and prepared betel-nut: had smoked a little of Colonel Gardner's *huqqa*, and had drank nothing but tea. Mr Gardner prepared some *pān* for me in a particular fashion: I ate it and found it very refreshing. *Pān*, so universally eaten in India, is made of the leaf of the *piper betel*, a species of pepper plant, called *pān supéarie* and betel-nut; but this betel-nut is not the nut of the *piper betel*, but of the *Areca catechu*, a palm fifty feet in height. The betel-nut is cut up in small bits and wrapped up in the *pān*-leaf with lime *cuttie*, which is a bitter gum resin, an astringent vegetable extract, the produce of a species of mimosa (*chadira Catechu japonica*); called *kuth* by the natives, and some slaked lime, or *chunā*. *Pān* at marriage feasts is tied up in packets of a triangular shape, and covered with gold and silver leaf and enamelled foil of bright colours: the lime *cuttie* dyes the gums and tongue a deep red.

I was quite fresh and free from headache: had I sat up all night in England, where we eat supper, it would have made me ill. Colonel Gardner came in to breakfast, and kissing me on the forehead, said, '*Mera beti* (my child), you are less fatigued than anyone.' The Prince lived with his bride at the tents for three days, after which they returned to Colonel Gardner's to perform the final ceremony of playing the *chāotree*.

CHAPTER XXXVII

THE CHĀOTREE

ONE SNAKE HAS BIT THEM ALL

THE PRINCESS HAS GROWN FOOLISH, SHE PELTS HER OWN
RELATIONS WITH SWEETMEATS, OTHERS WITH STONES

THEY HAVE SCATTERED DATURA (THORN APPLE) IN THE AIR
i.e. the people are all gone mad.

APRIL 2ND 1835 – The *chāotree* was to be played this day, it being the finale of
the wedding. When the Prince and Shubbeah arrived at Khasganj they
came into the *zenāna* and were seated on the *gaddī*; a large number of trays,
containing fruits and vegetables of every description fresh from the garden,
were placed before them, with sugar, etc. Shubbeah had divested herself of her
bridal attire, and wore the *peshwāz*, the court dress of Delhi, which was made
of Benares tissue of gold and silver, and she wore all her jewels. Nine fruits of
different sorts were wrapped in a cloth and suspended round her waist by her
attendants; it had a curious effect, because the whole was placed beneath her
garments; she arose, encumbered with these fruits, and made salam to each of
the four corners of the room. Her hair was then decked with natural flowers,
her face having previously been covered with silver dust, and she and the
Prince were both fed with sugar off a rupee. A stick ornamented with silver
tissue was given to him, and another to her, with which they pretended to beat
each other; these silver wands were presented to all the ladies, and wands
covered with flowers were given to the slaves. For some days before the
chāotree, the *begum* had been employed in teaching the ladies in the *zenāna*
and the slave girls a particular dance, the ancient Princess herself dancing with
them with a silver wand in her hand. I mentioned this to Colonel Gardner; he
said, 'It is very remarkable that, at weddings, all the ladies of this family
perform this particular *nāch*, but at no other time do they dance; it would
lower their dignity. This is an old Tartar dance and always performed at
weddings amongst the Timūrians; it is the *dasturi*. The *tamāshā* consisted in
beating each other with these silver sticks, and throwing handfuls of fruits, of
turnips, of oranges, of pomegranates, in fact, anything that could be seized

from the trays, at each other; the slaves joining in the fun, breaking the glass windows by accident, and doing much damage. The more you pelt a person, the greater the compliment; sharp jealousy was created in many a breast this day, the source of much anxiety afterwards. This is called playing the *chāotree*, and finishes the ceremonies of the wedding.

Soon after, a woman came in with a large basket full of *chūris* for the arms (bracelets), which were made of rings of glass, ornamented with beads. Everybody at the wedding, from the *begum* to the youngest slave, had *chūris* put on their arms; I was also decorated. These rings are extremely small; to put them on requires considerable art, it being necessary to mull the hand and render it very pliant before it can pass through so very small a circumference as that of the *churi*.

Thus ended the wedding of Prince Unjun Sheko and Shubbeah Begum. They quitted their tents and went to reside at a pretty little fort and indigo factory, the property of Colonel Gardner, at Moreechee.

The *dūlhan* (bride) visits her mother on the four first Fridays after her marriage, on each of which the *dūlhā* (bridegroom) is bribed with a full suit.

'A marriage may be celebrated with a *mŭn* of rice as well as a *mŭn* of pearls.'

Another wedding immediately began, that of Jhanee Khanum, an adopted daughter of Colonel Gardner's, a slave girl; but I did not stay to witness it, having before seen the grand display.

It is the custom in the *zenāna* for every young lady to adopt the child of a slave, which serves as a doll, an amusement for her. Shubbeah had an adopted child, for whom she will have eventually to provide; and every lady in the *zenāna* had an adopted daughter of the same description. The slaves are a set of the most idle, insolent, good-tempered, thievish, laughing girls I ever saw. I should think, counting babies, slaves and all, there must have been two hundred souls within the four walls of Colonel Gardner's *zenāna*.

The prince allowed his brothers to see the bride the day of the wedding, but said he should not allow them to see her in future. A native woman thinks this sort of jealousy very flattering, and prides herself upon it.

The mother of Shubbeah was the happiest of the happy: in her idea, her child had made the finest match in the world, by marrying a prince of the house of Delhi, although she was brought up a Christian, he a follower of the prophet. Her other daughter was happily married, her husband being very fond of native life and native customs.

At noon all the slave girls came for their dinners; each was given a great *chapati* (cake of flour) as large as a plate, and this was filled brim full from two great vessels of curry and rice. This repast took place again at eight in the evening. One day, just as they were beginning their meal, I sat down in the verandah and played an Hindustani air on a *sitar*; up started all the slaves in an instant and set to, dancing with their food in their hands and their mouths full. Each slave girl carried her curry and rice on the wheaten cake which was about the size of a plate, and used it as such; until having eaten the contents she finished with the cake. In spite of their dexterity in putting the food down their throats without dropping the rice or soiling their dresses, the fingers retain a considerable portion of the yellow turmeric and the greasy *ghee*! They eat custards, rice, and milk, and more fluid food with the hand, sucking the fingers to clean them, and afterwards wipe them dry with a *chapāti*! They were merry, and fat, and happy, unless the *begum* happened to catch one out in a theft, when the other girls punished her. Some of the slaves were pretty girls and great favourites. To show how little they had to do, the following anecdote may suffice. A pretty slave girl was sitting by my bedside; I held out my hand, and desired her to shampoo it: the girl's countenance became clouded, and she did not offer to do it – her name was Tara (the Star). 'Why do you not mull my hand, Tara?' said I. 'Oh,' she replied, 'I never mull the hand; the other girls do that; I only mull the Colonel Sāhib's eyebrows. I can take the pain from them when he is ill – that is my duty. I will not shampoo the hand.' I laughed at her description of the work that fell to her lot as a slave, and said, 'Well, Tara, mull my eyebrows; my head aches;' with the greatest good-humour she complied, and certainly charmed away the pain. It is the great luxury of the East.

I might have lived fifty years in India and never have seen a native wedding. It is hardly possible for a European lady to be present at one. Alaida and her sister the Evening Star learnt to read and write Persian; a very old *moonshee* was allowed to teach them. Musulmān ladies generally forget their learning when they grow up, or they neglect it. Everything that passes without the four walls is reported to them by their spies: never was any place so full of intrigue, scandal, and chit-chat as a *zenāna*. Making up marriages is their great delight, and the bustle attendant on the ceremonies. They dote upon their children, and are so selfish they will not part from them to allow them to go to school, if it be possible to avoid it. The girls, of course, never quit the *zenāna*. Within the four walls surrounding the *zenāna* at Khasganj is a pretty garden with a summer-house in the centre; fountains play before it, and they are fond of spending their time out of doors. During the rains they take great delight in swinging under the large trees in the open air. They never ride on horseback, or go on the water for pleasure. They are very fond of *atr* of all sorts, the scent of which is overpowering in their houses. They put scented oil on their hair; to eau-de-Cologne and lavender-water they have the greatest aversion, declaring it to be gin, to drink! The prophet forbade all fermented liquors, after a battle which he nearly lost by his soldiers getting drunk, and being surprised.

The old *begum* said to Colonel Gardner, 'They are curious creatures, these English ladies; I cannot understand them or their ways – their ways are so odd!' And yet the *begum* must have seen so many European ladies, I wonder she had not become more reconciled to our *odd ways*.

The conduct that shocked them was our dining with men not our relations, and that too with uncovered faces. A lady going out on horseback is monstrous. They could not comprehend my galloping about on that great English horse just where I pleased, with one or two gentlemen and the coachman as my attendants. My not being afraid to sleep in the dark without having half a dozen slave girls snoring around me surprised them. My remaining *alone* writing in my own room; in not being unhappy when I was alone – in fact, they looked upon me as a very odd creature. It was almost impossible to enjoy solitude, the slave girls were peeping under the corner of every *parda*. Someone or other was always coming to talk to me, sometimes asking me to make up a marriage! If a native lady is relating a story, and you look incredulous, she exclaims. 'I swear to God it is true.' They are very fond of this exclamation. One day, in the gardens, I was talking to Tara the pretty slave girl, when she darted away over the poppy beds, screaming out, 'I swear to God there is a ripe poppy-head! and she came back with her ripe poppy-head, out of which she beat the seeds on the palm of her hand, and ate them. She then brought some more for me, which I ate in her fashion. The half-ripe seeds of the poppy eaten raw, and fresh gathered, are like almonds; they do not intoxicate. 'Remember,' said Tara, 'after dinner you shall have a dish sent you; partake of it, you will like it.' It is made thus; gather three or four young poppy-heads when they are full of opium, and green; split each head into four parts, fry them in a little butter, *a very little*, only just enough to fry them, with some pepper and salt – send them to table, with the dessert. The flavour is very pleasant, and if you only eat enough, you will become as tipsy as a mortal may desire. We had them often at Colonel Gardner's; and I have felt rather sleepy from eating them. The old *nawāb* was in his glory when he had two or three spoonfuls of these poppy heads in his plate, one of which is a good dose. I was so fond of the unripe seeds that I never went into the garden, but the *mālī* brought me ten or twelve heads, which I usually finished at once. There were some beds of the double red poppy, especially set apart for the *begum*, the opium from that poppy being reckoned the finest; a couple of lumps of opium were collected and brought in daily. Colonel Gardner said to me, 'The *begum* is perplexed; she wants to know how you, a married woman, can have received the gift of a nose-ring from a gentleman not your husband? She says the nose-ring is the bridal ring. She is perplexed.' I had differed in opinion with a gentleman: he said, 'I will bet you a nose-ring you are in the wrong.' The native jewellers had been at the house that morning showing their nose-rings and other native ornaments. I accepted the bet, and was victorious: the gentleman presented me with a nose-ring, which I declined, because its value was Rs 160, i.e. £16. 'I will accept the *n'hut* I have won, but it must be one from the bazaar, which will be an exact imitation of this ring and will cost one rupee and a half.' It was accordingly procured for me. The *begum* having heard this story was perplexed until it was explained to her that I was not going to marry the gentleman, and had only accepted the nose-ring to make a native dress perfect.

Three of the slave girls, wishing to see the world I supposed went to the *begum* and asked her to give them to me. She laughed and told me their request.

Science has not yet entered the confines of the *zenāna*; nature and super-stition reign supreme; nevertheless, native women suffer less on the birth of a child than the women of Europe. The first nourishment given an infant medicinally is composed of *umaltass* (*cassia fistula*) sugar, aniseed water, and russote, from a colt just born! Native women do not approve of flannel for infants, thinking it excites the skin too much.

I remember the following remark by Colonel Gardner – 'Nothing can exceed the quarrels that go on in a *zenāna*, or the complaints the *begums* make against each other; a common complaint is, such an one has been practising witchcraft against me.'

[...]

Sons are of inestimable value; the birth of a daughter is almost a calamity; but even the mother blest with a son is not likely to remain long without a rival in the heart of her husband, since ninety-nine out of a hundred take new wives: besides the concubines given by the mother before marriage!

When a Mohammedan has sworn to separate himself from his wife, she retires to her own apartments and does not behold her husband for four months; if they are not reconciled by the end of that time, all their ties are broken; the woman recovers her liberty and receives, on quitting the house, the property settled on her by the contract of marriage. The girls follow the mother, the boys remain with the father. The husband cannot send her from his house until the expiration of the four months.

One day Colonel Gardner was ill; he was in the large garden without. The *begum* begged me to go to him; she *dared not* leave the *zenāna*, even to assist her husband who was so ill that his attendants had run in for aid! I went to him. After a time he was better and wished to return to the house; he leaned on my shoulder for support and led the way to the burial-ground of his son Allan, just without the garden. He sat down on a tomb, and we had a long conversation: 'If it were not for old age, and the illness it brings on,' said he, 'we should never be prepared, never ready to leave this world. I shall not last long; I shall not see you again, my *beti*; I wish to be buried by the side of my son; but I have spoken to James about it. The poor *begum*, she will not survive me long; mark my words – she will not say much, but she will take my death to heart, she will not long survive me: when her son Allan died she pounded her jewels in a mortar.' Shortly afterwards we returned to the house.

It may appear extraordinary to a European lady that the *begum*, in her affliction, should have pounded her jewels in a mortar: ornaments are put aside in times of mourning, and jewellery with native ladies is highly prized, not merely for its own sake – that of adding to their beauty, but as a proof of the estimation in which they are held by their husbands. If a man be angry with his wife, he will take away her jewels and not allow her to wear them; if pleased, it is his delight to cover her with the most valuable ornaments, precious stones set in pure gold. The quantity and value of the jewellery thus ascertains the rank to which a lady is entitled in this sort of domestic 'Order of Merit'; the women pride themselves upon this adornment, and delight in jewellery as much as the men of England in stars and garters.

A lady wears slippers only out of doors, and puts them off on entering the house; the slippers are of various forms and patterns; some of them are square at the toes and have iron heels. 'She combs his head with the iron heel of her slipper,' is applied to a woman who domineers over her husband. The slippers for the ladies are of cloth of the gayest colours, ornamented with embroidery of gold and silver, adorned with seed pearls and with beetle wings, which are worked into flowers upon the cloth, and cover the long peak that turns up over the toes.

Stockings are never worn; but I have seen little coloured socks, made of the wool of Kashmir, worn at times during the cold season. The ankles of a native lady are decorated with massive rings, called *kurrā*; those worn by the *begum* were of gold, thickly studded with jewels; the ladies had them of solid embossed gold; and for the slaves, they were of solid silver. These rings are generally hexagonal or octagonal, of an equal thickness throughout, and terminated by a knob at each end. The gold or the silver of which they are composed being pure metal, they may be opened sufficiently to be put on or off at pleasure; the ends being brought together by the pressure of the hand.

Another ornament consists of a great number of small bells, *ghoonghroo*, strung on a cord, and worn around the ankle, hanging to the heel. It is reckoned very correct to wear these tinkling bells; if a native wishes to praise a woman most highly, he says, 'She has never seen the sun, she always wears bells.'

In lieu of this string of bells, another ornament is often worn, called *pāezēb*, which consists of heavy rings of silver, resembling a horse's curb chain, but much broader, set with a fringe of small spherical bells, all of which tinkle at every motion of the limb; and all the toes are adorned with rings, some of which are furnished with little bells; such rings are called *ghoonghroo darchhallā*. The ladies wear their dresses, unless they be grand dresses for occasions of state, until they are dirty; perhaps for five or six days together; the dresses are then thrown away, and they put on new attire.

April 5th – I took leave of my dear Colonel Gardner, and quitted him with a heavy heart for I saw how feeble his health had become, how necessary quiet and attention were for him, and I knew that, left to the care of natives, his comfort would be little considered.

After my departure, I heard he endured much annoyance from domestic concerns and that it was too much for his feeble health. He suffered greatly from asthma and violent headaches, and had only recently recovered from an attack of paralysis. I was strongly tempted to return to Khasganj when I heard of his illness, but was deterred from a feeling of delicacy: an adopted child has a right to a portion of the inheritance, and my presence might have caused the ladies of the *zenāna* to imagine a sinister motive influenced me.

A gentleman who was with him afterwards told me 'During his last illness, Colonel Gardner often spoke of you in terms of the greatest affection, and expressed many times his wish for your presence; I did not write to tell you so, because the hot winds were blowing and the distance some five or six hundred miles.'

Had he only written to me, I would have gone *dāk* to Khasganj immediately; what would the annoyance of hot winds or the distance have been, in comparison with the satisfaction of gratifying the wish of my departing friend? I had lived for weeks in his house, enjoying his society, admiring his dignified and noble bearing and listening with delight to the relation of his marvellous escapes and extraordinary adventures. His chivalric exploits and undaunted courage deserve a better pen than mine, and he alone was capable of being his own historian.

Colonel Gardner told me, if I ever visited Delhi he would give me an introduction to the Nawāb Shāh Zamānee Begum the Emperor's unmarried sister; who would show me all that was worth seeing in the *zenāna* of the palace of the King of Delhi. This pleased me greatly; so few persons ever have an opportunity of seeing native ladies.

On the 29th of the following July my beloved friend, Colonel Gardner, departed this life at Khasganj, aged sixty-five. He was buried, according to his desire, near the tomb of his son Allan. From the time of his death the poor *begum* pined and sank daily; just as he said, she complained not, but she took his death to heart; she died one month and two days after his decease. Native ladies have a number of titles; her death, names and titles were thus announced in the papers: 'On the 31st of August, at her residence at Khasganj, Her Highness Furzund Azeza Zubdeh-tool Arrakeen Umdehtool Assateen Nawāb Matmunzilool Nissa Begum Delmī, relict of the late Colonel William Linnaeus Gardner.'

'The sound of the *Nakaras* and *Dumana* have ceased.'

Colonel Gardner's *begum* was entitled from her rank to the use of the *nalki*, the *morchhal* or fan of peacock's feathers, and the *nakara* and *dumana*, state kettle drums.

[...]

The sums of money and the quantity of food distributed by Colonel Gardner's *begum* in charity was surprising; she was a religious woman and fulfilled, as far as was in her power, the ordinances of her religion. The necessity of giving alms is strongly inculcated. 'To whomsoever God gives wealth, and he does not perform the charity due from it, his wealth will be made into the shape of a serpent on the day of resurrection, which shall not have any hair upon its head; and this is a sign of its poison and long life; and it has two black spots upon its eyes; and it will be twisted round his neck, like a chain, on the day of resurrection: then the serpent will seize the man's jaw-bones, and will say, "I am thy wealth, from which thou didst not give in charity; I am thy treasure, from which thou didst not separate any alms." After this the Prophet repeated this revelation. "Let not those who are covetous of what God of his bounty hath granted them imagine that their avarice is better for them: nay, rather it is worse for them. That which they have covetously reserved shall be bound as a collar about their necks on the day of resurrection." '

CHAPTER XXXVIII

THE MAHRATTA CAMP AND ZENĀNA

FOR WHOM SHALL I STAIN MY TEETH AND BLACKEN MY EYELASHES?
THE MASTER IS TURNED TO ASHES

APRIL 6TH 1835 – I arrived at Fatehgar, at the house of a relative in the Civil Service, the Judge of the Station and agent to the Governor-General. After a hot and dusty *dāk* trip, how delightful was the coolness of the rooms in which thermantidotes and *tattīs* were in full force! As may be naturally supposed, I could talk of nothing but Khasganj, and favoured the party with some Hindustanī airs on the *sitar*, which I could not persuade them to admire; to silence my *sitar* a dital harp was presented to me; nevertheless, I retained a secret fondness for the native instrument, which recalled the time when the happy slave girls figured before me.

Having seen Musulmān ladies followers of the Prophet, how great was my delight at finding native ladies were, at Fatehgar, worshippers of Ganesh and Krishna-ji!

Her Highness the Bāiza Bāī, the widow of the late Mahārāj Dāolut Rāo Scindia, was in camp at this place under the care of Captain Ross. Dāolut Rāo, the adopted son and grandnephew of Mahadajee Scindia, contested with the Duke of Wellington, then Sir Arthur Wellesley, the memorable field of Assaye. On the death of Scindia, by his appointment the Bāiza Bāī, having become Queen of Gwalior, ruled the kingdom for nine years. Having no male issue, her Highness adopted a youth, called Jankee Rāo, a distant relative of Scindia's, who was to be placed on the *masnad* at her decease.

A Rajpoot is of age at eighteen years: but when Jankee Rāo was only fourteen years old, the subjects of the Bāī revolted and placed the boy at the head of the rebellion. Had her Highness remained at Gwalior she would have been murdered; she was forced to fly to Fatehgar, where she put herself under the protection of the Government. Her daughter, the Chimna Rājā Sāhib, a lady celebrated for her beauty and the wife of Appa Sāhib, a Mahratta nobleman, died of fever brought on by exposure and anxiety at the time she fled from Gwalior, during the rebellion. It is remarkable that the ladies in this family take the title of Rājā, to which Sāhib is generally affixed. Appa Sāhib joined the Bāiza Bāī, fled with her, and is now in her camp at Fatehgar. The rebellion of her subjects, and her Highness being forced to fly the kingdom, were nothing to the Bāī in comparison to the grief occasioned her by the loss of her beloved daughter, the Chimna Rājā.

Her granddaughter, the Gaja Rājā Sāhib, is also living with her; she has been married two years but is alone, her husband having deserted her to join the stronger party.

The Bāī, although nominally free, is in fact a prisoner; she is extremely anxious to return to Gwalior, but is prevented by the refusal of the Government to allow her to do so; this renders her very unhappy.

April 8th – The Brija Bāī, one of her ladies, called to invite the lady with whom I am staying to visit the Mahārāj in camp; and gave me an invitation to accompany her.

April 12th – When the appointed day arrived, the attendants of her Highness were at our house at four o'clock to escort us to the camp.

It is customary for a visitor to leave her shoes outside the *parda*, when paying her respects to a lady of rank; and this custom is always complied with, unless especial leave to retain the shoes has been voluntarily given to the visitor, which would be considered a mark of great kindness and condescension.

We found her Highness seated on her *gaddi* of embroidered cloth, with her granddaughter the Gaja Rājā Sāhib at her side; the ladies, her attendants, were standing around her; and the sword of Scindia was on the *gaddi*, at her feet. She rose to receive and embrace us, and desired us to be seated near her. The Bāiza Bāī is rather an old woman, with grey hair, and *en bon point;* she must have been pretty in her youth; her smile is remarkably sweet, and her manners particularly pleasing; her hands and feet are very small and beautifully formed. Her sweet voice reminded me of the proverb, 'A pleasant voice brings a snake out of a hole.' She was dressed in the plainest red silk, wore no ornaments with the exception of a pair of small plain bars of gold as bracelets. Being a widow, she is obliged to put jewellery aside and to submit to numerous privations and hardships. Her countenance is very mild and open; there is a freedom and independence in her air that I greatly admire – so unlike that of the sleeping, languid, opium-eating Musulmāns. Her granddaughter, the Gaja Rājā Sāhib, is very young; her eyes the largest I ever saw; her face is rather flat and not pretty; her figure is beautiful; she is the least little wee creature you ever beheld. The Mahratta dress consists only of two garments, which are a tight body to the waist, with sleeves tight to the elbow; a piece of silk, some twenty yards or more in length, which they wind around them as a petticoat, and then, taking a part of it, draw it between the limbs and fasten it behind in a manner that gives it the effect both of petticoat and trousers; this is the whole dress unless, at times, they substitute *angiyas*, with short sleeves, for the tight long-sleeved body.

The Gaja Rājā was dressed in purple Benares silk, with a deep gold border woven into it; when she walked she looked very graceful and the dress very elegant; on her forehead was a mark like a spearhead, in red paint; her hair was plaited and bound into a knot at the back of her head, and low down; her eyes were edged with *surma*, and her hands and feet dyed with *hinnā*. On her feet and ankles were curious silver ornaments; toe-rings of peculiar form; which she sometimes wore of gold, sometimes of red coral. In her nostril was a very large and brilliant *n'hut*, of diamonds, pearls, and precious stones, of the particular shape worn by the Mahrattas; in her ears were fine brilliants. From her throat to her waist she was covered with strings of magnificent pearls and jewels; her hands and arms were ornamented with the same. She spoke but little – scarcely five words passed her lips; she appeared timid, but was pleased with the bouquet of beautiful flowers, just fresh from the garden, that the lady who presented me laid at her feet on her entrance. These Mahrattas are a fine bold race; amongst her ladies-in-waiting I remarked several fine figures, but their faces were generally too flat. Some of them stood in waiting with rich cashmere shawls thrown over their shoulders; one lady, before the Mahārāj, leaned on her sword, and if the Bāī quitted the apartment, the attendant and sword always followed her. The Bāī was speaking of horses, and the lady who introduced me said I was as fond of horses as a Mahratta. Her Highness said she should like to see an English lady on horseback; she could not comprehend how they could sit all crooked, all on one side, in the side-saddle. I said I should be too happy to ride into camp any hour her Highness would appoint, and show her the style of horsemanship practised by ladies in England. The Mahārāj expressed a wish that I should be at the Mahratta camp at four o'clock, in two days' time. *Atr*, in a silver filigree vessel, was then presented to the Gaja Rājā; she took a portion up in a little spoon and put it on our hands. One of the attendants presented us with *pān*, whilst another sprinkled us most copiously with rose-water: the more you inundate your visitor with rose-water, the greater the compliment.

This being the signal for departure, we rose, made our *bahut bahut adab* salam, and departed, highly gratified with our visit to her Highness the ex-Queen of Gwalior.

April 14th – My relative had a remarkably beautiful Arab, and as I wished to show the Bāī a good horse, she being an excellent judge, I requested him to allow me to ride his Arab; and that he might be fresh, I sent him on to await my arrival at the *zenāna* gates. A number of Mahratta horsemen having been

despatched by her Highness to escort me to the camp, I cantered over with
them on my little black horse, and found the beautiful Arab impatiently
awaiting my arrival.

> With the champèd bit, and the archèd crest,
> And the eye of a listening deer,
> And the spirit of fire that pines at its rest,
> And the limbs that laugh at fear.

Leetle Paul's description of his 'courser proud' is beautiful; but his steed was
not more beautiful than the Arab who, adorned with a garland of freshly-
gathered white double jasmine flowers, pawed impatiently at the gates. I
mounted him, and entering the precincts of the *zenāna* found myself in a large
court, where all the ladies of the ex-Queen were assembled and anxiously
looking for the English lady, who would ride crooked! The Bāī was seated in the
open air; I rode up and, dismounting, paid my respects. She remarked the
beauty of the Arab, felt the hollow under his jaw, admired his eye and, desiring
one of the ladies to take up his foot, examined it and said he had the small,
black, hard foot of the pure Arab. She examined and laughed at my saddle. I
then mounted, and putting the Arab on his mettle, showed her how English
ladies manage their horses. When this was over, three of the Bāiza Bāī's own
riding horses were brought out by the female attendants; for we were within the
zenāna, where no man is allowed to enter. The horses were in full caparison, the
saddles covered with velvet and *kimkhwab* and gold embroidery, their heads
and necks ornamented with jewels and chains of gold. The Gaja Rājā, in her
Mahratta riding dress, mounted one of the horses and the ladies the others; they
cantered and pranced about, showing off the Mahratta style of riding. On
dismounting, the young Gaja Rājā threw her horse's bridle over my arm and
said, laughingly, 'Are you afraid? Or will you try my horse?' Who could resist
such a challenge? 'I shall be delighted,' was my reply. 'You cannot ride like a
Mahratta in that dress,' said the Princess; 'put on proper attire.' I retired to
obey her commands, returning in Mahratta costume, mounted her horse, put
my feet into the great iron stirrups and started away for a gallop round the
enclosure. I thought of Queen Elizabeth, and her stupidity in changing the style
of riding for women. *En cavalier*, it appeared so safe, as if I could have jumped
over the moon. Whilst I was thus amusing myself, '*Shāh-bāsh! shāh-bāsh!*'
exclaimed some masculine voice; but who pronounced the words, or where the
speaker lay *perdu*, I have never discovered.

'Now,' said I to the Gaja Rājā, 'having obeyed your commands, will you
allow one of your ladies to ride on my side-saddle?' My habit was put on one of

them; how ugly she looked! 'She is like a black doctor!' exclaimed one of the girls. The moment I got the lady into the saddle, I took the rein in my hand, and riding by her side, started her horse off in a canter; she hung on one side, and could not manage it at all; suddenly checking her horse, I put him into a sharp trot. The poor lady hung half off the animal, clinging to the pummel and screaming to me to stop; but I took her on most unmercifully, until we reached the spot where the Bāiza Bāī was seated; the walls rang with laughter; the lady dismounted and vowed she would never again attempt to sit on such a vile crooked thing as a side-saddle. It caused a great deal of amusement in the camp.

Qui vit sans folie n'est pas si sage qu'il croit.

The Mahratta ladies live in *parda*, but not in such strict seclusion as the Musulmān ladies; they are allowed to ride on horseback veiled; when the Gaja Rājā goes out on horseback, she is attended by her ladies; and a number of Mahratta horsemen ride at a certain distance, about two hundred yards around her, to see that the *kurk* is enforced; which is an order made public that no man may be seen on the road on pain of death.

The Hindus never kept their women in *parda* until their country was conquered by the Mohammedans, when they were induced to follow the fashion of their conquerors; most likely, from their unveiled women being subject to insult.

The Bāiza Bāī did me the honour to express herself pleased, and gave me a title, 'The great-aunt of my granddaughter,' 'Gaja Rājā Sāhib ki par Khāla.' This was very complimentary, since it entitled me to rank as the adopted sister of her Highness.

A part of the room in which the ex-Queen sits is formed into a domestic temple, where the idols are placed, ornamented with flowers, and worshipped; at night they are lighted up with lamps of oil and the priests are in attendance.

The Mahratta ladies are very fond of sailing on the river, but they are equally in *parda* in the boats as on shore.

The next day the Bāiza Bāī sent down all her horses in their gay native trappings for me to look at; also two fine rhinoceroses, which galloped about the grounds in their heavy style, and fought one another; the Bāī gave Rs 5,000 (£500) for the pair; sweetmeats and oranges pleased the great animals very much.

When Captain Ross quitted, her Highness was placed under the charge of the agent to the Governor-General. I visited the Bāī several times and liked her better than any native lady I ever met with.

A Hindu widow is subject to great privations; she is not allowed to wear gay attire or jewels, and her mourning is eternal. The Bāiza Bāi always slept on the ground, according to the custom for a widow, until she became very ill from rheumatic pains; after which she allowed herself a hard mattress, which was placed on the ground, a *chārpāi* being considered too great a luxury.

She never smoked, which surprised me: having seen the Musulmān ladies so fond of a *huqqa*, I concluded the Mahratta ladies indulged in the same luxury.

The Mahratta men smoke the *huqqa* as much as all other natives; and the Bāi had a recipe for making tobacco cakes that were highly esteemed in camp. The cakes are, in diameter, about four inches by one inch in thickness; a small quantity added to the prepared tobacco usually smoked in a *huqqa* imparts great fragrance; the ingredients are rather difficult to procure.

Speaking of the privations endured by Hindu widows, her Highness mentioned that all luxurious food was denied them as well as a bed; and their situation was rendered as painful as possible. She asked me how an English widow fared?

I told her, 'An English lady enjoyed all the luxury of her husband's house during his life; but on his death she was turned out of the family mansion, to make room for the heir, and pensioned off; whilst the old horse was allowed the run of the park, and permitted to finish his days amidst the pastures he loved in his prime.' The Hindu widow, however young, must not marry again.

The fate of women and of melons is alike. 'Whether the melon falls on the knife or the knife on the melon, the melon is the sufferer.'

We spoke of the severity of the laws of England with respect to married women, how completely *by law* they are the slaves of their husbands, and how little hope there is of redress.

You might as well 'Twist a rope of sand', or 'Beg a husband of a widow' as urge the men to emancipate the white slaves of England.

'Who made the laws?' said her Highness. I looked at her with surprise, knowing she could not be ignorant on the subject. 'The men,' said I; 'why did the Mahārāj ask the question?' 'I doubted it,' said the Bāi, with an arch smile, 'since they only allow themselves one wife.'

'England is so small,' I replied, 'in comparison with your Highness's Gwalior; if every man were allowed four wives, and obliged to keep them separate, the little island could never contain them; they would be obliged to keep the women in vessels off the shore, after the fashion in which the Chinese keep their floating farmyards of ducks and geese at anchor.'

'Is your husband angry with you?' asked the Brija, the favourite attendant of her Highness. 'Why should you imagine it?' said I. 'Because you have on no ornaments, no jewellery.'

The Bāiza Bāī sent for the wives of Appa Sāhib to introduce them to me. The ladies entered, six in number; and walking up to the *gaddi*, on which the Bāī was seated, each gracefully bowed her head, until her forehead touched the feet of her Highness. They were fine young women, from fifteen to twenty-five years old. The five first wives had no offspring; the sixth, who had been lately married, was in expectation of a *bābā*.

Appa Sāhib is the son-in-law of the ex-Queen; he married her daughter, the Chimna Bāī, who died of fever at the time they were driven out of Gwalior.

[...]

CHAPTER XXXIX

THE NAWĀB HAKĪM MENHDI AND
THE CITY OF KANNAUJ

APRIL 15TH 1835 – I received an invitation to pay my respects to the Begum Moktar Mahal, the mother of the Nawāb of Fatehgar; she is connected with Mulka Begum's family but very unlike her, having none of her beauty, and not being a ladylike person. Thence we went to the grandmother of the Nawāb, Surfuraz Mahal, in the same *zenāna*. They were in mourning for a death in the family and wept, according to *dasturi* (custom), all the time I was there: they were dressed in plain white attire with no ornaments; that is their *mátim* (mourning). The young Nawāb, who is about twelve years old, is a fine boy; ugly, but manly and well-behaved.

The Nawāb Moontuzim Adowlah Menhdi Ali Khān Bahādur, commonly called Nawāb Hakīm Menhdi, lives at Fatehgar; he was unwell and unable to call, but he sent down his stud to be shown to me, my fondness for horses having reached his ears.

April 22nd – I visited a manufactory for Indian shawls, lately established by the Hakīm to support some people who, having come from Kashmir, were in distress; and as they were originally shawl manufacturers, in charity he gave them employment. This good deed is not without its reward; three or four hundred workmen are thus supported; the wool is brought from Kashmir and the sale of the shawls gives a handsome profit. I did not admire them; they are manufactured to suit the taste of the English and are too heavy; but they are handsome and the patterns strictly Indian. Colonel Gardner's *begum* said to me one day, at Khasganj, 'Look at these shawls, how beautiful they are! If you wish to judge of an Indian shawl, shut your eyes and feel it; the touch is the test of a good one. Such shawls as these are not made at the present day in Kashmir; the English have spoiled the market. The shawls made now are very handsome, but so thick and heavy they are only fit for carpets, not for ladies' attire.'

April 26th – The Nawāb Hakīm Menhdi called, bringing with him his son, a man about forty years of age, called the 'General'. He invited me to pay him and the *begum* a visit, and wished to show me his residence.

April 29th – We drove to the Nawāb's house, which is a good one; he received us at the door and took *my* arm, instead of giving me his. He is a fine-looking old man, older than Colonel Gardner, whom in style he some-what resembles; his manners are distinguished and excellent. He wore an embroidered cap, with a silver muslin twisted like a cord and put around it, as a turban; it was very graceful, and his dress was of white muslin. The rooms of his house are most curious; more like a shop in the China bazaar, in Calcutta, than anything else; full of lumber, mixed with articles of value. Tables were spread all down the centre of the room, covered with most heterogeneous articles: round the room were glass cases, full of clocks, watches, sundials, compasses, guns, pistols, swords; every thing you can imagine might be found in these cases.

The Hakīm was making all due preparation for celebrating the Muharram in the most splendid style; he was a very religious man, and kept the fast with wonderful strictness and fortitude. A very lofty room was fitted up as a *Taziya khāna*, or house of mourning; from the ceiling hung chandeliers of glass of every colour, as thickly as it was possible to place them, all the length of the spacious apartment; and in this room several *taziyas*, very highly decorated, were placed in readiness for the ceremony. One of them was a representation of the Mausoleum of the Prophet at Medina; another the tomb of Hussein at Karbala; a third, that of Kāsim; and there was also a most splendid Burāk, a facsimile of the winged horse on which the Prophet made an excursion one night from Jerusalem to Heaven, and thence returned to Mecca. The angel Gabriel acted as celestial *sā'is* on the occasion, and brought the animal from the regions above. He must have been a fiery creature to control that winged horse; and the effect must have been *more* than picturesque, as the Prophet scudded along on a steed that had the eyes and face of a man, his ears long, his forehead broad, and shining like the moon; eyes of jet, shaped like those of a deer, and brilliant as the stars; the neck and breast of a swan, the loins of a lion, the tail and the wings of a peacock, the stature of a mule, and the speed of lightning – hence its name Burāk.

In front of the *taziyas* and the flying horse were a number of standards; some intended to be facsimiles of the banner (*'alam*) of Hussein; and others having the names of particular martyrs. The banners of Ali were denominated, 'The Palm of the Hand of Ali the Elect'; 'The Hand of the Lion of God'; 'The Palm of the Displayer of Wonders'; and 'The Palm of the Disperser of Difficulties'. Then there was the 'Standard of Fatima', the daughter of the Prophet and wife of Ali; also that of Abbās-i-'alam-dār, the standard-bearer; with those of Kāsim, Ali-akbar, and others; the banner of the twelve Imāms; the double-bladed sword of Ali; and the *n'al-Sāhib*. There was also the *neza*, a spear or lance dressed up with a turban, the ends flying in the air, and a lime fixed at the top of it; emblematic, it is said, of Hussein's head, which was carried in triumph through different cities by the order of Yuzeed, the King of Shawm.

The *n'al-Sāhib* is a horseshoe affixed to the end of a long pole; it is made of gold, silver, metals, wood, or paper, and is intended as an emblem of Hussein's horse.

The 'Alam-i-Kāsim, or Standard of Kāsim the Bridegroom, is distinguished by its having a little *chatr* in gold or silver fixed on the top of it. All these things were collected in the long room in the house of the Nawāb, ready for the nocturnal perambulations of the faithful.

After the loss of the battle of Karbala, the family of Hussein were carried away captive with his son Zein-ool-Abaīdīn, the only male of the race of Alī who was spared, and they were sent to Medina. With them were carried the heads of the martyrs; and that of Hussein was displayed on the point of a lance, as the cavalcade passed through the cities. In consequence of the remonstrances and eloquence of Zein-ool-Abaīdīn, the orphan son of Hussein, the heads of the martyrs were given to him; and forty days after the battle they were brought back to Karbala and buried, each with its own body; the mourners then returned to Medina, visited the tomb of the Prophet, and all Medina eventually became subject to Zein-ool-Abaīdīn.

Alī, the son-in-law of Mohammed was, according to the Shī'as, the direct successor of the Prophet; they not acknowledging the other three caliphs; but, according to the Sunnīs, he was the fourth Khalifa, or successor of Mohammed.

The Muharram concludes on the fortieth day, in commemoration of the interment of the martyrs at Karbala, the name of a place in Iraq, on the banks of the Euphrates. At this place the army of Yuzeed, the King, was encamped; while the band of Hussein, including himself, amounting only to seventy-two persons, were on the other side of an intervening jungle, called Mareea.

The Nawāb is a very public-spirited man and does much good; he took me over a school he founded, and supports, for the education of native boys; showed me a very fine *chita* (hunting leopard), and some antelopes which were kept for fighting. For the public benefit, he has built a bridge, a *ghāt*, and a *sarāy*, a resting-place for travellers; all of which bear his name.

The *begum*, having been informed that I was with the Nawāb, sent to request I would pay a visit to the *zenāna*, and a day was appointed in all due form.

May 3rd – The time having arrived, the Nawāb came to the house at which I was staying to pay me the compliment of escorting me to visit the *begum*. The Muharram having commenced, all his family were therefore in mourning, and could wear no jewels; he apologised that, in consequence, the *begum* could not be handsomely dressed to receive me. She is a pretty looking woman, but has none of the style of James Gardner's *begum*; she is evidently in great awe of the Hakīm who rules, I fancy, with a rod of iron. The rooms in the *zenāna* are long and narrow, and supported by pillars on the side facing the enclosed garden, where three fountains played very refreshingly, in which golden fish were swimming. The *begum* appeared fond of the fish, and had some beautiful pigeons which came to be fed near the fountains; natives place a great value upon particular breeds of pigeons, especially those obtained from Lucknow, some of which bring a very high price. It is customary with rich natives to keep a number of pigeons; the man in charge of them makes them manoeuvre in the air by word of command, or rather by the motions of a long wand which he carries in his hand and with which he directs the flight of his pigeons; making them wheel and circle in the air, and ascend or descend at pleasure. The sets of pigeons consist of fifty, or of hundreds; and to fly your own in mock battle against the pigeons of another person is an amusement prized by the natives.

Several large glass cases were filled in the same curious manner as those before mentioned; and the upper panes of the windows were covered with English prints, some coloured and some plain. The Hakīm asked me if I did not admire them? There was Lord Brougham; also a number of prints of half-naked boxers sparring; Molineux and Tom Cribb, etc., in most scientific attitudes; divers characters of hunting celebrity; members of Parliament in profusion; and bright red and blue pictures of females as Spring, Summer, Autumn, and Winter: a most uncouth collection to be displayed around the walls of a *zenāna*! I was surprised to see pictures in the house of a man considered to be so religious as the Nawāb; because the Prophet said, 'Every painter is in hellfire, and God will appoint a person at the day of resurrection, for every picture he shall have drawn, to punish him in hell. Then, if you must make pictures, make them of trees, and things without souls.' 'And whoever draws a picture will be punished, by ordering him to blow a spirit into it; and this he can never do; and so he will be punished as long as God wills.'

'The angels do not enter the house in which is a dog, nor into that in which are pictures.'

I spent an hour in the *zenāna* talking to the old Nawāb; the *begum* scarcely ventured to speak. He took me over her flower garden, and made me promise I would never pass Fatehgar without paying him a visit. I told him that when the rains arrived, I should come up in the pinnace, having promised to revisit my relatives, when I should have the pleasure of seeing him and the *begum* again. He pressed me to stay and see the ceremonies of the Muharram; I regretted extremely I was obliged to return home, being very anxious to see the mourning festival celebrated in all state.

I happened to wear a *ferronière* on my forehead; it amused the *begum* very much, because it somewhat resembled the *tīka* worn by the women of the East.

His first *begum*, to whom he was much attached, died: he sent her body to Mekka: it went down at sea. This was reckoned a great misfortune and an omen of ill luck. Four years afterwards he married the present *begum*, who was slave girl to the former.

Between the pauses in conversation the Nawāb would frequently have recourse to his rosary, repeating, I suppose, the ninety-nine names of God, and meditating on the attributes of each. In the *Qanoon-e-islam* it is mentioned, 'To read with the use of a *tusbeeh* (or rosary) is meritorious; but it is an innovation, since it was not enjoined by the Prophet (the blessing and peace of God be with him!) or his companions, but established by certain *mushaeks* (or divines). They use the chaplet in repeating the *kulma* (confession of faith) or *durood* (blessing), one, two, or more hundred times.' On the termination of my visit to the *zenāna*, the Nawāb re-escorted me to the house of the friend with whom I was staying.

For the first time, I saw today a person in a *burkā* walking in the street; it was impossible to tell whether the figure was male or female; the long swaggering strut made me suppose the former. A pointed crown was on the top of the head, from which ample folds of white linen fell to the feet, entirely concealing the person. Before the eyes were two holes, into which white net was inserted; therefore the person within could see distinctly, while even the colour of the eyes was not discernible from without. The *burkā-posh*, or person in the *burkā*, entered the house of the Nawāb. The dress afterwards was sent me to look at, and a copy of it was taken for me by my *darzee* (tailor). It is often worn by respectable women who cannot afford to go out in a palanquin, or in a *dolī*.

The Hakīm was fond of writing notes in English, some of which were curious. When the office of Commissioner was done away with, he thought the gentleman who held the appointment would be forced to quit Fatehgar. The old Hakīm wrote a singular note, in which was this sentence: 'As for the man who formed the idea of doing away with your appointment, my dear friend, may God blast him under the earth.' However, as the gentleman remained at Fatehgar and the Government bestowed an appointment equally good upon him, the Hakīm was satisfied. On my return to Allahabad, he wrote to me and desired me 'not to bury his friendship and affection in oblivion'.

May 4th – Paid a farewell visit to her Highness the ex-Queen of Gwalior, in the Mahratta Camp, and quitted Fatehgar *dāk* for Allahabad. A brain fever would have been the consequence, had I not taken shelter during the day, as the hot winds were blowing and the weather intensely oppressive; therefore I only travelled by night, and took refuge during the day.

May 5th – I stopped during the day at the house of a gentleman at Mehndī Ghāt, which was built by the Nawāb, as well as the *sarāy* at Naramhow, which also bears his name. From this place I sent to Kannauj for a quantity of *chūris*, i.e., rings made of sealing-wax, very prettily ornamented with gold foil, beads, and colours: the old woman, who brought a large basketful for sale, put a *very expensive* set on my arms; they cost four ānās, or three pence! The price of a very pretty set is two ānās. My host appeared surprised; he must have thought me a Pukka Hindustanī. Kannauj is famed for the manufacture of *chūris*. I wore the bracelets for two days, and then broke them off because the sealing-wax produced a most annoying irritation of the skin.

May 6th – I spent the heat of the day with some kind friends at Cawnpore, and the next *dāk* brought me to Fatehpur. The day after, I spent the sultry hours in the *dāk* bungalow at Shāhzād-poor; and the following morning was very glad to find myself at home, after my long wanderings. The heat at times in the *pālkee* was perfectly sickening. I had a small thermometer with me which, at ten o'clock, often stood at 93°; and the sides of the palanquin were hot as the sides of an oven. The fatigue also of travelling so many nights was very great; but it did me no harm.

I found Allahabad greatly altered; formerly it was a quiet station, it had now become the seat of the Agra Government and Mr Blunt, the Lieutenant-Governor, was residing there. I had often heard Colonel Gardner speak in high praise of this gentleman who was a friend of his. My time was now employed in making and receiving visits, and going to parties.

May 13th – At the house of Mr F— I met the Austrian traveller, Baron H—; he requested to be allowed to call on me the next day to see my collection of curiosities. He pronounced them very good and promised to send me some idols to add to them. I gave him a set of Hindu toe-rings, the sacred thread of the Brahmans, and a rosary, every bead of which was carved with the name of the god Rām. Men were deceivers ever; the promised idols were never added to my collection. The Lieutenant-Governor's parties, which were very agreeable, rendered Allahabad a very pleasant station.

August 2nd – I went to the *melā* (Fair) held within the grounds at Papamhow. To this place we had sent the pinnace, *Seagull*, and on the 10th of the month my husband accompanied me two days' sail on my voyage to revisit my relations in Fatehgar, after which he returned to Allahabad, leaving me and the great spaniel Nero to proceed together.

[...]

August 16th – Anchored at Maigong in rather a picturesque spot, close to a *sati* mound. By the side of the mound I saw the trunk of a female figure beautifully carved in stone. The head, arms and part of the legs had been broken off. They said it was the figure of a *sati*. At the back of the mound was a very ancient banyan tree; and the green hills and trees around were in all the freshness and luxuriance of the rainy season.

The next morning, to my surprise, on going into the large cabin to breakfast, there was the figure of the headless *sati* covered with flowers, and at the spot where feet *were not*, offerings of *gram*, boiled rice, etc., had been placed by some of the Hindu *dāndis*. 'How came you possessed of the *satī*?' said I. 'The memsāhib admired her, she is here.' '*Chori-ke-mal nā'ich hazm hota*', 'Stolen food never digests', i.e., 'Ill deeds never prosper, the poor people will grieve for the figure; tell the *sarang* to lower sail and return her to them'. 'What words are these?' replied the *sarang*, 'we are miles from the spot; the *sati* has raised the wind'. The headless lady remained on board.

As we passed the residence of Rājā Budannath Singh, he came out with his family on three elephants to pay his respects, thinking my husband was on board. The ladies were peeping from the house-top. The pinnace passed in full sail, followed by ten immense country boats full of magazine stores, and the cook boat. Being unable at night to cross those rivers, we anchored on the Oude side. I did not much admire being in the domains of the King of Lucknow instead of those of the Company; they are a very turbulent set, those men of Oude, and often pillage boats. The vicinity of the Rājā's house was some protection. Rām Din had the matchlocks of the *sipāhi* guard fired off by way of bravado, and to show we were armed; the bamboos (*lathis*) were laid in readiness, in case of attack: the watch was set and, after these precautions, the memsāhib and her dog went to rest very composedly.

May 22nd – Not a breath of air! A sun intensely hot; the river is like a silver lake; but over its calm the vessel does *not* glide, for we are fast on a sandbank! Down come the fiery beams; several of the servants are ill of fever. Heaven help them; I doctor them all and have killed no one as yet! My husband will fret himself as he sits in the coolness of the house and thinks of me on the river. The vessel was in much difficulty this morning; the conductor of some magazine boats sent forty men and assisted her out of it. Lucky it was that chance meeting with the conductor in this Wilderness of Waters! One is sure to find someone to give aid in a difficulty, no doubt through the power of the *sati*, whom they still continue to adorn with fresh flowers.

May 25th – After a voyage of fifteen days and a half I arrived at Cawnpore; coming up the reach of the Ganges in front of Cantonments a powerful wind was in our favour. The *Seagull* gallantly led the way in front of the twelve magazine boats: a very pretty sight for the Cawnporeans, especially as a squall overtook us, struck us all into picturesque attitudes, and sunk one of the magazine boats containing Rs 16,000 worth of new matchlocks. When the squall struck the little fleet they were thrown one against another, the sails shivered and the centre boat sank like a stone. Being an eye-witness of this scene, I was afterwards glad to be able to bear witness, at the request of the conductor, to his good conduct and the care he took of the boats when called upon by the magistrate of the place.

May 28th – Anchored off Bittoor on the opposite side. I regretted being unable to see the place and Bajee Row, the ex-Peshwī who resides there on an allowance of eight *lakh* per annum. In 1818, he submitted to the Company, abdicated his throne, and retired to Bittoor for life. It would have given me pleasure to have seen these Mahrattas, but the channel of the stream forced me to go up the other side of the river.

The Government wish the Bāiza Bāī to live at Benares on six *lakh* a year; but the spirited old lady will not become a pensioner, and refuses to quit Fatehgar. She has no inclination, although an Hindu, to be satisfied with 'A little to eat and to live at Benares', especially as at this place she is no great distance from her beloved Gwalior.

September 2nd – A day of adventures. Until noon we battled against wind and stream: then came a fair wind which blew in severe squalls and storms. Such a powerful stream against us; but it was fine sailing and I enjoyed it very much. At times the squalls were enough to try one's courage. We passed a vessel that had just broken her mast: the stream carried us back with violence, and we ran directly against her; she crushed in one of the Venetian windows of the cabin and with that damage we escaped. Two men raising the sail of another vessel were knocked overboard by the squall, and were carried away with frightful velocity, the poor creatures calling for help: the stream swept them past us and threw them on a sandbank – a happy escape!

Anchored at Mehndī Ghāt; the moon was high and brilliant, the wind roaring around us, the stream, also, roaring in concert, like a distant waterfall; the night cold and clear, the stars bright and fine; but the appearance of the sky foretold more wind and squalls for the morrow. I had no idea, until I had tried it, how much danger there was on the Ganges during the height of the rains; in this vessel I think myself safe, but certainly I should not admire a small one. All the vessels today were at anchor; not a sail was to be seen but the white sails of the *Seagull*, and the dark ones of the cook boat, the latter creeping along the shore, her *mānjhī* following very unwillingly.

My *sarang* says the quantity of sail I oblige him to carry during high winds has turned 'his stomach upside down with alarm'.

September 3rd – For some hours the next morning the gale continued so violently we could not quit the bank; a gentleman came on board and told me, by going up a stream called the Kali Nadī I should escape the very powerful rush of the Ganges; that I could go up the Nadī twenty miles, and by a canal, cut in former days, re-enter the Ganges above.

I asked him to show me the ruins of Kannauj; we put off; it was blowing very hard: at last we got out safely into the middle of the stream. About a mile higher up, we quitted the roaring and rushing waters of the Ganges, and entered the placid stream of the Kali Nadī. Situated on a hill, most beautifully wooded with the winding river at its feet, stands the ancient city of Kannauj; the stream flowing through fine green meadows put me in mind of the Thames near Richmond. In the Ganges we could scarcely stem the current, even though the wind, which was fair, blew a gale; in the Nadī we furled every sail and were carried on at a good rate, merely by the force of the wind on the hull of the vessel, and the non-opposition of the gentle stream. My friend told me he had once thrown a net across the Kali Nadī, near the entrance, and had caught one hundred and thirty-two great *rhoee* fish. On the hill above stands the tomb of Colonel—, who, when Lord Lake's army were encamped here on their road to Delhi, attempted on horseback to swim the Nadī, and was drowned.

[...]

We anchored; and after tiffin, Mr M— accompanied me to see the tombs of two Mohammedan saints, on the top of the hill. Thence we visited a most singular Hindu building, of great antiquity, which still exists in a state of very tolerable preservation; the style of the building, one stone placed on the top of another, appeared to me more remarkable than any architecture I had seen in India.

The fort, which is in ruins, is on a commanding spot; the view from it all around is beautiful. The people sometimes find ancient coins amongst the ruins, and jewels of high value; a short time ago, some pieces of gold, in form and size like thin bricks, were discovered by an old woman; they were very valuable. The Brahmans brought to us for sale square rupees, old rupees and copper coins; but none of them were Hindu; those of copper, or of silver, not being more than three hundred years old, were hardly worth having. I commissioned them to bring me some gold coins, which are usually genuine and good. A regular trade is carried on at this place in the fabrication of silver and copper coins, and those of a mixed metal. The rose-water of Kannauj is considered very fine; it was brought, with other perfumed waters, for sale; also native preserves and pickles which were inferior. To this day the singers of Kannauj are famous. I am glad I have seen the ruins of this old city, which are well worth visiting; I did not go into the modern town; the scenery is remarkably pretty. I must revisit this place on my black horse; there are many parts too distant from each other for a walk; I returned very much fatigued to the pinnace. A great many Hindu idols, carved in stone, were scattered about in all directions, broken by the zeal of the Mohammedans when they became possessed of Kannauj. I shall carry some off should I return this way.

[...]

September 6th – After fighting with the stream all day, and tiring the crew to death on sandbanks and pulling against a terribly powerful current, we were forced back to within two miles of our last night's anchorage; we have happily found a safe place to remain in during the night; these high banks, which are continually falling in, are very dangerous. Fortunately in the evening, assisted by a breeze, we arrived at the canal; and having passed through it quitted the Kalī Nadī, and anchored in the deep old bed of the Ganges.

September 7th – With great difficulty we succeeded in bringing the pinnace to within three miles of Fatehgar, where I found a palanquin waiting for me; the river being very shallow, I quitted the vessel and, on my arrival at my friend's house, sent down a number of men to assist in bringing her up in safety.

CHAPTER XL

The Mahratta Camp and Scenes in the Zenāna

SEPTEMBER 8TH 1835 – A deputation arrived from her Highness the Bāiza Bāī claiming protection from the Agent to the Government on account of a mutiny in her camp. She was fearful of being murdered, as her house was surrounded by three hundred and fifty mutinous soldiers, armed with matchlocks and their *palitas* ready lighted. The mutineers demanded seven months pay, and finding it was not in her power to give it to them, they determined to have recourse to force, and seized her treasurer, her paymaster, and four other officers. These unfortunate men they had made prisoners for seven days, keeping them secured to posts and exposed the whole day to the sun, and only giving them a little sherbet to drink. The Agent to the Government, having called out the troops, marched down with them to the Mahratta Camp, where they seized the guns.

The mutineers would not come to terms or lay down their arms. The troops spent the night in the Camp; at daybreak they charged into the *zenāna* compound, killed eight mutineers, and wounded nine: the guns were fired at the Mahratta horsemen, who were outside; after which the men laid down their arms and tranquillity was restored.

The magistrate of the station, who had gone in with the troops, was engaged with two of the mutineers when all three fell into a well; a Mahratta from above having aimed his spear at him, an officer struck the weapon aside and killed the assailant; the spear glanced off and only inflicted a slight wound. The moment Colonel J— charged the mutineers in the *zenāna* compound, they murdered their prisoners, the treasurer and the paymaster, in cold blood; the other four officers escaped in the tumult. The greater part of her Highness's troops being disaffected, they could not be trusted to quell the mutiny; she was therefore compelled to ask for assistance. It was feared her troops, which amounted to eighteen hundred, might attempt to plunder the city and station and be off to Gwalior; and there being only two hundred of the Company's troops, and three guns at Fatehgar, the military were sent for from other stations and a large body of police called out. The Bāiza Bāī despatched a lady several times to say she wished me to visit her; this was during the time she was a prisoner in her house, surrounded by the mutineers with their matches lighted. The agent for the Government would not allow me to go, lest they should seize and keep me a prisoner with the Bāī's officers. I was therefore obliged to send word I could not obey the commands of her Highness on that account.

Emissaries from Gwalior are at the bottom of all this. The camp was in great ferment yesterday: it would be of no consequence if we had a few more troops at the station; but two hundred infantry are sad odds against eighteen hundred men, one thousand of whom are horsemen; and they have three guns also.

September 17th – Infantry have come in from Mynpooree and cavalry from Cawnpore, therefore every thing is safe in case the Mahrattas should mutiny again.

September 24th – The Governor-General's agent allowed me to accompany him to the camp. He took some armed horsemen from the police as an escort in case of disturbance. The Bāiza Bāī received me most kindly, as if I were an old friend. I paid my respects and almost immediately quitted the room, as affairs of state were to be discussed. The Gaja Rājā took me into a pretty little room, which she had just built on the top of the house as a sleeping-room for herself. Her *chārpāī* (bed) swung from the ceiling; the feet were of gold, and the ropes by which it swung were covered with red velvet and silver bands. The mattress, stuffed with cotton, was covered with red and blue velvet: the cases of three large pillows were of gold and red *kimkhwab*; and there were a number of small flat round pillows covered with velvet. The counterpane was of gold and red brocade. In this bed she sleeps, and is constantly swung during her repose. She was dressed in black gauze and gold, with a profusion of jewellery and some fresh flowers I had brought for her were in her hair. She invited me to sit on the bed, and a lady stood by swinging us. The Gaja Rājā has a very pretty figure and looked most fairylike on her decorated bed. When the affairs of state had been settled, we returned to the Bāī. Rose-water, *pān*, and *atr* of roses having been presented, I took my leave.

September 28th – I was one of a party who paid a visit of state to her Highness. Nothing remarkable occurred. As we were on the point of taking our departure, the Bāī said she had heard of the beauty of my pinnace and would visit it the next morning. This being a great honour, I said I would be in attendance and would have the vessel anchored close to the Bāī's own *ghāt*, at which place she bathes in the holy Ganges. On my return home, a number of people were set hard to work, to fit the vessel for the reception of the Bāī. Every thing European was removed, tables, chairs, etc. The floors of the cabins were covered with white cloth and a *gaddi* placed in each for her Highness.

September 29th – The vessel was decorated with a profusion of fresh flowers; she was drawn up to the *ghāt*, close to a flight of steps; and the canvas walls of tents were hung around her on every side, so that no spectators could see within. The sailors all quitted her, and she was then ready to receive the ladies of the Mahratta camp. Although I was at the spot at four o'clock, the Bāī and hundreds of her followers were there before me. She accompanied me on board with all her ladies, and on seeing such a crowd in the vessel, asked if the numbers would not sink her. The Bāī admired the pinnace very much; and observing the *sati* which stood in one corner of the cabin, covered with flowers, I informed her Highness I had brought the headless figure to *eat the air* on the river; that Ganges water and flowers were daily offered her; that her presence was fortunate, as it brought an easterly wind. The Bāī laughed; and, after conversing for an hour she quitted the vessel, and returned to her apartment on the *ghāt*. The Gaja Rājā and her ladies went into the inner cabin; Appa Sāhib, the Bāī's son-in-law, came on board with his followers, the vessel was unmoored, and they took a sail on the river. The scene was picturesque. Some hundreds of Mahratta soldiers were dispersed in groups on the high banks amongst the trees; their elephants, camels, horses and native carriages standing near the stone *ghāts*, and by the side of white temples. The people from the city were there in crowds to see what was going forward. On our return from the excursion on the river, I accompanied the Gaja Rājā to the Bāī; and, having made my salam, returned home, not a little fatigued with the exertion of amusing my guests. During the time we were on the water, Appa Sāhib played various Hindustani and Mahratta airs on the *sitar*. It must have been a great amusement to the *zenāna* ladies, quite a gaiety for them, and a variety in their retired mode of life. They were all in their holiday dresses, jewels and ornaments. Some wore dresses of bright yellow, edged with red, with black cashmere shawls thrown over their shoulders; this costume was very picturesque. The Gaja Rājā wore a dress of black and gold, with a yellow satin tight body beneath it; *enormous* pearls in profusion, ornaments of gold on her arms, and silver ornaments on her ankles and toes; slippers of crimson and gold.

October 2nd – The Ganges at Farrukhabad is so full of sandbanks, and so very shallow, that fearing if I detained the pinnace I might have some chance of being unable to get her down to Cawnpore, I sent her off with half the servants to that place to await my arrival; I shall go *dāk* in a palanquin, and the rest of the people can float down in the cook boat.

October 7th – I called on the Bāī; and while she was employed on state affairs retired with the Gaja Rājā to the pretty little room before mentioned. There I found a Hindu idol, dressed in cloth of gold and beads, lying on the floor on a little red and purple velvet carpet. Two other idols were in niches at the end of the room. The idol appeared to be a plaything, a doll: I suppose, it had not been rendered sacred by the Brahmans. An idol is of no value until a Brahman dip it, with divers prayers and ceremonies, into the Ganges; when this ceremony has been performed, the spirit of the particular deity represented by the figure enters the idol. This sort of baptism is particularly expensive, and a source of great revenue to the Brahmans. The church dues fall as heavily on the poor Hindu as on the people of England; nevertheless, the heads of the Hindu church do not live in luxury like the Bishops.

The *fakir*, who from a religious motive, however mistaken, holds up both arms until they become withered and immovable, and who, being in consequence utterly unable to support himself relies in perfect faith on the support of the Almighty, displays more religion than the man who, with a salary of £8,000 per annum, leaves the work to be done by curates on a pittance of £80 a year.

The Gaja Rājā requested me to teach her how to make tea, she having been advised to drink it for her health; she retired, changed her dress, returned, took her tea, and complained of its bitter taste.

'I am told you dress a camel beautifully,' said the young Princess; 'and I was anxious to see you this morning to ask you to instruct my people how to attire a *sawāri* camel.' This was flattering me on a very weak point: there is but one thing in the world that I *perfectly* understand, and that is how to dress a camel.

'I hope you do not eat him when you have dressed him!' said an English gentleman.

My relative had a fine young camel, and I was not happy until I had superintended the making the attire in which he – the camel, not the gentleman – looked beautiful! The Nawāb Hakīm Menhdi, having seen the animal, called, to request he might have similar trappings for his own *sawāri* camel; and the fame thereof having reached the Mahratta camp, my talents were called into play. I promised to attend to the wishes of the Gaja Rājā and, returning home, summoned twelve *mochīs*, the saddlers of India, natives of the Chamār caste, to perform the work. Whilst one of the men smokes the *nārjil* (coconut pipe), the remainder will work; but it is absolutely necessary that each should have his turn every half-hour, no smoke – no work.

Five hundred small brass bells of melodious sound; two hundred larger ditto, in harmony, like hounds well matched, each under each; and one large bell, to crown the whole; one hundred large beads of imitative turquoise; two snow-white tails of the cow of Tibet; some thousands of cowries, many yards of black and of crimson cloth and a number of very long tassels of red and black worsted. The *mochis* embroidered the attire for three days and it was remarkably handsome. The camel's clothing being ready, it was put into a box and the Gaja Rājā having appointed an hour, I rode over, taking it with me, at four o'clock.

In the courtyard of the *zenāna* I found the Bāī, and all her ladies; she asked me to canter round the enclosure, the absurdity of sitting on one side a horse being still an amusing novelty.

The Bāī's riding horses were brought out; she was a great equestrian in her youthful days and, although she has now given up the exercise, delights in horses. The ladies relate, with great pride, that in one battle her Highness rode at the head of her troops, with a lance in her hand and her infant in her arms!

A very vicious, but large and handsome camel was then brought in by the female attendants; he knelt down and they began putting the gay trappings upon him; his nose was tied to his knee to prevent his injuring the girls around him, whom he attempted to catch hold of, showing his great white teeth; if once the jaw of a camel closes upon you, he will not relinquish his hold. You would have supposed they were murdering not dressing the animal; he groaned and shouted as if in great pain, it was piteous to hear the beast; and laughable, when you remembered it was the '*dastūr*'; they always groan and moan when any load is placed on their backs, however light. When the camel's toilet was completed, a Mahratta girl jumped on his back and made him go round the enclosure at a capital rate; the trappings were admired, and the bells pronounced very musical.

They were eager I should mount the camel; I thought of Theodore Hook. 'The hostess said, "Mr Hook, will you venture upon an orange?" "No, thank you, ma'am, I'm afraid I should tumble off." ' *C'est beau çà, n'est pas?* I declined the elevated position offered me for the same reason.

The finest young *sawārī* camels, that have never been debased by carrying any burthen greater than two or three Persian cats, are brought down in droves by the Arabs from Kabul; one man has usually charge of three camels; they travel in single file, the nose of one being attached to the crupper of another by a string passed through the cartilage. They browse on leaves in preference to grazing. It was a picturesque scene, that toilet of the camel performed by the Mahratta girls, and they enjoyed the *tāmāsha*.

I mentioned my departure was near at hand; the Bāī spoke of her beloved Gwalior and did me the honour to invite me to pay my respects there, should she ever be replaced on the *gaddī*. She desired I would pay a farewell visit to the camp three days afterwards. After the distribution, as usual, of betel leaves, spices, *atr* of roses, and the sprinkling with rose-water, I made my salam. Were I an Asiatic, I would be a Mahratta.

The Mahrattas never transact business on an unlucky day; Tuesday is an unfortunate day and the Bāī, who was to have held a *durbār*, put it off in consequence. She sent for me, it being the day I was to take leave of her; I found her looking grave and thoughtful and her sweet smile was very sad. She told me the Court of Directors had sent orders that she was to go and live at Benares, or in the Deccan; that she was to quit Fatehgar in one month's time and should she refuse to do so, the Governor-General's agent was to take her to Benares by force, under escort of troops that had been sent to Fatehgar for that purpose. The Bāī was greatly distressed, but spoke on the subject with a command of temper and a dignity that I greatly admired. 'What must the Mahāraj do? Cannot this evil fate be averted? Must she go to Benares? Tell us, memsāhib, what must we do?' said one of the ladies in attendance. Thus called upon, I was obliged to give my opinion; it was an awkward thing to tell an exiled Queen she must submit – 'The cudgel of the powerful must be obeyed'. I hesitated; the Bāī looked at me for an answer. Dropping the eyes of perplexity on the folded hands of despondency, I replied to the Brija, who had asked the question, '*Jiska lāthi ooska bhains*' – i.e. 'He who has the stick, his is the buffalo!' The effect was electric. The Bāiza Bāī and the Gaja Rājā laughed, and I believe the odd and absurd application of the proverb half reconciled the Mahāraj to her fate.

I remained with her Highness some time, talking over the severity of the orders of Government, and took leave of her with great sorrow; the time I had before spent in the camp had been days of amusement and gaiety; the last day, the unlucky Tuesday, was indeed ill-starred and full of misery to the unfortunate and amiable ex-Queen of Gwalior.

CHAPTER XLI

The Mahrattas at Allahabad

OCTOBER 1835 – One day I called on the *begum*, the mother of the young Nawāb of Farrukhābād, and found her with all her relations sitting in the garden; they were plainly dressed and looked very ugly. For a woman not to be pretty when she is shut up in a *zenāna* appears almost a sin, so much are we ruled in our ideas by what we read in childhood of the *hooris* of the East.

One morning, the Nawāb Hakīm Menhdi called; his dress was most curious; half European, half Asiatic. The day being cold, he wore brown corduroy breeches with black leather boots and thick leather gloves; over this attire was a dress of fine white flowered Dacca muslin; and again, over that, a dress of pale pink satin, embroidered in gold! His turban was of gold and red Benares tissue. He carried his sword in his hand, and an attendant followed, bearing his *huqqa*; he was in high spirits, very agreeable, and I was quite sorry when he rose to depart. In the evening he sent down a charming little elephant, only five years old, for me to ride; which I amused myself with doing in the beautiful grounds around the house, sitting on the back of the little beauty and guiding him with cords passed through his ears.

The next evening the Nawāb sent his largest elephant, on which was an *amāri* – that is, a *howdah*, with a canopy – which, according to native fashion, was richly gilt, the interior lined with velvet, and velvet cushions; the elephant was a fast one, his paces very easy, and I took a long ride in the surrounding country.

[...]

October 15th – Having dispatched the pinnace to await my arrival at Cawnpore, I started dāk for that place which I reached the next day after a most disagreeable journey. I was also suffering from illness, but the care of my kind friends soon restored me to more comfortable feelings.

October 22nd – I accompanied them to dine with the Nawāb Zulfecar Bahādur, of Banda. The Nawāb is a Mohammedan, but he is of a Mahratta family, formerly Hindus; when he changed his religion and became one of the faithful, I know not. Three of his children came in to see the company; the two girls are very interesting little creatures. The Nawāb sat at table, partook of native dishes and drank sherbet when his guests took wine. The next day, the Nawāb dined with the gentleman at whose house I was staying, and met a large party.

[...]

October 26th – Here are we – that is, the dog Nero and the memsāhib – floating so calmly, and yet so rapidly, down the river; it is most agreeable; the temples and *ghāts* we are now passing at Dalmhow are beautiful; how pictur-esque are the banks of an Indian river! The flights of stone steps which descend into the water; the temples around them of such peculiar Hindu architecture; the natives, both men and women, bathing or filling their jars with the water of the holy Ganges; the fine trees and the brightness of the sunshine add great beauty to the scene. One great defect is the colour of the stream which, during the rains, is peculiarly muddy; you have no bright reflections on the Ganges, they fall heavy and indistinct.

[...]

1836, January 16th – The Bāiza Bāī arrived at Allahabad, and encamped about seven miles from our house, on the banks of the Jumna beyond the city. A few days after, the Brija Bāī, one of her ladies, came to me to say her Highness wished to see me; accordingly I went to her encampment. She was out of spirits, very unhappy and uncomfortable, but expressed much pleasure at my arrival.

February 5th – Her Highness requested the steam-vessel should be sent up the river opposite her tents; she went on board and was much pleased, asked a great many questions respecting the steam and machinery, and went a short distance up the river. Captain Ross accompanied her Highness to Allahabad, and remained there in charge of her whilst her fate was being decided by the Government.

February 9th – The Bāī gave a dinner party at her tents to twenty of the civilians and the military; in the evening there was a *nāch*, and fireworks were displayed; the ex-Queen appeared much pleased.

There is a very extensive enclosure at Allahabad, called Sultan Khusrū's garden; tents had been sent there and pitched under some magnificent tama-rind trees, where a large party were assembled at tiffin, when the Bāī sent down a Mahratta dinner to add to the entertainment. In the evening, her two rhinoc-eroses arrived; they fought one another rather fiercely; it was an amusement for the party. Captain Ross having quitted Allahabad, Mr Scott took charge of her Highness.

March 1st – The Brija Bāī called to request me to assist them in giving a dinner party to the Station, for which the Bāiza Bāī wished to send out invitations; I was happy to aid her. The guests arrived at about seven in the evening; the gentlemen were received by Appa Sāhib, her son-in-law; the ladies were ushered behind the *parda*, into the presence of her Highness. I have never described the *parda* which protects the Mahratta ladies from the gaze of the men: In the centre of a long room a large curtain is dropped, not unlike the curtain at a theatre, the space behind which is sacred to the women; and there the *gaddi* of the Bāī was placed, close to the *parda*; a piece of silver about six inches square, in which a number of small holes are pierced, is let into the parda; and this is covered on the inside with white muslin. When the Bāī wished to see the gentlemen, her guests, she raised the bit of white muslin, and could then see everything in the next room through the holes in the silver plate – herself unseen. The gentlemen were in the outer room, the ladies in the inner. Appa Sāhib sat close to the *parda*; the Bāī conversed with him, and, through him, with some of the gentlemen present, whom she could see perfectly well.

Dancing girls sang and *nāched* before the gentlemen until dinner was announced. Many ladies were behind the *parda* with the Bāiza Bāī, and she asked me to interpret for those who could not speak Urdu. I was suffering from severe rheumatic pain in my face; her Highness, perceiving it, took from a small gold box a lump of opium and desired me to eat it, saying she took as much herself every day. I requested a smaller portion; she broke off about one-third of the lump, which I put into my mouth, and as it dissolved the pain vanished; I became very happy, interpreted for the ladies, felt no fatigue and talked incessantly. Returning home, being obliged to go across the country for a mile in a palanquin to reach the carriage, the dust which rolled up most thickly half choked me; nevertheless, I felt perfectly happy, nothing could discompose me; but the next morning I was obliged to call in medical advice, on account of the severe pain in my head from the effect of the opium.

The table for dinner was laid in a most magnificent tent, lined with crimson cloth, richly embossed and lighted with numerous chandeliers. The *nāch* girls danced in the next apartment, but within sight of the guests; her Highness and her granddaughter, from behind the *parda*, looked on. About two hundred native dishes in silver bowls were handed round by Brahmans; and it was considered etiquette to take a small portion from each dish. On the conclusion of the repast, the Governor-General's agent rose and drank her Highness's health, *bowing to the parda*; and Appa Sāhib returned thanks in the name of the Bāī. The dinner and the wines were excellent; the latter admirably cooled. Fireworks were let off and a salute was fired from the cannon when the guests departed. Her nephew was there in his wedding dress – cloth of gold most elaborately worked. The Bāī expressed herself greatly pleased with the party, and invited me to attend the wedding of her nephew the next day, and to join her when she went in state to bathe in the Jumna. I was very glad to see her pleased, and in good spirits.

March 4th – This being the great day of the wedding, at the invitation of the Bāī we took a large party to the camp to see the ceremonies in the cool of the evening. Having made our salam to her Highness, we proceeded with the Gaja Rājā Sāhib to the tents of the bride, which were about half a mile from those of the bridegroom. The ceremony was going on when we entered. The bridegroom, dressed in all his heavy finery, stood amongst the priests who held a white sheet between him and the bride, while they chanted certain prayers. When the prayers were concluded, and a quantity of some sort of small grain had been thrown at the lady, the priest dropped the cloth and the bridegroom beheld his bride. She was dressed in Mahratta attire, over which was a *dupatta* of crimson silk, worked in gold stars; this covered her forehead and face entirely, and fell in folds to her feet. Whether the person beneath this covering was man, woman, or child, it was impossible to tell: bound round the forehead, outside this golden veil, was a *sihrā*, a fillet of golden tissue from which strings and bands of gold and silver fell over her face. The bridegroom must have taken upon trust that the woman he wished to marry was the one concealed under these curious wedding garments. It was late at night; we all returned to the Bāī's tent and the ladies departed, all but Mrs Colonel W— and myself; the Gaja Rājā having asked us to stay and see the finale of the marriage. The young Princess retired to bath, after which, having been attired in yellow silk with a deep gold border and covered with jewels, she rejoined us and we set out to walk half a mile to the tents of the bride; this being a part of the ceremony. The Gaja Rājā, her ladies, and attendants, Mrs W— and myself, walked with her in *parda*; that is, the canvas walls of tents having been fixed on long poles so as to form an oblong enclosure, a great number of men on the outside took up the poles and moved gently on; while we who were inside walked in procession over white cloths, spread all the way from the tent of the Bāī to that of the bride. It was past ten o'clock. Fireworks were let off and blue lights thrown up from the outside, which lighting up the procession of beautifully dressed Mahratta ladies, gave a most picturesque effect to the scene. The graceful little Gaja Rājā, with her slight form and brilliant attire, looked like what we picture to ourselves a fairy was in the good old times, when such beings visited the earth. At the head of this procession was a girl carrying a torch; next to her a *nāch* girl danced and figured about; then a girl in the dress of a soldier, who carried a musket and played all sorts of pranks.

Another carried a pole, on which were suspended onions, old shoes, and all sorts of queer extraordinary things to make the people laugh. Arrived at the end of our march, the Gaja Rājā seated herself and water was poured over her beautiful little feet. We then entered the tent of the bride, where many more ceremonies were performed. During the walk in *parda*, I looked at Mrs W— who had accompanied me, and could not help saying, 'We flatter ourselves we are well dressed, but in our hideous European ungraceful attire we are a blot in the procession. I feel ashamed when the blue lights bring me out of the shade; we destroy the beauty of the scene.'

I requested permission to raise the veil and view the countenance of the bride. She is young and, for a Mahratta, handsome. The Bāī presented her with a necklace of pure heavy red gold, and told me she was now so poor she was unable to give her pearls and diamonds. New dresses were then presented to all her ladies. We witnessed so many forms and ceremonies, I cannot describe one-fourth of them. That night the bridegroom took his bride to his own tents, but the ceremonies of the wedding continued for many days afterwards. I returned home very much pleased at having witnessed a *shādi* among the Hindus, having before seen the same ceremony among the Mohammedans.

The ex-Queen had some tents pitched at that most sacred spot, the Treveni, the junction of the three rivers; and to these tents she came down continually to bathe; her ladies and a large concourse of people were in attendance upon her, and there they performed the rites and ceremonies. The superstitions and the religion of the Hindus were to me most interesting subjects, and had been so ever since my arrival in the country. Her Highness was acquainted with this and kindly asked me to visit her in the tents at the junction whenever any remarkable ceremony was to be performed. This delighted me, as it gave me an opportunity of seeing the worship and conversing on religious subjects with the ladies, as well as with the Brahmans. The favourite attendant, the Brija Bāī never failed to call and invite me to join their party at the time of the celebration of any particular rite. At one of the festivals her Highness invited me to visit her tents at the Treveni. I found the Mahratta ladies assembled there: the tents were pitched close to the margin of the Ganges and the canvas walls were run out to a considerable distance into the river. Her Highness, in her usual attire, waded into the stream, and shaded by the *khanāts* from the gaze of men, reached the sacred junction where she performed her devotions, the water reaching to her waist. After which she waded back again to the tents, changed her attire, performed *pooja* and gave magnificent presents to the attendant Brahmans. The Gaja Rājā and all the Mahratta ladies accompanied the ex-Queen to the sacred junction, as they returned dripping from the river, their draperies of silk and gold clung to their figures; and very beautiful was the statue-like effect, as the attire half revealed and half concealed the contour of the figure.

[...]

May 9th – The Sohobut Melā, or Fair of Kites, was in Alopee Bāgh; I went to see it; hundreds of people, in their gayest dresses, were flying kites in all directions, so happily and eagerly; and under the fine trees in the mango *tope*, sweetmeats, toys and children's ornaments were displayed in booths erected for the purpose. It was a pretty sight, that Alopee ke Melā.

The kites are of different shapes, principally square, and have no tails; the strings are covered with *mānjhā*, a paste mixed with pounded glass and applied to the string to enable it to cut that of another by friction. One man flies his kite against another, and he is the loser whose string it cut. The boys, and the men also, race after the defeated kite, which becomes the prize of the person who first seizes it. It requires some skill to gain the victory; the men are as fond of the sport as the boys.

The string of a kite caught tightly round the tail of my horse Trelawny and threatened to carry away horse and rider tail foremost into midair! The more the kite pulled and danced about, the more danced Trelawny, the more frightened he became, and the tighter he tucked in his tail; the gentleman who was on the horse caught the string, and bit it in two, and a native disengaged it from the tail of the animal. A pleasant bite it must have been, that string covered with pounded glass! Yah! Yah! How very absurd! I wish you had seen the *tamāshā*. In the evening we dined with Sir Charles Metcalfe; he was residing at Papamhow. He told me he was thinking of cutting down the avenue of *neem* trees (*Melia azadirachta*) that led from the house to the river; I begged hard that it might be spared, assuring him that the air around *neem* trees was reckoned wholesome by the natives, while that around the tamarind was considered very much the contrary. In front of my rooms, in former days at Papamhow, was a garden full of choice plants and a very fine young India-rubber tree; it was pleasant to see the bright green of the large glossy leaves of the *caoutchouc* tree, which flourished so luxuriantly. In those days, many flowering trees adorned the spot; among which the *katchnar* (*Bauhinia*), both white and rose-coloured and variegated, was remarkable for its beauty. Sir Charles had destroyed my garden, without looking to see what trees he was cutting down; he had given the ruthless order. I spoke of and lamented the havoc he had occasioned; to recompense me, he promised to spare the avenue, which, when I revisited it years afterwards, was in excellent preservation.

May 14th – The Bāiza Bāī sent for me in great haste; she was in alarm respecting the Gaja Rājā, who was ill of epidemic fever. Having lost her daughter, the Chimna Bāī, of fever when she was driven out of Gwalior by her rebellious subjects, she was in the utmost distress, lest her only remaining hope and comfort, her young granddaughter, should be taken from her. I urged them to call in European medical advice; they hesitated to do so, as a medical man might neither see the young Princess, nor feel her pulse. I drove off and soon returned with the best native doctress to be procured; but, from what I heard at the consultation, it may be presumed her skill is not very great.

The Nawāb Hakīm Menhdi is very ill; I fear his days are numbered.

The murder of Mr Frazer by the Nawāb Sumshoodeen at Delhi, who bribed a man called Kureem Khān to shoot him, took place when I was at Colonel Gardner's; no one could believe it when suspicion first fell upon the Nawāb; he had lived on such intimate terms with Mr Frazer, who always treated him like a brother. The Nawāb was tried by Mr Colvin, the judge, condemned and executed. The natives at Allahabad told me they thought it a very unjust act of our Government, the hanging the Nawāb merely for bribing a man to murder another, and said the man who fired the shot ought to have been the only person executed. On Sunday, the 13th March, 1835, Kureem Khān was foiled in his attempt on Mr Frazer's life, as the latter was returning from a *nāch*, given by Hindu Rāo, the brother of the Bāiza Bāi. He accomplished his purpose eight days afterwards, on the 22nd of the same month. In the Hon. Miss Eden's beautiful work *The Princes and People of India*, there is a sketch of Hindu Rāo on horseback; his being the brother of the Bāiza Bāi is perhaps his most distinguishing mark; I have understood, however, he by no means equals the ex-Queen of Gwalior in talent.

June 7th – Sir Charles Metcalfe gave a ball to the station: in spite of all the thermantidotes and the *tattīs* it was insufferably hot; but it is remarkable that balls are always given and better attended during the intense heat of the hot winds than at any other time.

June 9th – The Bāiza Bāi sent word she wished to see me ere her departure, as it was her intention to quit Allahabad and proceed to the west: a violent rheumatic headache prevented my being able to attend. The next morning she encamped at Pādshāh Bāgh, beyond Allahabad on the Cawnpore road, where I saw her the next evening in a small round tent, entirely formed of *tattīs*. The day after she quitted the ground and went one march on the Cawnpore road, when the Kotwal of the city was sent out by the magistrate to bring her back to Allahabad, and she was forced to return. Her granddaughter is very ill, exposed to the heat and rains in tents. I fear the poor girl's life will be sacrificed. Surely she is treated cruelly and unjustly. She who once reigned in Gwalior has now no roof to shelter her: the rains have set in; she is forced to live in tents and is kept here against her will – a state prisoner, in fact.

The sickness in our farmyard is great: forty-seven *gram*-fed sheep and lambs have died of smallpox; much sickness is in the stable, but no horse has been lost in consequence.

June 25th – Remarkably fine grapes are selling at one rupee the *ser*; i.e. one shilling per pound. The heat is intolerable, and the rains do not fall heavily as they ought to do at this season. The people in the city say the drought is so unaccountable, so great, that some rich merchant, having large stores of grain of which to dispose, must have used *magic* to keep off the rains, that a famine may ensue and make his fortune!

CHAPTER XLII

Tufāns in the East

JUNE 28TH 1836 – A hurricane has blown ever since gunfire; clouds of dust are borne along upon the rushing wind; not a drop of rain; nothing is to be seen but the whirling clouds of the *tufān*. The old *peepal* tree moans and the wind roars in it as if the storm would tear it up by the roots. The pinnace at anchor on the Jumna below the bank rolls and rocks; the river rises in waves, like a little sea. Some of her iron bolts have been forced out by the pressure of the cables, and the *sarang* says she can scarcely hold to her moorings. I am watching her unsteady masts, expecting the next gust will tear her from the bank and send her off into the rushing and impetuous current. It is well it is not night or she would be wrecked to a certainty. I have not much faith in her weathering such a *tufān* at all, exposed as she is to the power of the stream and the force of the tempest. High and deep clouds of dust come rushing along the ground which, soaring into the highest heaven, spread darkness with a dull sulphurous tinge, as the red brown clouds of the *tufān* whirl swiftly on. It would almost be an inducement to go to India, were it only to see a hurricane in all its glory: the might and majesty of wind and dust: just now the fine sand from the banks of the river is passing in such volumes on the air, that the whole landscape has a white hue and objects are indistinct; it drives through every crevice and, although the windows are all shut, fills my eyes and covers the paper. It is a fearful gale. I have been out to see if the pinnace is likely to be driven from her moorings. The waves in the river are rolling high with crests of foam; a miniature sea. So powerful were the gusts, with difficulty I was able to stand against them. Like an Irish hurricane it blew up and down. At last the falling of heavy rain caused the abatement of the wind. The extreme heat passed away, the trees, the earth, all nature, animate and inanimate, exulted in the refreshing rain. Only those who have panted and longed for the fall of rain can appreciate the delight with which we hailed the setting in of the rains after the *tufān*.

July 3rd – This morning the Bāī sent down two of her ladies, one of whom is a celebrated equestrian, quite an Amazon, nevertheless, in stature small and slight, with a pleasant and feminine countenance. She was dressed in a long piece of white muslin, about eighteen yards in length; it was wound round the body and passed over the head, covering the bosom entirely: a part of it was brought up tight between the limbs, so that it had the appearance of full trousers falling to the heels. An embroidered red Benares shawl was bound round her waist; in it was placed a sword and a pistol and a massive silver bangle was on one of her ankles. Her attendants were present with two saddle horses, decked in crimson and gold and ornaments of silver, after the Mahratta fashion. She mounted a large bony grey, astride of course, and taking an extremely long spear in her hand, galloped the horse about in circles, performing the spear exercise in the most beautiful and graceful style at full gallop; her horse rearing and bounding and showing off the excellence of her riding. Dropping her spear, she took her matchlock, performing a sort of mimic fight, turning on her saddle as she retreated at full gallop, and firing over her horse's tail. She rode beautifully and most gracefully. When the exhibition was over, we retired to my dressing-room: she told me she had just arrived from Jaganāth, and was now *en route* to Lahore to Runjeet Singh. She was anxious I should try the lance exercise on her steed, which I would have done had I possessed the four walls of a *zenāna* within which to have made the attempt.

What does Sir Charles Metcalfe intend to do with the poor Bāī? What will be her fate? This wet weather she must be wretched in tents. The Lieutenant-Governor leaves Allahabad for Agra in the course of a day or two.

In the evening I paid my respects to her Highness. I happened to have on a long rosary and cross of black beads; she was pleased with it, and asked me to procure some new rosaries for her that they might adorn the idols, whom they dress up, like the images of the saints in France, with all sorts of finery.

She showed me a necklace of gold coins which appeared to be Venetian: the gold of these coins is reckoned the purest of all, and they sell at a high price. The natives assert they come from the eastward, and declare that to the East is a miraculous well into which, if copper coins be thrown, they come out after a time the very purest of gold.

[...]

The necklace, which was a wedding present to the bride, consisted of three rows of silken cords as thickly studded with these coins as it was possible to put them on, the longest string reaching to the knees: it was very heavy and must have been valuable. Another Mahratta lady wore a necklace of the same description, but it consisted of a single row which reached from her neck to her feet: people less opulent wear merely one, two, or three *putlīs* around the neck.

An old Muhammadan *darzī* of the Shīā sect asked me one morning to be allowed to go to the bazaar to purchase a *putlī* (a doll) to bind upon his forehead, to take away a violent pain in his head. This request of his puzzled me greatly: at the time I was ignorant that *putlī* was also the name of the charmed coin, as well as that of a doll. He told me he had recovered from severe headache before in consequence of this application, and believed the remedy infallible. The Bāi mentioned that she struck *mohurs* and half *mohurs* at Gwalior, in her days of prosperity. I showed her some new rupees struck by the East India Company with the king's head upon them which, having examined, she said, 'These rupees are very paltry, there is so little pure silver in them.'

[...]

July 8th – Sir Charles quitted this station for Agra, leaving Allahabad to return to its usual routine of quietness. The thermantidotes have been stopped, rain has fallen plentifully, the trees have put on their freshest of greens and the grass is springing up in every direction. How agreeable, how pleasant to the eye is all this luxuriant verdure!

The report in the bazaar is, that a native of much wealth and consideration went into his *zenāna* tents, in which he found two of his wives and a man; the latter escaped; he killed both the women. A *zenāna* is a delightful place for private murder, and the manner in which justice is distributed between the sexes is so impartial! A man may have as many wives as he pleases and mistresses without number – it only adds to his dignity! If a woman take a lover, she is murdered and cast like a dog into a ditch. It is the same all the world over; the women, being the weaker, are the playthings, the drudges or the victims of the men; a woman is a slave from her birth; and the more I see of life, the more I pity the condition of the women. As for the manner in which the natives strive to keep them virtuous, it is absurd; a girl is affianced at three or four years old, married without having seen the man, at eleven, shut up and guarded and suspected of a wish to intrigue which, perhaps, first puts it into her head; and she amuses herself with outwitting those who have no dependence upon her, although, if discovered, her death generally ends the story.

[...]

July 23rd – During the night it began to blow most furiously, accompanied by heavy rain and utter darkness; so fierce a *tufān* I never witnessed before. It blew without cessation, raining heavily at intervals; and the trees were torn up by their roots. At four o'clock the storm became so violent, it wrecked twenty large native salt boats just below our house; the river roared and foamed, rising in high waves from the opposition of the wind and stream. Our beautiful pinnace broke from her moorings, was carried down the stream a short distance, driven against the broken bastions of the old city of Prāg which have fallen into the river, and totally wrecked just off the Fort; she went down with all her furniture, china, books, wine, etc., on board, and has never been seen or heard of since; scarcely a vestige has been discovered. Alas! my beautiful *Seagull*; she has folded her wings for ever and has sunk to rest! We can only rejoice no lives were lost and that we were not on board; the *sarang* and *khalāsis* (sailors) swam for their lives; they were carried some distance down the stream, below the Fort, and drifted on a sandbank. The headless image of the *sati* that graced the cabin had brought rather too much wind. When the *sarang* lamented her loss, I could only repeat, as on the day he carried off the lady, '*Chori ke mal nāich hazm hota*' – stolen food cannot be digested: i.e. ill deeds never thrive.

The cook-boat was swamped. On the going down of the river, although she was in the mud with her back broken, she was sold, and brought the sum we originally gave for her when new – such was the want of boats occasioned by the numbers that were lost in the storm! The next morning, three of the Venetians and the companion-ladder of the pinnace were washed ashore below the Fort, and brought to us by a fisherman. We were sorry for the fate of *Seagull*; she was a beautifully built vessel, but not to be trusted, the white ants had got into her. The mischief those white ants do is incalculable; they pierce the centre of the masts and beams working on in the dark, seldom showing marks of their progress outside, unless during the rains. Sometimes a mast, to all appearance sound, will snap asunder, when it will be discovered the centre had been hollowed by the white ants, and the outside is a mere wooden shell. Almost all the trees in the garden were blow down by the gale.

[...]

August 7th – Some friends anchored under our garden on their way to Calcutta; the sight of their little fleet revived all my roaming propensities and, as I wished to consult a medical man at the Residency in whom I had great faith, I agreed to join their party and make a voyage down the river. The Bāiza Bāī was anxious to see my friends; we paid her a farewell visit; she was charmed with Mr C—, who speaks and understands the language like a native, and delighted with the children.

August 13th – Our little fleet of six vessels quitted Allahabad and three days afterwards we arrived at Mirzapur, famous for its beautiful *ghāts* and carpet manufactories.

August 17th – Anchored under the Fort of Chunar, a beautiful object from the river; it was not my intention to have anchored there, but the place looked so attractive I could not pass by without paying it a visit. The goats and sheep, glad to get a run after their confinement in the boat, are enjoying themselves on the bank; and a boy with a basket full of snakes (*cobra di capello*), is trying to attract my attention. In the cool of the evening we went into the Fort, which is situated on the top of an abrupt rock which rises from the river. The view, coming from Allahabad, is very striking; the ramparts running along the top of the rising ground, the broad open river below; the churchyard under the walls, on the banks of the Ganges, with its pretty tombs of Chunar stone rising in all sorts of pointed forms, gives one an idea of quiet, not generally the feeling that arises on the sight of a burial-place in India; the ground was open and looked cheerful as the evening sun fell on the tombs; the hills, the village, the trees all united in forming a scene of beauty. We entered the magazine and visited the large black slab on which the deity of the Fort is said to be ever present, with the exception of from daybreak until the hour of nine, during which time he is at Benares. Tradition asserts that the Fort has never been taken by the English, but during the absence of their god Burtreenath. We walked round the ramparts and enjoyed the view. The church, the houses which stretch along the riverside for some distance and the Fort itself looked cheerful and healthy; which accounted for the number of old pensioners to be found at Chunar, who have their option as to their place of residence.

As you approach Benares, on the left bank of the river stands the house of the Rājā of Benares, a good portly looking building. The appearance of the Holy City from the river is very curious and particularly interesting. The steep cliff on which Benares is built is covered with Hindu temples and *ghāts* of all sizes and descriptions; the first *ghāt*, built by Appa Sāhib from Poona, I thought handsome; but every *ghāt* was eclipsed by the beauty of the one which is now being built by her Highness the Bāiza Bāī; the scale is so grand, so beautiful, so light, and it is on so regular a plan, it delighted me; it is the handsomest *ghāt* I have seen in India; unfinished as it is, it has cost her Highness fifteen *lakh*; to finish it will cost twenty *lakh* more; should she die ere the work be completed it will never be finished, it being deemed unlucky to finish the work of a deceased person. The money, to the amount of thirty-seven *lakh*, which the Bāī had stored in her house at Benares to complete the *ghāt* and to feed the Brahmāns, whose allowance was Rs 200, i.e. £20 a day, has been seized by the Government and put into the Company's treasury, where it will remain until the point now in dispute is settled; that is, whether it belong to the Bāī or to her adopted son, the present Mahārāj of Gwalior, who forced her out of the kingdom. Several Hindu temples are near this *ghāt*; a cluster of beauty. Two *chirāghdāns*, which are lighted up on festivals, are curious and pretty objects; their effect, when glittering at night with thousands of little lamps, must be beautiful, reflected with the temples and crowds of worshippers on the waters below; and great picturesque beauty is added to the scene by the grotesque and curious houses jutting out from the cliff, based on the flights of stone steps which form the *ghāts*. How I wished I could have seen Benares from the river during the Dewalī, or Festival of Lights! At sunset we went up the Minarets, built by Aurangzeb; they are considered remarkably beautiful, towering over the Hindu temples; a record of the Muhammadan conquest.

On my return to my *budjerow*, a number of native merchants were in waiting hoping to dispose of their goods to the strangers; they had boxes full of Benares turbans, shawls, gold and silver dresses, *kimkhwāb* and cloth of gold. This place is famous for its embroidery in gold, and for its tissues of gold and silver. I purchased some to make a native dress for myself, and also some very stiff ribbon, worked in silk and gold, on which are the names of all the Hindu deities; the Hindus wear them round their necks; they are holy, and called *junéoo*. The English mare and my little black horse met me here, *en route* to Calcutta.

The Bāiza Bāī told me by no means to pass Benares without visiting her *ghāt* and her house; some of her people having come down to the river, I returned with them to see the house; it is very curiously situated in the heart of the city. Only imagine how narrow the street is which leads up to it; as I sat in my palanquin, I could touch both the sides of the street by stretching my arms out, which I did to assure myself of its extreme narrowness. All the houses in this street are five or six storeys high. We stopped at the house of the Bāī; it is six storeys high and was bought by her Highness as a place in which to secure her treasure. It is difficult to describe a regular Hindu house such as this, which consists of four walls, within and around which the rooms are built storey above storey; but from the foundation to the top of the house there is a square in the centre left open, so that the house encloses a small square court open to the sky above, around which the rooms are built with projecting platforms on which the women may sit, and *eat the air* as the natives call it, within the walls of their residence. I clambered up the narrow and deep stone stairs, storey after storey, until I arrived at the top of the house the view from which was unique: several houses in the neighbourhood appeared much higher than the one on which I was standing, which was six storeys high. The Mahratta who did the honours on the part of her Highness took me into one of the rooms and showed me the two chests of cast iron, which formerly contained about eighteen thousand gold *mohurs*. The Government took that money from the Bāī by force and put it into their treasury. Her Highness refused to give up the keys and also refused her sanction to the removal of the money from her house; the locks of the iron chests were driven in and the tops broken open; the rupees were in bags in the room; the total of the money removed amounted to thirty-seven *lakh*. Another room was full of copper coins; another of cowries. The latter will become mouldy and fall into dust in the course of time. One of the gentlemen of the party went over the house with me and saw what I have described. *Atr* and *pān* were presented, after which we took our leave and proceeded to the marketplace. The braziers' shops were open but they refused to sell anything, it being one of the holidays on which no worker in brass is allowed to sell goods.

[...]

August 19th – The hour was too early, and but few shops were open, which gave a dull look to this generally crowded and busy city.

The air is cool and pleasant; we float gently down the river; this quiet, composed sort of life, with a new scene every day, is one of great enjoyment.

I must not forget to mention that, after a considerable lapse of time, the treasure that was detained by the Government on behalf of the young Mahārāj of Gwalior, was restored to her Highness the Bāiza Bāī.

CHAPTER XLIII

FROM GHAZIPUR TO BALLIA

NOVEMBER 21ST 1836 – Arrived early at Ghāzipur, the town of Ghāzī, also called, as the Hindus assert, Gādhpūr, from Gādh, a Rājā of that name. We went on shore to view the tomb of a former Governor-General, the Marquis Cornwallis, who lies buried here, aged sixty-seven. The sarcophagus is within a circular building surmounted by a dome, and surrounded by a verandah; it is of white marble, with appropriate figures in half relief by Flaxman. In front is a bust of the Marquis; the coronet and cushion surmount it; the iron railings are remarkably handsome and appropriate; the whole is surrounded by a plantation of fine young trees, and kept in excellent order; in front is a pedestal intended, I should imagine, for a statue of the Marquis. The view from the building is open and pretty; it is situated in the cantonment on the banks of the Ganges. There are four figures in mourning attitudes on the tomb, in half relief; that of a Brahman is well executed. The *pukka* houses of the European residents at Ghāzipur, stretching along the river's side, have pleasing effect.

The ruins of the palace of the Nawāb of Ghāzipur are situated on a high bank, in front of which the rampart, with four bastions, faces the river. The house is falling into ruins. I admired it very much, the plan on which it is built is charming; what a luxurious abode during the hot winds! It is situated on a high bank overlooking the Ganges; in the centre is an octagonal room; around this, four square rooms alternate with four octagonal rooms which are supported on light and handsome arches. There are no walls to the rooms, but each is supported on arches. Around the centre room is a space for water, and a great number of fountains played there in former times. Between the arches hung rich *pardas*; how delightfully suited to the climate! Imagine the luxury of sitting in the centre room, all the air coming in cooled by the fountains and screened from the glare by the rich *pardas*! One of the octagonal rooms has fallen in completely. A gentleman of our party, not finding any game in the surrounding fields, shot five *anwari* fish that were sporting about on the surface of the river. Rosewater and cloth was brought for sale in abundance. The fields by the riverside are in parts a perfect Golgotha, strewn with human skulls. The Company's stud is here, but we did not visit it.

Off the village of Beerpūr I saw from ten to twenty *sati* mounds, under some large trees by the riverside; the idea of what those wretched women must have suffered made me shudder.

Off Chounsah I was most thoroughly disgusted; there is on the bank of the river a *murda ghāt*, or place for burning the dead bodies of the Hindus; about twenty *chārpāis* (native beds) were there cast away as unclean, the bodies having been carried down upon them. Some of the bodies had hardly been touched by the fire, just scorched and thrown into the water. The dogs and crows were tearing the flesh from the skeletons, growling as they ate to deter other dogs that stood snarling around from joining in the meal. A gentleman fired at them, drove off some of the dogs and killed others; you have no idea how fierce and hungry the wretches were; a bullet from a musket only scared them for a moment and then they returned to the corpse. I was glad to get beyond the *murda ghāt*; the sight and smell of such horrors made me ill.

Anchored at Buxar and visited the stud; the only stable I went into was a most admirable one, lofty, airy, ventilated, clean, and spacious. It contained two hundred horses, all looking clean and in excellent condition; the horses in this stable are all three years old, remarkably fine young animals. You may have the choice of the stable for £100, Rs 1,000; these horses ought to be good, they come from the best imported English, Arab and Persian horses and are reared with great care. The animals stand in a long line without any separation or bar between them in the stable; the head is tied to the manger, the heels at liberty, no heel-ropes. They appear perfectly quiet although they stand so close to each other. About six hundred horses are at Buxar, and more on the other side of the river; I derived much pleasure from seeing the stud at this place and regret I did not visit that at Ghāzipur. Every day, from seven o'clock to eight, the whole of the young horses are turned loose into a paddock, to run and gallop about at pleasure; it must be a pretty sight.

November 23rd – The *melā* at Ballia is held on this day, the last of the month of Kartik. The scene for five miles was very gay; a great Hindu fair and bathing day; boats full of people going to the fair, numbers on the cliff, and crowds in the river at their devotions – an animated scene. The gentlemen are firing ball at the great crocodiles as they lie basking on the sandbanks; they have killed a very large one. When crocodiles are cut open, silver and gold ornaments are sometimes found in the interior; the body of a child – the whole body – was found in a crocodile, a short time ago, at Cawnpore.

[. . .]

CHAPTER XLIV

SKETCHES IN BENGAL – THE SUNDERBANDS

DECEMBER 9TH 1836 – Arrived at Jungipūr, where a toll was levied of Rs 6 on my *bajrā*, usually called *budjerow*, and Rs 2 on the cook boat – a tax for keeping open a deep channel in the river. During the hour we anchored there and the servants were on shore for provisions, I was much amused watching the women bathing; they wade into the stream, wash their dresses, and put them on again all wet as they stand in the water; wash their hair and their bodies, retaining all the time some part of their drapery which assumes the most classical appearance. They wear their hair fastened behind in the Grecian fashion, large silver nose-rings, a great number of white ivory bracelets (*churis*) on their arms, with a pair of very large silver bangles on the wrists, and massive ornaments of silver on their ankles; their drapery white with, perhaps, an edge of some gay colour; bright brass vessels for water (*gāgrī*) or of porous red earthenware (*gharā*), in which they carry back the river water to their dwellings. Having bathed, they repeat their prayers with their hands palm to palm raised to their faces, and turning in *pooja* to particular points. After sipping the water a certain number of times, taking it up in their hands, they trip away in their wet drapery which dries as they walk. The skin of the women in Bengal is of a better tinge than that of the up-country women; they are small, well-formed and particularly graceful in their movements.

December 10th – The Bhaugruttī, as you approach Moorshadabad is remarkably picturesque, and presents a thousand views that would make beautiful sketches. At this moment we are passing the Nawāb's residence, or rather the palace that is building for him; it is situated on the side of the river, which presents a beautiful expanse of water, covered with vessels of all sorts and sizes, of the most oriental and picturesque form. A fine breeze is blowing, and the vessels on every side and all around me are in every sort of picturesque and beautiful position. The palace, which is almost quite completed, is a noble building, an enormous and grand mass of architecture reared under the superintendence of Colonel Macleod.

The *mor-pankhi*, a kind of pleasure boat, with the long neck and head of a peacock, most richly gilt and painted, and the snake boats, used on days of

festival, are fairy-like, picturesque, fanciful and very singular. Pinnaces for hire
are here in numbers. The merchant-boats built at this place are of peculiar and
beautiful form, as if the builder had studied both effect and swiftness; the small
boats, over which rafts are fastened to float down wood; the fishermen's little
vessels, that appear almost too small and fragile to support the men, and which
fly along impelled only by one oar; the well-wooded banks, the mosques, and
the *mut'hs* (Hindu temples), mixed with curiously built native houses – all
unite in forming a scene of peculiar beauty. Kāsim Bazaar adjoins Moorshadabad; both are famous for silk of every sort. In the evening we anchored at
Berhampūr; the *budgerow* was instantly crowded with people bringing carved
ivory toys, chessmen, elephants, etc., for sale, and silk merchants with handker-
chiefs and Berhampūr silk in abundance; all asking more than double the price
they intended to take. Four more *dāndis* having deserted, I have been obliged to
apply to the Judge Sāhib to procure other men.

The most delicious oranges have been procured here, the rinds fine and
thin, the flavour excellent; the natives call them '*cintra*'; most likely they were
introduced by the Portuguese. The station extends along the side of the river,
which is well banked and offers a cool and refreshing evening walk to the
residents. I was tempted to buy some of the carved ivory chessmen, an elephant,
etc. all very cheap and well carved in good ivory; nor could I resist some silk nets
for the horses.

[...]

December 15th – This evening we anchored at Chandar-nagar, the town of
Chandar, *the moon*, commonly called Chandar-nagore, and took a walk to see
a Bengāli temple which looked well from the river. The building consisted of a
temple in the centre containing an image of the goddess Kalī, and five smaller
temples on each side, each containing an image of Mahadēo; a little further on
were two images, gaily dressed in tarnished silk and tinsel; the one a female
figure, Unapurna, the other Mahadēo, as a Bairāgī or religious mendicant. The
village was pretty. I stopped at a fisherman's to look at the curiously-shaped
floats he used for his very large and heavy fishing nets; each float was formed of
eight pieces of *sholā*, tied together by the ends, the four smaller within the four
larger. When this light and spongy pith is wetted, it can be cut into thin layers
which, pasted together, are formed into hats; Chinese paper appears to be
made of the same material. The banks of the river, the whole distance from
Hoogly to Chinsurah and Chandar-nagar, presents a view of fine houses
situated in good gardens and interspersed with the dwellings of the natives.
There is a church at Chandar-nagar where there are also cantonments; and the
grand depôt for the wood from the up-country rafts appears to be at this place;

the riverside was completely covered with timber for some distance. The natives were amusing themselves as we passed, sending up small fire balloons and brilliantly blue sky rockets.

The view is beautiful at Barrackpūr; the fine trees of the park stretching along the side of the river; the bright green turf that slopes gently down to the water; the number of handsome houses with their lawns and gardens; the Government-house and the buildings around it, stuccoed to resemble white stone; the handsome verandahs which surround the houses, supported by pillars; and the great number of boats gliding about render it peculiarly pleasing.

In front, on the opposite side of the river, is the Danish settlement of Serampūr; its houses, which are large and handsome, are two or three storeys high. We are floating gently down with the tide; I can scarcely write, the scenery attracts me so much – the Bengali *mandaps* (places of worship) close to the water, the fine trees of every description and the pretty stone *ghāts*. We have just passed a ruined *ghāt*, situated in the midst of fine old trees; at the top of the flight of steps are the ruins of two Hindu temples of picturesque form; an old *peepal* tree overshadows them; its twisted roots are exposed, the earth having been washed away during the rains. A number of women are bathing, others carrying water away in *gharās* poised on their heads: the men take it away in water vessels which are hung to either end of a split bamboo, called a *bahangī*, which is carried balanced on the shoulder. We fly past the objects with the ebbing tide; what an infinity of beauty there is in all the native boats! Could my pencil do justice to the scenery, how valuable would be my sketchbook!

The Governor-General, Lord Auckland, lives partly in Calcutta and partly at the Government-house at Barrackpūr. At Cassipūr is the house of the agent for gunpowder, its white pillars half-hidden by fine trees. At Chitpore is a high, red, Birmingham-looking, long-chimnied building with another in the same style near it; the high chimneys of the latter emitting a dark volume of smoke such as one only sees in this country pouring from the black funnel of a steamer: corn is here ground in the English fashion, and oil extracted from divers seeds. The establishment cost a great sum of money and I think I have heard it has failed, owing to each native family in India grinding their own corn in the old original fashion of one flat circular millstone over another, called a *chakki*.

From this point I first caught a view of the shipping off Calcutta: for ten years I had not beheld an English vessel: how it made me long for a glimpse of all the dear ones in England! 'The desire of the garden never leaves the heart of the nightingale.'

Passing through the different vessels that crowd the Hoogly off Calcutta gave me great pleasure; the fine merchant-ships, the gay, well-trimmed American vessels, the grotesque forms of the Arab ships, the Chinese vessels with an eye on each side the bows to enable the vessel to see her way across the deep waters, the native vessels in all their fanciful and picturesque forms, the pleasure-boats of private gentlemen, the beautiful private residences in Chowringhee, the Government-house, the crowds of people and vehicles of all descriptions, both European and Asiatic, form a scene of beauty of which I know not the equal.

We anchored at Chandpaul *ghāt*, amidst a crowd of vessels. The river-beggars fly about in the very smallest little boats in the world, paddled by one tiny oar: a little flag is stuck up in the boat and on a mat at the bottom, spread to receive offerings, is a collection of copper coins, rice and cowries, thrown by the pious or the charitable to these *fakirs*; who, if fame belie them not, are rascals. 'A guru at home, but a beggar abroad.' I forgive them the sin of rascality, for their picturesque appearance; the gifts they received were very humble. 'A *kuoree* is a gold *mohur* to a pauper.'

There not being room that night for our party at Spence's hotel, I was forced to sleep on board the *budjerow*, off Chandpaul *ghāt*. What a wretched night it was! The heat was intolerable. I could not open a window because the *budjerows* on either side were jammed against mine: the heat, the noise, the mooring and unmooring according to the state of the tide rendered it miserable work. I wished to anchor lower down, but the answer was '*Budjerows* must anchor here; it is the Lord Sāhib's *hukm* (order).'

December 17th – I took possession of apartments in Spence's hotel: they were good and well furnished. Since I quitted Calcutta a great improvement has taken place: a road has been opened from the Government-house to Garden Reach, by the side of the river; the drive is well-watered, the esplanade crowded with carriages and the view of the shipping beautiful.

M. le Général Allard, who had just returned from France and was in Calcutta *en route* to rejoin Runjeet Singh, called on me; he is the most picturesque person imaginable; his long forked beard, divided in the centre, hangs down on either side his face; at dinner-time he passes one end of his beard over one ear, and the other end over the other ear. The General, who was a most agreeable person, regretted he had not seen me when he passed Allahabad but illness had prevented his calling and delivering, in person, the bows and arrows entrusted to his charge.

I was much delighted with the General: he asked me to visit Lahore, an invitation I told him I would accept with great pleasure should I ever visit the

Hills, and he promised to send an escort for me. The General took with him to Europe some fine jewels, emeralds and other valuable stones; he brought them back to India, as they were of less value in Europe than in the East.

I could have remained contentedly at the hotel myself, but my up-country servants complained there was no comfort for them; therefore I took a small house in Chowringhee, and removed into it the furniture from the *budjerow*. It was comfortable also to have my horses, which had arrived, in the stables.

Went to a ball given in the English style by a rich Bengāli Baboo, Rustam-jee Cowsajee. The Misses Eden were there, which the Baboo ought to have thought a very great honour.

[...]

January 15th 1837 – Accompanied Mr W— and a party over his racing stables: the sight of the racers all ready for the contest in the morning was pleasing. We then visited a number of imported English and Cape horses that were for sale.

In the evening I drove to see the far-famed Bengāli idol Kali Māi, to which, in former times, human sacrifices were publicly offered; and to which, in the present day and in spite of the vigilance of the magistrate, I believe, at times, a human being is offered up – some poor wretch who has no-one likely to make inquiries about him. The temple is at Kali Ghāt, about two miles from Calcutta. The idol is a great black stone cut into the figure of an enormous woman, with a large head and staring eyes; her tongue hangs out of her mouth, a great broad tongue down to her breast. The figure is disgusting. I gave the attendant priests a rupee for having shown me their idol, which they offered with all reverence to Kali Māi. The instruments with which, at one stroke, the priest severs the head of the victim from the trunk are remarkable.

January 16th – A cup of silver, given by a rich Bengāli, Dwarkanāth Tagore, was run for: the cup was elaborately worked and the workmanship good; but the design was in the excess of bad taste and such as only a Baboo would have approved. It was won by Absentee, one of the horses I had seen in the stable the day before, contrary to the calculation of all the knowing ones in Calcutta.

January 17th – The inhabitants of Calcutta gave a ball to the Miss Edens. I was too ill to attend.

January 30th – Dined with an old friend at Alipūr some two miles from Calcutta. The coachman, being unable to see his way across the *maidān* (plain), stopped. The *sā'ises*, who were trying to find out where they were, ran directly against the walls of the hospital; the fog was so dense and white you could not see a yard before you; it made my cough most painful, and the carriage was two hours returning two miles.

February 4th – I spent the day at the Asiatic Society. A model of the foot of a Chinese lady in the collection is a curiosity, and a most disgusting deformity. The toes are crushed up under the foot so as to render the person perfectly lame: this is a less expensive mode of keeping a woman confined to the house than having guards and a *zenāna* – the principle is the same.

Having bid *adieu* to my friends in Calcutta, I prepared to return to Allahabad and took a passage in the Jellinghy flat. The servants went up the river in a large baggage boat with the stores, wine and furniture. I did not insure the boat, insurance being very high and the time of the year favourable. The horses marched up the country.

March 6th – I went on board the Jellinghy flat, established myself and my *ayha* in a good cabin and found myself, for the first time, located in a steamer. She quitted Calcutta in the evening, and as we passed Garden Reach, the view of handsome houses in well-wooded grounds which extend along the banks of the river was beautiful. The water being too shallow at this time of the year for the passage of the steamer up the Bhaugrutti, or the Jellinghy, she was obliged to go round by the sunderbands (*sindhū-bandh*). The steamer herself is not the vessel in which the passengers live; attached to, and towed by her, is a vessel as large as the steamer herself, called a flat, built expressly to convey passengers and Government treasure. It is divided into cabins, with one large cabin in the centre in which the passengers dine together.

[...]

March 9th – Last night two boats full of woodcutters passed us; they said several of their men had been carried off by tigers. We have only overtaken four boats all this time in the sunderbands. During the hot weather people dare not come through this place; fevers are caught from the malaria: at the present time of the year it is safe enough. There are no inhabitants in these parts, the people finding it impossible to live here. We have a very pleasant party on board, most of whom are going to Allahabad. The vessel is a good one; the accommodation good, the food also. It is very expensive, but as it saves one a *dāk* trip this hot weather, or a two or three months' voyage in a country vessel, it is more agreeable. The heat in these vile sunderbands is very great; during the day, quite oppressive; when we enter the Ganges we shall find it cooler. As we were emerging from the sunderbands and nearing the river, the banks presented a scene which must resemble the back settlements in America. Before this time we had scarcely met with a good-sized tree. Here the trees partook of the nature of forest: some people were burning the forest and had made a settlement. Barley was growing in small portions and there were several dwarf cows. The scene was peculiar; a little bank of mud was raised to prevent the overflow of the tide; the stumps of the burned and blackened trees remained standing, with the exception of where they had been rooted out and a paddy field formed. Places for look-out erected on high poles were numerous and thatched over: there a man could sit and watch all night, lest a tiger should make his appearance. There were a few miserable huts for the men, no women were to be seen; nothing could be more primitive and more wretched than these young settlements in the sunderbands. On the morning of the 10th we quitted this vile place and anchored at Culna to take in a fresh supply of coals.

[...]

March 26th – Passed Chunar – the place had lost much of the beauty it displayed during the rains. A *khidmatgār* fell overboard, passed under the vessel from head to stern, and was picked up by the boat just as he was on the point of sinking. The skin was torn off the old man's scalp; he received no further injury. The next day, to my astonishment, he was in attendance on his master at dinner-time and seemed to think nothing of having been scalped by the steamer!

March 27th – Received fruit and vegetables from an old friend at Mirzapur. I am weary of the voyage, the heat for the last few days has been so oppressive: very gladly shall I return to the quiet and coolness of my own home. Aground several times on sandbanks.

March 29th – Started early and arrived within sight of the Fort; were again fixed on a sandbank; the river is very shallow at this time of the year. With the greatest difficulty we reached the *ghāt* on the Jumna, near the Masjid, and were glad to find ourselves at the end of the voyage. My husband came down to receive and welcome me, and drive me home. The great dog Nero nearly tore me to pieces in his delight. Her Highness the Bāiza Bāi sent her people down to the *ghāt* to make salam on my landing, to welcome and congratulate me on my return, and to say she wished to see me.

It was pleasant to be thus warmly received and to find myself once more in my cool and comfortable home on the banks of the Jumna-ji after all the heat and fatigue of the voyage.

The Brija Bāi, one of the Mahratta ladies, was delighted to see me once again and performed a certain sort of blessing called *balaiyā lenā*, or taking all another's evils on one's self; which ceremony she performed by drawing her hands over my head and cracking her fingers on her own temples, in token of taking all my misfortunes upon herself. This mode of blessing I have many times seen performed both by men and women, our dependants and servants, both towards my husband and myself, on our bestowing any particular benefit upon them; it expressed the depth of their gratitude.

April 6th – The smallpox is making great ravages; some of our friends have fallen victims. Lord William Bentinck did away with the vaccine department to save a few rupees; from which economy many have lost their lives. It is a dreadful illness, the smallpox in this country. People are in a fright respecting the plague; they say it is at Palee, and has approached the borders of the Company's territories; we have fevers, cholera and deadly illnesses enough without the plague; it is to be trusted *that* will not be added to the evils of this climate.

The Palee plague, they say, after all, is not the *genuine* thing: it has not as yet entered our territories; however, the Government of Agra have very wisely adopted preventive measures, and have established boards of health, cordons, and quarantine, with the usual measures as to fumigations and disinfectants. It would be really *too bad* to give this stranger a playground, in addition to our old friends fever and cholera, already domesticated.

April 15th – The first time of using the thermantidote was this morning: how delightful was the stream of cool air it sent into the hot room! How grateful is the coolness and darkness of the house, in contrast to the heat and glare on the river!

[...]

The Hon. Miss Frances Eden has been with a party at Moorshadabad, tiger shooting; they had indifferent sport and only killed five tigers, one of which had the happiness of dying before the eyes of the fair lady. They have returned to Calcutta. It must have been warm work in the jungles after the tigers; but when one has an object in view, one is apt to forget the power of an Indian sun until a good fever reminds one of the danger of exposure.

April 21st – Last night, at midnight, the moon was completely eclipsed and darkness fell over the land. The natives are horror-struck; they say it foretells sickness, disease and death to a dreadful extent. It is not unlikely their fears may be verified: the plague is raging at Palee; it is expected it will spread ere long to the Company's territories. Then, indeed, will the natives believe in the direful presages of the eclipse, forgetting the plague was the forerunner not the follower of the signs of wrath in the heavens. Sir Charles Metcalfe has issued all necessary orders to prevent the intercourse of persons from the infected cities with those of the surrounding country. The smallpox is carrying off the young and the healthy; in every part of the country you hear of its fatal effects.

The Brija Bāī, one of the favourite attendants on the Baīza Bāī, came to see me; I showed her a prize I had won in a lottery at Calcutta; a silver vase beautifully enamelled in gold, value £40. She was much pleased with it and anxious to procure tickets in the next lottery for mechanical curiosities.

[...]

April 24th – The Brija came to request I would visit the camp to show them how to use a magic-lantern; I did so, but it was a failure, being dim and indistinct. In the course of conversation, wishing to remember a circumstance related by one of the ladies in attendance, I noted it in my pocketbook on a little slate of white china. Her Highness, who observed the action, asked for the pocketbook, examined it, admired the delicately white china and asking for a pencil wrote her own name upon it. She appeared surprised at my being able to read and write, accomplishments possessed by herself but uncommon among the Mahratta ladies who are seldom able to attain them, it being the system of eastern nations to keep their women in ignorance, imagining it gives them greater power over them. They are taught to consider it unfit for ladies of rank, and that it ought to be done for them by their writers and *moonshees*; nevertheless, they were proud of the accomplishments possessed by the Bāiza Bāī. Her Highness returned me the pocketbook, which I received with pleasure, and value highly for the sake of the autograph.

All the needlework is done by women in the *zenāna*: to allow a tailor to make your attire would be considered indelicate, and their clothes are never allowed to be shown to men lest they should thus be able to judge of the form of the lady *parda-nishīn*, i.e. behind the curtain. Imagine the disgust an Asiatic lady would feel if placed in Regent Street, on beholding figures displayed in shop windows intended to represent English ladies in corsets, bustles and under petticoats, turning round on poles, displaying for the laughter and criticism of the men the whole curious and extraordinary *arcana* of the toilet of an European!

May 5th – The Bāiza Bāī was unable to get the thirty tickets she sent for in the lottery; eighteen were all that were unsold and these were taken by her. She was very fortunate and won two prizes; one was an ornament in diamonds attached to a necklace of two strings of pearls and a pair of diamond earrings, valued at Rs 2,000, i.e. £200; the second a clock, valued at Rs 400, £40: my own ticket proved a blank. [. . .] The Mahrattas were charmed with [the clock]: it is a good specimen, but they will spoil it in a month.

[*An entire chapter is omitted here*]

CHAPTER XLV

The Famine at Kannauj

HEALTH ALONE IS EQUAL TO A THOUSAND BLESSINGS

[...]

SEPTEMBER 24th 1837 – The Nawāb Hakīm Menhdi has been re-appointed minister in Oude; how happy the old man must be! He has been living at Fatehgar, pining for a restoration to the honours at Lucknow. The Nawāb quitted for Oude; on the first day of his march, the horse that carried his *nakaras* (state kettledrums) fell down and died and one of his cannon was upset – both most unlucky omens. The Camp and the Minister were in dismay! To us it is laughable, to the natives a matter of distress. The right to beat kettledrums, and to have them carried before you, is only allowed to great personages. Therefore the omen was fearful; it will be reported at Lucknow, will reach the ears of the King, and perhaps produce a bad effect on his mind – the natives are so superstitious.

The Mahārāj of Gwalior, the Bāiza Bāi's adopted son who drove her out of the kingdom, announced a few days ago that a son and heir was born unto him. The Resident communicated the happy news to the Government; illuminations took place, guns were fired, every honour paid to the young heir of the throne of Gwalior. The Bāi sent her granddaughter on an elephant in an *amārī* (a canopied seat), attended by her followers on horseback, to do *pooja* in the Ganges and to give large presents to the Brahmans. As the Gaja Rājā passed along the road, handfuls of rupees were scattered to the crowd below from the seat on the elephant. Six days after the announcement of the birth of a son, the King sent for the Resident and, looking very sheepish, was obliged to confess the son was a daughter! The Resident was much annoyed that his beard had been laughed at; and, in all probability, the King had been deceived by the women in the *zenāna*: perhaps a son had really been born, and having died, a girl had been substituted – the only child procurable, perhaps, at the moment, or approved of by the mother. A *zenāna* is the very birthplace of intrigue.

September 30th – I am busy with preparations for a march; perhaps, in my rambles, I shall visit Lucknow, see the new King and my old friend the Nawāb Hakīm Menhdi in all his glory. I should like very much to visit the *zenāna* for, although the King be about seventy, there is no reason why he may not have a large *zenāna*, wives of all sorts and kinds – 'the black, the blue, the brown, the fair' – for purposes of state and show.

[...]

December 1st – The Governor-General Lord Auckland, the Hon. the Misses Eden and Captain Osborne arrived at Allahabad with all their immense encampment. The gentlemen of the Civil Service and the military paid their respects. Instead of receiving morning visits, the Misses Eden received visitors in the evening, transforming a formal morning call into a pleasant party – a relief to the visitors and the visited.

December 7th – I made my salam to Miss Eden at her tents; she told me she was going to visit her Highness the Bāiza Bāi with the Governor-General, asked me to accompany her and to act as interpreter to which I consented with pleasure.

December 8th – The Gaja Rājā Sāhib went on an elephant in state to bring the Misses Eden to call on the Bāiza Bāi. They arrived with Lord Auckland in all due form: his Lordship and Appa Sāhib sat in the outer room, and conversed with her Highness through the *parda*. I introduced the Misses Eden to the Bāiza Bāi and her granddaughter, with whom they appeared pleased and interested. Twenty-two trays, containing pairs of shawls, pieces of cloth of gold, fine Dacca muslin and jewels were presented to the Governor-General; and fifteen trays, filled in a similar manner, to each of the Misses Eden. They bowed to the presents when they were laid before them, after which the trays were carried off and placed in the treasury for the benefit of the Government.

December 15th – I quitted Allahabad on my road to the Hills, under the escort of our friend Mr F—, near whose tents my own were to be pitched: the country was swarming with robbers; they follow the camp of the Governor-General wherever it may be.

December 16th – Arrived at my tents at Fatehpur; the scene in the camp was very picturesque; the troops were drawn out before the tents of the Governor-General and all was state and form for the reception of the Chiefs of Bandelkhand; the guns were firing salutes; it was an animated and beautiful scene.

December 18th – I mounted my black horse and rode at daybreak with some friends. From the moment we left our tents we were passed, during the whole march, by such numbers of elephants, so many strings of camels, so many horses and carts and so many carriages of all sorts, attendant on the troops and the artillery of the Governor-General and his suite, that the whole line of march, from the beginning to the end, was one mass of living beings. My tents were pitched near the guns of the artillery, outside the camp at Mulwah: a Rājā came to call on Lord Auckland, a salute was fired; my horses, being so near, became alarmed; the grey broke from his ropes, fell on the pegs to which he was picketed, and lamed himself; another broke loose; a camel lamed himself and we had some difficulty in quieting the frightened animals.

December 19th – I was unwell from over-fatigue, most uncomfortable. In the evening I roused myself to dine with Lord Auckland to meet Prince Henry of Orange. His Royal Highness entered the navy at eight years of age and has been in the service ten years, in the *Bellona* frigate. Accompanied by his captain, he came up *dāk* to spend a few days with Lord Auckland. The Prince is a tall, slight young man and, apparently, very diffident.

December 21st – Arrived at Cawnpore, and paid a long promised visit to a relative. As the Misses Eden were at home in the evening, I accompanied Major P— to pay my respects. We lost our way in the ravine from a dense fog: when we reached the tents the whole station was assembled there, quadrilles and waltzing going forward.

December 25th – On Christmas-day the old Nawāb Hakīm Menhdi, the minister of Oude of whom I have so often spoken, breathed his last at Lucknow. His death was announced to me in a very original note from his nephew and heir, the General Sāhib:

'Dear Madam – I have to inform you that my poor uncle Nawāb Moontuzim-ood-Dowlah Bahadur departed this life at the decree and will of Providence, at half-past three o'clock A.M. the day before yesterday, Monday, the 25th inst., after a short illness of six days only; consequently seeing him any more in this world is all buried in oblivion. The Begum Sāhiba tenders her kind remembrances to you. With best wishes, believe me to be, dear Madam, yours very faithfully, Ushruff-ood-Dowla Ahmed Ally Khān Bahadur.'

I was sorry to hear of the death of the Nawāb. How soon it has followed on the bad omens of his march!

December 26th – Received an invitation to breakfast with the son of the King of Oude, who had arrived from Lucknow to meet the Governor-General's party: went there on an elephant: at immense party were assembled in a very fine tent. Shortly after, breakfast was announced: when it was over we returned to the former tent when the presents were brought forth; they consisted of a fine elephant with a *howdah* on his back, and the whole of the trappings of red cloth and velvet richly embroidered in gold. Two fine horses next appeared, their housings of velvet and gold, and the bridles were studded with rows of turquoise. A golden palanquin was next presented. On the ground, in front of the party, were twenty-three trays, the present to Lord Auckland; they were filled with cashmere shawls in pairs, pieces of *kimkhwāb*, and necklaces of pearls emeralds and diamonds. Fifteen trays of shawls and cloth of gold, with fine pieces of Dacca muslin, were presented to each of the Misses Eden; two of the trays contained two combs set in superb diamonds, and two necklaces of diamonds and emeralds such as are hardly ever seen even in India. All these fine things were presented and accepted; they were then carried off and placed in the Government treasury. The Government make presents of equal value in return.

[. . .]

January 6th – At six o'clock, when I quitted my tent to mount my horse, it was bitterly cold; the poor starving wretches had collected on the spot which my horses had quitted and were picking up the grains of *gram* that had fallen from their nosebags; others were shivering over a half-burned log of wood my people had lighted during the night. On the road I saw many animals dead from over-exertion and famine; carts overturned; at one place a palanquin *gari* had been run away with, the wheels had knocked down and passed over two camel drivers; one of the men was lying on the roadside senseless and dying.

On reaching the Stanhope, which had been laid half way for me, the horse gave some annoyance while being put into harness; when once in, away he went, pulling at a fearful rate, through roads half way up the leg in sand, full of great holes and so crowded with elephants, camels, artillery, cavalry and infantry, and all the camp followers, it was scarcely possible to pass through such a dense crowd; and in many places it was impossible to see beyond your horse's head from the excessive dust. Imagine a camp of eleven thousand men all marching on the road, and such a road!

Away rushed the horse in the Stanhope, and had not the harness been strong, and the reins English, it would have been all over with us. I saw a beautiful Persian kitten on an Arab's shoulder; he was marching with a long string of camels carrying grapes, apples, dates and Tusar cloth for sale from Kabul. Perched on each camel were one or two Persian cats. The pretty tortoiseshell kitten, with its remarkably long hair and bushy tail caught my eye – its colours were so brilliant. The Arab ran up to the Stanhope holding forth the kitten; we checked the impetuous horse for an instant and I seized the pretty little creature; the check rendered the horse still more violent, away he sprang, and off he set at full speed through the encampment which we had just reached. The Arab thinking I had purposely stolen his kitten ran after the buggy at full speed, shouting as he passed Lord Auckland's tents, *'Dohā'i,*

Dohā'i, sāhib! Dohā'i, Lord sāhib!' 'Mercy, mercy, sir! Mercy, Governor-General!' The faster the horse rushed on, the faster followed the shouting Arab, until on arriving at my own tents, the former stopped of his own accord and the breathless Arab came up. He asked ten rupees for his kitten but at length, with well-feigned reluctance, accepted five, declaring it was worth twenty. 'Who was ever before the happy possessor of a tortoiseshell Persian cat?' The man departed. Alas! for the wickedness of the world! Alas! for the Pilgrim! She has bought a cocky-olli-bird!

The cocky-olli-bird, although unknown to naturalists by that name, was formerly sold at Harrow by an old man to the boys who were charmed with the brilliancy of its plumage – purple, green, crimson, yellow, all the colours of the rainbow united in this beautiful bird; nor could the wily old fellow *import* them fast enough to supply the demand, until it was discovered they were *painted sparrows!*

The bright burnt sienna colour of the kitten is not tortoiseshell, she has been dyed with hinnā, her original colour was white, with black spots; however, she looks so pretty, she must be fresh dyed when her hair falls off; the *hinnā* is permanent for many months. The poor kitten has a violent cold, perhaps the effect of the operation of dyeing her: no doubt, after having applied the pounded *menhdī*, they wrapped her up in fresh castor-oil leaves, and bound her up in a handkerchief, after the fashion in which a native dyes his beard. Women often take cold from putting hinnā on their feet.

[. . .]

January 7th – This day, being Sunday, was a halt – a great refreshment after toil; and Divine Service was performed in the tent of the Governor-General; after which, at three o'clock, I went on an elephant to see two most ancient and curious specimens of Hindu sculpture, the figures of Rām and Lutchman, which are about five feet in height, carved on separate stones, and surrounded by a whole heaven of gods and goddesses: the stones themselves, which are six or seven feet high, are completely covered with numerous images; and a *devi* (goddess), rather smaller, is on one side.

Passing through the bazaar at Kannauj was a fearful thing. There lay the skeleton of a woman who had died of famine; the whole of her clothes had been stolen by the famished wretches around, the pewter rings were still in her ears, but not a rag was left on the bones that were starting through the black and shrivelled skin; the agony on the countenance of the corpse was terrible. Next to her a poor woman, unable to rise, lifted up her skinny arm and moaned for food. The unhappy women, with their babies in their arms, pressing them to their bony breasts, made me shudder. Miserable boys, absolutely living skeletons, pursued the elephant imploring for bread: poor wretches, I had but little money with me and could give them only that little and my tears: I cannot write about the scene without weeping, it was so horrible and made me very sick. Six people died of starvation in the bazaar today. Lord Auckland daily feeds all the poor who come for food, and gives them blankets; five or six hundred are fed daily – but what avails it in a famine like this? It is merciful cruelty, and only adds a few more days to their sufferings; better to die at once, better to end such intolerable and hopeless misery: these people are not the beggars but the tillers of the soil. When I was last at Kannauj the place was so beautiful, so luxuriant in vegetation – the bright green trees, the river winding through low fields of the richest pasture: those fields are all bare, not a blade of grass. The wretched inhabitants tear off the bark of the wild fig tree (*goolèr*) and pound it into food; in the course of four or five days their bodies swell and they die in agonies. The cultivators sit on the side of their fields and, pointing to their naked bodies, cry, 'I am dying of hunger.' Some pick out the roots of the bunches of coarse grass and chew them. The people have become desperate; sometimes, when they see a *sipāhi* eating they rush upon him to take his food; sometimes they fall one over the other as they rush for it, and having fallen, being too weak to rise, they die on the spot, blessed in finding the termination of their sufferings. The very locusts appear to have felt the famine; you see the wings here and there on the ground, and now and then a weak locust pitches on a camel. Every tree has been stripped of its leaves for food for animals. The inhabitants of Kannauj, about a *lakh* of people, have fled to Oogein and to Saugar. The place will be a desert; none will remain but the grain merchants who fatten on the surrounding misery. There is no hope of rain for five months; by that time the torments of these poor wretches will have ended in death – and this place is the one I so much admired from the river, with its rich fields and its high land covered with fine trees and ruins!

[...]

CHAPTER XLVI

Pleasant Days in Camp

JANUARY 8TH 1838 – Arrived at Jelalabad without any adventures. Went to hear the band in the evening, but felt weary from not having slept the night before on account of the yells of the packs of jackals in every direction round the tent, and the noise of the sentries keeping off the people from Kannauj. We were in a complete *jangal*: a wolf came up to my tent at midday, then trotting over to the opposite tent carried off my neighbour's kid.

[...]

January 12th – Dined with Major Sutherland, the Resident of Gwalior, who was in attendance on the Governor-General. A number of friends were assembled; a bright fire blazed in the tent; our host was the life of the party; the dinner was excellent. I have seldom passed a more agreeable evening.

[...]

January 19th – Finished a march of fifteen miles before half-past eight; halted at Nawābganj; breakfasted with my friends; a most kind welcome, a bright fire and an excellent breakfast made me quite happy. The formality of the great camp I had just quitted formed a strong contrast to the gaiety and cheerfulness of marching under the flag of the Resident of Gwalior.

January 23rd – We arrived at Khasganj, and encamped in the *mango tope* just beyond the village. After breakfast, I drove four miles to see Mr James Gardner, who had succeeded to his father's property and was living at his house. I found the place quite deserted; Mr Gardner was at one of his villages some miles off but his wife, Mulka Begum, was at home. I sent word I would pay my respects to her if she could receive me. In the meantime I went into the garden and visited all those spots where I had so often enjoyed the society of my dear friend Colonel Gardner. The pavilion in the centre of the garden, in which I had nursed him when he was so ill, recalled to mind the conversation we then had which ended in his taking me to the tomb of his son just beyond the garden; we sat on that tomb and the dear old man said, pointing to the spot, 'I wish to be buried there, by the side of my son; another year will not pass ere I shall be placed there; you are very kind in trying to persuade me, my dear daughter, that I have still many years before me, but I feel I am going, my constitution is gone; it is well that with old age we feel all these pains and the ills that accompany it; were it not so, we should never be willing to quit this world.' Our conversation lasted some time, afterwards he took my arm and we returned slowly to the house. I visited his grave: his son had raised a tomb on the spot selected by his father; it was not quite finished. I knelt at the grave of my kind, kind friend and wept and prayed in deep affliction. His *begum* had only survived him a few days. She was buried in the same tomb, with her head to Mecca, towards which place the face of a true believer is always turned when laid in the grave. The corpse of a Muhammadan is laid on its back in the grave, with the head to the north and feet to the south, turning its face towards the *kibla* (or Mecca, i.e. west). The Shī'as make their tombs for men of the same shape as the Sunnīs make those for females; and for women like those of the Sunnīs for men, but with a hollow, or basin, in the centre of the upper part.

Mulka Begum received me very kindly; she showed me her little girl, the youngest, about two years old, whom she said was reckoned very like me. The child was shy and clung to her *ayah*, frightened at a stranger; I could scarcely catch a glimpse of her face. The eldest boy was from home with his father; the second son, William Linnaeus, so called after his grandfather, was at home; he is a very fine, intelligent boy. I requested leave to bring Mrs H— to pay her a visit that evening, and then asking permission to depart I returned to the tents. In the evening, our party set off for Khasganj: we walked in the garden and visited the tomb. Major Sutherland spoke of Colonel Gardner as a most gallant officer, and recorded several most dashing actions in which he had distinguished himself in many parts of the country; gallantry that had not met the recompense due to it from Government – the value of a spirit such as Colonel Gardner's had not been properly appreciated by the rulers of the land.

When the evening closed in, the gentlemen went into the outer house and I took Mrs H— into the *zenāna*: as dark beauties always look best by candlelight, I had selected a late hour to visit the *begum*; she was sitting on her *gaddi* when we went in, surrounded by her three beautiful children and was in herself a picture. The little girl, my likeness, had lost all her shyness and was figuring about like a dancing girl; on remarking the extraordinary change from shyness to such violent spirits, Mulka said, 'She has had some opium, that makes her so fearless.' We sat an hour with the *begum* and then took our leave. We found the gentlemen in the outer house, sitting over a warm fire and an excellent dinner of native dishes was ready; having dined, we returned by torchlight to the tents.

My friends were much gratified with their visit to Khasganj; I had spoken so warmly of the beauty of Mulka Begum, that I was pleased to find Mrs H— admired equally both her person and manners.

January 25th – Our morning march was thus: Mr H—, Major Sutherland and myself on horseback; Mrs H— in a palanquin-carriage that rivalled Noah's ark; it held herself, three children, three *ayahs*, two dogs and packages without number; four good Arab horses had hard work to pull it six miles over such roads: the rest of the march was performed in buggies, with a relay of horses on the road. Major Sutherland, on his beautiful Arab, used to fly over the country in true Pindaree style; some of his Arabs I coveted exceedingly. In the evening the gentlemen took their guns; no game was to be found – the land was generally perfectly bare, not a blade of grass – the game had perished for want of food. The whole country around Zezaree was very flat and uninteresting; the only picturesque object we could find during these evening rambles was an old well; these wells we used to seek out and peer into as if we belonged to the Thuggee department and were searching for dead bodies. Our life in tents was very agreeable and I believe the whole party were sorry the next march would bring us to Aligarh, and once more into the form and stupidity of life in a house; for myself, the idea of having any roof over my head but that of a tent fell like a nightmare on my spirits; and the giving up hunting for old wells was a complete sacrifice.

January 26th – Arrived at Aligarh; were kindly welcomed by Mr and Mrs H—, and pitched our tents in the Compound; in the evening we visited the fort, rendered famous for the gallant style in which it was taken, in Lord Lake's time, from General Perron. The fort was strong and surrounded by a fine ditch; to have approached it in a regular manner would have taken a month. A party of the — regiment had a skirmish with some of the men belonging to the fort; as these men retreated over the first bridge the English fought with and entered the first gate with them. When within the gate they were exposed to a heavy fire on every side; just under a large *peepal* tree, close to the gate, six of the officers were killed; the rest crossed the second bridge and fixed their ladders on the wall; but by their own ladders the enemy descended upon them. After dreadful slaughter, the second gate was entered and the English took possession of the fort.

General M— was wounded in the assault and obliged to retire; it was fortunate for his memory he was an actor in one scene of gallantry, for his after-conduct gave rise to a song that is known to every *sipahi* in the service.

> *Hathi par howda*
> *Ghore par zin*
> *Jaldí bhāgiya*
> *Gen'ral Monsin.*

The English lowered the walls of the fort, but left one small portion standing to show their great original height. The fort formerly had but one entrance, which opened on the ditch; the English built another gate on the opposite side and another bridge across the ditch; the place was kept in repair for a short time but is now in ruins. Within the fort, on the right, is a model of the ground plan. I only regret I cannot very well remember all that was told me at the time in the most animated manner by Major Sutherland who, himself a distinguished officer, was greatly interested in the Fort of Aligarh.

[...]

January 31st – Encamped at Bulandsher; quitted the good Delhi road to turn to Meerut; the wind very high and miserably cold, the sand flying like dust, covering every thing in the tent and filling my eyes. The servants annoyed me by disobeying orders; the food was bad – the Arab's saddle wrung his back – everything went wrong. What a distance I have marched! How generally barren, flat and uninteresting the country has been! I saw a very fine banyan tree a day or two ago, but the general face of the country is a sandy plain, interspersed with a few green fields near the wells, and *topes* of mango trees: in one of these *topes* my tent is pitched today. My beautiful dog Nero is dead. What folly in this climate to be fond of anything! It is sure to come to an untimely end.

[...]

February 4th – Arrived at Meerut, pitched my tents in the Compound, i.e. the grounds around the house.

February 6th – The Governor-General and the Camp arrived.

February 7th – Attended a ball given by the officers of the artillery to the Governor-General; Lord Auckland and the Misses Eden were gracious, and had I not been suffering from illness, I should have enjoyed the party.

February 9th – Drove to the Sūraj Kūnd, or Spring of the Sun, a remarkably large tank; a little further on are a great number of *sati* mounds of peculiar construction. In the evening attended a ball, given by the station to the Governor-General and his party.

February 12th – Dined with General and Mrs R— to meet the Governor-General and his party; the dinner was given in one great tent, which held eighty guests at table. In the evening the party went to a ball given by the Buffs to the Governor-General; the room was gay and well-lighted, ornamented with rays of steel, formed of bayonets and ramrods; a sort of throne was decorated with the colours of the regiment for the Governor-General. The dancing was carried on with spirit; the finale an excellent supper.

Mr W— invited me to Lahore to witness the meeting of the Governor-

General and Ranjit Singh. I promised to accept the invitation if in that part of the world in November, but I fear I shall be far distant. Captain O— sent me three Italian greyhound pups; they dart about in the most amusing manner. I hope the little delicate creatures will live. Wishing to view the ruins of Delhi, I sent off my tents one march to await me. In the evening I went to the theatre, to see the performance of the privates of the artillery. The men built their own theatre, painted their own scenes and are themselves the performers. The scenery is excellent, the house crowded; the men acted remarkably well; and the ladies, strapping artillery men, six feet high, were the cause of much laughter. A letter from Allahabad informed me, 'the 12th of January was one of the great bathing days, the river and its banks were covered with the pilgrims; for days and days we saw them passing in one almost continued line, very few rich people amongst them, principally the lower orders. There is no tax now levied by the Government, but an officer is sent down with a guard as usual. There was a storm in the morning, and the rain had been pouring ever since. The poor creatures now on their way in thousands for tomorrow's bathing will suffer dreadfully, and all their *tamāshā* be spoiled.'

CHAPTER XLVII

RUINS OF DELHI

VEDI NAPOLI, E POI MORI .

FEBRUARY 1838 – With the Neapolitan saying 'Vedi Napoli, e poi mori', I beg leave to differ entirely, and would rather offer *this* advice – 'See the Tāj Mahal, and then – see the Ruins of Delhi.' How much there is to delight the eye in this bright, this beautiful world! Roaming about with a good tent and a good Arab, one might be happy for ever in India: a man might possibly enjoy this sort of life more than a woman; he has his dog, his gun and his beaters, with an open country to shoot over, and is not annoyed with 'I'll thank you for your name, Sir.' I have a pencil instead of a gun, and believe it affords me satisfaction equal, if not greater, than the sportsman derives from his Manton.

On my return from the theatre I sought my *chārpāī*, and slept – Oh, how soundly! – was dressed and on my horse by six o'clock, having enjoyed four hours and a half of perfect rest. 'Sleep is the repose of the soul.' I awoke from my slumber perfectly refreshed and my little soul was soon cantering away on the back of an Arab, enjoying the pure, cool, morning breeze. Oh! the pleasure of vagabondising over India!

February 16th – We rode part of the distance and drove the remainder of the march, sixteen miles; found the tents ready, and the *khidmatgārs* on the look out. Took a breakfast such as hungry people eat, and then retired to our respective tents. The fatigue was too much; the novel dropped from my hand, and my sleepy little soul sank to repose for some hours.

When the sun was nearly down, we roamed over the fields with the gentlemen and their guns, but found no game. Thus passed the day of the first march on the road to Delhi at Begumabad.

February 17th – Arrived early at Furrudnagar, another long distance; a high wind, clouds of dust, and a disagreeable day. During the night the servants were robbed of all their brass *lotas* and cooking utensils. A thief crept up to my camels, that were picketed just in front of the tent, selected the finest, cut the rope and strings from his neck; then, having fastened a very long thin rope to the animal, away crept the thief. Having got to the end of the line, the thief gave the string a pull, and continued doing so until he rendered the camel uneasy;

the animal got up – another pull – he turned his head, another – and he quietly followed the twitching of the cord that the thief held, who succeeded in separating him from the other camels and got him some twenty yards from the tent; just at this moment the sentry observed the camel quietly departing, he gave the alarm, the thief fled and the animal was brought back to the camp – a few yards more the thief would have been on his back and we should have lost the camel.

February 18th – Marched into Delhi: the first sight of the city from the sands of the Jumna is very imposing; the fort, the palace, the mosques and minarets, all crowded together on the bank of the river, is a beautiful sight. 'In the year of the Hijerah, 1041 (AD 1631–2), the Emperor Shāhjahān founded the present city and palace of Shāhjahānabad, which he made his capital during the remainder of his reign. The new city of Shāhjahānabad lies on the western bank of the Jumna, in latitude 28° 36' North. The city is about seven miles in circumference and is surrounded on three sides by a wall of brick and stone; a parapet runs along the whole, but there are no cannon planted on the ramparts. The city has seven gates: viz., *Lahore* Gate, *Delhi* Gate, *Ajimere* Gate, *Turkoman* Gate, *Moor* Gate, *Kabul* Gate, *Kashmir* Gate; all of which are built of freestone and have handsome arched entrances of stone, where the guards of the city kept watch.'

We entered the town by the Delhi Gate: during the rains, when the river flows up to and by the walls of the city, the view from a boat must be beautiful; at present the river is shallow, with a great sandbank in the centre. We crossed a bridge of boats and encamped in front of the church.

The church was built by Colonel Skinner, planned by Colonel S—; I do not like the design: it was put into execution by Captain D—. The dome appears too heavy for the body of the church, and in the inside it is obliged to be supported by iron bars – a most unsightly affair. A man should visit the ruins of Gaur, and there learn how to build a dome ere he attempt it. Colonel Skinner is a Christian; the ladies of his family are Muṣalmāns, and for them he has built a mosque opposite the church. In the churchyard is the tomb of Mr William Frazer, who was murdered by the Nawāb Shumsheodin: Colonel Skinner has erected a monument to the memory of his friend; it is of white marble, in compartments, which are inlaid with green stones, representing the weeping willow; the whole was executed at Jaipur, and cost, it is said, Rs 10,000. On the top is a vase, and, in a compartment in front of the church is a Persian inscription. Below are these lines, and in front of the lines are two lions reposing: to none but an Irishman would it be clear that the *us* in the epitaph proceeds from the lions:

Deep beneath this marble stone
A kindred spirit to our own
Sleeps in death's profound repose,
Freed from human cares and woes;
Like *us* his heart, like *ours* his frame,
He bore on earth a gallant name.
Friendship gives to *us* the trust
To guard the hero's honour'd dust.

On the other side the monument is another inscription, also written by Colonel Skinner.

THE REMAINS

INTERRED BENEATH THIS MONUMENT

WERE ONCE ANIMATED

BY AS BRAVE AND SINCERE

A SOUL

AS WAS EVER VOUCHSAFED TO MAN

BY HIS

CREATOR!

A BROTHER IN FRIENDSHIP

HAS CAUSED IT TO BE ERECTED,

THAT, WHEN HIS OWN FRAME IS DUST,

IT MAY REMAIN

AS A

MEMORIAL

FOR THOSE WHO CAN PARTICIPATE IN LAMENTING

THE SUDDEN AND MELANCHOLY LOSS

OF ONE

DEAR TO HIM AS LIFE.

WILLIAM FRAZER

DIED MARCH 22ND, 1835.

In the evening the brother of the Bāiza Bāi, Hindu Rāo, sent me an elephant, and Colonel Skinner sent another; on these we mounted and went through all the principal streets of the city. Dehlī or Dillī, the metropolis of Hindustan, is generally called by Musulmāns Shāhjahānābād and, by Europeans, Delhi. The Chāndnī Chauk, a very broad and handsome street, is celebrated; it has a canal that runs through and down the centre of it; but such is the demand for water, that not a drop now reaches Delhi, it being drawn off for the irrigation of the country, ere it arrive at the city. This fine stream is called *Nahr-i-Bihisht*, or 'Canal of Paradise'. 'In the reign of Shāh-jahān, Ali Merdan Khān, a nobleman, dug, at his own expense, a canal, from the vicinity of the city of Panniput, near the head of the Doo-ab, to the suburbs of Delhi – a tract of ninety miles in extent. This noble canal is called by the natives the 'Canal of Paradise', and runs from north to south, in general about ten miles distant from the Jumna, until it joins that river nine miles below the city of New Delhi: it yielded formerly fourteen *lakh* of rupees per annum. At present it is out of repair, and in many places almost destroyed.'

As we went round the Jáma Masjid, a fine mosque, I thought of the words of the Prophet – 'Masjids are the gardens of Paradise, and the praises of God the fruit thereof.' On the high flight of steps leading to the mosque were hundreds of people in gay dresses, bargaining for cloth, sweetmeats, etc.

The inhabitants of Delhi appear to delight in dresses of the gayest colours, and picturesque effect is added to every scene by their graceful attire. Native gentlemen of rank, attended by large *sawāris* (retinues) on horseback, on elephants or on camels, are met at every turn, rendering the scene very amusing and animated. Nevertheless, in spite of all this apparent splendour, a proverb is used to express the vanity and indigence prevalent in that city: '*Dilli ke dilwāli munh chiknā pet khāli;*' 'The inhabitants of Dilli appear to be opulent when, in fact, they are starving.' A little beyond the Jáma Masjid is the wall of the palace – a most magnificent wall; I was delighted with it and its gateways. Shortly afterwards we turned our elephants towards the tents and returned, considerably fatigued, to dinner.

February 19th – This morning we had decided on visiting the tomb of Humaioon but, on mounting our horses, hearing firing at a distance, we rode off to see what amusement was going forward, leaving the visit to the tomb for another day. It was lucky we did so, I would not on any account have missed the scene. We galloped away to save time, and found Lord Auckland and his party at a review; after looking at the review a short time Captain S—, himself an engineer, took me to see a very interesting work: the sappers and miners had erected a mud-fort; trenches were regularly formed in front of the fort to cover the attacking party, and mines were formed underground to a considerable distance. We walked through the long galleries, which were all lighted up, and Captain S— explained the whole to me. On our return, Lord Auckland came up, examined the fort, and walked through the miners' galleries. The attack commenced, the great guns blazed away at the bastion which was blown up in good style by the miners; the soldiers mounted the breach and took the fort whilst, on the right, it was scaled by another party. This mimic war was very animated; I like playing at soldiers and it gave me an excellent idea of an attack, without the horror of the reality: another mine was sprung and the warfare ended. The sun was high and very hot – we rode home as fast as our horses could carry us – only stopping on the top of a rocky hill near the late Mr Frazer's house to admire the view of Delhi, which lay below a mass of minarets and domes, interspersed with fine trees. Near this spot Mr Frazer was shot. The house was bought by Hindu Rāo for Rs 20,000. Out of this rocky hill a sort of red gravel is dug, which forms the most beautiful roads.

After breakfast we struck our tents and came to stay with a friend, who has a fine house in beautiful grounds, with a garden filled to profusion with the gayest flowers, situated just beyond the Kashmir Gate of the city. Colonel Edward Smith, of the engineers, deserves great credit for the style and good taste he has displayed in the architecture of this gate of Delhi, and for several other buildings which were pointed out to me as of his design in other parts of the city. We found the tents very hot within the walls, with flies innumerable, like the plague of Egypt; at least, they must be quite as bad during the hot season. In the evening we went to a ball, given by Mr Metcalfe to the Governor-General and his party.

February 20th – The ball gave me a headache, and I was suffering a good deal of pain when a native lady came to see me on the part of the Nawāb Shāh Zamānee Begum, the Emperor's unmarried sister, from whom she brought a complimentary message and a request that I would call upon her at the palace. The lady, finding me in pain, most kindly shampooed and mulled my forehead so delightfully that my headache was charmed away – shampooing is the great luxury of the East.

Mausoleum of Humaioon

In the evening we drove through the ruins of old Delhi to the tomb of the Emperor Humaioon. The drive is most interesting; you cannot turn your eye in any direction but you are surrounded by ruins of the most picturesque beauty. The tomb of Humaioon is a fine massive building, well worth visiting: it is kept in good repair. There are several monuments within the chambers of the mausoleum that are of carved white marble. The tomb of the Emperor is very plain and without any inscription. On the terrace is a very elegant white marble monument, richly carved, of peculiar construction, over the remains of a *begum*. The different and extensive views from the terrace over the ruins of old Delhi are very beautiful.

[...]

Masjid of Roshan-ool-Dowla.

We observed with great interest the gilded domes of the mosque of Roshan-ool-Dowla, at one end of the Chandnī Chauk; it is of the common size, built of red stone, and surmounted by three domes. The King of Persia took Delhi, in AD 1739. Nādir Shāh, on hearing of a tumult that broke out in the great marketplace, in which two thousand Persians were slain, marched out at night with his men as far as this Masjid; here he thought it prudent to halt until daylight. When daylight began to appear, a person from a neighbouring terrace fired upon the king and killed an officer by his side. Nādir Shāh was so much enraged that although the tumult had by this time totally subsided, he sent out his soldiers and ordered a general massacre of the inhabitants. This order was executed with so much rigour that before two o'clock above one hundred thousand, without distinction of age, sex, or condition, lay dead in their blood, although not above one-third part of the city was visited by the sword. Nādir Shāh sat during this dreadful scene in the Masjid of Roshan-ool-Dowla; none but slaves dared approach him. At length the unfortunate Emperor of Delhi, attended by a number of his chief *omrah*, ventured before him with downcast eyes. The *omrah*, who preceded the king, bowed their foreheads to the ground. Nādir Shāh sternly asked them what they wanted? They cried out with one voice, 'Spare the city.' Mohammed said not a word, but the tears flowed fast from his eyes. The tyrant, for once touched with pity, sheathed his sword and said, 'For the sake of the prince Mohammed I forgive.' The massacre was instantly stopped.

Since that dreadful carnage, this quarter of Delhi has been but very thinly inhabited.

[. . .]

CHAPTER XLVIII

ANCIENT DELHI – THE ZENĀNA GHAR

FEBRUARY 22ND 1838 – In the cool of the evening we mounted our horses and rode to Ancient Delhi, or Indrapesta, now called Marowlie, the capital of the former Rajas. At this place many houses were pointed out to us as having belonged to the mighty dead; but my attention was arrested by a *bā'olī*, an immense well. From the top of the well to the surface of the water the depth is sixty feet, and the depth of water below forty feet; just above the surface of the water the side of the well opens on a flight of stone steps, which lead to the upper regions. I peered over the well to see the water, and shuddered as I looked into the dark cold depth below; at that instant a man jumped from the top into the well, sank a great depth, rose again, and swimming to the opening, came up the steps like a drenched rat; three more immediately followed his example, and then gaily claimed a *bakshish*, or reward, begging a rupee, which was given: we did not stay to see the sport repeated, at which the jumpers appeared disappointed.

Quitting the *bā'olī*, we visited the tombs of the three last emperors of Delhi – Bahādur Shāh, Shāh'ālam, and Akbar Shāh. The latter had been placed there within a few weeks; the tomb of Shāh'ālam is of white marble, and about eighteen inches distant from that of the Emperor Bahādur Shāh, over whose tomb flourishes a white jasmine. How are the mighty fallen! I had visited the tomb of Humaioon and the still grander monument of Akbar at Sikandra; had admired the magnificent building, its park and portal. The last Akbar reposes side by side with the two former emperors. Three marble tombs, prettily sculptured in a small open court the walls of which are of white marble, is all that adorns the burial-place of the descendants of Tamurlane!

The building that most interested me was the Royal Zenāna Ghār. At certain times of the year the Emperor of Delhi used to retire to this spot with all his ladies; the place is prettily situated amidst rocks and trees: there, seated at ease on his cushions of state, his amusement was to watch the sports of the ladies of the *zenāna*, as they jumped from the roof of a verandah into the water below and then came up to jump in again. On the other side is another tank, with a sloping bank of masonry; on this slope the ladies used to sit and slide down into the tank. In the water, amidst the trees, the graceful drapery of the Musulmān and Hindu ladies clinging to their well-formed persons must have had a beautiful effect. During these sports guards were stationed around to prevent the intrusion of any profane eye on the sacredness of the *zenāna*.

At nine o'clock we revisited the *minār*: the night was remarkably fine, no moon, but a dark blue, clear starlight. The *minār* is fine by day, its magnitude surprising; but by night a feeling of awe is inspired by its unearthly appearance. If you ask a native, 'Who built the Kutab?' His answer will generally be – 'God built it – who else could have built it?' And such is the feeling as you stand at the base, looking up to the top of the column of the polar star, which appears to tower into the skies: I could not withdraw my eyes from it; the ornaments, beautiful as they are by day, at night, shadowed as they were into the mass of building, only added to its grandeur. We roamed through the colonnades, in the court of the beautiful arches, and returned most unwillingly to our tents.

February 23rd – Quitted the Kutab without revisiting Tuglukabad, our time not admitting of it; and I greatly regretted not having the power of visiting the tombs that surrounded us on every side – the ruins of Ancient Delhi. The extent of these ruins is supposed not to be less than a circumference of twenty miles, reckoning from the gardens of Shalimar on the northwest, to the Kutab Minār on the southeast, and proceeding thence along the centre of the old city, by way of the mausoleum of Nizam-al-Deen, the tomb of Humaioon, which adjoins, and the old fort of Delhi, on the Jumna, to the Ajmeer gate of Shāhjahānābād. The environs to the north and west are crowded with the remains of the spacious gardens and country houses of the nobility, which in former times were abundantly supplied with water by means of the noble canal dug by Ali Merdān Khān.

Franklin remarks – 'Ancient Delhi is said by historians to have been erected by Rajah Delu, who reigned in Hindustan prior to the invasion of Alexander the Great: others affirm it to have been built by Rajah Pettouvar, who flourished at a much later period. It is called in Sanscrit *Indraput*, or the Abode of *Indra*, one of the Hindu deities, and is thus distinguished in the royal diplomas of the Chancery office.'

The Observatory

On our road home, about a mile and a half from the present city of Delhi, we stopped to visit the Observatory, *Jantr-Mantr*, a building well worthy the inspection of the traveller. The name of Jayasinha, the Rajah of Ambhere, or Jayanagar and his astronomical labours, are not unknown in Europe; but yet the extent of his exertions in the cause of science is little known; his just claims to superior genius and zeal demand some enumeration of the labours of one whose name is conspicuous in the annals of Hindustan. Jey-sing or Jayasinha succeeded to the inheritance of the ancient Rajahs of Ambhere in the year of Vicramadittya 1750, corresponding to 1693 of the Christian era. His mind had been early stored with the knowledge contained in the Hindu writings, but he appears to have peculiarly attached himself to the mathematical sciences and his reputation for skill in them stood so high, that he was chosen by the Emperor Mahommed Shāh to reform the calendar which, from the inaccuracy of the existing tables, had ceased to correspond with the actual appearance of the heavens. Jayasinha undertook the task and constructed a new set of tables; which, in honour of the reigning prince, he named Zeej Mahommedshāhy. By these, almanacs are constructed at Delhi and all astronomical computations made at the present time.

The five observatories, which were built and finished by Jayasinha, still exist in a state more or less perfect; they were erected at Jaipur, Matra, Benares, Oujein, and Delhi.

[...]

After this most interesting visit to the Observatory, we returned to Delhi.

The Zenāna

During my visit at Khasganj, Mr James Gardner gave me an introduction to one of the princesses of Delhi, Hyāt-ool-Nissa Begum, the aunt of the present, and sister of the late king. Mr James Gardner is her adopted son. The princess sent one of her ladies to say she should be happy to receive me, and requested me to appoint an hour. The weather was excessively hot, but my time was so much employed I had not an hour to spare but one at noonday, which was accordingly fixed upon.

I was taken in a palanquin to the door of the court of the building set apart for the women, where some old ladies met and welcomed me. Having quitted the palanquin, they conducted me through such queer places, filled with women of all ages; the narrow passages were dirty and wet – an odd sort of entrance to the apartment of a princess!

Under a verandah, I found the princess seated on a *gaddi*, of a green colour. In this verandah she appeared to live and sleep, as her *charpaāi*, covered with a green *razā'i*, stood at the further end. She is an aged woman; her features, which are good, must have been handsome in youth; now they only tell of good descent. Green is the mourning worn by the followers of the Prophet. The princess was in mourning for her late brother, the Emperor Akbar Shāh. Her attire consisted of trousers of green satin, an *angiya*, or bodice of green, and a cashmere shawl of the same colour: jewels are laid aside during the days of mourning (*mātam*). I put off my shoes before I stepped on the white cloth that covered the carpet, and advancing, made my *bahut bahut adab* salam, and presented a *nazr* of one gold mohur. The princess received me very kindly, gave me a seat by her side, and we had a long conversation. It is usual to offer a gold mohur on visiting a person of rank; it is the homage paid by the inferior to the superior: on the occasion of a second visit it is still correct to offer a *nazr*, which may then consist of a bouquet of freshly-gathered flowers. The compliment is graciously received, this homage being the custom of the country.

I had the greatest difficulty in understanding what the *begum* said, the loss of her teeth rendering her utterance imperfect. After some time, she called for her women to play and sing for my amusement. I was obliged to appear pleased but my aching head would willingly have been spared the noise. Her adopted son, the son of the present King Bahādur Shāh, came in; he is a remarkably fine, intelligent boy, about ten years old, with a handsome countenance. Several other young princes also appeared and some of their betrothed wives, little girls of five and six years old: the girls were plain. The princess requested me to spend the day with her, saying that if I would do so, at four o'clock I should be introduced to the Emperor (they think it an indignity to call him the king), and if I would stay with her until the evening, I should have *nāchs* for my amusement all night. In the meantime she desired some of her ladies to show me the part of the palace occupied by the *zenāna*. Her young adopted son, the heir-apparent, took my hand and conducted me over the apartments of the women. The ladies ran out to see the stranger: my guide pointed them all out by name and I had an opportunity of seeing and conversing with almost all the *begums*. A plainer set I never beheld: the verandahs, in which they principally appeared to live, and the passages between the apartments, were *mal propre*. The young prince led me through different parts of the palace and I was taken into a superb hall: formerly fountains had played there; the ceiling was painted and inlaid with gold. In this hall were three old women on *chārpāis* (native beds) looking like hags; and over the marble floor, and in the place where fountains once played, was collected a quantity of offensive black water as if from the drains of the cook rooms. From a verandah, the young prince pointed out a bastion in which the king was then asleep, and I quitted that part of the palace, fearing the talking of those who attended me, and the laughing of the children might arouse His Majesty from his noonday slumbers.

On my return to the princess I found her sister with her, a good-humoured, portly-looking person. They were both seated on chairs and gave me one. This was in compliment, lest the native fashion of sitting on the ground might fatigue me. The heat of the sun had given me a violent headache. I declined staying to see the king and requested permission to depart.

Four trays, filled with fruit and sweetmeats, were presented to me; two necklaces of jasmine flowers, fresh gathered and strung with tinsel, were put round my neck; and the princess gave me a little embroidered bag filled with spices. It is one of the amusements of the young girls in a *zenāna* to embroider little bags, which they do very beautifully; these they fill with spices and betel-nut, cut up into small bits; this mixture they take great delight in chewing. An English lady is not more vain of a great cat and kitten with staring eyes, worked by herself in Berlin wool, than the ladies behind the *parda* of their skill in embroidery. On taking my departure the princess requested me to pay her another visit; it gave her pleasure to speak of her friends at Khasganj. She is herself a clever, intelligent woman and her manners are good. I had satisfied my curiosity and had seen native life in a palace; as for beauty, in a whole *zenāna* there may be two or three handsome women and all the rest remarkably ugly. I looked with wonder at the number of plain faces round me.

When any man wishes to ascend the minarets of the Jāma Masjid, he is obliged to send word to the captain of the gate of the palace that the ladies may be apprised and no veiled one may be beheld, even from that distance: the fame of the beauty of the *generality* of the women may be continued, provided they never show their faces. Those women who are beautiful are very rare, but then their beauty is very great; the rest are generally plain. In England beauty is more commonly diffused amongst all classes. Perhaps the most voluptuously beautiful woman I ever saw was an Asiatic.

I heard that I was much blamed for visiting the princess, it being supposed I went for the sake of presents. Natives do not offer presents unless they think there is something to be gained in return; and that I knew perfectly well. I went there from curiosity, not avarice, offered one gold *mohur* and received in return the customary sweetmeats and necklaces of flowers. Look at the poverty, the wretched poverty of these descendants of the emperors! In former times strings of pearls and valuable jewels were placed on the necks of departing visitors. When the Princess Hyāt-ool-Nissa Begum in her fallen fortunes put the necklace of freshly-gathered white jasmine flowers over my head, I bowed with as much respect as if she had been the queen of the universe. Others may look upon these people with contempt, I cannot; look at what they are, at what they have been!

The indecision and effeminacy of the character of the Emperor is often a subject of surprise. Why should it be so? Where is the difference in intellect between a man and a woman brought up in a *zenāna*? There they both receive the same education, and the result is similar. In Europe men have so greatly the advantage of women from receiving a superior education, and in being made to act for, and depend upon themselves from childhood, that of course the superiority is on the male side; the women are kept under and have not fair play.

One day a gentleman, speaking to me of the *extravagance* of one of the young princes, mentioned he was always in debt, he could never live upon his allowance. The allowance of the prince was Rs 12 a month! – not more than the wages of a head servant!

With respect to my visit, I felt it hard to be judged by people who were ignorant of my being the friend of the relatives of those whom I visited in the *zenāna*. People who themselves had, perhaps, no curiosity respecting native life and manners and who, even if they had the curiosity, might have been utterly unable to gratify it unless by an introduction which they were probably unable to obtain.

It is a curious fact that a native lady in a large house always selects the smallest room for her own apartment. A number of ladies from the palace at Delhi were staying in a distant house, to which place a friend having gone to visit them, found them all in the bathing-room, they having selected that as the smallest apartment in which they could crowd together.

I will here insert an extract from the *Delhi Gazette* of January 13th 1849.

'On Thursday morning, departed this life, Prince Dara Bukht, heir-apparent to the throne of Delhi, and with him, we have some reason to believe, all the right of the royal house to the succession, such having been guaranteed to him individually, and to no other member of the family. We sincerely trust that such is really the case, and that our Government will now be in a position to adopt steps for making efficient arrangements for the dispersion, with a suitable provision, of the family on the death of the present king. The remains of the deceased prince were interred near Cheeragh Delhi within a few hours of his death. It is a curious fact, that nearly all the native papers have long since omitted the designation of "Pādshāh" when alluding to the King of Delhi, styling him merely "Shāh".'

[...]

It was my intention to have gone round the walls in the cool of the evening, with my relative, but I was so much disgusted with the ill-natured remarks I had heard, I would not enter the place again.

The gardens of Shalimar are worthy of a visit, from which the prospect to the south, towards Delhi as far as the eye can reach, is covered with the remains of extensive gardens, pavilions, mosques and burial-places. The environs of this once magnificent city appear now nothing more than a heap of ruins, and the country around is equally desolate and forlorn:

> The spider hath woven his web in the royal palace of the Caesars,
> The owl standeth sentinel on the watchtowers of Afrāsiāb!
>
> *Sadi*

[...]

Near the Ajimere Gate is a Madrasa, or college, erected by Gazooddeen Cawn, nephew of Nizam-ool-Mooluk; it is built of red stone and situated in the centre of a spacious quadrangle, with a fountain, lined with stone. At the upper end of the area is a handsome mosque, built of red stone and inlaid with white marble. This college is now uninhabited.

[...]

Exclusive of the mosques before described, there are in Shāhjahānābād and its environs above forty others; most of them of inferior size and beauty, but all of them of a similar fashion. In the evening, we drove to the Turkoman Gate of the city, to see the Kala Masjid or Black Mosque. We found our way with difficulty into the very worst part of Delhi: my companion had never been there before and its character was unknown to us; he did not much like my going over the mosque, amid the wretches that surrounded us; but my curiosity carried the day. The appearance of the building from the entrance is most singular and extraordinary; it would form an excellent subject for a sketch. You ascend a flight of stone steps, and then enter the gateway of the *masjid*: the centre is a square; the pillars that support the arches are of rude construction – stone placed upon stone without mortar between; there are twelve or fifteen small domes on three sides of the square. I wished to sketch the place, but my relative hurried me away, fearful of insult from the people around. The *masjid* was built four hundred and fifty years ago, before the building of the modern Delhi. The tradition of the place is this:

In former times the *masjid* was built of white stone. A father committed a horrible crime within its walls. The stones of the *masjid* turned from white to black. It obtained the name of the black mosque. No service was ever performed there, and the spot was regarded as unholy: none but the lowest of the people now frequent the place; and any stranger visiting it might as well take a *barkandāz* as a protection against insult. Hindu Rāo, the brother of the Bāiza Bāi, lives near Delhi in the house of the late Mr Frazer; he came in his curricle to call on Captain S—: I saw him; he is a short, thickset, fat Mahratta, very independent in speech and bearing. After some conversation, he arose to depart, shook hands with me and said, 'How do you do?' Thinking he was bidding me 'good-night'. This being all the English he has acquired, he is very fond of displaying it. Some young officer, in a fit of *tāmashā* (i.e. fun) must have taught him his 'How do you do?'

[...]

CHAPTER XLIX

Departure for the Hills – Landowr

M ARCH 16TH 1838 – We drove out twenty miles to the place where the palanquins awaited us, travelled *dāk* all night, found a buggy ready for us at the last stage and reached our friend's house at Saharanpūr the next morning by eight o'clock. On the road, about five o'clock in the morning, I was much delighted with the first view of the snowy ranges; I never anticipated seeing mountains covered with snow again and, as I lay in my palanquin, watching the scene for miles, breathing the cool air from the hills, and viewing the mountains beyond them, I felt quite a different being, charmed and delighted. Mr and Miss B— received us very kindly; and I had the pleasure of meeting an old friend, Captain Sturt, of the engineers – the man whose noble conduct distinguished him so highly and who was shot during the fatal retreat of the army in Afghānistan. In the evening we visited the Botanical Garden; it is an excellent one and in high order; some tigers were there, fiercely growling over their food, several bears and a porcupine. The garden is well watered by the canal which passes through it. The Governor-General broke up his camp at Saharanpūr and quitted, with a small retinue, for Mussoorie the day before we arrived.

March 14th – We took leave of our friends, and resumed our *dāk* journey at four o'clock; during the night we passed Lord Auckland's camp, which was pitched in a very picturesque spot at Mohunchaukī: the tents, the elephants and the camels formed beautiful groups among the trees, and I stopped the palanquin a short time to admire them. We passed through a forest – or *sāl jangal*, as they call it – in which wild elephants are sometimes found, and met with a little adventure: a tiger was lying by the roadside; the bearers put down the palanquin, waved their torches, and howled and screamed with all their might: the light and noise scared the animal – he moved off. I got out of the palanquin to look at a tiger *au naturel*, saw some creature moving away, but could not distinguish what animal it was; the bearers were not six feet from him when they first saw him; it was a fine, clear, moonlight night. The *jangal* looked well, and its interest was heightened by the idea you might now and then see a wild beast. A number of fires were burning on the sides of the hills and running up in different directions; these fires, they tell me, are lighted by the *zamindars*, to burn up the old dry grass; when that is done, the new grass springs up and there is plenty of food for the cattle; the fires were remarkable in the darkness of the night. For some miles up the pass of Keeree, our way was over the dry bed of a river; on both sides rose high cliffs, covered with trees; the moonlight was strong and the pass one of great interest; here and there you heard the noise of water, the pleasing sound of a mountain stream turning small mills for grinding corn, called *Panchakki*. In the morning we arrived at the Company's bungalow at Rājpūr.

Rājpūr is situated at the foot of the Hills: I was delighted with the place; the view from the bungalow put me in mind of Switzerland. We went to Mrs Theodore's hotel, to see her collection of stuffed birds and beasts; a complete set costs Rs 1,600 (£160). At the bottom of the valley between the Hills I heard the most delightful sound of rushing waters: taking a servant with me, I went down the steep footpath, irresistibly attracted by the sound, and found the mountain rill collected into a mill-dam from which, rushing down, it turned several mills; and one of the streams was turned off into the valley, forming the little cascade the sound of which had attracted me. How bright, clear, cold, and delicious was the water! Being too unwell to bear the fatigue of climbing the hill, I sent for a hill-pony, called a *gūnth*; he was brought down; the little fellow never had a woman on his back before, but he carried me bravely up the sheep-path, for road there was none. Motī, the name of the handsome *gūnth*, is an iron-grey hill-pony – more like a dwarf-horse than a pony; he has an exceedingly thick, shaggy mane, and a very thick, long tail – the most sure-footed sagacious animal; he never gets tired, and will go all day up and down hill; seldom fights, and is never alarmed when passing the most dangerous places. Give your *gūnth* his head, and he will carry you safely. Horses are dangerous – even the most quiet become alarmed in the hills. Captain S— bought this *gūnth* at the Hurdwar fair; he came from Almorah, cost Rs 160 (£16); and Rs 300 rupees have been refused for him.

[...]

The whole day I roamed about Rājpūr; the *Paharis* (the Hill-men), who had come down to bring up our luggage, were animals to stare at: like the pictures I have seen of Tartars – little fellows, with such flat ugly faces, dressed in black woollen coarse trousers, a blanket of the same over their shoulders; a black, greasy, round leather cap on their heads, sometimes decorated all round their faces with bunches of hill-flowers, freshly gathered; a rope round their waists. Their limbs are stout, and the sinews in the legs strongly developed from constantly climbing the Hills. They are very honest and very idle; moreover, most exceedingly dirty. Such were the little Hill fellows we met at Rājpūr.

March 16th – This morning the *gūnth* came to the door for my companion to ride up the Hills: I was to be carried up in a *jampān*. A *jampān* is an armchair, with a top to it, to shelter you from the sun or rain; four long poles are affixed to it. Eight of those funny little black Hill fellows were harnessed between the poles, after their fashion, and they carried me up the hill. My two women went up in *dolīs*, a sort of tray for women, in which one person can sit native fashion; these trays are hung upon long poles and carried by Hill-men. The ascent from Rājpūr is seven miles, climbing almost every yard of the way. The different views delighted me: on the side of the Hills facing Rājpūr the trees were stunted and there was but little vegetation; on the other side, the north-ern, we came upon fine oak and rhodedendron trees – such beautiful rhodedendrons! They are forest trees, not shrubs as you have them in England. The people gathered the wild flowers and filled my lap with them. The *jangal* pear, in full blossom, the raspberry bushes and the nettles delighted me; I could not help sending a man from the plains, who had never seen a nettle, to gather one; he took hold of it and, relinquishing his hold instantly in excessive surprise, exclaimed – 'It has stung me; it is a scorpion plant.' Violets were under every rock; and the wild, pleasing notes of the Hill birds were to be heard in every direction. The delicious air, so pure, so bracing, so unlike any air I had breathed for fifteen years – with what delight I inhaled it! It seemed to promise health and strength and spirits: I fancied the lurking fever crept out of my body as I breathed the mountain air; I was so happy, so glad I was alive; I felt a buoyancy of spirit, like that enjoyed by a child.

The only bungalow we could procure was one on the top of the hill of Landowr; it was an uncomfortable one, but a roof was not to be despised in such cold weather: we had a fire lighted instantly and kept it burning all day. Where now was the vile fever that had bowed me down in the plains? It had vanished with the change of climate, as if by magic. The Hill air made me feel so well and strong, we set off on our ponies in the evening to visit Mr E—'s house; it is beautiful, built with great taste and highly finished; its situation is fine, on a hill, at the further end of Landowr. Thence we went to Colonel P—'s bungalow, a good house, well situated, but very far from supplies; he offered it to me for the season for Rs 1,200 – £120 for seven months. From the barracks at the top of Landowr, the view of the Snowy Ranges is magnificent. In any other country these hills would be called mountains; but, being near the foot of the Himalaya that in the distance tower above them, they have obtained the title of the 'Hills.' Landowr, Bhadràj, Ben Oge, are covered with oak and rhodo-dendron trees; the valleys between them, by the Hill people called *khuds*, are extremely deep: at the bottom of these *khuds* water is found in little rills, but it is very scarce. About two thousand feet below Landowr water is abundant, and there are some waterfalls. The Hills are very grand, but have not the picturesque beauty of the valley of Chamonix– and yet it is unfair to make the comparison at Landowr; Chamonix is at the foot of Mont Blanc: to compare the two, one ought to proceed to the foot of the Snowy Ranges, where their solitary grandeur would overpower the remembrance of Mont Blanc. I long to go there: the difficulties and privations would be great; I could not go alone and the fatigue would be excessive; nevertheless, I long to make a pilgrimage to Gangotrī, the source of the Ganges.

March 17th – Started on our ponies at seven o'clock to ride to Mussoorie, which is only a short distance from Landowr. The scenery at that place is of a tamer cast; the southern side of the hill, on which most of the houses are situated, puts me in mind of the back of the Isle of Wight, but on a larger scale; the projecting rocks and trees, with gentlemen's houses in every nook, all built on the side of the hill, give the resemblance. The northern side is called the Camel's Back, from a fancied resemblance of the hill to the shape of that animal; there the scenery differs entirely. The southern side, on which Mussoorie is situated, has few trees and looks down on the valley of the Doon; the northern side is covered with fine trees, the hills abrupt; a wildness and grandeur, unknown on the southern side, is all around you; the valleys fearfully deep, the pathway narrow, and in some parts so bad, only one foot in breadth is left for a pony. At first I felt a cold shudder pass over me as I rode by such places; in the course of a week I was perfectly accustomed to the sort of thing, and quite fearless. A pathway three feet in width at its utmost breadth is a handsome road in the Hills; a perpendicular rock on one side, and a precipice, perhaps three or four hundred feet deep, may be on the other. It is all very well when the road is pretty open; but when you have to turn the sharp corner of a rock, if looking over a precipice makes you giddy, shut your eyes and give your *gūnth* the rein, and you will be sure to find yourself safe on the other side. The little rascals never become giddy; and after a short time you will turn such corners at a canter as a thing of course. I was delighted with the wildness of the scenery – it equalled my expectations. In front of Mussoorie you are in high public, the road called the Mall is from eight to ten feet wide, covered with children, nurses, dogs and sickly ladies and gentlemen, walking about gaily dressed. I always avoid the Mall; I go out for enjoyment and health and do not want to talk to people. The children! It is charming to see their rosy faces; they look as well and as strong as any children in England; the climate of the Hills is certainly far superior to that of England. Not liking my bungalow, I changed it for another half way up the hill of Landowr.

March 17th – Lord Auckland and the Misses Eden arrived today, and took up their residence at Colonel Young's, a little below, on the hill of Landowr.

From my bungalow the view is beautiful, and we have as much air as man can desire. The first thing was to get *pardas*, stuffed with cotton, for every window and door; the next, to hire a set of Hill-men to cut and bring wood from the *khuds*, and water and grass for the ponies. A long ride round Waverly was the evening's amusement; then came a dinner of excellent Hill-mutton, by the side of a blazing fire of the *beautiful rhododendron wood!* The well-closed doors kept out the cold, and my kind relative congratulated me on having lost my fever and being so comfortable in the Hills.

Visited Mr Webb's hotel for families; it is an excellent one and very commodious. There is a ballroom and five billiard tables with slate beds; these slate beds have only just arrived in India and have very lately been introduced in England.

March 19th – During the time I was waiting for my relative, who had accompanied Lord Auckland, to show him the hospital and the different buildings at Landowr which were under his charge, my attention was arrested by a great number of Hill-men, carrying large bundles of moss down to the plains; they grind up the moss with barley-meal and use it as soap; it is in great repute at weddings.

Rode my little black horse but found him not so pleasant in the Hills as a *gūnth*, and more fatiguing. At the foot of Landowr there is an excellent bazaar: everything is to be had there – *Pâtée foie gras, bécasses truffées, shola* hats covered with the skin of the pelican, champagne, bareilly couches, shoes, Chinese books, pickles, long poles for climbing the mountains and various incongruous articles. Many years ago, a curious little rosary had been brought me from the *santa casa* of our Lady of Loretto – a facsimile of the little curiosity was lying for sale in the Landowr bazaar, amongst a lot of Hindustani shoes!

[...]

March 23rd – Captain E. S— has an estate in the Hills called Cloud End – a beautiful mountain of about sixty acres covered with oak trees. On this spot he had long wished to build a house and had prepared the plan but his duties as an engineer prevented his being long enough at a time in the Hills to accomplish the object. I offered to superintend the work during his absence, if he would mark out the foundations: a morning's ride brought us to his estate situated between a hill called the 'Park' and Ben Oge, with Bhadráj to the west; the situation beautiful – the hills magnificent and well-wooded. Having fixed on the spot for the house – the drawing-room windows face a noble view of the

Snowy Ranges – the next things was to mark a pathway to be cut into the *khud*, a descent of two miles for the mules to bring up water.

The plan of the house was then marked out and a site was selected for my hill-tent commanding a view of the Himalayas. This little tent was made to order at Fatehgar – it is twelve feet square, has walls four feet high and two doors. A storm wall is to be built around it, a chimney at one end and a glass door at the other; a thatch will be placed over it and this will be my habitation when I go to Cloud End or when I make excursions into the Hills; my kitchen will be an old oak tree.. The Hills are so steep a single-pole tent of the usual size can be pitched in very few places. Under an old oak, on a rock covered with wild flowers, I sat and enjoyed the scene; the valley of the Doon lay stretched before me and the Hills around me. There is a rhododendron tree on this estate that bears *white* flowers – it is a great rarity and highly prized – all the flowers of the other rhododendron trees are a magnificent crimson. The Hill-men are fond of sucking the juice from the petals which it is said possess an intoxicating quality.

Stormy-looking clouds were rolling up from the valley towards the Hills: returning home, we were caught in as fine a storm as I almost ever beheld; it was a glorious sight – the forked lightning was superb, the thunder resounded from hill to hill, the hail and rain fell heavily: for about two hours the storm raged. We took shelter in a Europe shop; towards night it decreased; wrapped in black blankets, which we procured from the bazaar, we got home in safety; the rain could not penetrate the black blankets, the wool of which is so oily. The storm raged with violence during the night, but I heard it not: in the morning the hilltops were covered with snow: at seven o'clock the thermometer was 38° in the verandah; in the room at noon with a fire it stood at 57°.

[...]

CHAPTER L

PICTURESQUE SCENES IN THE HILLS

APRIL 17TH 1838 – Started on my gūnth, the day being cloudy and cold, to make a call some miles off down the hill, at Jerrīpānī. The elevation of Jerrīpānī is much less than that of Landowr and the difference in the vegetation remarkable: here, the young leaves of the oaks are just budding – there, they are in full leaf; here, the raspberry is in flower – there, in fruit.

> The clematis, the favoured flower,
> That boasts the name of Virgin's Bower,

was at Jerrīpānī in beautiful profusion, sometimes hanging its white clusters over the yellow flowers of the barbery. The woodbine delighted me with its fragrance, and the remembrance of days of old; and the rhododendron trees were in full grandeur. Near one clump of old oaks, covered with moss and ivy, I stopped to listen to the shrill cries of the *cicala*, a sort of transparently-winged beetle: the sounds are like what we might fancy the notes would be of birds gone crazy.

> The shrill cicalas, people of the pine –
> Making their summer lives one ceaseless song,
> Were the sole echoes, save my steed's and mine.

The road was remarkably picturesque, the wind high and cold – a delightful breeze, the sky cloudy, and the scenery beautiful: I enjoyed a charming ride, returned home laden with wild flowers, and found amusement for some hours comparing them with Loudon's *Encyclopedia*. A pony that was grazing on the side of Landowr close to my house fell down the precipice and was instantly killed: my *ayah* came to tell me that the privates of the 16th Lancers and of the Buffs ate horseflesh, for she had seen one of them bring up a quantity of the pony's flesh in a towel – I ventured to observe, the man might have dogs to feed.

View from the Pilgrim's Banglā

April 19th – The view from the verandah of my *banglā* or house is very beautiful: directly beneath it is a precipice; opposite is that part of the hill of Landowr on which stands the sanatorium for the military, at present occupied by the invalids of the 16th Lancers and of the Buffs. The hill is covered with grass and the wild potato grows there in profusion; beyond is a high steep rock, which can only be ascended by a very precipitous path on one side of it; it is crowned by a house called Lall Tība, and is covered with oak and rhodo-dendron trees. Below, surrounded with trees, stands the house of Mr Connolly; and beyond that, in the distance, are the snow-covered mountains of the *lower* range of the Himalaya. The road – if the narrow pathway, three feet in breadth, may deserve so dignified an appellation – is to the right, on the edge of a precipice, and on the other side is the perpendicular rock out of which it has been cut. This morning I heard an outcry and ran to see what had happened; just below, and directly in front of my house, an accident had occurred: an officer of the Buffs had sent a valuable horse down the hill, in charge of his groom; they met some mules laden with water-bags where the path was narrow, the bank perpendicular on the one side, and the precipice on the other; the groom led the horse on the side of the precipice, he kicked at the mules, his feet descended over the edge of the road, and down he went – a dreadful fall, a horrible crash; the animal was dead ere he reached a spot where a tree stopped his further descent: the precipice is almost perpendicular.

[...]

April 25th – Accompanied some friends to breakfast in my cottage-tent at Cloud End. We laid out a garden and sowed flower seeds around the spot where my little tent is pitched beneath the trees; while thus employed, I found a scorpion among the moss and leaves where I was sitting, which induced me to repeat those lines of Byron:

> The mind that broods o'er guilty woes
> Is like the scorpion girt by fire –
> In circle narrowing as it glows,
> The flames around their captive close,
> Till, inly search'd by thousand throes,
> And maddening in her ire,
> One sad and sole relief she knows,
> The sting she nourish'd for her foes,
> Whose venom never yet was vain,
> Gives but one pang, and cures all pain,
> And darts into her desperate brain.

My memory was a source of woe to the scorpion at Bhadráj; they surrounded him with a circle of fire; as the heat annoyed him he strove to get over the circle, but the burning charcoal drove him back; at last, mad with pain, he drove his sting into his own back; a drop of milk-white fluid was on the sting, and was left on the spot which he struck; immediately afterwards the scorpion died: Mr R— saw him strike the sting into his own back. When it was over we felt a little ashamed of our scientific cruelty, and buried the scorpion with all due honour below the ashes that had consumed him: a burnt sacrifice to science. In a note in the *Giaour*, the idea is mentioned as an error, of the scorpion's committing suicide, but I was one of the witnesses to the fact.

[...]

May 18th – My fair friend and myself having been invited to a picnic at a waterfall, about two thousand feet below Landowr, we started on our *gūnths* at five o'clock; the tents, servants and provisions had gone on the day before; none of us knew the way but we proceeded, after quitting the road, by a footpath that led up and down the steepest hills; it was scarcely possible for the *gūnths* to go over it. At eight o'clock we arrived, completely tired, and found an excellent breakfast ready. The waterfall roared in the *khud* below, and amidst the trees we caught glimpses of the mountain torrent chafing and rushing along. After breakfast the gentlemen went out to explore the path to the waterfall; we soon grew too impatient to await their return and followed them.

We descended into the *khud*, and I was amusing myself jumping from rock to rock, and thus passing up the centre of the brawling mountain stream, aided by my long *pahari* pole of *rous* wood, and looking for the picturesque, when my fair friend, attempting to follow me, fell from the rocks into the water – and very picturesque and very Undine-like she looked in the stream! We returned to the tents to have her garments dried in the sun, and while the poor little lady was doing penance, I wandered down the stream, of which the various water-falls are beautiful; and, although there was a burning sun on the top of the Hills, down below, by the water, it was luxuriously cool. The path I took was straight down the torrent; I wandered alone for three hours, refreshing myself with wild strawberries, barberries, raspberries and various other Hill fruits that hung around the stream on every side. The flowers were beautiful, the wild ferns luxuriant, the noise of the torrent most agreeable – in fact, all was charming. On my return, I found the party at the foot of a beautiful waterfall, eighty feet in height; the spot was lovely, it was overhung with trees, from the topmost boughs of which gigantic climbers were pendant. How gaily did we partake of excellent wine and good fare on that delicious spot! It was nearly sunset ere we mounted our *gūnths*, and took the path through the village of Būttah.

This village is inhabited by Hill people; I saw a very good-looking woman at a cottage door, in a very picturesque dress, and wished to go and speak to her, but was deterred from so doing, as the Hill-men appeared to dislike the gentlemen passing near the village: I must go alone some day and see her again. By mistake we lost the path and got into paddy fields, where we were obliged to dismount and take the ponies down the most dangerous places. My fair companion was on a mare from the plains; we were obliged to tie a rope to the animal and leap her down those places over which the ponies scrambled; we went down the dry bed of a torrent for some distance, and it was most curious to see how the *gūnths* got over and down the rocks. Walking fatigued me to excess; I mounted my *gūnth*, and rode up some frightful places, up the bed of a small torrent, where there was no path; the *gūnth* clambered up the rocks in excellent style. Presently Mrs B— thought she would do the same; she had not been on the mare ten minutes when I heard a cry, 'The memsāhib has fallen into the *khud*!' Her horse had refused to clamber up a rocky ascent, I suppose she checked him, he swerved round and fell down the *khud*; fortunately he fell on his right side, therefore her limbs were above him, and they slipped down together, the horse lying on his side until, by the happiest chance, his downward course was stopped by a tree. The *sā'ises* ran down, pulled her off and brought her up the Hill; afterwards they got the horse up again in safety. But for the tree, the lady and her steed would have been dashed to pieces; she was bruised, but not much hurt. Her scream alarmed me – I thought it was all over. We returned completely tired; but the day had been one of great delight, the scenery lovely and the air delicious.

From Landowr, looking towards Hurdwar, the isolated hill of Kalunga or Nālāpanī, with its table-land and fortress on the highest extremity, is visible. When the steady coolness and bravery of the Ghurkhas, united with insurmountable obstacles, compelled our troops to fall back, General Gillespie determined to carry the place; and, at the head of three companies of the 53rd Regiment, reached a spot within thirty yards of a wicket defended by a gun; there, as he was cheering the men, waving his hat in one hand, and his sword in the other, he was shot through the heart and fell dead on the spot. Thus died as brave and reckless a cavalier as ever put spur on heel; his sword is one of the interesting relics of my museum. I never meet a hardy, active little Ghurkha, with a countenance like a Tartar, and his *kookree* at his side, but I feel respect for him, remembering the defence of Kalunga. The women showed as much bravery as the men; showers of arrows and stones were discharged at the enemy: the women threw the stones dexterously – severe wounds were inflicted by them; and they undauntedly exposed themselves to the fire of the enemy; they acted with the natural courage inherent in us all, never having been taught that it was pretty and interesting to be sweet, timid creatures!

[...]

June 1st – The weather is hot during the middle of the day, the thermometer 70°; one cannot go out with comfort, unless the day be cloudy or stormy; it is very hot for the Hills.

June 5th – A very hot day – the Hills covered with a fog-like smoke, occasioned by the burning of the *jangal* in the valley below; hot and smoky air comes up in volumes. Mrs M— was riding this evening when a leopard seized her spaniel, which was not many yards in front of her pony; the shouts of the party alarmed the animal and he let the dog drop; however, the poor spaniel died of his wounds. Some officers laid wait for the leopard and shot it; I saw it, coming up the Hill, fastened on a bamboo, to be stuffed and prepared with arsenical soap.

[…]

June 11th – A letter from Allahabad tells me a most severe storm took place there on the third of this month – more severe than the one in which *Seagull* was wrecked; it only lasted an hour. It blew down one of the verandahs of our house, unroofed the cow-house, the meat-house, the wild-duck-house, the sheep-house, etc.: the repairs will not cost us less than Rs 700 (£70).

June 13th – Accompanied Mr R— to see the Botanical Garden, which is small, but interesting: I ate cherries from Kashmir, saw a very fine hill lily from the interior and gathered many beautiful-flowers. Some peaches, from the Doon valley, very large and fine, like English peaches, were sent me today.

[…]

June 24th – A delightful day! How fine, how beautiful are the Snowy Ranges! In consequence of the heavy rain the roads have become very rotten and dangerous; in many parts, half the road has fallen into the *khud*; and where the path is often not three feet in width, it leaves but a small space for a man on his *gŭnth*. Mr T—, of the artillery, met with a serious accident this morning; the road was much broken and as he attempted to ride over it, it gave way; he and his pony went down the precipice. Mr T— was stopped in his descent, after he had gone one hundred feet, by a tree, was brought up and carried to a surgeon. He was much hurt in the head, but is expected to recover in two or three weeks; no bones were broken: the pony went down two hundred and fifty feet, and was found alive!

One of my men was brought in for medical aid. He had been employed in charge of a gang of Hill-men, cutting slates for the roof of the new house in a deep *khud*, and had caught a fever. The slates found in the Hills are very good, but more brittle than those of Europe. The houses formerly were all thatched at Landowr; a thatched roof is dangerous on account of the lightning which so often strikes and sets fire to it. Captain S— introduced slated roofs, and several people have followed the good example he has set them.

CHAPTER LI

LIFE IN THE HILLS

The Kharitā

JUNE 29TH 1838 – Her Highness the Bāiza Bāi did me the honour to send me a *kharitā*, that is, a letter enclosed in a long bag of *kimkhwāb*, crimson silk, brocaded with flowers in gold, contained in another of fine muslin: the mouth of the bag was tied with a gold and tasselled cord to which was appended the great seal of her Highness – a flat circular mass of sealing-wax, on which her seal was impressed. Two smaller bags were sent with it each containing a present of bonbons. The letter was written in Urdū (the court language), in the Persian character, by one of her Highness's *moonshees*, and signed by the Bāi herself: the paper is adorned with gold devices. The letter commenced in the usual complimentary style; after which her Highness writes, that – 'The light of my eyes – the Gaja Rājā – has been very ill; she has recovered and her husband, Appa Sāhib Kanulka, having heard of her illness, has come from Gwalior to see her.' *Kharitās* of this sort pass between the mighty men of the East, and between them and the public functionaries of Government.

July 3rd – I rode over to Cloud End, inspected the new house and trained young convolvulus plants over the bamboo hedge around the garden: the rain descended in torrents; it was very cold and uncomfortable. At seven o'clock, being anxious to get home before dark, although it was still raining, I ordered my *gūnth*; my relative wrapped me up in his military cloak and put a large Indian-rubber cape above it; in this attire I hoped to keep myself dry during my ride home of seven miles. I had not proceeded a mile from the estate when the storm came on in the fearful style of mountain tempests; the thunder burst roaring over my head, the lightning spread around in sheets of flame and every now and then the flashes of forked lightning rendered me so blind I could not see the path for some minutes. I had two servants with me; they walked before the *gūnth*, but were unable very often to trace the road, it was so dark amidst the trees, and the whole time the rain fell in torrents. I saw a dark space in front of the horse, and asked, 'What is that?' 'Oh, nothing,' said the *sā'is*, 'ride on.' But I stopped, and sent him forward. At this spot three or four trees had been thrown across a precipice; over these earth had been laid to some depth to form a road;

the earth had been entirely washed away by the force of a stream of water, produced from the heavy rain, and had fallen into the precipice: the darkness was the hollow produced by the chasm! I dismounted; the trees were still below, across the hollow; with difficulty I clambered down, got over the trunks, and up the other side; it was almost perfectly dark. I called the *gūnth*; the cunning little fellow looked at the hollow, stamped his fore-feet on the ground as if he disliked it, sprang up the bank on the other side, and was in safety by me. I remounted him and proceeded – an act that required a good deal of quiet courage.

'The darkness of the night is a collyrium to the eyes of the mole.' It certainly was not to mine: after I had been out two hours I found that I had advanced four miles on a path that was covered by high trees on every side, rendering it the more dangerous; the lightning was very vivid, and I saw a flash strike the roof of a house; suddenly a faintness came over me, with difficulty I kept in my saddle, and feeling ill, I desired the servant to lead the *gūnth* to the first gentleman's house he came near. As soon as we arrived at a bungalow we went up to the verandah, when an officer, hearing a lady was exposed to such a storm and wished for shelter, came out and took me into the house: I was so much exhausted the tears ran down my face and I almost fainted away. They gave me wine and took off the Indian-rubber cloak which, most likely, was the cause of the extreme oppression that overcame me.

The lady and gentleman in whose house I had taken refuge were very kind; dry clothes soon replaced my wet habit and they gave me a bed; however, I was far too much excited to go to sleep, and was disturbed by queer sounds in an outhouse not far from my sleeping room. I got up, opened my door, wished to call my host, but not knowing his name lay down again and listened. In the morning the mystery was explained: a lady staying at the house had two she-asses for her baby, which were in an outhouse near my room; the night before my arrival a leopard had broken into the outhouse in which the donkeys were fastened and had killed them both; they were found dead with their halters on. The night I was there the leopard came again, tore one of the carcases from the halter and carried it down the *khud* – this was the strange noise that prevented my sleeping. Quite a night of adventures. The carcases had been left on purpose, and some of the officers of the Buffs were to have laid wait for the leopard that night, but the storm prevented their quitting their houses.

Captain S— came to Landowr the next day: he was surprised at my having passed the broken road in the darkness of the storm; even by daylight he passed over it with difficulty – perhaps the darkness aided me, as it prevented my being giddy.

July 11th – Rode to the Botanical Gardens; observed several young tea plants, which were flourishing. The bright yellow broom was in full flower; it put me in mind of the country by the seaside at Christchurch, Hampshire, where the broom is in such luxuriance. We feasted on Kashmir apricots which, though not to be compared to those of Europe, were agreeable to the taste.

July 12th – Storms, storms – rain, rain – day by day – night by night: thermometer at noon, 66°.

July 17th – A bear having been killed, I procured several bottles of bear's grease. Apricot oil was recommended also for the hair.

I bought some *dēodar* oil, made from the white cedar; the smell is vile; it is good for rheumatic pains; if rubbed in *too much* it will produce a blister.

Baskets full of currants were brought for sale; they were only fit for tarts. Fresh figs, pretty good, were sent me, also some tolerable pears of good size. Tar, called *cheer-ke-tel*, is excellent in the Hills.

July 25th – Was persuaded to go to a ball given by the bachelors of Landowr and Mussoorie, an event in my quiet life. Cholera has appeared in the bazaar: the Hill-men are so much alarmed that they run away from service. My *paharis* came to request I would let them all depart and pay them their wages: this I refused to do: they pleaded their fear of the cholera. At length they agreed to remain, if I would give them a kid to sacrifice to the angry goddess who resides in the mountain, and whom they believe has brought the illness amongst them – they are extremely superstitious. What can you expect from uneducated men? 'If grass does not grow upon stones, what fault is it in the rain?' – i.e. it is unreasonable to expect learning from him who has not the means or capacity to acquire it.

[...]

July 31st – A most fearful storm during the night – one that was sufficient to make me quit my bed, to look after my little widow and the *bābās*, i.e., children. The *paharis* informed me a few days ago that the banglā or thatched house in which I am living has been three times struck by lightning, and twice burned to the ground! – an agreeable reminiscence during so violent a storm. As the lightning, if it strike a house, often runs round the walls of a room, from the iron of one wall shade to that of another, and then pursuing its course down to the grate, tears out the bars and descends into the earth, we took the precaution of sitting in the centre of the room, avoiding the sides. My fair friend laughed, in spite of her alarm, when I repeated the old verses:

> Ellen, from lightning to secure her life,
> Draws from her pocket the attractive knife;
> But all in vain, my fair, this cautious action,
> For you can never be without attraction.

[...]

September 5th – A letter informed me of the bursting of the Mahratta Bāndh at Allahabad: the Ganges poured through the gap, inundating the whole country, until it reached the Jumna just above the Fort, leaving the latter completely insulated. Our house, being close to the bank of the Jumna, escaped, but was on every side surrounded by water. *Monsieur mon mari* had two large boats anchored near, to receive himself, his horses, his flocks and his herds should the river rise any higher. The Bāndh burst on the 23rd of August; it swept away the villages of Kyd and Mootī Gunge, carrying away all the thatched huts, the brick houses alone escaping. The Jumna rose to within seven feet of the top of the very high bank on which the terrace (*chabūtara*) in our garden is placed. The damage done to the crops and villages is estimated at four *lakh*; besides this, the force of the water rushing upon the bastion of the Fort has caused it to fall in; it will cost Rs 40–50,000 to repair the bastion.

September 6th – Ill: my *ayah* is so kind and so careful of me: what a good servant I find her! *Apropos* – grain is at present very dear at Landowr; *gram*, twelve seer per rupee.

'One wife is enough for a whole family.' 'Where do you live?' said I to one of my servants, a *paharī* (mountaineer) who had just deposited his load of rhododendron wood, or, as he calls it, flower wood, in the verandah. 'Three days' journey from this, in the *pahar* (mountain),' said the man. 'Are you married?' said I. The man looked annoyed; 'Who will marry me? How can I have a wife? There are but three of us.' Having heard of the singular customs of the *paharis* with regard to marriage, I pursued my interrogation. 'Why cannot you marry?' We are only three brothers; if there were seven of us we might marry, but only three, who will marry us?' The greater the number of the family the more honourable is the connection, the more respected is the lady. 'But who claims the children?' 'The first child belongs to the eldest brother, the second to the second brother and so on, until the eighth child is claimed by the eldest brother, if there be a family of seven.'

I have heard that the Hill women destroy their female offspring, thinking the lot of woman too hard to endure. The price of a wife is high, from the scarcity of women, and may account for the disgusting marriages of the *paharis*.

[...]

I am told that honesty was the distinguishing characteristic in former times of the *paharis*, but intercourse with civilised Europeans has greatly demoralised the mountaineers.

[*An entire chapter is omitted here*]

CHAPTER LII

DEPARTURE FROM THE HILLS

HE ONLY IS DEAD WHOSE NAME IS NOT MENTIONED WITH RESPECT

THE DAYS OF DISTRESS ARE BLACK.

S EPTEMBER 8TH 1838 – I made arrangements with my relative to march across the mountains to Simla, a journey of fifteen days from Landowr, and was looking forward with delight to all the adventures we should meet with, and the crossing the river in a basket suspended on a rope fastened across the stream; but he, an old mountaineer, would not permit me to begin the journey until the *khuds* – which are unwholesome during the rains, and full of fever – should be fit to pass through. A friend had given me the use of a house for some months beyond Simla and I was anxious to visit that part of the country. In the interval we formed a party to see the mountains at the back of Landowr, and I sent out my hill tents to the interior.

In the evening I was riding alone at Mussoorie, when I met Captain L—; there was an embarrassment and distress in his manner that surprised me: he quitted his party and led my pony away from the walk, where the people were in crowds, and when we were alone informed me of the death of my beloved father. I had received no letters from home: this melancholy event had been known some days at Mussoorie but no one had had the courage to tell his child. With what pain I reflected on having so long postponed my return home! Letters from Allahabad confirmed the melancholy news, and my kind husband urged my return to England instantly to see my remaining and widowed parent.

I recalled my tents and people from the interior; and from that moment the thoughts of home, and of what time it would take from the Himalaya to Devonshire, alone filled my thoughts. It was decided I should sail from Calcutta the next cold season.

The weather had become most beautiful; the rains had passed away and the most bracing air was over the Hills. I spent my time chiefly in solitude, roaming in the Hills at the back of Landowr; and where is the grief that is not soothed and tranquillised by the enjoyment of such scenery? The rains had

passed away and had left the air clear and transparent; the beauty of the Snowy
Ranges, whose majestic heads at intervals flushed brightly with the rose-tints
that summer twilight leaves upon their lofty brows – or rising with their snowy
peaks of glittering whiteness high above the clouds, was far greater than I ever
beheld before the departure of the rains.

[...]

September 23rd – Colonel Everest has a fine estate near Bhadráj, called the
'Park'; I rode over with a most agreeable party to breakfast there this morning,
and to arrange respecting some boundaries which, after all, we left as unsettled
as ever; it put me in mind of the child's play:

> Here stands a post.' – 'Who put it there?'
> 'A better man than you, touch it if you dare.

Boundaries in the Hills are determined not by landmarks but by the fall of
the rain; in the division of a mountain, all that land is yours down which the
rain water runs on your side, and on the opposite side, all the land is your
neighbour's over which the water makes its way downwards.

Colonel Everest is making a road – a most scientific affair; the obstacles to
be conquered are great – levelling rocks, and filling up *khuds*. The Park is the
finest estate in the Hills.

September 25th – I was fortunate in being able to procure camels and sent
off my baggage from Rājpūr in time to allow the animals to return to Meerut to
be in readiness to march with the army there collecting for Afghānistan.

[...]

September 29th – Having ascertained that the water in the Keeree Pass had
subsided, and that it had been open for three days, we determined to quit
Landowr for Meerut: accordingly a *dāk* and horses having been laid for us, our
party went down this morning to Rājpūr. It was a beautiful ride, but when we
reached the foot of the Hill the heat became most unpleasant: such a sudden
change from fires and cold breezes, to the hot winds – for such it felt to us at
Rājpūr when we took refuge at Mrs Theodore's hotel. She has stuffed birds for
sale; her Moonāl pheasants are very dear, sixteen rupees a pair; but they are not
reckoned as well prepared as those of Mr Morrow, the steward at the hospital.
Our party being too large to proceed *dāk* in a body, it was agreed I should lead
the way, with Captain L— as my escort. At four o'clock we got into our
palanquins and commenced the journey: crossing the Deyra Doon it was hot,
very hot, and the sides of the palanquin felt quite burning. As the sun sank we
entered the Keeree Pass, where I found the air very cold; and it struck so chillily
upon me that I got out of the palanquin, intending to walk some distance. The

pass is the dry bed of a mountain torrent, passing through high cliffs, covered with fine trees and climbers; a stream here and there crosses the road. During a part of the year it is impassable, but the water having subsided, the road had been open three days.

It was a beautiful night and a beautiful scene; I enjoyed it extremely and walked some distance, aided by my long *pahari* pole. Wishing my escort to partake in the pleasure to be derived from such romantic and picturesque scenery, I asked him if he would walk. He partially opened the doors of his palanquin and, looking out, expressed his astonishment at the madness of my walking in the Pass; said the malaria was so great he had shut the doors of the *palkee* and lighted a cigar to secure himself from its influence, begged I would get into my palanquin and keep the doors closed as long as I was in the pass. I followed his advice, but the moonlight night often tempted me to open the doors, and I became completely ill at times from the chill that fell upon my chest, like the deadly chill of a vault, in spite of having wrapped myself up in a blanket. At first I was unwilling to attribute it to the effect of the air of the Keeree Pass, but having arrived at the end of it, these uncomfortable feelings instantly disappeared.

An instance of the danger of the Pass is that Mrs T— was detained for two hours at the entrance of it for want of bearers – she took a fever and died. The wife of the *behishti*, who was with our servants, was detained at the same place – she took the fever and it killed her. To sleep in the pass one night is to run the pretty certain chance of fever, perhaps death: there is something in the air that almost' compels one to sleep. With the very greatest difficulty I kept my eyes open, even when in pain from a chilly sickness that had crept over me: I thought of Corinne and the Pontine Marshes, in passing which she could scarcely resist the spell that induced her to long for sleep, even when she knew that sleep would be the sleep of death. Quitting the pass, we entered on the plains where the sun was burningly hot – how fierce it was! We did not arrive at Dēobund, where we were to take shelter, until noon the next day; I felt sick and faint from the excessive heat and was very glad to gain the shelter of a roof.

September 30th – At four o'clock our palanquins were ready; getting into them was like going into an oven. We had taken the precaution of having no dinner during the heat of the day; in the cool of the evening refreshment was welcome, in the shade of the *jangal* by the roadside. The bearers were good, and at two o'clock we arrived at the spot to which a buggy had been sent, and horses laid on the road: how gladly I left the hot palanquin for the cool air in the buggy! The roads were so bad, they were absolutely dangerous, and the moonlight so puzzling, we could not see the holes into which the buggy was continually going bump bump, to the infinite hazard of breaking the springs; nevertheless, we arrived in safety at Meerut.

[...]

October 17th – Colonel Arnold gave a farewell ball to his friends at Meerut. The Lancers are to march for Afghānistan on the 30th. His house is built after his own fancy: from without it has the appearance of Hindu temples that have been added to a bungalow; nevertheless, the effect is good. The interior is very unique. The shape of the rooms is singular; the trellis work of white marble between them, and the stained glass in the windows and over the doors, give it an Eastern air of beauty and novelty. Fire-balloons were sent up, fireworks displayed; the band was good and the ball went off with great spirit.

October 18th – The evening after this fête, during the time Colonel Arnold was at dinner, and in the act of taking wine with Sir Willoughby Cotton, he burst a blood-vessel on his lungs and was nearly choked. Medical aid was instantly called in; he was in extreme danger during the night and was bled three times. A hope of his recovery was scarcely entertained: never was more interest or more anxiety felt by any people than by those at Meerut for Colonel Arnold. He had just attained the object of his ambition, the command during the war of that gallant regiment the 16th Lancers; and he was beloved both by the officers and the men. At three o'clock he parted with the guests in his ballroom in high health and spirits: at seven that evening he lay exhausted and apparently dying. When at Waterloo he was shot through the lungs, and recovered. It was one of those remarkable instances of recovery from a severe gunshot wound, and as that had gone through the lungs, the breaking of the blood-vessel was a fearful occurrence.

[...]

October 21st – My boats being ready at Ghurmuktesur Ghāt, I started *dāk* to join them; on my arrival a fine breeze was blowing, a number of vessels of every description were at anchor; the scene was picturesque and my people were all ready and willing to start. Messrs Gibson and Co. of Meerut have furnished me with two large flat-bottomed country boats on each of which a house is built of bamboo and mats, which is well thatched; the interior of the one in which I live is divided into two large rooms and has two bathing rooms; the floor is of planks covered with a gaily-coloured *satrangi*, a cotton carpet; and inside is fitted up with white cloth – sometimes the rooms are fitted up with the coloured chintz used for tents. The other large boat contains the servants, the horses and the dogs. The sort of boat generally used for this purpose is called a *surri* which is a *patelī* that draws very little water and is generally rowed from the top of a platform above the roof on which the *dāndīs* live.

October 23rd – Started from Ghurmuktesur Ghāt the moment it became possible to see the way down the river, and to avoid the sandbanks. At three o'clock the thermometer was 82° – a most oppressive heat for one just arrived from the Hills. *Lugoed* on a sandbank, and walked with the dogs until ten at night when I went to rest and dreamed of thieves, because this part of the Ganges is dangerous, and I have no guard on board the boats. From a fisherman on the bank I have purchased fish enough for myself and all the crew, a feast for us all and a piece of good luck.

[...]

October 31st – Reached Bitoor at breakfast time; a large fair was being held on the banks of the river. Here we nearly lost the horse-boat; a strong wind carried the boats against a high bank, which was falling in every second; just as the horse-boat ran foul of it the bank fell in; the *chaprāsi* on deck cut the towing-line with his sword, and the boat swerved off from the bank; she was filled with earth and all but swamped. The horses, feeling the violent rocking of the vessel, neighed loudly several times as if conscious of danger and willing to remind us of their existence. The boat righted and was got off with some difficulty.

On our arrival at Cawnpore we were detained by the bridge of boats, which was closed, and would not be opened until noon the next day.

[...]

November 4th – On the top of the thatch of the house which is built on my boat is a platform on which the people sit; when the wind is in a particular direction all that is said above is plainly heard in the cabin below. A most theological discourse has amused me for the last hour carried on between my *khidmatgār*, one of the Faithful, and a staunch Hindu, one of my *chaprasis*. The question under consideration was, whether God made Hindus or Musulmāns first; and whether you ought to say 'By the blessing of Allah,' or 'By the blessing of Vishnă.' These points the Musulmān undertook to explain. The questions of the Hindu were simple but most puzzling; nor could the man refrain from a laugh now and then, when some curious point of faith was explained to him by the follower of the Prophet. It ended by the *khidmatgār* saying, 'If you do not believe in Allah and the Qur'an, they will take you by that Hindu topknot of yours, hold you by it whilst they fill your mouth with fire, and pitch you to *Jahannam*.' I laughed – the people heard me, and being aware that their conversation was overheard dropped the subject. The follower of Mohammed worked so hard and so earnestly to gain a convert, it was unfortunate his opponent should have been so utterly incapable of understanding what he considered the true faith.

The Musulmāns are anxious for converts; the Hindus will neither make proselytes, nor be converted themselves. Deism is the religion of well-educated Hindus, they leave idolatry to the lower orders. When conversing with a lady one evening, the priest's bell was heard; she said, 'I must attend – will you come with me?' Accordingly we entered the small room which contained the idols; they were lighted up and the Brahmans in attendance. The worship proceeded: I said to the lady, 'Is it possible that *you* can believe in the power of brazen images, the work of men's hands?' She answered, 'I believe in one great and eternal God; as for these images, it is the custom of the country to worship them; the lower orders believe in their power.' 'Why do you attend such *poojā*?' said I. She looked at the Brahmans as if she feared our conversation might be overheard and answered, 'Their power is great; if I were not to appear it would soon be over; they — ' she ceased speaking and drew her forefinger across her throat with a significant gesture. The conversation dropped; and I observed the Brahmāns 'cast camel's glances' both on her and me.

The clergyman at Allahabad converted a Hindu to the Christian faith; consequently, the man became an outcast – he could neither eat, drink, nor smoke with his own family; he complained to the clergyman and was taken into service. His attendance at church was constant. His patron died: the man was never seen afterwards at Divine Service. The newly appointed clergyman inquired the reason and this answer was returned: 'I received Rs 8 a month from your predecessor; if you will give me the same I will go to church every Sunday!' So little did the man comprehend his adopted religion, or the kindness that induced the Clergyman to support him!

Passed Manucpūr with a fine breeze and a powerful stream in our favour; *lugoed* below Kurrah, where the people cooked on shore and as soon as the moon was high we turned the boat into the current and allowed her to drift; the helmsman ties the rudder up in the centre and usually lies down to sleep by its side; if the vessel run ashore, he starts up and marvels at the occurrence. We drifted the whole night by moonlight; at one time I told them to anchor, but the bank kept falling in in so fearful a manner we were obliged to put off again.

Just as we came to the bank to *lugoe* the men suddenly shoved the boat back into the stream saying, 'Someone has sneezed, we cannot anchor here at present.' A few moments afterwards they anchored. They are superstitious respecting a sneeze, and by waiting for a short time fancy the evil influence passes away. 'After sneezing you may eat or bathe, but not go into any one's house' because it is considered an omen of ill luck.

A fair breeze is springing up; we are near home and they will be looking for the return of the wanderer. We are off Papamhow; the river is very shallow and very broad. We passed the *ghāt* and moored while the people ate their dinners. I would have proceeded by moonlight, but was deterred from doing so by the advice of the fishermen on the banks, who said it would be very dangerous then to go on, as the stream was very fierce and shallow below.

November 6th – Arrived at Raj-Ghāt, at which place the carriage was waiting for me; but I found it impossible to reach the *ghat*, the force of the current drove us off; therefore, taking the crew of the horse-boat to aid our own, we dropped down into the Jumna below the Fort; in doing this, we ran against another vessel and did our own some damage. At this moment we are making our way slowly and with difficulty up the stream against the current of the Jumna, just below the Fort; the view is interesting, and the pilgrim will reach the landing-place, below her own old *peepal* tree, within an hour. I have at this moment but little energy left wherewith to pursue my homeward voyage, but my promise is yours, my beloved mother, and your child would not disappoint you for all the wealth of Ormus or of Ind. She who ventures on the waters must take patience and await the good pleasure of the wind and tides; but there is the Fort and the great Masjid, and the old *peepal* tree, and the memsāhib's home, and the *chabūtara* (a terrace to sit and converse on), the bank of the river, which is crowded with friends on the look out for the pilgrim and ready to hail her return with the greatest pleasure.

[*An entire chapter is omitted here*]

CHAPTER LIII

Departure from Allahabad

NOVEMBER 1838 – On my first arrival at Allahabad I thought I should never get through all the arrangements necessary before my departure for England; so many farewell visits were to be paid to my old friends, and so many preparations were to be made for the voyage. Her Highness the Bāiza Bāī was still at Allahabad, and she sent for me. One of the Italian greyhounds given me by Captain Osborne having died, I took the other two and presented them to the Gaja Rājā Sāhib, the young princess having expressed a wish to have one: I gave her also a black terrier and one of King Charles's spaniels.

One day a Mahratta lady came to my house, riding *en cavalier* on a camel, which she managed apparently with the greatest ease; she told me her Highness requested I would call immediately upon her. On my arrival in camp, after the ceremony of meeting had passed, the Bāiza Bāī said, 'You are going to England – will you procure for me three things? The first is a perfectly high caste Arabian mare; secondly, a very, very little dog, just like a ball, covered with long hair, perfectly white and having red eyes; and thirdly, a mechanical figure that, standing on a slack rope with a pole in its hand, balances itself, and moves in time to the music that plays below it.'

I thought of the fairy tales, in which people are sent to roam the world in search of marvellous curiosities, and found myself as much perplexed as was ever a knight of old by the commands of a fairy. The Bāī added, 'You know a good Arab, I can trust your judgment in the selection, the little dogs, they say, come from Bombay: you can bring them all with you in the ship on your return.'

I informed her Highness that very few Arabs were in England; that in her Majesty's stud there were some, presents from Eastern Princes, who were not likely to part with the apple of their eyes: that I did not think an Arab mare was to be had in the country. With respect to the little powder-puff dog with the red eyes, I would make enquiries: and the mechanical figure could be procured from Paris.

A few days after this visit one of her ladies called on me, and the following conversation ensued:

Mahratta Lady – 'You are going to England – you will be absent eighteen months or two years – have you arranged all your household affairs? You know how much interest I take in your welfare; I hope you have made proper arrangements.'

I assured her I had.

'Yes, yes, with respect to the household, that is all very well; but with respect to your husband, what arrangement have you made? It is the custom with us Mahrattas, if a wife quit her husband, for her to select and depute another lady to remain with him during her absence – have you selected such a one?'

'No,' said I, with the utmost gravity; 'such an arrangement never occurred to me – will you do me the honour to supply my place?'

She laughed and shook her head. 'I suppose you English ladies would only select one wife; a Mahratta would select two to remain with her husband during her absence.'

I explained to her the opinions of the English on such subjects: our ideas appeared as strange to her as hers were to me; and she expressed herself grieved that I should omit what they considered a duty.

November 27th – I called on the ex-Queen of Gwalior and took leave in all due form; the dear old lady was very sorry to part with me – the tears ran down her cheeks and she embraced me over and over again. I was sincerely grieved to part with her Highness, with whom and in whose camp I had passed so many happy hours, amused with beholding native life and customs and witnessing their religious ceremonies. The next day she sent me the complimentary fare-well dinner, which it is the custom to present to a friend on departure: I partook of some of the Mahratta dishes, in which, to suit my taste, they had omitted musk or *assafoetida*; the cookery was good; *pān, atr,* and rose-water, as usual, ended the ceremony.

Those ladies who are kind enough to support and educate the orphan children of natives are startled at times by curious occurrences. A lady at this station lately married one of her orphans to a drummer in the 72nd regiment, and gave Rs 20 as a portion; the man was drunk for about a week; in a fortnight he made over his wife to another drummer, and in a month came to the lady saying, 'If you please, Ma'am, I should like to marry again.' 'Why, John Strong, you were married a few days ago!' 'Yes, Ma'am, but I made over she to my comrade.' Imagine the lady's amazement and horror! The man John Strong went away and told his officers he thought he had been very ill-used. The man was a half-caste Christian, the girl a converted native.

[...]

November 28th – My friend Mrs B— and her four children arrived; she is to accompany me to Calcutta: and a *manis* has been sent me to add to my collection.

December 1st – We quitted Allahabad, and proceeded down the river, calling on those friends *en passant* of whom I wished to take leave. At Mirzapur the head of a ravine deer was given me. Off Patna a quantity of *arwarī* fish were brought alongside for breakfast; they were delicious; the remainder we had smoked in *shakar* and *chokar* – that is, coarse sugar and wheat bran: let no one neglect this economical luxury – the smoked *arwarī* are delicious.

December 17th – Both the boys being very ill of fever, we hastened on for medical assistance. At night, as Mrs B—was quitting my boat to go to her own, passing down the plank, it upset and she was thrown into the river; it was as deep as her waist; the night was dark and the stream strong; she was saved by a bearer's catching her gown as she was sinking; fortunately the bearer was in attendance, carrying a lantern. The rest of the people were on the shore eating their dinners, which they had just cooked. I called to the *dāndīs* to assist, not a man would stir; they were not six yards from he and saw her fall into the river. I reprimanded them angrily, to which they coolly answered, 'We were eating our dinners, what could we do?' Natives are apathetic with respect to all things, with the exception of rupees and *khānā-pinā* – that is, 'meat and drink'.

December 18th – To avoid the return of the accident of yesterday, this evening our vessels were lashed together; I went to my friend's boat to see the poor boys who were delirious; on my return I did not see that the hold of my boat was open; the shadows deceived me in the uncertain light and meaning to jump from the railing of her vessel upon the deck of my own, I took a little spring and went straight down the hold: falling sideways with my waist across a beam, the breath was beaten out of my body for a moment and there I hung like the sign of the golden fleece. The people came to my assistance and brought me up again; it was fortunate the beam stopped my further descent. I was bathed with hot water, and well rubbed with *dēodar* oil, which took off the pain and stiffness very effectually.

[...]

December 31st – Quitted Berhampūr. I have suffered so much during the last twelvemonth from the death of relatives and friends, that I now bid adieu to the past year without regret. May the new one prove happier than the last!

CHAPTER LIV

Arrival in Calcutta – the Madagascar

JANUARY 1st 1839 – We flew down the river on a powerful wind until we reached Cutwa, where we moored, to purchase a *gāgrā*, a brass vessel for holding water; *gāgrās* and *lotas* are manufactured at this place, as are also *churis*, bracelets made of the *sankh*, the conch shell which the Hindus blow. These *churis* are beautifully white, very prettily ornamented, and are worn in sets: above them, some of the women wore immense bracelets of silver or of pewter, according to the rank of the wearer; those bracelets stand up very high, and the pewter ones shine like silver, from being scrubbed with sand daily in the river. At this place a number of people were bathing; one of the Bengalī women was remarkably well formed, my attention was attracted by the beauty of her figure; her skin was of a clear dark brown, with which her ornaments of red coral well contrasted; her dress, the long white *sari* hanging in folds of graceful drapery around her; but her face was so ugly, it was quite provoking – so plain a face united to so well-formed a figure.

January 2nd – At Nuddea the tide was perceptible, and the smell of the burnt bodies on the opposite side of the river most annoying.

January 3rd – Anchored at Culwa, to get the wooden anchor filled with mud and bound up with ropes; the process was simple and curious, but it took five hours to accomplish the work. Bamboos were tied to the cross of the anchor, which was of heavy wood – a bit of old canvas was put inside, and filled with lumps of strong clay – the bamboos were then pressed together, and the whole bound with ropes; a very primitive affair. I had a new cable made before quitting Prāg – a necessary precaution; for unless you have it done beforehand they will detain you at Culwa to do it, as the hemp is a little cheaper there than in the up-country, and the *mānjhis* do not care for the annoyance the detention of three or four days may occasion. At Culwa I saw a shocking sight: a dying Bengalī woman was lying on a mat by the river side, her head supported by a pillow, and a woman sitting at her side was fanning her with a *pankha*. At a certain time the body is laid in the water up to the waist, prayers are repeated; and at the moment of dying the mud of the holy Ganges is stuffed into the nose and mouth, and the person expires in the fullness of righteousness. My people told me that if the woman did not die by night-time, it was very likely they would stuff her nose and mouth a little too soon with the holy mud, and expedite her journey rather too quickly to another world! The Hindus, up-country men, who were with me, were disgusted with the Bengalee customs, and violent in their abuse. Should she recover she will take refuge, an outcast in the village of Chagdah.

We anchored at Santipūr. The water of the river at the *ghāt* was covered with drops of oil, from its being a bathing-place, and the Bengalis having the custom of anointing their bodies daily with oil.

A *chaprāsi* of mine, seeing a skull, struck it with a bamboo and cursed it.

'Why did you strike and curse the skull?' said I.

'It is a vile Bengali skull; and those sons of slaves, when we ask a question, only laugh and give no answer.'

'Perhaps they do not understand your up-country language.'

'Perhaps not, that may be the reason; but we hate them.'

January 6th – Two miles above Calcutta: the day was fine, the wind very heavy, but favourable: the view of the shipping beautiful; I enjoyed it until I remembered my crew were up-country men, from Hurdwar, who had never seen the sea and knew not the force of the tides. We drifted with fearful velocity through the shipping; they threw the anchor overboard, but it would not hold; and away we went, our great unwieldy boat striking first one ship then another; at length a gentleman, seeing our danger as we were passing his pinnace, threw a rope on board, which the men seized and, having fastened it, brought up the vessel. All this time I was on deck, under a burning sun, and we did not anchor until twelve noon; consequently that night I was very ill, the beating in my head fearfully painful, and I fainted away three times; but it was of no consequence, I was in the hands of a kind friend, and soon recovered.

January 9th – The ships lie close to the drive near the Fort, and visiting them is amusement for a morning. I went on board the *Earl of Hardwicke* – she could not accommodate me; thence I proceeded to the *Madagascar*, and took one of the lower stern cabins for myself, for which I was to give Rs 2,500; and a smaller cabin, at Rs 1,300 for my friend's three children, who were to accompany me to England. At the same time I engaged an European woman to attend upon me and the young ones. Going to sea is the only chance for the poor boys, after the severe fever they had on the river, from the effects of which they are still suffering.

The larboard stern cabin suits me remarkably well; it is very spacious, sufficient to contain a number of curiosities; and before the windows I have arranged a complete *forest* of the horns of the buffalo, the stag and the antelope.

January 20th – A steamer towed the *Madagascar* down the river, and the pilot quitted us on the 22nd, from which moment we reckoned the voyage actually commenced; it is not counted from Calcutta, but from the Sandheads, when the pilot gives over the vessel to the captain, and takes his departure. Suddu Khān, my old *khānsāmān*, who had accompanied me thus far now returned with the pilot: the old man must have been half-starved, he would eat nothing on board but a little parched grain, and slept outside my cabin-door; he is an excellent servant, and says he will take the greatest care of the sāhib until my return.

I suffered severely at the Sandheads from *mal de mer*, on account of the heavy ground-swell; perhaps no illness is more distressing – to complain is useless and only excites laughter; no concern on the subject is ever felt or expressed. Why is blind man's buff like sympathy?

Let no one be tempted to take a lower stern cabin; mine was one of the largest and best, with three windows and two ports; nevertheless it was very hot, the wind could not reach it; it was much less comfortable than a smaller cabin would have been on the poop.

January 30th – Very little wind in the early morning; during the day a dead calm – very hot and oppressive. How a calm tries the temper! Give me any squall you please, but spare me a calm.

January 31st – The ship rolling and pitching most unmercifully; there is scarcely wind enough to move her; she lies rolling and pitching as if she would send her masts overboard; thermometer 87° – the heat is most distressing – no wind: caught a shark and a sucking fish.

February 1st – Thermometer 87°, the heat is distressing: a return voyage is much hotter than one from England. Captain Walker is very attentive to his passengers; he keeps an excellent table and every thing is done to render them comfortable. We have sixty invalids on board – wretched-looking men; one of them, when the ship was going seven knots an hour, threw himself overboard; a rope was thrown out, to which he clung, and they drew him in again; he came up sober enough, which it was supposed he was not when he jumped overboard. Fortunate was it for the man that the voracious shark we afterwards caught, whose interior was full of bones, did not make his acquaintance in the water.

March 4th – The morning was fine, the sea heavy, and we came in delightfully towards the Cape: the mountains of Africa were beautiful, with the foaming breakers rushing and sounding at their base. The lighthouse and green point, with its white houses, were pleasing objects. The view as you enter the Cape is certainly very fine: the mountains did not appear very high to my eye, accustomed to the everlasting snows of the Himalaya, but they are wild, bold and picturesque, rising directly from the sea – and such a fine, unquiet, foaming and roaring sea as it is! The Devil's Peak, the Lion, and Table Mountain were all in high beauty; not a cloud was over them. The wreck of the *Juliana* lay near the lighthouse; and the *Trafalgar* was also there, having been wrecked only a week before.

March 5th – Breakfasted at the George Hotel; fresh bread and butter was a luxury. Drove to Wineburgh to see a friend, and not finding him at home we consoled ourselves with making a *tiffin* – that is, luncheon – on the deliciously fine white water grapes from his garden. Proceeded to Constantia, called on a Dutch lady; the owner of the vineyard, whose name I forget; she, her husband, and daughter were very civil, and offered us refreshment. We walked over the vineyard; the vines are cut down to the height of a gooseberry bush, short and stumpy; the blue grapes were hanging on them half dried up, and many people were employed picking off the vine leaves, to leave the bunches more exposed to the sun; the taste of the fruit was very luscious, and a few grapes were sufficient, they were too cloying, too sweet. They told us it took an amazing quantity of grapes to make the Constantia, so little juice being extracted in consequence of their first allowing the bunches to become so dry upon the vine; but as that juice was of so rich a quality, it rendered the Constantia proportionably expensive. The old Dutchman took us up a ladder into an oak tree, in which benches were fixed all round the trunk; he took great pride in the breadth of it, and the little verdant room formed of the branches was his favourite place for smoking. The acorns I picked up were remarkably large, much larger than English acorns. Oaks grow very quickly at the Cape, three times as fast as in England; but the wood is not so good and they send to England for the wood for the wine-casks, which is sent out ready to be put together; they think their wine too valuable for the wood at the Cape. There was no wine-making going on at the time, but the lovers of Constantia may feel some disgust at knowing that the juice is pressed out by trampling of the grapes in a tub – an operation performed by the naked feet of the Africanders, who are not the most cleanly animals on earth.

How much the freshness of the foliage and the beauty of the country through which we drove delighted me! The wild white geranium and the myrtle were both in flower in the hedges. After a sea-voyage we devoured the vegetables, the fish and the fruit, like children turned loose amongst dainties.

Our voyage from Calcutta to the Cape had been a very fine one – forty-two days; the shortest period in which it has been accomplished was thirty-one days by a French vessel. The *mal de mer* that had made me miserable from the time the pilot quitted us never left me until we were within four or five days' sail of the Cape; then image to yourself the delight with which I found myself on shore. Eatables – such as sardines, anchovies, etc. – are more reasonable than in Calcutta; one shilling is equivalent to a rupee. Visited a shop where there is a good collection of stuffed birds; bought a Butcher bird – it catches its prey, sticks it upon a thorn and devours it at leisure: small birds are one shilling each; but I know not if they are prepared with arsenical soap, like those to be purchased at Landowr. No good ostrich feathers were to be had at the Europe shops: there is a shop, kept by a Dutchwoman, near the landing-place, where the best – the uncleaned ostrich feathers – are sometimes to be bought; the price about five guineas per pound. My man-servant gave twenty shillings for eighteen very fine large long feathers in the natural state, and he told me he made a great profit by selling them in town.

[. . .]

March 7th – Quitted Cape Town on a fine and powerful wind; we were all in good spirits; the change had done us good and we had gathered fresh patience – the worst part of the voyage was over – for a man in bad health what a trial is that voyage from Calcutta to the Cape!

March 12th – Very cold weather; this frigate-built ship is going nine knots an hour and rolling her main chains under water. In the evening, as I was playing with the children on deck at oranges and lemons, we were all thrown down from the ship having rolled heavily; her mizen-top-gallant mast and the main-top-gallant mast both broke; one spar fell overboard, and the broken masts hung in the rigging.

March 18th – At eight o'clock we arrived at St Helena: the view of the island is very impressive; it rises abruptly from the sea – a mass of wild rocks, the heavy breakers lashing them; there appears to be no shore, the waves break directly against the rocks. The highest point is, I believe, two thousand feet; the island appears bare and desolate as you approach it. A white heavy cloud hung over the highest part of the mountain; the morning was beautiful and many vessels were at anchor. I sketched the island when off Barn's Point. The poles of the flagstaffs still remain, on which a flag was hoisted whenever the Emperor appeared, that it might tell of his whereabouts, giving him the unpleasant feeling that spies were perpetually around him. I went on shore in a bumboat that had come alongside with shells. Landing is difficult at times when the waves run high; if you were to miss your footing on the jetty from the rising and sinking of the boat, you would fall in and there would be little chance of your being brought up again. There are only two points on the island on which it is possible to land, namely, this jetty and one place on the opposite side, both of which are strongly guarded by artillery. Batteries bristle up all over the rock like quills on a porcupine. The battery on the top of Ladder Hill may be reached by the road that winds up its side, or by the perpendicular ladder of six hundred and thirty-six steps. We went to Mr Solomon's Hotel and ordered a late dinner; the prices at his shop and at the next door are very high: he asked twelve shillings for articles which I had purchased for five at the Cape.

Procured a pass for the tomb, and a ticket for Longwood, for which we paid three shillings each. Next came a carriage drawn by two strong horses, for which they charged three pounds. We ascended the hill from James's Hotel; from the summit, as you look down, the view is remarkably beautiful; the town lying in the space between the two hills, with the ocean in front, and a great number of fine vessels at anchor. The roads are good, and where they run by the side of a precipice are defended by stone walls.

The tomb of the Emperor is situated in a quiet retired spot at the foot of, and between, two hills. Three plain large flagstones, taken from the kitchen at Longwood, cover the remains of Napoleon: there is no inscription, nor does there need one; the tomb is raised about four inches from the ground, and surrounded by an iron palisade formed at the top into spearheads. Within the palisade is still seen a geranium, planted by one of the ladies who shared his exile. The old willow has fallen and lies across the railing of the tomb, withered, dead and leafless. Many young willows reared from the old tree shade the tomb, and every care is taken of the place by an old soldier, who attends to open the gate and who offers to visitors the water from the stream which now flows out of the hill by the side of the tomb. Its course was formerly across the spot where the tomb is now placed; it was turned to the side to render it less damp: the water is remarkably pure, bright and tasteless. It was under these willows, and by the side of this little clear stream, that Bonaparte used to pass his days in reading, and this spot he selected as his burial-place.

A book is here kept in which visitors insert their names; many pages were filled by the French with lamentations over their Emperor, and execrations upon the English. Many people have made a pilgrimage from France to visit the tomb, and on their arrival have given way to the most frantic grief and lamentations.

Having pleased the old soldier who has charge of the tomb with a present in return for some slips of the willow, we went to a small and neat cottage hard-by for grapes and refreshment. It is inhabited by a respectable widow who, by offering refreshment to visitors, makes a good income for herself and family. We had grapes, peaches and pears, all inferior, very inferior to the fruit at the Cape. After tiffin we proceeded to Longwood, and passed several very picturesque points on the road. Around Longwood there are more trees, and the appearance of the country is less desolate than in other parts of the island. We were first taken to the old house in which the Emperor lived; it is a wretched place, and must ever have been the same. The room into which you enter was used as a billiard-room: the dining-room and the study are wretched holes. The Emperor's bedroom and bath is now a stable. In the room in which Bonaparte expired is placed a corn-mill! I remember having seen a picture of this room: the body of the Emperor was lying near the window from which the light fell upon the face of the corpse. The picture interested me greatly at the time, and was vividly brought to my recollection as I stood before the window; whilst in imagination the scene passed before me. How great was the power of that man! With what jealous care the English guarded him! No wonder the women used to frighten their children into quietness by the threat that Bonaparte would come and eat them up, when the men held him in such awe. Who can stand on the desolate and picturesque spot where the Emperor lies buried and not feel for him who rests beneath? How much he must have suffered during his sentry-watched rambles on that island, almost for ever within hearing of the eternal roar of the breakers, and viewing daily the vessels departing for Europe!

In the grounds by the side of the house are some oak trees planted by his own hands; there is also a fishpond, near which was a birdcage. The Emperor used to sit here under the firs, but as he found the wind very bleak, a mud wall was raised to protect the spot from the sharp gales of the sea. After the death of Napoleon the birdcage sold for £175.

We quitted the old house and went to view the new one, which was incomplete at the time of the death of the Emperor; had he lived another week he would have taken possession of it. The sight of this house put me into better humour with the English; in going over the old one, I could not repress a feeling of great disgust and shame. The new house is handsome and well finished; and the apartments, which are large and comfortable, would have been a proper habitation for the exiled Emperor. The bath daily used by him in the old dwelling has been fitted up in the new; everything else that could serve as a relic has been carried away.

In the grounds were some curious looking gum trees covered with long shaggy moss. The heat of the day was excessive; we had umbrellas but I had never before been exposed to such heat, not even in India. The sea-breeze refreshed us, but the sun raised my skin like a blister; it peeled off after some days quite scorched.

We returned to dinner at Mr Solomon's Hotel. Soup was placed on the table. Dr G— said, 'This soup has been made of putrid meat.' 'Oh no, Sir,' said the waiter, 'the soup is very good; the meat smelt, but the cook took it all out before it came to table!' A rib of beef was produced with a flourish; it was like the soup – we were very glad to send it out of the room. We asked to see the landlord; the waiter said he was over at the mess: we desired him to be sent for, of course supposing he was sending up dinner to the officers of a Scotch regiment, whose bagpipe had been stunning our ears, unaccustomed to the silver sound. What was our surprise when we found the hotel and shopkeeper was dining with the officers of the regiment! King's officers may allow of this, but it would never be permitted at the mess of a regiment of the Honourable Company; perhaps his being sheriff formed the excuse. It was too late to procure dinner from another house; the boatmen would wait no longer and our hungry party returned on board to get refreshment from the steward.

The night was one of extreme beauty – the scene at the jetty under the rocks was delightful; the everlasting roar of the breakers that at times dash over the parapet wall, united with the recollections awakened by the island, all produce feelings of seriousness and melancholy.

[...]

CHAPTER LV

Departure from St Helena

MARCH 19TH 1839 – A fine and favourable breeze bore the *Madagascar* from St Helena, and gave us hopes of making the remainder of the voyage in as short a space of time as that in which the first part had been accomplished. The only really good fruit we got at James's Town was the plantain. Some mackerel was baked and pickled on board, but we were recommended not to eat it after the first day as the St Helena mackerel, if kept, is reckoned dangerous.

April 11th – How glad I was to see the polar star, visible the first time this evening! I thought of my dear mother and how often we had watched it together; and the uncertainty of what might have occurred during my voyage to the dear ones at home rendered me nervous and very unhappy. The southern hemisphere does not please me as much as the northern; the stars appear more brilliant and larger in the north.

April 18th – The ship was passing through quantities of seaweed, supposed to be drifted from the Gulf of Mexico; it is always found in this latitude. The children amused themselves with writing letters to their mother and sending them overboard, corked up in empty bottles.

[...]

May 13th – For some time we had been busy arranging for going on shore, which I determined to do if possible at Plymouth; therefore my packages of curiosities were got up – at least as many as I thought I could take with me, being nine chests; and all the buffalo and *stags'* horns were in readiness. About thirty-five miles from Plymouth a pilot vessel came alongside, and we calculated on landing in her in four hours. At five o'clock, having taken leave of the captain who had shown us the greatest attention during the voyage, we went – a large party – on board the pilot vessel: no sooner did we enter her than the wind changed, the rain fell, it was very cold; we were forced to go below into a smoky cabin, the children squalled and we all passed a most wretched night.

May 14th – We arrived at six o'clock. May-flowers and sunshine were in my thoughts. It was bitterly cold walking up from the boat – rain, wind and sleet, mingled together, beat on my face. I thought of the answer of the French ambassador to one of the *attachés*, who asked why the Tower guns were firing – '*Mon ami, c'est peut-être qu'on voit le soleil.*'

Everything on landing looked so wretchedly mean, especially the houses, which are built of slate stone, and also slated down the sides; it was cold and gloomy – no wonder on first landing I felt a little disgusted. I took a post-chaise, and drove to the house of that beloved parent for whose sake I had quitted the Hills and had come so far. The happiness of those moments must be passed over in silence: she laid back the hair from my forehead and looking earnestly at me, said 'My child, I should never have known you – you look so anxious, so careworn!' No wonder – for years and anxiety had done their work.

The procession from the Custom House was rather amusing; the natural curiosities passed free, and as the buffalo and stag-horns were carried through the streets, the people stopped to gaze and wonder at their size. Having left my young friends in the *Madagascar*, it was necessary to go to town to receive them. I went up in the mail from Devonport; its fine horses pleased me very much, and at every change I was on the look out for the fresh ones. We went on an average ten miles an hour. One gentleman was in the mail. I was delighted with the sides of the hedges covered with primroses, heatherbells and wild hyacinths in full bloom; nor could I repress my admiration; 'Oh! what a beautiful lane!' 'A *lane!*' said the man with frowning astonishment, 'this is the Queen's highway.' I saw the error I had committed; but who could suppose so narrow a road between two high banks covered with primroses was the Queen's highway? Everything looked on so small a scale; but everything brought with it delight. When the gruff gentleman quitted the mail, he gathered and gave me a bunch of primroses; with them and a bouquet of lilies-of-the-valley I was quite happy, flying along at the rate of a mile in five minutes. In the cold of the raw dark morning they took me out of the mail thirty miles from London and placed me in a large coach, divided into six stalls, somewhat like those of a cathedral: a lamp was burning above, and in a few minutes we were going through a long, dark, dreary tunnel. It was very cold and I felt much disgusted with the great fearful-looking monster of a thing called a train: in a short time we were at the end of the thirty miles, and I found myself once again in London. On my arrival I was exceedingly fatigued; all the way from Landowr I had met with nothing so overcoming as that day and night journey from Devonport to town. To every person on a return from India, all must appear small by comparison. Devonshire, that I had always heard was so hilly, appeared but little so; and although I was charmed with a part of the drive from Devonport to Exeter, with the richness of the verdure and the fine cows half hidden in rich high grass, and the fat sheep, still I was disappointed – Devon was not as hilly a country as I had fancied. Oh the beauty of those grass fields, filled as they were with buttercups and daisies! During seventeen years I had seen but one solitary buttercup, and that was presented to me by Colonel Everest in the Hills. The wild flowers were delightful, and the commonest objects were sources of the greatest gratification. I believe people at times thought me half mad, being unable to understand my delight.

At the time I quitted England it was the fashion for ladies to wear red cloaks in the winter – and a charming fashion it was: the red or scarlet seen at a distance lighted up and warmed the scenery – it took from a winter's day half its dullness. The poor people, who always imitate the dress of those above them, wore red, which to the last retained a gay and warm appearance, however old or threadbare. On my return all the women were wearing grey, or more commonly very dark blue cloaks. How ugly, dull, dingy and dirty the country people generally looked in them! Even when perfectly new they had not the pleasant and picturesque effect of the red garment.

In Wales I was pleased to see the women in black hats, such as men usually wear, with a white frilled cap underneath them: it was national, but not a red cloak was to be seen.

What can be more ugly than the dress of the English? I have not seen a graceful girl in the kingdom: girls who would otherwise be graceful are so pinched and lashed up in corsets, they have all and every one the same stiff dollish appearance; and that dollish form and gait is what is considered beautiful! Look at the outline of a figure; the corset is ever before you. In former days the devil on two sticks was a favourite pastime. The figure of the European fair one is not unlike that toy. Then the *bustle* – what an invention to deform the shape! It is a pity there is no costume in England as on the Continent for the different grades in society. Look at the eyes of the women in church – are they not generally turned to some titled fair one, or to some beautiful girl, anxious to catch the mode of dressing the hair, or the tie of a ribbon that they may all and each imitate the reigning fashion, according to the wealth they may happen to possess? This paltry and wretched mimicry would be done away with if every grade had a fixed costume.

I went to Mr Greville's, Bond Street, to look at some birds and took a list of his prices. My scientific friends preferred the birds in the state in which they came from India, therefore they remain *in statu quo*.

Of all the novelties I have beheld since my return, the railroads are the most surprising and have given me the best idea of the science of the present century.

The rate at which a long, black, smoking train moves is wonderful; and the passing another train is absolutely startling. The people at the stations are particularly civil; there is no annoyance, all is pleasant and well conducted. From the velocity with which you move, all near objects on the side of the railroad look like anything turned quickly on a lathe – all long stripes; you cannot distinguish the stones from the ground, or see the leaves separately, all run in lines from the velocity with which at full speed you pass near objects. The New Police, now so well regulated, also attracted notice; their neat uniform renders them conspicuous; a wonderful improvement on the watchmen of former days. The beautiful flowers, the moss-roses and the fine vegetables in town were most pleasing to the eye. The height of the carriage horses in the Park attracted my attention; they are fine, powerful animals, but their necks are flat, and their heads generally appeared very coarse. They wanted the arched neck and the fire of the horses of India.

Visited the British Museum; the new rooms that have been added are handsome and well filled with Egyptian curiosities; mummies in crowds, and very fine ones. The Elgin marbles, in a handsome hall, are also shown to great advantage. My collection of Hindu idols is far superior to any in the Museum; and as for Ganesh, they never beheld such an one as mine, even in a dream!

[...]

THE FAREWELL

AND NOW the pilgrim resigns her staff and plucks the scallop-shell from her hat – her wanderings are ended – she has quitted the East, perhaps for ever: surrounded in the quiet home of her native land by the curiosities, the monsters, and the idols that accompanied her from India, she looks around and dreams of the days that are gone.

The resources she finds in her recollections, the pleasure she derives from her sketches and the sad sea waves (written at St Leonard's-on-Sea), her constant companions, form for her a life independent of *her own* life.

> THE NARRATION OF PLEASURE IS BETTER
> THAN THE PLEASURE ITSELF

And to those kind friends at whose request she has published the history of her wanderings, she returns her warmest thanks for the pleasure the occupation has afforded her. She entreats them to read the pilgrimage with the eye of indulgence, while she remembers at the same time that,

> HAVING PUT HER HEAD INTO THE MORTAR, IT IS USELESS TO
> DREAD THE SOUND OF THE PESTLE

To her dear and few surviving relatives – and to her friends of many years – the Pilgrim bids adieu:

> THE BLESSING OF HEAVEN BE UPON THEIR HEADS
> 'Āp ki topiyan par salāmat rahi.'

> THE PEN ARRIVED THUS FAR AND BROKE ITS POINT

> i.e. It is finished.

> Salām! Salām!

ELAND

61 Exmouth Market, London EC1R 4QL
Fax: 020 7833 4434
Email: info@travelbooks.co.uk

Eland was started in 1982 to revive great travel books
that had fallen out of print. Although the list has diversified
into biography and fiction, it is united by a quest to define the
spirit of place. These are books for travellers, and for readers who aspire
to explore the world but who are also content to travel in their own
minds.

Eland books open out our understanding of other
cultures, interpret the unknown and reveal different environments
as well as celebrating the humour and occasional horrors of travel. We
take immense trouble to select only the most readable
books and therefore many readers collect the entire series.

All our books are printed on fine, pliable, cream-coloured paper.
Most are still gathered in sections by our printer and sewn as well
as glued, almost unheard of for a paperback book these days.
This gives larger margins in the gutter, as well as
making the books stronger.

You will find a very brief description of all our books on the
following pages. Extracts from each and every one of them can be
read on our website, at www.travelbooks.co.uk. If you would
like a free copy of our catalogue, please fax, email
or write to us (details above).

ELAND

'One of the very best travel lists' WILLIAM DALRYMPLE

Memoirs of a Bengal Civilian
JOHN BEAMES
Sketches of nineteenth-century India painted with the richness of Dickens

Jigsaw
SYBILLE BEDFORD
An intensely remembered autobiographical novel about an inter-war childhood

A Visit to Don Otavio
SYBILLE BEDFORD
The hell of travel and the Eden of arrival in post-war Mexico

Journey into the Mind's Eye
LESLEY BLANCH
An obsessive love affair with Russia and one particular Russian

Japanese Chronicles
NICOLAS BOUVIER
Three decades of intimate experiences throughout Japan

The Way of the World
NICOLAS BOUVIER
Two men in a car from Serbia to Afghanistan

Persia: through writers' eyes
ED. DAVID BLOW
Guidebooks for the mind: a selection of the best travel writing on Iran

The Devil Drives
FAWN BRODIE
Biography of Sir Richard Burton, explorer, linguist and pornographer

Turkish Letters
OGIER DE BUSBECQ
Eyewitness history at its best: Istanbul during the reign of Suleyman the Magnificent

My Early Life
WINSTON CHURCHILL
From North-West Frontier to Boer War by the age of twenty-five

Sicily: through writers' eyes
ED. HORATIO CLARE
Guidebooks for the mind: a selection of the best travel writing on Sicily

A Square of Sky
JANINA DAVID
A Jewish childhood in the Warsaw ghetto and hiding from the Nazis

Chantemesle
ROBIN FEDDEN
A lyrical evocation of childhood in Normandy

Croatia: through writers' eyes
ED. FRANKOPAN, GOODING & LAVINGTON
Guidebooks for the mind: a selection of the best travel writing on Croatia

Viva Mexico!
CHARLES FLANDRAU
A traveller's account of life in Mexico

Travels with Myself and Another
MARTHA GELLHORN
Five journeys from hell by a great war correspondent

The Weather in Africa
MARTHA GELLHORN
Three novellas set amongst the white settlers of East Africa

The Last Leopard
DAVID GILMOUR
The biography of Giuseppe di Lampedusa, author of The Leopard

Walled Gardens
ANNABEL GOFF
An Anglo-Irish childhood

Africa Dances
GEOFFREY GORER
The magic of indigenous culture and the banality of colonisation

Ask Sir James
MICHAELA REID
The life of Sir James Reid,
personal physician to Queen Victoria

A Funny Old Quist
EVAN ROGERS
A gamekeeper's passionate evocation
of a now-vanished English rural lifestyle

Meetings with Remarkable Muslims
ED. ROGERSON & BARING
A collection of contemporary travel
writing that celebrates cultural difference
and the Islamic world

Marrakesh: through writers' eyes
ED. ROGERSON & LAVINGTON
Guidebooks for the mind: a selection
of the best travel writing on Marrakesh

Turkish Aegean: through writers' eyes
ED. RUPERT SCOTT
Guidebooks for the mind: a selection
of the best travel writing on Turkey

Valse des Fleurs
SACHEVERELL SITWELL
A day in St Petersburg in 1868

Living Poor
MORITZ THOMSEN
An American's encounter with
poverty in Ecuador

Hermit of Peking
HUGH TREVOR-ROPER
The hidden life of the scholar
Sir Edmund Backhouse

The Law
ROGER VAILLAND
The harsh game of life played in
the taverns of southern Italy

Bangkok
ALEC WAUGH
The story of a city

The Road to Nab End
WILLIAM WOODRUFF
The best selling story of poverty and
survival in a Lancashire mill town

The Village in the Jungle
LEONARD WOOLF
A dark novel of native villagers struggling
to survive in colonial Ceylon

Death's Other Kingdom
GAMEL WOOLSEY
The tragic arrival of civil war in an
Andalucian village in 1936

The Ginger Tree
OSWALD WYND
A Scotswoman's love and survival
in early twentieth-century Japan

Poetry of Place series

London: Poetry of Place
ED. BARING & ROGERSON
A poetry collection like the city itself, full of
grief, irony and delight

Andalus: Poetry of Place
ED. TED GORTON
Moorish songs of love and wine

Venice: Poetry of Place
ED. HETTY MEYRIC HUGHES
Eavesdrop on the first remembered glimpses
of the city, and meditations on her history

Desert Air: Poetry of Place
ED. MUNRO & ROGERSON
On Arabia, deserts and the Orient of
the imagination

Istanbul: Poetry of Place
ED. ATES ORGA
Poetry from her long history, from paupers to
sultans, natives and visitors alike

The Ruins of Time
ED. ANTHONY THWAITE
Sized to fit any purse or pocket, this is just the
book to complement a picnic amongst the
ruins of time